I0567019

THE EPISTLE TO THE
ROMANS

Other works by Dr. Surrendra Gangadean & The Logos Foundation:

Philosophical Foundation: A Critical Analysis of Basic Beliefs

History of Philosophy: A Critical Analysis of Unresolved Disputes

Theological Foundation: A Critical Analysis of Christian Belief

Philosophical Foundation: Trivium Study Guide

The Logos Papers: To Make the Logos Known

The Westminster Confession: A Doxological Understanding

*The Westminster Shorter and Larger Catechisms:
A Doxological Understanding*

*On Natural and Revealed Theology:
Collected Essays of Surrendra Gangadean*

*The Logos Curriculum:
Grammar Catechisms: Philosophical, Theological, and
Historical Foundations*

The Contradictoriness of Sin: A Reading of Paradise Lost

Fundación Filosofica: Un Análisis Crítico de Creencias Básicas

DOXOLOGICAL REFORMED SERMON SERIES:

*The Biblical Worldview: Creation, Fall, Redemption—
Genesis 1–3: Scripture in Organic Seed Form*

The Unity of the Church: That They May Be One That the World May Believe

*The Epistle to the Hebrews: Christ Is Superior in Every Way—
Foundation to Persevere in Biblical Faith*

*The Person and Work of Christ: To Undo What Adam Did and To Do What
Adam Failed to Do—A Summary Exposition*

*The Gospel of Matthew: The Person and Work of Christ—
The Fulfillment of Redemption Through the One to Come*

*The Book of Revelation: What Must Soon Take Place—
Doxological Postmillennialism*

The Natural Moral Law: The Foundation for Lasting Culture, Volumes 1–6

Biblical Foundation: In Narrative and Theological Form

The Seven Pillars of the Faith: The Theological Foundation of Scripture

PHILOSOPHICAL FOUNDATION DIALOGUE SERIES:

Introduction to Philosophy: The Basic Things Are Clear to Reason

DOXOLOGICAL REFORMED SERMON SERIES

THE EPISTLE TO THE
ROMANS

The Righteousness of God Revealed from Faith to Faith

The Gospel According to St. Paul

SURRENDRA GANGADEAN

LOGOS PRESS PAPERS

LOGOS

A DIVISION OF THE LOGOS FOUNDATION

Phoenix, Arizona

The Epistle to the Romans: The Righteousness of God Revealed from Faith to Faith—The Gospel According to St. Paul

Copyright © 2025 Surrendra Gangadean

Logos Papers Press 2025
Phoenix, Arizona
logospaperspress.com
thelogosfoundation.org

All Scripture quotations, unless otherwise indicated, are taken from the Holy Bible, New International Version®, NIV®. Copyright ©1973, 1978, 1984, 2011 by Biblica, Inc.™ Used by permission of Zondervan. All rights reserved worldwide. www.zondervan.com The "NIV" and "New International Version" are trademarks registered in the United States Patent and Trademark Office by Biblica, Inc.™

Scripture quotations marked KJV are taken from the King James Version. Public Domain.

Printed in the United States of America

All rights reserved. No part of this publication may be reproduced, stored in a retrieval system, or transmitted in any form or by any means—electronic, mechanical, photocopy, recording, scanning, or otherwise—without prior written permission from the publisher, Logos Papers Press. It is illegal to copy this book, post it to a website, or distribute it by any other means without permission.

Cover design: Beth Ellen Nagle
Typesetting: Matthew P. Hicks & Brian J. Phelps

Library of Congress Cataloging-in-Publication Data pending

Gangadean, Surrendra, 1943–2022.
    The epistle to the Romans: the righteousness of God revealed
    from faith to faith—the gospel according to St. Paul
    Includes Index
    ISBN: 978-1-965685-06-8 (hbk.)
    ISBN: 978-1-965685-07-5 (pbk.)
    ISBN: 978-1-965685-08-2 (e-book)

1. Bible. N.T. Epistle to the Romans 2. Theology—Clarity and Inexcusability 3. Romans—Sermons 4. Historic Christianity 5. Doxological Reformed I. Title

For those looking for
the city whose architect
and builder is God

CONTENTS

APPENDICES

SERIES PREFACE

THE *DOXOLOGICAL REFORMED SERMON SERIES*[1] is a collection of Pastor Surrendra Gangadean's sermons during his over two-decade tenure as the founder and senior pastor of Westminster Fellowship Church. During this period, he delivered over 1,000 sermons, preserved through audio recordings, handwritten outlines, and congregants' notes. These sermons now form the basis of dozens of books, offering a Doxological Reformed exposition of the Scripture, the moral law, and foundational theological doctrines.

The significance of this collection lies in its pioneering nature—in seeking to advance the kingdom of God—providing the groundwork for future hermeneutical works. Pastor Gangadean developed and applied Rational Presuppositionalism[2] to general revelation in his work *Philosophical Foundation*,[3] addressing enduring challenges of the modern and postmodern world. Similarly, he tackled central questions concerning the content and application of Scripture. Recognizing the impracticality of writing full commentaries, Pastor Gangadean utilized sermon delivery to engage with the meaning of Scripture, foundational doctrines, and moral law as they apply to all of life.

Consequently, The Logos Foundation Editorial Board has unanimously decided to present the sermon series in its original form. Minor grammatical changes aside, the content remains untouched, accurately reflecting Pastor Gangadean's ongoing thought process. We aim to prepare the way for future generations to connect directly with the mind that shaped these doctrines. This original preservation will also

---

1. Surrendra Gangadean, *The Westminster Shorter and Larger Catechisms: A Doxological Understanding* (Phoenix: Logos Papers Press, 2023), xv–xxxii.

2. Surrendra Gangadean, "Paper No. 101: Rational Presuppositionalism: Critically Examining Assumptions for Meaning," in *The Logos Papers: To Make the Logos Known* (Phoenix: Logos Papers Press, 2022), 521–526; "Paper No. 52: Common Ground (Part III)," 281–282; "Paper No. 2: Common Ground," 9–13; "Paper No. 95: Rational Presuppositional Apologetics," 503–506; "Paper No. 96: The Project of Rational Presuppositional Apologetics," in *The Logos Papers*, 507–508.

3. Surrendra Gangadean, *Philosophical Foundation: A Critical Analysis of Basic Beliefs*, Second Edition (Phoenix: Public Philosophy Press, 2022).

aid the Editorial Board in capturing the diverse contexts in which ideas were expounded. These sermons, coupled with foundational work in philosophy, theology, the humanities, and history, form the basis for forthcoming biblical commentaries. While each book is not exhaustive in itself, the series collectively reflects Pastor Gangadean's distilled wisdom throughout his body of work. As more books are published, a complete tapestry of his understanding will gradually unfold.

We regard the content of these sermons as invaluable contributions to the Next Reformation.[4] They illustrate how contextual thinking can illuminate the organic content of Scripture, reaching across every book and addressing even the most disputed passages that have troubled the Church throughout history. Through these sermons, the perspicuity of Scripture is meticulously brought into focus, shedding light on the clarity derived from general revelation, special revelation, and the cumulative insights of the Historic Christian Faith.[5] The convergence of the doxological focus, the doctrine of clarity and inexcusability, the knowledge of God as the good, and Rational Presuppositionalism collectively work to unveil the profound meaning of Scripture and encapsulate the essence of its truth.

Pastor Gangadean's preaching approach unfolds with a discernible progression. In the earlier sermons from 1993 to 2004, the emphasis rests on biblical exposition, laying a robust foundation by elucidating fundamental doctrines such as clarity and inexcusability, the divine image in man, the knowledge of God, church authority, and worship. Delivered with rapidity, these sermons were densely packed and aimed at a comprehensive exposition.

From 2005 to 2014, a pronounced shift occurred in Pastor Gangadean's sermons with a heightened focus on the need for sanctification within the context of discipleship. This period aimed to equip the congregation to grasp the interplay between foundational truths and personal application, fostering maturity. These sermons naturally evolved from the preceding foundational exposition of Scripture. After a decade of delving into the objective and subjective facets of biblical truths and

---

4. Gangadean, "Paper No. 62: The Next Reformation," in *The Logos Papers*, 335–337.

5. Surrendra Gangadean, *The Westminster Confession of Faith: A Doxological Understanding* (Phoenix: Logos Papers Press, 2023); *The Westminster Catechisms*, Surrendra Gangadean.

their integration, the imperative to address remaining sin within the congregation became increasingly apparent.

The subsequent phase of preaching, spanning 2015 to 2022, witnessed a shift towards existential hermeneutics, emphasizing the moral law, the unity of the Church, public witness, and adopting a more deliberate and rhetorical expository style. While his pace slowed, Pastor Gangadean's focus intensified on discerning how to apply truths to dismantle self-deception and self-justification among congregants and within the broader Church. The doctrine of repentance of root sin and an in-depth analysis of the doctrine of clarity and inexcusability assumed central significance.

The essence of these sermons constitutes the most profound exposition of the Word of God in its fullness to date. The expositor lived an exemplary life, building upon the cumulative insights from the three foundations, and endeavored to equip God's people with a clear understanding of Scripture amidst its myriad challenges, facilitating enduring responses.

Anticipating that this sermon series will serve as an essential source for crafting a biographical account of Pastor Gangadean's life and work, it becomes evident in these sermons how providence in his life, the challenges inherent in shepherding the flock, the practical application of doctrinal principles to the life of the Church, and a continuous response to the prevailing state of the Church and culture are interwoven. They stand as a testament to the life of a faithful servant who fought the good fight, finished the race, and kept the faith.[6]

These sermons, given initially to the congregants of Westminster Fellowship over the years, are deemed blessings that must be shared with the broader body of Christ. We consider it imperative to extend these blessings to our fellow brothers and sisters, and view it as our duty to contribute to the spiritual enrichment of the larger Christian community.

May the Lord bless the preaching and hearing of His Word, and may this compilation serve as the foundation for the contextual interpretation of Scripture for generations to come, and persist until the fulfillment

---

6. *2 Timothy 4:7–8.*

of the dominion[7] and mission[8] mandates in the earth being filled with the knowledge of the glory of the Lord as the waters cover the sea.

—THE LOGOS FOUNDATION
EDITORIAL BOARD
Phoenix, Arizona
November 2024

---

7. *Genesis 1:26–28.*

8. *Matthew 28:18–20.*

THE EPISTLE TO THE ROMANS
A Brief Summary

THE EPISTLE TO THE ROMANS IS A SYSTEMATIC statement of the Christian faith. All men have clear general revelation of the nature and existence of God and the law of God, and so are without excuse for unbelief and sin (1–2). Since no one is righteous, a person is accepted by God on the basis of the righteousness of God, which comes through faith in Jesus Christ. Abraham, too, was accepted by faith (3–4). This reconciliation by grace through Christ's atoning death has benefits far greater than the effects of Adam's sin. It not only forgives sin but frees from the power of sin. It extends to the whole of creation and triumphs over every opposition (5–8). This grace comes into a person by God's sovereign choice, and though Israel does not now believe, God will bring both the Gentiles and Israel to believe (9–11). In view of God's mercy, men are to devote themselves to God and to do His will in all things. The will of God in many applications of the law is urged upon those who believe (12–16).

INTRODUCTION

THE CENTRALITY OF ROMANS
TO THE REFORMATION

S T. PAUL'S EPISTLE TO THE ROMANS TOOK CENTER place in the development of the theology of the Reformation. Both the *Five Solas*[1] and the acronym TULIP,[2] summarizing the context of the bestowal of grace, find their source in the content of the Epistle to the Romans. Both Martin Luther and John Calvin wrote commentaries on this epistle. In his *Preface to the Epistle of St. Paul to the Romans*, Luther describes, "This letter is truly the most important piece in the New Testament. It is purest Gospel."[3] Similarly, in the preface to his *Commentary on Romans*, Calvin writes: "If we have gained a true understanding of this Epistle, we have an open door to all the most profound treasures of Scripture."[4]

The insights derived during the Reformation underwent development. Luther and Calvin were responsible for formulating the primary focus of the two phases of the Reformation. Under Luther, the first phase concerned the ultimate authority of Scripture versus the teaching authority of the Church; that justification is by faith alone, apart from works and sacrament; and the priesthood of every believer versus the need for priests as intermediaries with God. The focus of the Reformation under Calvin broadened to the divine sovereignty over all aspects of life; the purity of worship apart from human traditions; and that Church order is synodical—the joint rule of all pastor-teachers—rather than hierarchical or locally independent. Both phases culminated in the *doxological focus* of the Westminster Confession of Faith, the high-water

---

1. Gangadean, "Paper No. 17: The Five Solas," in *The Logos Papers*, 115–118.

2. Gangadean, "Paper No. 18: Salvation by Grace," in *The Logos Papers*, 119–122.

3. Martin Luther, *Preface to the Epistle of St. Paul to the Romans*, trans. Andrew Thornton (Grand Rapids, MI: Christian Classics Ethereal Library), accessed February 26, 2025, https://www.ccel.org/l/luther/romans/pref_romans.html.

4. John Calvin, *Commentary on the Epistle of Paul the Apostle to the Romans*, trans. John Owen (Grand Rapids, MI: Christian Classics Ethereal Library), accessed February 26, 2025, https://www.ccel.org/ccel/calvin/calcom38.html.

mark of the Historic Christian Faith.[5] The Westminster Confession of Faith built upon earlier creeds of the Reformation—Augsburg (Lutheran), Thirty-Nine Articles (Anglican), Belgic (French), Helvetic (Swiss), Heidelberg (German), and Dort (Dutch)—making it the last and most conscious and consistent creed of the Reformation and of Church History. The understanding attained by the Westminster Divines and the doctrines they set forth constitutes the historical foundation upon which Pastor Gangadean built his philosophical and theological works, including the present work.

The understanding attained by the Westminster Divines, as expressed in the Westminster Standards (the Westminster Confession of Faith and its Catechisms), includes the affirmation of the clarity of general revelation and the inexcusability of unbelief; the use of reason—the light of nature and good and necessary consequences—to understand general revelation and special revelation; the doxological focus on the knowledge of the glory of God; divine sovereignty in creation–fall–redemption; and the law of God for all of life.

This work seeks to apply these doctrines to St. Paul's Epistle to the Romans as an attempt to faithfully continue the work the Westminster Divines accomplished. Pastor Gangadean recognized the need to advance the work of the kingdom by building on the foundation attained at the end of the Reformation and by responding to the challenges that have arisen since. Others who continued the work of the Reformation did not build upon this foundation, and the Church has keenly felt the effects—in its divisions, in the loss of its headship in the culture, and in its displacement as the pillar and ground of the truth. Uncritically held assumptions remain in the Church and have caused further divisions, which have scandalized the world. This reality sets the stage for the need for a second Reformation, which, in turn, calls for a fuller and clearer justification and exposition of the gospel. That is the aim and the hope for which this work was formulated and is now being published.

---

5. Gangadean, *The Westminster Confession*, xxix–xxxii, 347–348; Gangadean, "Paper No. 115: Doxological Christianity," in *The Logos Papers*, 595–596.

THE NEED FOR A SECOND REFORMATION

We need a second Reformation because the first Reformation has lost its impact. After 500 years, the Church's message is no longer influential—it is ignored, or even mocked, by those who were once its strongest supporters. The Church is deeply divided and widely perceived as irrelevant, merely following cultural trends rather than leading them. It has lost its authority and become entangled in the world's unbelief. In reaction to centuries of empiricism and skepticism, the Church has fallen into fideism—belief without understanding. In response to naturalism and secularism, it has turned to superstitious supernaturalism and mystical escapism. Confronted with the relativism of political correctness and the despair of nihilism, the Church has embraced legalism and pietism. As a result, the gospel's power to transform lives and cultures is no longer being proclaimed.

The need for a second Reformation is urgent. The first Reformation has lost its vitality; it is time for a new movement to revive and restore the Church's influence and power through the gospel. In essence, the first Reformation is spent—it is over; it is dead. Long live the second Reformation!

It is clear what is needed for a second Reformation: to establish the very foundation upon which the first Reformation should have been built. The Church's foundation must be laid again—this time more deeply—and it must be built upon the rock, not upon sand. That rock is clarity, not fideism. Only by the clarity of general revelation can the inexcusability of unbelief be understood. The basic things about God and man, and about good and evil, are clear to reason. The Church must repent of its root sin: not seeking and not understanding what is clear to reason.

THE GOSPEL OF THE FIRST REFORMATION:
Focused on Salvation by Faith

Paul begins his proclamation of the gospel by asserting, "I am not ashamed of the gospel" (Rom. 1:16a), emphasizing his unwavering confidence in its power. This confidence is grounded in the reality that the gospel is "the power of God for the salvation of everyone who believes" (Rom. 1:16b). To understand why Paul is not ashamed, we must recognize the necessity of the gospel in light of two fundamental revelations: the righteousness of God and the wrath of God. "For in the gospel a righteousness from God is revealed" (Rom. 1:17a). This is not human righteousness, but the righteousness that originates from God and is received "by faith from first to last" (Rom. 1:17). It is necessary because humanity lacks righteousness and stands condemned under "the wrath of God [that] is being revealed from heaven against all the godlessness and wickedness of men" (Rom. 1:18a). There is a deliberate parallel here: *righteousness* is revealed in the gospel, and *wrath* is revealed against sin. This contrast is central to understanding the need for the gospel.

Paul's argument is definitive: if humanity is under God's wrath due to sin, then salvation requires a righteousness that meets God's standard. This righteousness is both imputed and worked out. It is imputed—credited to believers, justifying them before God on the basis of Christ's righteousness alone—and it is received by faith alone. It is also worked out in personal sanctification, producing a transformed life and making one actually righteous. Paul states, "The righteous will live by faith" (Rom. 1:17b), emphasizing that righteousness is both the means and the ongoing experience of salvation. This righteousness is "by faith from first to last" or "from faith to faith,"[6] showing that faith is the continuous source of life and growth in righteousness. This understanding of righteousness is deepened when we see the severity of God's wrath. The wrath of God is not merely future judgment, but a present reality, manifesting as spiritual death and moral decay. It is God's response to human rebellion and suppression of the truth. The depth of this wrath shows the necessity of the righteousness revealed in the gospel—only righteousness from God can save.

THE GOSPEL OF THE SECOND REFORMATION:
Focus on Justifying the Need for the Gospel

Romans 1:17 requires the truth of Romans 1:18–20. The basis for our sin before God is the foundation needed to justify the need for the gospel. The clarity of the existence and nature of God is the basis for the inexcusability of unbelief. God has made His existence *maximally*

---

6. *Romans 1:17* NKJV.

clear and has written the law on our hearts, leaving us without excuse. The gospel that emerged from the Reformation emphasized the gift of salvation by faith but neglected to establish the doctrine of clarity and inexcusability. Although this doctrine—assumed as the basis for our inexcusability from general revelation—is clearly stated by Paul in Romans 1:18–20, and affirmed in the opening words of the Westminster Confession of Faith, it was largely lost from view due to the Reformation's soteriological focus on individual salvation.

Rather than pursuing the need to articulate the doctrine of clarity and establish the basis for our inexcusability, the gospel was advanced primarily as a means of escape from the wrath of God in the hereafter—in hell—rather than as the means of fulfilling the doxological aim: that the earth be filled with the knowledge of God. This doxological focus entails the work of dominion—bringing glory to God by taking every thought captive and rendering it subject to Christ. In the end, soteriological concerns displaced the doxological focus that had been attained at the end of the Reformation, as summarized in the Westminster Confession of Faith.

Since the Reformation, because of its misplaced focus, the Church has lost its position of headship in the culture and is now in captivity to fideism and mystical otherworldliness. In addition, it is surrounded by unbelief in the form of skepticism and secularism. The Church has not taken unbelief captive; it has not demolished all arguments and pretensions raised against the knowledge of God and, therefore, has fallen captive to unbelief. The doctrine of clarity and inexcusability is the cornerstone—the bedrock of the foundation. By this doctrine, all else comes into place. If there is no clarity and inexcusability, then there can be no sin and no Christianity in which Christ is the Lamb of God who takes away the sin of the world. The stone which the builders rejected has become the head stone of the corner.[7]

The doctrine of clarity states that the basic things about God and man, and good and evil, are clear to reason.[8] The existence and nature of God, as well as the moral law written on the heart, are clear to reason. This doctrine becomes the basis for the justification of the gospel and the

---

7. *Psalm 118:2.*

8. Gangadean, *Philosophical Foundation*, 3–5, 287–292; Gangadean, *The Westminster Confession*, 1–13; Gangadean, "Paper No. 53: Common Ground (Part IV)," in *The Logos Papers*, 283–286.

means of advancing the work of the kingdom in discipling the nations. Therefore, it is to take center place in establishing and advancing the work of the kingdom.

In *The Epistle to the Romans: The Righteousness of God Revealed from Faith to Faith—The Gospel According to St. Paul,* Pastor Gangadean brings into focus the centrality of the doctrine of clarity and inexcusability. Both in 1994 and 2013, and throughout his pastoral and academic life, he faithfully pursued the establishment of the truth of God grounded in this doctrine. In this book, the reader is afforded an exposition of Romans developed over a span of twenty years, drawing from a variety of approaches—ranging from sermons to academic papers—to incorporate theological, philosophical, and pastoral insights into a single work. It is intended to equip God's people for works of service by distilling doctrine into theological and ethical principles and their practical implementation in the life of the Church.

ELEMENTS OF THIS WORK

A prolegomena to Romans explains the centrality of the doctrine of clarity in understanding the content of the epistle. It also alerts the reader to the ongoing dispute between two competing epistemological views regarding the inexcusability of unbelief: the voluntarist view of *willful suppression* versus the view of *culpable ignorance* in the face of clear and present truth unacknowledged. This dispute, concerning the unity and order of human personality, currently divides those within the Reformed faith and carries significant implications for the Christian faith more broadly.

The exposition of Romans consists of sermons delivered in 1994, 2000, 2003, 2011, and 2013. While most of the 1994 sermons are preserved in The Logos Archives, those on Romans 7 and 15 remain unaccounted for. In the case of Romans 7, The Logos Foundation Editorial Board composed a brief exposition of its main ideas based on Pastor Gangadean's notes and related comments made elsewhere. For Romans 15, a post-sermon discussion was used to convey the substance of the sermon, as well as Pastor Gangadean's pedagogical approach to mentorship through dialogue—a hallmark of his mastery of dialectic and rhetoric.

Four sermons from 2013 were incorporated—specifically, the pivotal chapters 1–2, 5, and 16. During that year, younger apprentices delivered sermons as part of their *practicum*, a structured component of their preparation for teaching within the church. While it would undoubtedly have been a great blessing for Pastor Gangadean to have preached through the entirety of Romans in 2013, his commitment to training the next generation of leaders compelled him, in wisdom, to proceed as he did. In addition, two sermons were added. One, from 2003 on Romans 12:1–8, titled *Sacrifice: The Way to Life*, was included to underscore the theme of sanctification through knowledge of the truth and suffering in the Christian life. Another sermon, from 2011 on Romans 8:28–39, titled *Christ's Victory and Ours: Crossing the Finish Line*, illustrates endurance, victory, and completion of the work as embodied in Christ, Paul, and believers.

Four appendices have been added to provide the reader with additional resources:

Appendix A is an exposition of Romans 1 in connection with the work of the Church. Delivered within weeks of the founding of Westminster Fellowship in 2000, this sermon contextualizes the importance of the doctrine of clarity in relation to spiritual maturity and the equipping of God's people for works of service in the kingdom. *Appendix B* addresses the long-standing dispute regarding voluntarism. In 1994–1995, Pastor Gangadean engaged several pastors within the Reformed tradition in an effort to settle this debate. This lecture, given to a small group, reflects his thinking at a time when the issue was increasingly coming into focus in his mind. *Appendices C* and *D* are polished expositions of the plan of natural theology and the responsibility of Christians regarding philosophy. Since the doctrine of clarity is foundational to this book, and to the Christian faith, The Logos Foundation Editorial Board thought it fitting to include these writings to demonstrate how the doctrine of clarity and inexcusability can be proven. While Paul speaks of these doctrines in Romans, their proof must be derived from general revelation through natural theology. These appendices serve as invaluable guides for establishing the foundational doctrines of the Christian faith in our time and for reversing the Church's ongoing retreat from its God-appointed role as the pillar and ground of the truth in culture.

Laying the foundation more deeply requires answering the most explicit challenges of unbelief since the first Reformation. Both Modernity and Postmodernity demand a philosophical response grounded in the clarity of general revelation. May these sermons serve to edify the body of Christ, and may they stand as a foundation for establishing the doctrine of clarity and inexcusability—securing a lasting framework for life and culture.

—THE LOGOS FOUNDATION
EDITORIAL BOARD
Phoenix, Arizona
March 2025

PROLEGOMENA TO PAUL'S GOSPEL

The Biblical Doctrine of Clarity and Inexcusability

THE BASIS OF INEXCUSABILITY

Willful Suppression of the Knowledge of God: Knowingly Doing Evil

NO INTELLIGENT CHRISTIAN WILL ARGUE THAT unregenerate sinners are without excuse for their unbelief. Paul makes this all too abundantly clear in Romans 1:20. However, debate does exist about the basis of inexcusability. The majority of Protestants, Arminian and Reformed, presuppositional and evidential, believe that inexcusability rests fundamentally in the truth that all sinners willingly suppress the knowledge of God within themselves, sinning, in effect, against their better knowledge. Mired in destructive self-deception, what the unbeliever knows of God and will not accept he knowingly rejects.

Culpable Ignorance: Clear and Present Truth Unacknowledged

In opposition to the idea that unbelievers know God deep down inside and suppress that truth in sinful rebellion, is the idea that unbelievers in spiritual death do not seek after the clear truth of God and, therefore, do not know God deep down inside. In other words, the objective revelation of God is never subjectively realized—it fails to "get through" apart from seeking. Here, inexcusability is not a matter of knowledge knowingly suppressed or rejected but is a matter of clear and present truth unacknowledged. In effect, sinners in unbelief are primarily accountable for not understanding and not believing what is clearly revealed of God.

CLARITY AND INEXCUSABILITY
BEGINS IN THE GARDEN ACCOUNT

The doctrines of both clarity and inexcusability do not first surface with Romans 1:18–21, but spring from the beginning of redemptive revelation in Genesis 3.[1] It is from within this context, as well as the rest of Scripture that follows, that we must eventually come to and uncover the coherent meaning of Romans 1:18–21.

The Temptation: Willful Suppression or Culpable Ignorance?

From Genesis 3, we see that God's testing of Adam in the Garden was designed to reveal where Adam was in his seeking the clear truth of God. Was he seeking the good, the knowledge of God, or was he seeking to determine the good for himself in autonomous rebellion? From the beginning, the serpent's temptation was directed at the heart of what Adam understood to be true regarding the nature of God and himself. Directly contradicting God's command that both Adam and Eve would surely die upon eating of the forbidden fruit, the serpent tactfully insinuated that God is either ignorant or a liar, both of which God clearly cannot be. The crux of the matter is whether Adam ate the fruit of the tree because he wanted to be autonomous and suppress what he deep down knew to be true of God or whether he, in spiritual death, had not sought after the knowledge of God and, thus, did not know what is clear of God, or at least had neglected what perhaps he did at one time know to be true of God.

Adam and Eve Failed to Seek and Understand the Nature of God and Man

When we do not diligently seek to know God, our knowledge of Him can be missed or lost altogether. Therefore, we need not insist that Adam paradoxically knew deep down that God could not lie or be ignorant, yet still agreed with the serpent's appeal, as though the test was a matter of the heart and not of the head/the understanding. Furthermore, the serpent's temptation also incorporated a suggestion that both Adam

---

1. Surrendra Gangadean, *The Biblical Worldview: Creation, Fall, Redemption—Genesis 1–3: Scripture in Organic Seed Form* (Phoenix: Logos Papers Press, 2024).

and Eve, though created, could be like God knowing good and evil. As both Adam and Eve were responsible to know that God cannot lie or be ignorant, both were likewise responsible to know the clear truth that as finite beings they could not be as God, who is eternal. Likewise, because God is eternal, He alone determines good and evil. He does not discover it, as Adam and Eve would have had to if the serpent's lie were the truth. Moreover, clear thinking on the part of both husband and wife would also have kept them from trying to hide from an omniscient and omnipresent God, which showed yet an even greater deficiency in their understanding of the nature of God. If Adam and his wife had been seeking to know the clear truth concerning the nature of God and man, they would have rejected the serpent's lie; they would have seen the temptation as complete nonsense, an impossible suggestion.

INEXCUSABILITY ASSUMES CLARITY RATHER THAN SUPPRESSED KNOWLEDGE

The Universality of Root Sin: The Sin of Not Seeking to Know God and His Creation[2]

The original sin of our first parents, the sin of not seeking to know what is clear of God and His creation, is with all of us today, both believers and unbelievers. The idea that inexcusability assumes clarity rather than a suppressed knowledge of God coherently demonstrates how unbelievers and believers sin alike; sin is fundamentally not seeking to know God as He has revealed Himself, both generally and specially. Paul speaks to this in Romans 3:10–11: "As it is written: 'There is no one righteous, not even one; there is no one who understands, no one who seeks God.'"

Regarding how Paul's analysis relates to sin in both the believer and the unbeliever, it is shown in how Peter, though clearly regenerate, insisted that Jesus as Messiah could not be made to suffer. Peter's attempted suppression of the truth of Christ's mission stemmed from

---

2. Root sin is not seeking and not understanding what is clear about God. Root sin leads to fruit sin (not doing what is right). It is the original sin, is universal in all as unbelief, and is inexcusable in light of the objective clarity of general revelation. Root sin blinds man to the reality of sin. Root sin is the first sin historically (in Eden), ontologically (in the first commandment), and existentially (in human self-awareness).

a false assumption that was born of not seeking what God had clearly revealed of His redemptive plan in Scripture. Shall we assume that Peter was rebelliously suppressing an innate understanding that the Messiah had to suffer, or shall we instead assume that Peter wrongly believed that the atonement for sin would come without the shedding of the Messiah's blood? Though Peter came to see the error of his uncritically held assumptions, unbelievers are forever unwilling to seek after and acknowledge the clear truth of God. Both the Old and New Testaments speak to this matter.

Culpable Ignorance in the Unbeliever, the Teachers of the Law, and Paul

Isaiah in 44:18 writes, "They know nothing, they understand nothing; their eyes are plastered over so they cannot see, and their minds closed so they cannot understand." Clearly, this verse is best interpreted to mean that God's objective revelation is not subjectively realized by the unbeliever.

This same sentiment is mirrored by Paul in 2 Corinthians 4:3–4. Paul writes, "And even if our gospel is veiled, it is veiled to those who are perishing. The god of this age has blinded the minds of unbelievers, so they cannot see the light of the gospel of the glory of Christ, who is the image of God." We see an example of Paul's above emphasis nowhere better than with the teachers of the law. These individuals were operating from age-old assumptions about the nature of the Messiah that ran in direct contrast with the life and teachings of Christ. Their problem was that in light of their own entrenched assumptions, they would not and could not see the truth and consistency of Christ's claims. They hated Christ not because they knew He spoke the truth and could not stomach it; they hated Him because what He preached did not align with their beliefs (Messianic and otherwise) and also because He brilliantly exposed their illegitimate authority. We should expect the spiritually blind to be unwilling to seek after and understand spiritual truths—resorting instead to blind authoritarianism and militant self-justification.

Continuing with his general point about not seeking, and not understanding, Paul writes in 1 Corinthians 2:14, "The man without the Spirit does not accept the things that come from the Spirit of God, for they are foolishness to him, and he cannot understand them, because they are spiritually discerned." What is foolishness to those in unbelief is such because they have not understood it, and they have not understood it because they have not sought the clear truths of God. This notion that unbelieving man in spiritual death is unwilling and unable to know God is not entirely foreign to Hebrew thought. While not of canonical authority, the apocryphal book of Wisdom states in chapter 13:1, "For all men were by nature foolish who were in ignorance of God, and who from the good things seen did not succeed in knowing him who is, and from studying the works did not discern the artisan." Concerning his own life in sinful unbelief, Paul writes in 1 Timothy 1:13, "Even though I was once a blasphemer and a persecutor and a violent man, I was shown mercy because I acted in ignorance and unbelief." Clearly, ignorance is a matter of not knowing what is true—not a matter of suppressing what is true. One who knowingly suppresses the truth cannot also be suppressing the truth ignorantly.

JESUS CONFRONTS SINNERS FOR THEIR CULPABLE IGNORANCE

Though what Paul stresses must not be overlooked, we cannot help but see that Jesus Himself confronts the sinner as ignorant and unwilling to know the truths of God. Christ speaks in Matthew 13:14–15:

> You will be ever hearing but never understanding; you will be ever seeing but never perceiving. For this people's heart has become calloused; they hardly hear with their ears, and they have closed their eyes. Otherwise they might see with their eyes, hear with their ears, understand with their hearts and turn, and I would heal them.

The emphasis of Christ's words here seems to reveal a problem with the cognition of the truth and not a willful rejection of it. Furthermore, in Luke 23:34, Jesus declares, "Father, forgive them; for they know not what they do."[3] Here, we see that the greatest rebellion against God is not chalked up to the willful suppression of the truth but to culpable ignorance. This flows perfectly with how Jesus' apologetic efforts were consistently aimed at showing where the assumptions of others were

---

3. KJV.

clearly at fault and how they were responsible for their obstinacy in not seeking and not knowing the clear truths of God. When Christ asked whether John's baptism was of God or of man, and who David's Lord was in Psalm 110, He knew that the questions He raised would serve to expose and demolish the uncritically held assumptions of those in authority, those who were in positions of instruction in the faith.[4] In fact, many of Christ's debates ended in silence, revealing that the truth is clear and that sinful man must turn off his mind not to see it.

Time and time again, the gospels reveal a Christ who taught people what they did not already know or realize, yet ought to have. Luke in chapter 24:27 writes, "And beginning with Moses and all the Prophets, he explained to them what was said in all the Scriptures concerning himself," and verse 45, "Then he opened their minds so they could understand the Scriptures." The gospels reveal the same psychological effect of regeneration time and time again—coming to see the truth of what had not before been understood because of a lack of seeking to know the truth of God. Even in everyday life, it is common that when believers come to the Lord they do so through a process of realizing that their past assumptions and basic beliefs no longer make any sense in the light of God's clear and compelling truth. What Nicodemus[5] did not understand about regeneration is the effect of having not diligently sought out the clear truth of God and cannot be attributed to any type of suppressed knowledge. Furthermore, time and time again we see Christ admonishing His followers for being of dull mind and slow in understanding,[6] but never do we see Christ admonishing them for anything that can be categorized as willful suppression of the truth. Never do we see Christ appealing to suppressed knowledge, but always to the blindness of unbelief and the unwillingness of sinful man to seek after the clear truth of God. In John 8:43, Christ speaks to this: "Why is my language not clear to you? Because you are unable to hear what I say." What else could our Lord have said to make Himself any clearer?

---

4. Surrendra Gangadean, *The Gospel of Matthew: The Person and Work of Christ—The Fulfillment of Redemption Through the One to Come* (Phoenix: Logos Papers Press, 2025).

5. *John 3:1–21.*

6. *Matthew 8:26, 14:31, 15:16, 16:8–9, 17:17; Mark 4:40, 6:52, 7:18, 8:17–18, 9:41; Luke 24:25; John 3:10.*

INTERPRETATION OF ROMANS 1:18–21

It is now appropriate to give an interpretation of Romans 1:18–21 in light of the above analysis that men are without excuse for not understanding and believing in what God has clearly revealed of Himself.

The Wrath of God Versus Unbelief in Men (Romans 1:18)

"The wrath of God is being revealed from heaven against all the godlessness and wickedness of men who suppress the truth by their wickedness." We need not assume here that unbelievers suppress the truth while at the same time knowing it, but instead, suppress and hinder the truth of God principally by the mountain of lies and falsehood they concoct out of their darkened and ignorant minds. Paul's emphasis is to set up the idea that the truth of God, both specially and generally revealed, has been systematically suppressed, hindered, and held down by false assumptions and lies. Helmut Thielicke remarks,

> The fact that the divine majesty is objectively presented in the works of creation (Rom. 1:18 ff.) by no means implies a corresponding capacity in man to lay hold of this presentation and, as it were, put it to fruitful effect. It is quite possible for God's revelation to be objectively given while it is subjectively obstructed. Hence the revealing of revelation takes place only in the miracle of the Holy Spirit.[7]

In connection with Thielicke's last point, a robust Reformed apologetic must never be willing to grant too much to the unregenerate mind in terms of what it knows to be true of God. If it is the case that the unregenerate does not seek and does not understand God's revelation,[8] why ought we to insist that they know the truth of God? After all, the Holy Spirit not only regenerates our deadened minds so that we may confess belief in Christ, but He also must first work in opening our minds to seek and understand what we before did not comprehend about the truths of the Spirit, as Paul speaks about in 1 Corinthians.[9]

---

7. Helmut Thielicke, *Theological Ethics*, vol. 1, *Foundations*, trans. William H. Lazareth (Grand Rapids, MI: Eerdmans, 1979), 164.

8. *Romans 3:10.*

9. *1 Corinthians 2:6–16.*

The Perspicuity of General Revelation (Romans 1:19)

"Since what may be known about God is plain to them, because God has made it plain to them." God's wrath against unbelief is made all the more understandable in light of the fact that the truth of God is and has been clearly manifested to all persons, universally in the form of general revelation and non-universally in the form of special revelation. Regardless of the particular mode of God's revelation, it has been made clear and intelligible.

The Existence and Nature of God Understood from the Creation (Romans 1:20)

"For since the creation of the world God's invisible qualities—his eternal power and divine nature—have been clearly seen, being understood from what has been made, so that men are without excuse." This verse can be understood as emphasizing the general or universal manifestation of God's clear revelation of Himself. Since the beginning of history up until this present day, God's clear universal revelation of Himself has been manifested to all rational persons. Not only is it clear that God exists, it is clear that all opposing beliefs are incoherent and false. The Christian must be able to demonstrate the substantial incoherence of all ideas raised up against the knowledge of God. From what is clear generally, the Christian is called to silence the spiritual monist, as well as the material monist. It is our task to rout the Mormon and completely demolish the strongholds of Islam. The truth of God is clear; and the Church's apologetic must be reinvigorated in that truth. As Christ our Lord took all thoughts captive and did not appeal to a suppressed knowledge within the unbeliever, so too must we fight.

Corporate Apostasy of Mankind (Romans 1:21)

"For although they knew God, they neither glorified him as God nor gave thanks to him, but their thinking became futile and their foolish hearts were darkened." Undoubtedly, Romans 1:21 is the *locus classicus* for those who assert that all persons in unbelief willingly suppress what they know to be true of God as their Creator. Upon first impression, this passage appears to say as much and nothing less. What alternate interpretation can be given that does not unnecessarily twist the immediate sense of the verse, yet still makes room for the assumption that the unbeliever does not know God deep down inside? To begin, while Paul uses Romans 1:20 to speak of that clear universal revelation of God that holds all men without excuse to this very day, verse 21 can be understood as documenting how God's clear special revelation has undergone an unmistakable pattern of generational decay in what people knew to be true of God and of His commands. In short, since none seek and none understand, what God has specially revealed of Himself has been just as neglected from the beginning as has His general revelation.

Starting from a truly biblical framework, the reader of Romans 1:21 would have to admit that all persons descended from Adam and that there was a slow, but progressive neglect, distortion, and dissolution of God's special revelation originally transmitted to our first father. While it is demonstrably true that God has not manifested Himself specially to all persons, the entire human race does spring from an original historical point that was saturated with God's special revelation. For example, because of the effects of spiritual death (not seeking, not understanding), what Cain learned from his father concerning God quickly became something less than glorifying to God. While Cain knew enough to bring sacrifice, he did not care enough to understand, in contrast to Abel, the tremendous significance of the blood sacrifice. More or less, this generational pattern of revelation decay carried all the way to the Flood, where only Noah and his sons were left with God's original and undistorted special revelation. As also occurred with the immediate descendants of Adam, from this post-Flood historical point, the generations of men slowly moved further and further away from what Noah and his sons had preserved of God's special revelation. On this matter, Henry M. Morris comments,

> Accordingly, we are on solid ground when we adopt Genesis 1–11 as the true framework of ancient history. When we take our stand on this fundamental premise, we find that all the phenomena of mythology and all the discoveries of archaeology and geology correlate with each other and with the Bible in a most satisfying way. These data, when carefully examined, all point to a world where the people first knew the true God, then rapidly corrupted that knowledge into pantheism, polytheism, occultism, and idolatry, with

all the evil practices these encourage. This was true in the primeval world and then again in the postdiluvian world.[10]

While it is true that an Aztec warrior could not be held personally accountable for what Ham and his descendants once knew of God, he is held accountable for failing to know of what God has clearly revealed of Himself generally. What Paul says in Romans 1 concerning the debasing practices of mind and body committed by those of darkened intellect can be easily interpreted as a pre-Flood and post-Flood indictment of how sinful man slowly but surely dissolves the truth of God, turning it into a detestable and distorted lie.

The history of Israel shows time and time again that although they knew of God as a nation and as individuals, they consistently failed to seek after the knowledge of God, wherein the truth dissolved into gross idolatry. Whereas all persons are responsible to see what is clear of God from general revelation, there are those specifically who are under special indictment for their failure to seek after and understand God's special revelation as well. The generational decay in the Book of Judges is a perfect example of how special revelation can be both known and disregarded because of a lack of seeking God earnestly. Judges 2:10–12 reads,

> After that whole generation had been gathered to their fathers, another generation grew up, who knew neither the LORD nor what he had done for Israel. Then the Israelites did evil in the eyes of the LORD and served the Baals. They forsook the LORD, the God of their fathers, who had brought them out of Egypt. They followed and worshiped various gods of the peoples around them. They provoked the LORD to anger.

Furthermore, Hosea 4:6–7 reads,

> My people are destroyed from a lack of knowledge. Because you have rejected knowledge, I also reject you as my priests; because you have ignored the law of your God, I also will ignore your children.

---

10. Henry M. Morris, *The Long War Against God: The History and Impact of the Creation/Evolution Conflict* (Grand Rapids, MI: Baker Book House, 1989), 263.

The more the priests increased, the more they sinned against me;
they exchanged their Glory for something disgraceful.

And lastly, Jeremiah 2:11 reads, "Has a nation ever changed its gods?
(Yet they are not gods at all.) But my people have exchanged their
Glory for worthless idols." One may neglect or distort what they have
been taught of God, not so much because they rebelliously loathe its
content, but because in spiritual death, they have not uncovered its
true significance and, thus, cannot discern its meaningfulness for their
lives. One can see a pattern emerge in the Bible regarding complacency
and pseudo-religiosity in the life of God's people that inevitably leads
to a defective reinterpretation of God's revealed will.

From the history of Israel alone, the reader of Romans 1:21 need not
assume that Paul is speaking about first-century Gentiles who willingly
suppress an innate knowledge of God. Instead, one need only assume
that Paul is alluding to God's historical special revelation, which, though
clearly given to the race of man at times, has been systematically debased
and forgotten by generation after generation.[11]

CONCLUSION

There are four principal benefits in assuming that unbelievers in spiritual death do not know God. One, the Christian is not stuck with
the ugly paradox of the unbelieving believer. Because of this awkward
predicament, Cornelius Van Til, the great presuppositional apologist,
spoke of Romans 1:18–22 as "this most difficult passage."[12] It need not
be. The perspicuity of Scripture demands that such a crucial issue as
this be relatively easy to comprehend, as opposed to being intrinsically
enigmatic. Two, this position is consistent with the whole of Scripture,

---

11. Along with verse 21, verse 32 has been used to help substantiate the theory that men willingly suppress what they know to be true of God. Nowhere does verse 32 allude to the
idea of man possessing a formal and specific knowledge of God; for it is quite easy to see
how man can have the law of God in the very structure of their being (written on their
hearts) and have no understanding of God specifically as Creator. Though nearly all soci-
eties demonstrate a universal law code, and all men act against their consciences, it is not
the same thing to suggest that all men willingly suppress a formal and immediate knowledge of God within them.

12. Cornelius Van Til, *An Introduction to Systematic Theology*, 2nd ed. (Phillipsburg, NJ: Presbyterian and Reformed Publishing, 1974), 93.

and is not primarily founded on one particular verse. Moreover, there is nothing heretical in this position that makes it immediately less appealing than the assumption that unbelievers knowingly reject the truth of God. Three, as opposed to the assumption that unbelievers resist the truth of what they know about God, this position carries with it no voluntaristic baggage—the will warring against the intellect.[13] The issue is an intellectual one, not a moral one. And fourth, this position upholds the cultural mandate, whereby we master the lies that suppress the truth and expose the incoherence of those thoughts raised up against the knowledge of God.

---

13. Gangadean, "Paper No. 120: Contra Voluntarism," in *The Logos Papers*, 611–647.

———

THE EPISTLE TO THE
ROMANS

———

1

THE GOSPEL ACCORDING TO ST. PAUL

The Wrath and Righteousness of God Are Being Revealed

1994

Romans 1

¹Paul, a servant of Christ Jesus, called to be an apostle and set apart for the gospel of God—²the gospel he promised beforehand through his prophets in the Holy Scriptures ³regarding his Son, who as to his human nature was a descendant of David, ⁴and who through the Spirit of holiness was declared with power to be the Son of God by his resurrection from the dead: Jesus Christ our Lord. ⁵Through him and for his name's sake, we received grace and apostleship to call people from among all the Gentiles to the obedience that comes from faith. ⁶And you also are among those who are called to belong to Jesus Christ.

⁷To all in Rome who are loved by God and called to be saints: Grace and peace to you from God our Father and from the Lord Jesus Christ.

⁸First, I thank my God through Jesus Christ for all of you, because your faith is being reported all over the world. ⁹God, whom I serve with my whole heart in preaching the gospel of his Son, is my witness how constantly I remember you ¹⁰in my prayers at all times; and I pray that now at last by God's will the way may be opened for me to come to you.

¹¹I long to see you so that I may impart to you some spiritual gift to make you strong—¹²that is, that you and I may be mutually encouraged by each

other's faith. 13I do not want you to be unaware, brothers, that I planned many times to come to you (but have been prevented from doing so until now) in order that I might have a harvest among you, just as I have had among the other Gentiles.

14I am obligated both to Greeks and non-Greeks, both to the wise and the foolish. 15That is why I am so eager to preach the gospel also to you who are at Rome.

16I am not ashamed of the gospel, because it is the power of God for the salvation of everyone who believes: first for the Jew, then for the Gentile. 17For in the gospel a righteousness from God is revealed, a righteousness that is by faith from first to last, just as it is written: "The righteous will live by faith."

18The wrath of God is being revealed from heaven against all the godlessness and wickedness of men who suppress the truth by their wickedness, 19since what may be known about God is plain to them, because God has made it plain to them. 20For since the creation of the world God's invisible qualities—his eternal power and divine nature—have been clearly seen, being understood from what has been made, so that men are without excuse.

21For although they knew God, they neither glorified him as God nor gave thanks to him, but their thinking became futile and their foolish hearts were darkened. 22Although they claimed to be wise, they became fools 23and exchanged the glory of the immortal God for images made to look like mortal man and birds and animals and reptiles.

24Therefore God gave them over in the sinful desires of their hearts to sexual impurity for the degrading of their bodies with one another. 25They exchanged the truth of God for a lie, and worshiped and served created things rather than the Creator—who is forever praised. Amen.

26Because of this, God gave them over to shameful lusts. Even their women exchanged natural relations for unnatural ones. 27In the same way the men also abandoned natural relations with women and were inflamed with lust for one another. Men committed indecent acts with other men, and received in themselves the due penalty for their perversion.

28Furthermore, since they did not think it worthwhile to retain the knowledge of God, he gave them over to a depraved mind, to do what ought not to be done. 29They have become filled with every kind of wickedness, evil, greed and depravity. They are full of envy, murder, strife, deceit and malice. They are gossips, 30slanderers, God-haters, insolent, arrogant and boastful; they invent ways of doing evil; they disobey their parents; 31they are senseless, faithless, heartless, ruthless. 32Although they know God's righteous decree that those who do such things deserve death, they not only continue to do these very things but also approve of those who practice them.

THE CENTRALITY OF THE GOSPEL

Paul Is Set Apart for the Gospel

THE GOSPEL ACCORDING TO ST. PAUL. We are accustomed to thinking of the gospel as focusing on the historic life of Jesus. That is certainly true, but the gospel is presented here in another manner, and we will see how Paul develops it. The centrality of the gospel comes through very clearly throughout the introductory part of this chapter. He says that he is "**a servant of Christ Jesus, called to be an apostle and set apart for the gospel of God**" (v. 1). He focuses on this point—that he is "**set apart for the gospel.**" He speaks about this gospel briefly and it will be opened up more and more as we go through the epistle.

Promised Beforehand Through the Prophets

The gospel was "**promised beforehand through his prophets in the Holy Scriptures**" (v. 2). The gospel is not something new. If we were to go back to the prophets of the Old Testament, we should find the gospel there. This is the gospel he is "**set apart for.**" This is the sense in which he is "**a servant of Christ Jesus.**"

Regarding His Son

This gospel comes to focus on the Son of God: "**regarding his Son.**" This is the gospel of God; it is "**regarding his Son,**" and it is the good news concerning His Son. Paul specifies clearly who this Son is. He says, "**regarding his Son, who as to his human nature was a descendant of David**" (v. 3). He is the Son of Man; He is the son of David. He is human; He has human nature. Not only that, but He, "**through the Spirit of holiness was declared with power to be the Son of God by his resurrection from the dead**" (v. 4a). So He is both the Son of Man and the Son of God. And the resurrection of the dead vindicated His claim that He had fully satisfied the penalty of sin as the Son of God incarnate, as this One of *unsurpassed* dignity was subject to *unsurpassed* humiliation. In that humiliation, our penalty is borne, and He bore it completely, fully, as the Son of God incarnate. He was raised from the dead. No mere man could pay that penalty. It took the humiliation of the Son of God to fully pay that penalty, and that it was fully paid is shown by the fact that He was raised from the dead. He "**was declared with power to be the Son of God by his resurrection from the dead: Jesus Christ our Lord**" (v. 4). The Son of God, both man and God: He is Jesus Christ our Lord.

To Call the Gentiles

"**Through him and for his name's sake**"—for His glory to be made known—"**we received grace and apostleship to call people from among all the Gentiles to the obedience that comes from faith**" (v. 5). Paul is set apart for the gospel, but particularly, he says, "**to call all the people from among the Gentiles**"—not exclusively, but particularly. He identifies his being set apart to call the Gentiles, the nations, and call them to the "**obedience that comes from faith.**"

To the Obedience from Faith

Paul is going to make the point that "**the righteous will live by faith**" (v. 17b). It is "**a righteousness that is by faith from first to last**" (v. 17a). Here, he speaks about "**obedience that comes from faith**" (v. 5b). Later on, we will speak about the righteousness that comes by faith imputed to us—by Christ's perfect obedience—but here, Paul says that in the gospel we are called to the "**obedience that comes from faith.**" That is our *own* obedience that comes from faith in Jesus Christ. Having been justified by faith,[1] we live accordingly, and we become obedient.[2]

Greetings: To All in Rome, Loved and Called

Paul is set apart for the gospel, which was promised from before. The gospel is regarding the Son of God, who is also the Son of Man, and Paul is taking this message to the Gentiles. It is appropriate that he identifies his calling to the Gentiles here, because he will speak to

---

1. Gangadean, *The Biblical Worldview*, 295–309; Gangadean, *The Westminster Confession*, 149–156; Gangadean, *The Westminster Catechisms*, 193–198.

2. Gangadean, *The Westminster Confession*, 161–166; Gangadean, *The Westminster Catechisms*, 45–49; Gangadean, *The Biblical Worldview*, 311–328.

the church in Rome—the Romans. He wants to see that this faith is bearing fruit in obedience. Those in Rome, who have come to Christ already, "**are called.**" They have already been called. "**And you also are among those who are called to belong to Jesus Christ. To all in Rome who are loved by God**"—with an everlasting love from before the foundations of the world—"**and called to be saints**" (vv. 6–7a). Later on, Paul is going to speak about God's predestinating work: "For those God foreknew he also predestined . . . And those he predestined, he also called" (Rom. 8:29a, 30a).

We know the historical significance of Rome and the Roman Church. It is interesting, then, to see how far the Church of Rome today has continued with this message: "**a righteousness that is by faith from first to last**" (v. 17). Compare this passage to what is taught in the Roman Catholic Church today. Also, we should note that it is Paul who is writing to the church in Rome and not Peter. We have no evidence that Peter was in Rome[3] or that he wrote to that church. This is a ministry that is particularly given to Paul.

To those in Rome, he brings the blessing of God: "**Grace and peace to you from God our Father and from the Lord Jesus Christ**" (v. 7b). Grace and peace—fullness of blessing—from both God the Father and the Lord Jesus Christ. We should note this is also put into effect by the work of the Holy Spirit in regenerating us and in sanctifying us through the truth.[4]

PAUL'S HEART FOR ROME

Thanksgiving for Their Faith

Paul is set apart for the gospel, and what we should expect, from what he said, is that he will declare the gospel to the Church of Rome. He particularly gives thanks to God for their faith. "**First, I thank my God through Jesus Christ for all of you, because your faith is being**

---

3. Paul makes no mention of Peter having a ministry in Rome and explicitly states that no other apostle had established a ministry there. "It has always been my ambition to preach the gospel where Christ was not known, so that I would not be building on someone else's foundation" (Rom. 15:20).

4. Gangadean, *The Westminster Confession*, 143–148; Gangadean, *The Westminster Catechisms*, 191–192; Surrendra Gangadean, *The Epistle to the Hebrews: Christ Is Superior in Every Way—Foundation to Persevere in Biblical Faith* (Phoenix: Logos Papers Press, 2024), 306–309.

reported all over the world" (v. 8). In a vital congregation, this is how it should be. There should be a witness to others. Individuals should know and truly understand their faith and who God is—we will see how Paul will open up the content of this faith. When we witness to the truth in this way, it should be real news coming to people, and reports should be going out. 'Have you heard about that church in Phoenix? They have some real understanding about this Word of God and the truth of God.' That is the way it should be. He gives thanks to God for this: "**your faith is being reported all over the world.**" The church in Rome had a particular opportunity, being in Rome. Rome was the center of the Empire. People would come and go from the city and reports would go out. People would come and visit Rome, go to the church, and take that word back with them.

Constant Remembrance in Prayer

Paul says, "**God, whom I serve with my whole heart in preaching the gospel of his Son, is my witness how constantly I remember you in my prayers at all times**" (vv. 9–10a). No work of God goes forward without prayer, and notice how Paul puts it. He calls God solemnly to witness: "**God, whom I serve with my whole heart in preaching the gospel of his Son . . .**" He is reiterating what he said before, that the gospel concerns God's Son. Paul focused on that gospel and he is doing that work.

"**God . . . is my witness.**" Paul is not merely saying this, he is very solemnly saying it. "**God, whom I serve with my whole heart in preaching the gospel of his Son, is my witness how constantly I remember you in my prayers at all times.**" It is in this context that he is writing to the Romans, and it is in this context that the work will bear fruit. If the Word of God will bear fruit in those to whom we bring it, we must be *constantly* in prayer for these persons. If we are not in prayer, the witness will not bear fruit; that is not how God works. God is pleased to hear and answer our prayer so that when it comes to pass, we will see that it is God who has done the work. God is pleased to do the work for those who constantly seek Him. "Ask and it will be given to you; seek and you will find; knock and the door will be opened to you" (Matt. 7:7). If you want someone to come to the Lord, you should be in prayer about them. It may delay; we do not know what the Lord will do, but we ultimately commit it to the Lord. We might say that this is the ordinary way in which God works. It does not mean it absolutely always works in that way. Some may come without prayer, and others may have bestowed labor on them, but if we are going to see someone come to the Lord, it must be in connection with a great deal of prayer. Paul considers this so significant that he calls God to be his witness, as he says this to the Romans: **"how constantly I remember you in my prayers at all times."**

To Come, to Strengthen, to Be Mutually Encouraged

"I pray that now at last by God's will the way may be opened for me to come to you" (v. 10b). Paul had been trying for a long time to come to the Romans. He had been praying about it. Again, though it delays, we pray, and trust God to eventually bring it about. When God did so for Paul, He brought it about that Paul went to Rome in chains—but God brought it about. While in chains, he was in a position where he had the freedom to speak the gospel. It went out through the palace of Caesar, through the Praetorian guard, to the Romans. Think about that guard who was constantly with Paul, hearing the Word. Paul says, "I am suffering even to the point of being chained like a criminal. But God's word is not chained" (2 Tim. 2:9). The Word of God cannot be chained; we should speak that Word boldly.

Paul had prayed to come to them. **"I long to see you so that I may impart to you some spiritual gift to make you strong"** (v. 11). This is the concern that Paul had as the apostle to the Gentiles to the church in Rome; he wanted to speak so that he may impart some spiritual gift, in this case, understanding, to make them strong. As a result of that understanding, he says, **"that you and I may be mutually encouraged by each other's faith"** (v. 12). That is the most encouraging thing as we meet with others. We see God working in their heart to bring them to understand the Word; that is very encouraging. Insofar as we see genuine faith issuing in obedience, we are encouraged by one another. Paul is aware of this. He says, **"That is, that you and I may be mutually encouraged by each other's faith."** Notice how often Paul brings faith into focus. It is certainly true that righteousness comes by faith in Christ—justifying faith—but there is also faith that is lived out in our lives, increasing and showing itself in obedience. He wants them to know this faith.

Delayed Yet Desiring a Harvest Among Them

Sometimes, it is appropriate for us to communicate to others how we desire to be with them. People may not know our interest and desire and how we may have tried. He says, "**I do not want you to be un-aware, brothers, that I planned many times to come to you (but have been prevented from doing so until now) in order that I might have a harvest among you, just as I have had among the other Gentiles**" (v. 13). God has blessed him elsewhere in his ministry, and he desires to minister in Rome, also, and have a harvest. Paul, especially, was singled out as the apostle to the Gentiles, though we have good reason to believe from history that many of the other apostles went all over the world preaching the gospel.

PAUL IS OBLIGATED AND EAGER
TO PREACH THE GOSPEL

Concerning this gospel, Paul said, "I am *obligated* both to Greeks and non-Greeks, both to the wise and the foolish. That is why I am so *eager* to preach the gospel also to you who are in Rome" (vv. 14–15).[5] Remember, this is the gospel according to St. Paul. He speaks about being set apart for this gospel. He says, "**I am obligated both to Greeks and non-Greeks.**" These are general categories among the Gentiles. Later on, he is going to say Jews and Gentiles. He says, "**I am obligated both to Greeks and non-Greeks, both to the wise and the foolish.**" The Greeks were reputed for their wisdom and seeking wisdom. They set themselves apart from other nations as being particularly given to wisdom. Their chief city, Athens, was devoted to the goddess of wisdom—Athena. They believed they had dedicated themselves to being guided by reason, rather than being led by superstitions and passions.[6] When Paul refers to "**the Greeks and non-Greeks,**" it includes all those belonging to the

---

5. Emphasis added.

6. Surrendra Gangadean, *History of Philosophy: A Critical Analysis of Unresolved Disputes* (Phoenix: Public Philosophy Press, 2022), 81–85.

Hellenistic world. Rome had been influenced by Greece, having been taught by the Greeks and imbibing their philosophy.

Paul is obligated to the Gentiles, both to the Greeks and the non-Greeks, to the wise and the foolish—to all the nations. He is obligated to them—obligated to preach the gospel. **"That is why I am so eager to preach the gospel also to you who are in Rome"** (v. 15). There is not the slightest shadow of tension between duty, obligation, and desire. The person who is devoted to God will delight in their obligation. Sometimes, we create tensions between obligation and desire. There is none of that tension in Paul: he is **"obligated,"** and so he is **"eager."** He is looking forward to it and holding to it, and so it should be; our desires and eagerness should flow out of a sense of obligation to proclaim the gospel.

Not Ashamed of the Gospel: It Is the Power of God for Salvation

Paul then says, **"I am not ashamed of the gospel"** (v. 16a). Notice how Paul keeps focusing on the gospel: **"set apart for the gospel of God . . . regarding his Son . . . obedience that comes from faith."** He is **"obligated"** and **"eager"** to preach the gospel, and he is **"not ashamed of the gospel."** Why is he not ashamed? **"Because it is the power of God for the salvation of everyone who believes"** (v. 16a). Sometimes, we may feel hesitant about the gospel. Perhaps we should feel a little bit hesitant about the gospel that *we* may be preaching, but Paul is preaching *the* gospel, and he does not have the slightest hesitation. It is stated negatively, but the positive is meant. Sometimes the negative statement brings out an aspect that we overlook if stated positively. There is no hesitation; there is no apology for preaching the gospel. 'Would you please give me a few minutes of your time to listen to this? Are you interested in spiritual things, maybe?' There is none of that, so to speak, apologetic for the gospel that 'maybe I could get a little bit of hearing from you.' Instead, there is an alacrity, an enthusiasm, as when we hear the best possible news, and we are ready to go out and speak that news to others. We are bringing life to a dying person. This should be the very best possible news you could imagine—just as a man dying would be overjoyed to see you, if he recognizes he is dying. Of course, if he does not recognize he is dying, then we have to do preliminary work.

In that sense, Paul is not ashamed of the gospel. **"It is the power of God for the salvation of everyone who believes."** There is no other way in which men will come to salvation and come to life. This is **"first to the Jew, then to the Gentile"** (v. 16b). Paul makes this point throughout the epistle. The proclamation of the gospel comes first to those who had the Scriptures previously; it begins there. It begins "in Jerusalem, and in all Judea and Samaria, and to the ends of the earth" (Acts 1:8b). There is a pattern that Paul will develop throughout the epistle. Later, he is going to ask, 'If it is to the Jews first and then to the Gentiles, why is it that so many of the Jews have not come?'[7] He is going to deal with that later on, but it is for the Jews first, *then* for the Gentiles.

In the Gospel, the Righteousness of God Is Revealed

"For in the gospel a righteousness from God is revealed" (v. 17a). This is the need of man: the need for righteousness. We will show how it is the case that there is a need. Paul, in the rest of Romans 1–2 and the early part of Romans 3, is going to establish the need for righteousness.

If we understand how the righteousness in the gospel is revealed, we understand how Paul continues with the parallel statement in verse 18: **"The wrath of God is being revealed"** (v. 18a). The antithesis, or contrast, is this: a righteousness from God is revealed in the gospel, and that is what is needed for those upon whom the wrath of God is being revealed. Special revelation is the answer to what we see in general revelation: the wrath of God, sin, and death.[8] We need to keep in mind this intentional contrast: the righteousness from God is revealed in the gospel, and the wrath of God *is*—present tense—being revealed now upon men.

Righteousness by Faith: The Righteous Will Live by Faith

"A righteousness that is by faith from first to last" (v. 17a). Paul could not emphasize more strongly that the righteousness of the gospel is by faith. He will develop this in Romans 3–12. From this righteousness,

---

7. *Romans 9:30–33.*

8. Gangadean, *The Westminster Confession,* 14–18; Gangadean, *The Biblical Worldview,* xvii–xix.

or *by* this righteousness, there is life. He says, "**Just as it is written: 'The righteous will live by faith'**" (v. 17b). This was the message that sunk into Luther's heart and produced the Reformation. That is, we are justified by faith. We are not justified by our own works; we cannot be justified by our own works. To paraphrase Luther, it is not *do penance*, but *repent and believe*. This one truth brought about a tremendous change in the history of Christianity. We should not underestimate the power of truth when clearly seen and declared to bring about change.

What I am going to say next, what I am going to place before you, is the truth that is needed to bring about the next major change.[9] In the Reformation, the truth that "**the righteous will live by faith**" was established, and it is truth, and it is needed. The context in which that truth is to be understood is being developed next. If we try to establish that "**the righteous will live by faith**" without understanding the condition of man, we will lose even the power of that truth. Historically, we have seen the results. We have had about 477 years of the teaching of "**the righteous shall live by faith**," but because the context that Paul goes to next—immediately, in the next word—has not been maintained, we have not been able to hold on to the truth that "**the righteous shall live by faith**." Notice that life comes by this faith.

THE WRATH OF GOD REVEALED:
The Reality of Sin and Death

Is Presently Being Revealed

In verse 18, Paul begins to explain why there is a need for righteousness from God. He says, "**The wrath of God is being revealed from heaven against all the godlessness and wickedness of men who suppress the truth by their wickedness**" (v. 18). The first point to note is that the wrath is presently being revealed. It is being revealed, and it is presently being revealed, and it is being revealed on all men who are in a state of unbelief. If we do not understand that, and we make God's wrath something in the future, after this life, in purgatory or in hell, we are going to miss the power of the gospel. It is absolutely essential to understand the wrath of God being revealed *now* in order to understand the need

---

9. Gangadean, "Paper No. 62: The Next Reformation," in *The Logos Papers*, 335–337.

for the gospel. It is spiritual death that exists now, and is manifesting itself now, and it is from spiritual death that we are delivered.[10] It is not some external punishment in the future from which we are delivered.[11]

This is spoken of as **"the wrath of God"** to emphasize not only the infinite justice of God but the attitude of God toward human sin—God is *always* angry at sin. Whenever there is sin, there is God's wrath. It is a sense of anger felt—injustice. We sometimes speak about human anger. We need to realize that we are reckoning with the divine anger and wrath on sin, and we have to see exactly what this wrath is.

The Basis of the Gospel

"The wrath of God is being revealed," and the gospel, **"a righteousness that is by faith,"** is the answer to the wrath that is being revealed. If you speak to others about the righteousness from faith without clearly establishing the wrath of God that is being revealed, people are going to say, 'What are you talking about?' Whatever it is that they may receive will not be the gospel; it will be something less than the gospel.[12]

This is the gospel according to St. Paul, and the gospel requires us to establish the need for righteousness by faith. To proclaim the gospel, we *must* go through this. It is not that this is an option which we might take. Some people ask, 'Must all go through the Wicket-gate?'[13] Some may say that there are many paths to God, but all must come through repentance of sin, repentance of works that lead to death, and faith in Christ.[14] We have to establish the reality of sin. This is what Paul is doing here. Not only is he establishing the *reality* of sin, but he is also establishing the *result* of sin, which is death. To see the

---

10. Gangadean, *The Biblical Worldview,* 37–54, 197–217; Gangadean, *The Westminster Confession,* 103–110; Surrendra Gangadean, *The Contradictoriness of Sin: A Reading of Paradise Lost* (Phoenix: Logos Papers Press, 2024), 1–34.

11. Gangadean, *Philosophical Foundation,* 195–197; Gangadean, *The Epistle to the Hebrews,* 357–371.

12. Gangadean, "Paper No. 56: The Gospel (Summary)," in *The Logos Papers,* 303–313.

13. A reference to John Bunyan's *Pilgrim's Progress.*

14. Gangadean, *The Epistle to the Hebrews,* 271–286; Gangadean, *The Westminster Confession,* 173–180; Gangadean, *The Westminster Catechisms,* 83–86.

connection between sin and death,[15] to see that particular connection, is to understand the wrath of God. To see the particular connection between sin and death is to have and to understand the fear of God, which is the beginning of wisdom.[16]

Anyone who tries to preach the gospel without the reality of sin and death is preaching the gospel without a basis, and as such, when pressure is put on, that gospel will collapse. Even if it takes 200 years, that gospel will collapse. The 400 years of history since the Reformation shows us that that teaching has collapsed, or is collapsing. In many places, it has been shattered. People are trying to pick up and go on in various ways, in even less adequate ways than the Reformation did, and *that* gospel will collapse.

What May Be Known Is Manifest

How does Paul establish the reality of sin and death? Why is God so angry, and exactly what is His anger? How is the anger of God, the wrath of God, manifested? **"The wrath of God is being revealed from heaven against all the godlessness and wickedness of men who suppress the truth by their wickedness"** (v. 18). Now, this statement is going to be opened up again and again. There are all sorts of ways in which we have tried to understand this statement: **"of men who suppress the truth by their wickedness."** Some suggest that men actually know the truth, they know it as the truth, and they are suppressing the truth.[17] Alternatively, it is said that men are holding back the truth and the progress of the truth by their unrighteousness. I am inclined to take the latter position and show how and to what extent it is that men do know the truth.

Why is this wrath being revealed? **"Since what may be known about God is plain to them, because God has made it plain to them"** (v. 19). We will see how this is explained further. Because the Scripture says that the truth is plain to men, or manifest to them, as some translations put it, some say that men actually know the truth. We will talk about

---

15. Gangadean, *The Biblical Worldview,* 37–54, 197–217; Gangadean, *The Westminster Confession,* 103–110; Gangadean, *The Contradictoriness of Sin,* 1–34; Gangadean, *The Epistle to the Hebrews,* 253–269.

16. Gangadean, *The Biblical Worldview,* 69–87.

17. Gangadean, "Paper No. 120: Contra Voluntarism," in *The Logos Papers,* 611–647.

that position another time.[18] At least, clearly, Paul says it is **"plain to them."** It is revealed clearly; it is manifest to them, and it is precisely in connection with it being **"plain"** that the Scriptures speak about this **"wrath . . . being revealed."** Men are rejecting, failing to see what is plain, and God has made it plain.

Paul explains what is meant by God making it plain to them: **"For since the creation of the world God's invisible qualities—his eternal power and divine nature—have been clearly seen, being understood from what has been made, so that men are without excuse"** (v. 20). Twice, then, he makes the point that it is clearly revealed. First, he says, **"What may be known about God is plain to them."** Second, he says, **"God's invisible qualities . . . have been clearly seen"**—this is the explanation of why the wrath of God is upon men.

The Eternal Power and Divine Nature

A few more points can be made about this passage: **"For since the creation of the world God's invisible qualities—his eternal power and divine nature—have been clearly seen, being understood from what has been made, so that men are without excuse."** The existence and nature of God have been known since the creation and are known from the creation. We do not know God apart from the creation. God's qualities are invisible, and cannot be known directly, but they are known *by* creation. Creation reveals God.[19] We have to look at the creation to see God. Paul specifies **"God's invisible qualities,"** and the specific quality that is made known is **"his eternal power."** Whenever we witness, we must come back to this basic truth: that God is eternal, and only God is eternal.[20] That establishes God as Creator.

---

18. The content regarding voluntarism and willful suppression of the truth is addressed in "Prolegomena to Paul's Gospel: The Biblical Doctrine of Clarity and Inexcusability" and "Appendix B: Contra Voluntarism: On Knowing and Not Doing," in this book.

19. Gangadean, *The Biblical Worldview,* 21–36; Gangadean, *The Westminster Confession,* 75–79; Gangadean, *Philosophical Foundation,* 144, 211–212; Surrendra Gangadean, *On Natural and Revealed Theology: Collected Essays of Surrendra Gangadean* (Phoenix: Logos Papers Press, 2023), 197.

20. Gangadean, *Philosophical Foundation,* 71–161; Gangadean, *History of Philosophy,* 47–58; Gangadean, *The Westminster Confession,* 1–13; Gangadean, "Paper No. 3: The Principle of Clarity," 15–20; "Paper No. 39: Clarity," in *The Logos Papers,* 217–220.

The opening words of the Bible make it very clear that God is eternal: "In the beginning, God . . ." (Gen. 1:1a). It could not be any clearer than to say that heaven and earth began and God did not begin. "I Am That I Am,"[21] the self-existent one, the eternal one, as is translated in places—that is the name of God. If we are going to make God known, we have to speak about His eternality.

Objectively Clear and So Without Excuse

When it says, "**so that men are *without excuse*,**"[22] the literal term in the Greek is ἀναπολόγητος (*anapologētos*), which means, without *logos*; without an apology; without reason. They do not have any reason for their unbelief.

We are not only to know God's eternality but His divine nature. I have received letters recently concerning witnessing from someone who has been with us in the past. This person said that it is one thing to argue to show the existence of God, but the nature of God is difficult to show. They get bogged down at that point. Here, it says not only the eternal power, but the divine nature in God, is clearly revealed, so that men are without excuse, and that is why the wrath of God is being revealed.

Men are holding back this truth by their unrighteousness. By their whole way of life, they are keeping this truth from being spoken and known. They cannot keep it from being revealed, because it is already revealed, but by their lifestyle, unbelievers hold back the efforts of those who would carry the truth forward. Whether it is reincarnation theory, or whether it is a dualist theory, materialist theory, or whatever theory it is that people are proclaiming, they are holding back the truth by their unrighteousness—by their way of life, by their walk, and by their deeds.

---

21. *Exodus 3:14.*

22. Emphasis added.

THE DOWNWARD PROGRESSION OF SIN AND DEATH:
Unbelief, Unholiness, and Unrighteousness

The Knowledge of God: Immediate or Inferred?

Paul further develops the point about unbelief and unrighteousness. He says, "For although they knew God, they neither glorified him as God . . ." and in verse 22, "Although they claimed to be wise, they became fools." There is a parallel statement here and it is developing the point that the wrath of God is presently being revealed. He says, "For although they knew God, they neither glorified him as God nor gave thanks to him, but their thinking became futile and their foolish hearts were darkened" (v. 21). Some say, 'Well, they knew God.' Some argue that everyone already knows God deep down, so there is no point in trying to bring the truth of God or show the clarity of God's existence. Paul says, "his eternal power and divine nature—have been clearly seen, *being understood from what has been made*" (v. 20b),[23] and some try to say that this truth is already in the heart of man as an innate belief: 'Deep down, all men know God.'

The passage says it is "being understood from what has been made." There is an *inference* that is needed in that understanding, *from* the things that are made. There has been a dispute about whether: (1) This understanding is an immediate knowledge of God already in the hearts of men, and they already know it, or (2) this understanding is by a clear revelation that men *can* know by inference from the creation. I believe it is a clear revelation that they can know by inference from the creation.

A Corporate Apostasy

Some appeal to verse 21 to argue that deep down, all men know God: "For although they knew God, they neither glorified him as God nor gave thanks to him." We will see the reasons to say that they knew, just as Adam knew, and changed,[24] because in the next two verses, he says, "They became fools and exchanged the glory of the immortal God for images made to look like mortal man." Further, we are going to say that this passage is speaking about mankind *as a whole*. It is

---

23. Emphasis added.
24. Gangadean, *The Biblical Worldview*, 159–195.

certainly true that the revelation is made clear to each and every one, but the things that are being said here speak about a *corporate* apostasy. He says, **"Although they claimed to be wise, they became fools and exchanged the glory of the immortal God for images made to look like mortal man and birds and animals and reptiles"** (vv. 22–23). It is not the case that each and every person makes the image of God into a reptile, but there is a progression referred to here. It begins with man exchanging **"the glory of the immortal God for images made to look like mortal man,"** and from that, there is a progression further downward. When Paul says that they knew God, I believe he is saying that *historically*, they knew God. After the Flood, mankind knew God, but they departed from that knowledge. In Israel, at times, they knew God, and they departed from that knowledge. He says in verse 28, **"Furthermore, since they did not think it worthwhile to retain the knowledge of God . . ."** They had it and departed from it. That is what apostasy is. Adam had it, and Adam departed from it.

Their Thinking Became Futile, Their Foolish Hearts Darkened

There is no use arguing that man always has the knowledge of God deep down, or that Adam had it, retained it, and simply acted contrary to it. That view is saying, in other words, that man's will rebels against his intellect. We do not affirm this. We believe in total depravity; the change originates from the thinking, not the will.[25] The thinking is what is being emphasized here: **"their *thinking* became futile and their foolish hearts were *darkened*"** (v. 21).[26] We move from the light of life to the darkness of death. This is the spiritual death that is coming upon them.

Notice that the downward progression starts with the heart being darkened: **"Their thinking became futile and their foolish hearts were darkened."** This is referring to the ability to see and understand. When we give up belief in God, we fail to see. Historically there has been a turning away, but also each one has a clear revelation, and left to ourselves, each one fails to see it. Psalm 14:1 and Psalm 53:1 state, "The fool says in his heart, 'There is no God.' They are corrupt, their deeds are vile; there is no one who does good." The wrath of God is

---

25. Gangadean, "Paper No. 18: Salvation by Grace," 119–122; "Paper No. 103: The Noetic Effect of Sin," in *The Logos Papers,* 531–538.

26. Emphasis added.

manifest in that "**their thinking became futile and their foolish hearts were darkened,**" and out of this darkness of the heart comes all the lust that we see in the lives of human beings. In the heart of darkness, there are unspeakable, vile lusts. "**Although they claimed to be wise, they became fools.**" They "**exchanged the glory of the immortal God for images made to look like mortal man.**" They changed it. They had greater knowledge and glory of God at one time, and departed from it. We are not saying that they had it, and retained it, and acted contrary to it. They did not retain it; they turned away.

There are those who take the interpretation that it is *immediate* knowledge and not inferred knowledge. They interpret it as immediate knowledge that is in the heart and is always in the heart: 'Deep down everyone knows.' They think, therefore, there is no point in talking to someone about what is deep down in the heart. Those persons sidestep the need to show the clarity of general revelation. They need to show how it is clear—especially when Paul underscores "**being understood from the things that are made.**" Furthermore, Psalm 19:1 says, "The heavens declare the glory of God; the skies proclaim the work of his hands." They need to show from the heavens how the glory of God is being declared.

A lot of people in the Church—staunch Reformed people—have tried to make the claim that it is immediate knowledge, already there, known deep down. Cornelius Van Til makes that claim. John Frame also makes that claim. Greg Bahnsen makes that claim. While a different claim is made by R. C. Sproul, he says, in effect, 'The knowledge is there, the problem is in the heart—the *desire* is not there.' We need to respond and show the clarity of general revelation; we cannot bypass this need. If we do not show the clarity of general revelation, we will not understand how it is that death comes in. We will not understand how it is that men have shut their eyes and what it means to shut their eyes.[27]

"**Although they claimed to be wise, they became fools and exchanged the glory of the immortal God for images made to look like mortal man and birds and animals and reptiles**" (vv. 22–23). Throughout history, there have been all kinds of animal depictions, such as bulls, creeping things, and serpents. Zeus is represented as a swan that rapes Leda. The same thing that happened in the Garden by blurring the

---

27. *Isaiah 6:9–10; Matthew 13:15.*

distinction between God and man, "You will be like God" (Gen. 3:5b), is the thing that continues to happen in history.

Therefore, God Gave Them Over

Paul says, "Therefore God gave them over" (v. 24a). Notice that they changed the glory; God gave them over. They did not want to retain the knowledge of God, so "God gave them over." That giving over is the wrath of God, and this expression is repeated three times: "God gave them over" (v. 24a), "God gave them over" (v. 26a), "He gave them over" (v. 28a). That is where the wrath of God is being revealed, and we see how they are being given over in the fruit of their ways. One of the ways in which this is shown is "in the sinful desires of their hearts to sexual impurity for the degrading of their bodies with one another" (v. 24b). This is the first manifest state of being given over—sexual immorality.

People press the sexual practice in all sorts of ways; it becomes degrading, and they degrade themselves by this. Sexual degradation is a manifestation of the wrath of God—that persons are being given over to the desires of their hearts. Again, "They exchanged the truth of God for a lie" (v. 25a). Notice, if they had the truth, it is not the case that they continue to have it, but they *exchange* it for a lie. "You will not surely die" (Gen. 3:4a) was the lie that they accepted in place of "in the day that you eat of it you shall surely die" (Gen. 2:17b NKJV). They "worshiped and served created things rather than the Creator—who is forever praised. Amen" (v. 25b).

We often worship the creature in terms of some other person, first and foremost. Some people say, 'I would do anything to be with that person, to have that person,' or 'If I could only have that person.' Then, when that other person does not satisfy us, we turn on them. We are really serving ourselves. This is why it says, "Because of this, God gave them over to shameful lusts" (v. 26a). Some of the most hideous abuses and perversions come into sexual practice as it is pressed for more and more. There is no satisfaction without the knowledge of God. We cannot get back to the tree of life;[28] no pleasure in the creature can be a substitute for the life in the knowledge of God.

---

28. *Genesis 3:24.*

"**Even their women exchanged natural sexual relations for unnatural ones**" (v. 26b). If we had spoken of this 30 years ago, people would have responded, 'What are you talking about?' Today, lesbianism and homosexuality have become rampant and have become very bold, pressing themselves into the Church and claiming to have equal status and wanting equal acceptance. Perhaps things have even been reversed, and people will respond, 'You guys are homophobic.' You begin to understand the insolence of those who would try to live their lives without God.

"**In the same way the men also abandoned natural relations with women and were inflamed with lust for one another**" (v. 27a). This lust is rushing in as a flood upon them and cannot be resisted. Why? Because they gave up the knowledge of God. They were not seeking God. If we try to speak to this generation without coming back to the failure to seek God, we are not adequately accepting the reality of sin and death and we are not paving the way for the gospel and faith by righteousness. "**Men committed indecent acts with other men, and received in themselves the due penalty for their perversion**" (v. 27b). They violate God's order and subject themselves to all sorts of problems; diseases that we hear about connected with this are certainly part of those problems.

"**Furthermore, just as they did not think it worthwhile to retain the knowledge of God . . .**" (v. 28a). This is the one central thing that is important in establishing sin and death. "**They did not think it worthwhile to retain the knowledge of God.**" They turned away from what is clear. It is absolutely essential, in proclaiming the gospel, to establish that the knowledge of God is clearly revealed, that this knowledge is what people do not want to retain, and that this knowledge is what they change over from. If we do not establish this, we cannot preach. This is the gospel; this is how Paul preaches the gospel. He does not just start out with the gospel; he establishes the *need* for the gospel. Once we establish the need for the gospel, we proclaim the gospel, and then we can see how we are not ashamed of it. Without establishing the need for the gospel, then we approach it apologetically. Without establishing the need, it is said, 'Maybe give Jesus a try.' The Epistle to the Romans is the gospel according to St. Paul, and this is how the gospel ought to be preached. This is how he preaches the gospel. We make no apology for what we have preached at Westminster Fellowship for the past months and years, saying, 'This is the Word of God.'

"**Furthermore, just as they did not think it worthwhile to retain the knowledge of God, he gave them over to a depraved mind**" (v. 28a). Notice Paul keeps coming back to the mind, and then from the mind to the desires, and from the desires to the will: "**to do what ought not to be done**" (v. 28b). "**They have become filled with every kind of wickedness, evil, greed and depravity**" (v. 29a). In the King James, the word is "**fornication.**" There is every kind of greed or covetousness, not being satisfied, and depravity. It is a flood of wickedness. It builds, increases, and then, like a dam, it breaks. What has happened in the 60s, 70s, 80s, and 90s is that the dam has been breaking, and the flood has been rising, and it can overwhelm—we have not seen the end of it yet.

Wickedness can become such a great flood that the whole world can be inundated with it, as it was in the days of Noah.[29] The world can become like it was in the days of Noah. We should not deceive ourselves. Human nature has not changed. It can become like that. God restrained that flood of wickedness by the flood of judgment—they are to be cut off. Paul says,

> They are full of envy, murder, strife, deceit and malice. They are gossips, slanderers, God-haters, insolent, arrogant and boastful; they invent ways of doing evil; they disobey their parents; they are senseless, faithless, heartless, ruthless (vv. 29b–31).

Every form of wickedness flows from not retaining the knowledge of God. And the churches that have not retained the knowledge of God—along with the doctrine that has been preached—have drifted further from godliness. Churches have bypassed the work of the pastor-teachers in Church history, the Historic Christian Faith, and even in the Church, the flood of godlessness is coming in. Because they have not shown the clarity of general revelation, they cannot resist the flood of wickedness that is coming in.

---

29. Gangadean, "Paper No. 58: The Spiritual War (Church and World)," in *The Logos Papers,* 317–322.

Worthy of Death

"Although they know God's righteous decree that those who do such things deserve death, they not only continue to do these very things but also approve of those who practice them" (v. 32). As godlessness increases, God Himself will intensify the curse—through war, famine, and plague. During the time of the Flood, sin advanced to the point where people hardened themselves against God, refusing to seek Him, and ultimately were cut off. We must remember this, for these are the very people to whom the gospel is preached. Paul reminds us in the next verse—the first verse of Romans 2—that if we make a judgment on these persons in a way that we put ourselves apart from and above them without recognizing that we, too, have that same failure to seek God, we condemn ourselves. He says, "You, therefore, have no excuse, you who pass judgment on someone else, for at whatever point you judge the other, you are condemning yourself" (Rom. 2:1a).

This is the state of mankind. This is the state in which we were before our conversion, and there are still remnants of sin in us. We are sinners, saved by grace, and yet God is pleased to use us to bring the gospel to others. This is the Gospel according to St. Paul.

2

THE GOSPEL ACCORDING TO ST. PAUL

The Righteousness of God Is the Answer to the Wrath of God

2013

Romans 1

INTRODUCTION

WE ARE GOING TO BE LOOKING AT THE GOSPEL according to St. Paul. In his introduction, in verses 1–17, Paul speaks about the gospel several times. Then he speaks about why that gospel is needed: because **"the wrath of God is being revealed from heaven"** (v. 18). The only answer to that wrath is the righteousness of God that is revealed in the gospel. We will closely examine why that wrath is upon us, try to see where we are, and break through any blocks that may prevent us from seeing where we are. We will look at our need to repent of the sin that remains, and we will seek to know the status of our repentance by looking at whether there is fruit in keeping with repentance. Then, we will see how God's wrath is revealed, how it is connected with the sin of man, and in verses 21–32, we will see how sin progresses up to the state of the fullness of the wrath of God.

Paul speaks about being called to preach the gospel. He speaks about what the gospel is, his prayer for the preaching of the gospel, and his longing to preach that gospel. He was not merely longing to preach the gospel, but it was something planned and then hindered. Paul speaks about the mutual and shared faith that may be increased through the preaching. Paul prays for what is according to his calling, and he longs for and desires that. Then, he speaks about his obligation, or his duty, to preach the gospel. He says that he is not ashamed of the gospel. We will speak about why exactly he expresses himself in that way, and how it affects us.

Called to Preach the Gospel

In verse 1, he says, "**Paul, a servant of Christ Jesus, called to be an apostle and set apart for the gospel of God . . .**" So, he is called to be an apostle, and he is called to preach the gospel. He says it is "**the gospel he promised beforehand through his prophets in the Holy Scriptures**" (v. 2). It is not something originating now, but it was there before, through the prophets in the Holy Scriptures. It is focused on the Son, the eternal Son of God, who in His human nature is descended from David: "**regarding his Son, who as to his human nature was a descendant of David, and who through the Spirit of holiness was declared with power to be the Son of God by his resurrection from the dead: Jesus Christ our Lord**" (vv. 3–4). The gospel is centered on the person and work of Christ promised in the Scriptures through the prophets, now made manifest.[1] Paul speaks about having grace to call people from among all the Gentiles. "**Through him and for his name's sake, we received grace and apostleship to call people from among all the Gentiles to the obedience that comes from faith. And you also are among those who are called to belong to Jesus Christ**" (vv. 5–6). The grace received is a grace to proclaim this gospel message to the Gentiles, and the result of this gospel message is obedience. He speaks about preaching, faith increasing, and out of that increase of faith, obedience comes.

To All in Rome for the Abundance of Their Faith

Paul is addressing this letter to those in Rome. He is called to be an apostle. God has also called those in Rome, and they belong to Jesus,

---

1. *The Gospel of Matthew*, Surrendra Gangadean.

and Paul will speak now to those in Rome. You might say, 'Well, they are already believers; what is Paul doing preaching the gospel to those who are believers?' Clearly, he says, **"To all in Rome who are loved by God and called to be saints"** (v. 7a); they are already believers. But Paul wants to go there also to preach, and we will see how this is going to result in obedience and praise to God. He pronounces grace upon them: **"Grace and peace to you from God our Father and from the Lord Jesus Christ"** (v. 7b). He tells the Roman believers, **"First, I thank my God through Jesus Christ for all of you, because your faith is being reported all over the world"** (v. 8). I want you to notice that not only is the word *gospel* mentioned, but *faith*, and in connection with faith, *obedience*. When we come to verse 17, **"The just shall live by faith"** (v. 17b NKJV), we have to take into account what he is saying about faith here in verse 8; this is the context. **"God, whom I serve with my whole heart in preaching the gospel of his Son, is my witness how constantly I remember you in my prayers at all times"** (vv. 9–10a). In connection with the preaching of the gospel, Paul remembers them in his prayers and prays that a way may be opened for him to come to them. He is praying that he may go to Rome and preach the gospel.

God Worked His Purpose: Longing, Planned, Hindered, Yet Preserved

We know from the Book of Acts that Paul does go to Rome, but he goes in chains from Jerusalem.[2] That seems to have been his first visit to Rome, but he seems to know a number of the people. Even though he wanted to go to Rome in person, as it turns out, this letter to the Romans is how he goes to them, to bring a blessing to them and an increase of faith. And not only to them—but to all of us. Think about this. Paul wants to go to Rome to build them up in their faith in the gospel, and he is writing a letter, which is not the same as going there in person. It is this work, this letter, that remains. It is this letter that was a blessing to the Romans then, and has been a blessing to the Church in every age. When Paul says, **"I planned many times to come to you (but have been prevented from doing so until now)"** (v. 13a), we can see God's hand in preventing him. Perhaps if he had not been

---

2. *Acts 28.*

prevented, Paul would have visited with them, and like so many of the churches he visited, he would have spoken to them. When that generation died, except for what they passed on, what he had spoken to them about would have been lost. We should be encouraged, even when we are called to do something, and we are praying for that to occur, and longing for it, but then we are hindered—God is working in the midst of that hindrance.

Prayer for the Gospel of Faith

Paul is called to preach the gospel; he desires to visit Rome, he is praying for it, and he is longing for it.

> **I pray that now at last by God's will the way may be opened for me to come to you. I long to see you so that I may impart to you some spiritual gift to make you strong—that is, that you and I may be mutually encouraged by each other's faith (vv. 10b–12).**

The spiritual gift is connected with faith, and notice, mutual faith, that they may come to a common understanding, which will be an encouragement. Paul wants to impart some spiritual gift to make them strong, that is, encouraged by their faith. He had planned to visit: "**I do not want you to be unaware, brothers, that I planned many times to come to you (but have been prevented from doing so until now)**" (v. 13a). God prevented Paul from visiting in person, and God called Paul to write, and it will be a stupendous blessing. Most of the advances that have occurred in the history of the Church originated from this writing of Paul to the Romans. I believe that will continue to be true. What is stated here in the gospel according to St. Paul in Romans goes to a depth of understanding that allows the foundational work to be done.

We know that Paul influenced Luke, his companion, and that influence came out in Luke's gospel, just as Peter influenced Mark in his gospel. We see something about the depth of the Word of God, the gospel of God, the working of God in John's gospel, in the *logos*. It is said of Moses that he saw the form of God, or the essence of God, not in types and shadows.[3] It seems that something like that is happening

---

3. *Numbers 12:6–8.*

here in Paul's gospel. The essence of the gospel is distilled. He is called, he is praying, he is longing, and he is obligated.

Obligated to Preach: His Duty Before God

> I planned many times to come to you (but have been prevented from doing so until now) in order that I might have a harvest among you, just as I have had among the other Gentiles. I am obligated both to Greeks and non-Greeks, both to the wise and the foolish. That is why I am so eager to preach the gospel also to you who are in Rome (vv. 13b–15).

It is not only a longing, but also a sense of duty before God. Paul says of this gospel in verse 16: "I am not ashamed of the gospel, because it is the power of God for the salvation of everyone who believes" (v. 16a). It is the power of God for the salvation of everyone who believes, with understanding, what this gospel is about, "first for the Jew, then for the Gentile" (v. 16b). We will see that the Jews need the preaching of the gospel. They have misunderstood, and he is going to especially address this in Romans 2:9–11: "There will be trouble and distress for every human being who does evil: first for the Jew, then for the Gentile; but glory, honor and peace for everyone who does good: first for the Jew, then for the Gentile. For God does not show favoritism."

THE NEED FOR THE GOSPEL OF RIGHTEOUSNESS BY FAITH

Verse 17 says, "For in the gospel a righteousness from God is revealed," and verse 18 says, "The wrath of God is being revealed." We will see how important this righteousness is when we see how deep, how severe, this wrath of God is, and how deep it is in terms of where we are. Righteousness from God is revealed: "a righteousness that is by faith from first to last, just as it is written: 'The righteous will live by faith'" (v. 17b). Notice the connection between faith and righteousness. Paul will open this up in the remainder of the letter. We will see that there is a righteousness that is imputed to us and received by faith alone. There is also an actual righteousness that comes by personal sanctification—that is also part of the gospel. Paul says that this righteousness, not distinguishing one kind from the other, **"is by faith from first to last,"** or, **"from faith to faith."**[4] Which is to say, as we grow in our faith, that righteousness will increase. There is a connection between faith and righteousness: both a received righteousness that is imputed to us and a righteousness that is worked out in us and through us. **"The righteous will live by faith"**—in every sense of the word *live*. The righteous will not merely be justified by faith; **"the righteous will *live* by faith."**[5] In the Reformation, the emphasis was justification by faith, and we will see that this letter of Paul includes justification by faith, but it is much more. The gospel that is to be preached by Paul is to increase their faith and bring righteousness.

The Wrath of God: Sin Leads to Death

Paul says that the wrath of God *is*, present tense, being revealed from heaven **"against all the godlessness and wickedness of men who suppress the truth by their wickedness"** (v. 18b). We are going to go into some detail now and look at this wrath of God. The focus of this wrath is on sin that leads to death. Paul begins by speaking about sin. He says, **"I am not ashamed of the gospel"** (v. 16a)—the gospel according to Paul. There are others who preach the gospel, but they do not begin with the *need* for the gospel and the wrath of God. They sometimes begin with the love of God. They believe that by beginning with love, they are making it easy to hear. Some may even preach the gospel according to the Roman Catholic way, and they begin with the conclusion that "all have sinned and fall short of the glory of God" (Rom. 3:23), but the premises are not there, so you are left hanging. It is a truncated proclamation of the gospel. It is a kind of alternative gospel, a cheap imitation gospel, a 'third-world knock-off' of the gospel. But when Paul says, **"I am not ashamed of the gospel, because it is the power of God that brings salvation to everyone who believes"** (v. 16a), he is speaking that truth of the gospel as it should be. I cannot think of anything lacking—I find that all the questions I have ever had are answered in this gospel of Paul. I have had questions, and I will bring them to your attention. So that is the gospel of which Paul speaks that

---

4. KJV.

5. Emphasis added.

he is not ashamed, and I can say, by God's grace, with the Apostle, that I am not ashamed of *that* gospel. Other versions of the gospel are, frankly, embarrassing. Just because it goes by the word 'gospel' does not mean it is the same in content. Paul begins his gospel by speaking about the wrath being revealed and its connection with the godlessness and wickedness of men who suppress the truth by their wickedness. We want to ask, what is this suppression of the truth? What exactly could that be?[6]

Definition of Clarity and Inexcusability: *Anapologētos*

Paul opens up what is meant by the wrath of God further by speaking about clarity and inexcusability in verses 19–20.

> Since what may be known about God is plain to them, because God has made it plain to them. For since the creation of the world God's invisible qualities—his eternal power and divine nature—have been clearly seen, being understood from what has been made, so that men are without excuse.

This idea of being without excuse is a Greek term, *anapologētos*, which means, without the *logos*, without a reason. Men are without excuse for not believing what has been revealed. They are not without excuse for not believing the gospel; the doctrine of clarity and inexcusability is establishing their need for the gospel. It is because they did not believe what is clear from general revelation[7] that they are under the wrath of God and need the gospel. We are not to confuse the need for the gospel and the gospel itself. Human beings are in sin not because they reject Jesus Christ. Why would they need Jesus Christ in the first place? They have never heard of Him. They are in sin because they have clear general revelation, and God has made it **"plain to them,"** and they **"suppress the truth by their wickedness."**

---

6. This question is more fully addressed in "Prolegomena to Paul's Gospel: The Biblical Doctrine of Clarity and Inexcusability" and "Appendix B: Contra Voluntarism: On Knowing and Not Doing," in this book.

7. Gangadean, "Paper No. 102: The Clarity of General Revelation," 527–529; "Paper No. 41: What Is Clear About God," 225–229; "Paper No. 112: Why General Revelation Is Basic in the Christian Worldview," in *The Logos Papers*, 583–585.

Paul brings into focus the teaching of clarity and inexcusability when he begins to speak about sin and death. Sin is being opened up under the heading of *clarity and inexcusability*. Please note that we will be using the word *inexcusable* many times and will continue to come back to it. To be inexcusable is to be without reason, without the *logos*. We define inexcusability as unbelief—a failure to believe what is true and a suppression of the truth by believing what is not true. That unbelief to which men are holding to suppress the truth is inexcusable. Those in unbelief can and should see that it does not hold up. They have to neglect, avoid, resist, and deny reason—*anapologētos*, being without reason—in the face of what is clear in order to hold on to their unbelief. It is important to see that Paul is not trying to account for belief in God. Inexcusability is connected with believing what is *false* in place of believing in God, and using that falsehood to suppress the truth of God.

The Content of Clarity: The Existence and Nature of God

What is the content of what is clear? Paul focuses on the invisible qualities, and specifies further, God's eternal power *and* divine nature. We should express this in the way in which God is commonly spoken of: God is infinite, eternal, and unchanging in His being, wisdom, power, holiness, justice, goodness, and truth.[8] Those are the things that are clear about God because in creating the world, God has made His revelation clear. It specifically says it is **"being understood from what has been made."** This involves inference. Noting that knowledge comes by inference is important, because when we ask ourselves whether we see clarity, all of these particulars that we are bringing out will come into the picture. Do we understand God's **"eternal power and divine nature"** from what has been made? We are to understand that if we fail to acknowledge God's eternal power and divine nature, and we believe something else in its place, we are without excuse, which brings God's wrath upon us.

What is clear, according to Romans 1, is **"his eternal power and divine nature."** What is clear, according to Romans 2, is the law of God that is written on the hearts of all men.[9] This leads Paul to say, in

---

8. Gangadean, *The Westminster Catechisms*, 119–122.

9. *Romans 2:14–15.*

Romans 3, "There is no one righteous, not even one; there is no one who understands, no one who seeks God. All have turned away, they have together become worthless; there is no one who does good, not even one" (Rom. 3:10–12).

What is meant by clarity? First, it is what is clear to reason, or, the laws of thought. Since we are thinking beings, that is where we begin. What do we mean by clarity? We could say, by example, that the opposite of *something is clear* is *nothing is clear*.[10] We know, beyond a shadow of a doubt, that those two statements are contradictory. We also know, beyond a shadow of a doubt, that they cannot both be true, and they cannot both be false. We begin with that as an example of what is clear to reason as the laws of thought. We might even add that it is clear that we are thinking beings; it is self-evident. In the very act of wondering whether we are thinking beings, we are thinking. We can know that reason is the laws of thought. Descartes should have added that to the list of clear and distinct ideas.[11] Do not minimize that; just keep that as a start for what we mean by clarity. Certain things about the laws of thought are clear.

Second, another sense of clarity is that we do not need an education to know what is clear. It can be known by all persons, everywhere, at all times.[12] Everyone is being held accountable for knowing what is clear. Anyone who has come to the age of thinking and can form a contrary belief about the existence and nature of God is responsible. Psalm 8 says, "Out of the mouth of babes and sucklings hast thou ordained strength because of thine enemies, that thou mightest still the enemy and the avenger" (Ps. 8:2 KJV). Psalm 19 says, "The heavens declare the glory of God" (Ps. 19:1a), particularly the sun and the heat from which

---

10. Gangadean, *Philosophical Foundation*, 61–65; Gangadean, *History of Philosophy*, 40–44.

11. René Descartes identifies four *clear and distinct ideas* as the foundation of knowledge: (1) the certainty of one's own existence (*cogito, ergo sum*), as even doubt requires a thinking self; (2) mathematical and logical truths, such as the sum of a triangle's angles equaling two right angles, which are self-evident and immutable; (3) the idea of God as a perfect being, whose existence is necessary and innate to human reason; and (4) the essence of material objects, which consists of extension, shape, and motion, independent of sensory perception. See: René Descartes, *Discourse on the Method*, trans. John Veitch (Chicago, IL: Open Court Publishing Company, 1903), 32; René Descartes, *Meditations on First Philosophy*, trans. John Cottingham (Cambridge, UK: Cambridge University Press, 1996), 33, 45–46.

12. Gangadean, "Paper No. 102: The Clarity of General Revelation," 527–529; "Paper No. 41: What Is Clear About God," 225–229; "Paper No. 112: Why General Revelation Is Basic in the Christian Worldview," in *The Logos Papers*, 583–585.

nothing is hidden. "There is no speech nor language, where their voice is not heard" (Ps. 19:3 KJV). When persons bow down and worship the sun, they are without excuse. Many nations have worshiped the heavenly bodies. We can and should know that the heavenly bodies are not eternal; they will pass away. We can and should know what is eternal, because the Scripture specifies "**his eternal power and divine nature.**" Not just His power but His divine nature, as well.

Third, we can speak about clarity as something made so clear that the only way you can get around it is to deny your reason. It is *maximally* clear, and only by shutting our eyes do we not see. As Scripture states it, "They do not know nor understand; For He has shut their eyes, so that they cannot see, And their hearts, so that they cannot understand" (Is. 44:18 NKJV). One may shut their eyes, and one may go on to deny the idea of any common ground and the possibility of discussion.[13] It is important to understand what clarity is, because inexcusability comes out of failing to know and acknowledge what is clear, and death comes out of inexcusability. The wrath of God is seen in the connection between clarity and inexcusability, and sin and death. This is what is being opened up in the remainder of this chapter.

Examples of the Refusal to Engage with Clarity

These are a few examples I have encountered in my own personal contact with others on the matter of the gospel.

Before my conversion, someone who was with a certain Christian organization said to me, 'God loves you and has a wonderful plan for your life.' I said, 'How do you know that God exists?' I have asked that question many times, of many persons, and I have never gotten an answer. Later, I had a meeting with the leadership of that organization at the Sedona Retreat. I was hoping that they might answer my questions. I never got an answer to that question. It was avoided by those who were proclaiming the gospel that 'God loves you and has a wonderful plan for your life.'

Later on, when I was in contact with a certain branch of the Christian faith, and I told them I came to believe in the doctrine of predestination, the pastor said to me, 'God showed me your deceit.' That was the end

---

13. Gangadean, "Paper No. 2: Common Ground," 9–13; "Paper No. 50–53: Common Ground (Part I–IV)," in *The Logos Papers*, 275–286.

of the discussion. Where is the reasoning connected with clarity? It is not there. These are Christians, and they are not engaged with showing the clarity of God's existence and the inexcusability of unbelief.

I was once in a church and left that church because of the pastor's misconduct. This pastor wrote a 35-page paper to explain his position, which was like Aaron explaining how the golden calf came to be. Where is the reasoning there, among Christians in the Reformed faith? At the latter end of my contact with this group, I was told that the doxological focus of the Historic Christian Faith[14] was 'novel theology' and that I should go elsewhere. Where is the reasoning in that statement? These persons *excused* themselves from having to engage with questions 1, 46, and 101 of the Westminster Shorter Catechism, which say that man's chief end is to glorify God, in all that whereby he makes himself known, in all of his works of creation and providence.[15]

I was in an online private forum with members of this same church for six months, preparing to show the need to show how it is clear that God exists. And after six months, I dropped the question: 'How do you show what is clear regarding the existence and nature of God?'—the whole forum went silent.[16] Where is knowing and seeing what is clear among those who profess faith?

Remember, there were persons in our midst who left and tried to discredit the work by arguing that 'only Presbyterian ordination is lawful.'[17] That would mean that the ordination going on through the centuries, which was hierarchical, was not lawful. It would mean that congregational ordination was not lawful. To say that there are no grounds to start a new work unless there is apostasy would mean the whole Presbyterian Church in England, which started up over and against the Anglican Church, was in apostasy. Where is the reasoning in that unwillingness to discuss? Nine people sat in front of these three persons who were trying to discredit the work, asking them to discuss, and they were unwilling to discuss. I am laying the groundwork because

---

14. Gangadean, *The Westminster Confession*, xxix–xxxii, 347–348; Gangadean, "Paper No. 115: Doxological Christianity," 595–596; "Paper No. 118: Eschatology (Seven Points)," in *The Logos Papers*, 603–607.

15. Gangadean, *The Westminster Catechisms*, 3–4, 57–59, 100.

16. This was called "Covie Forum" after the Covenanters, and the records of the exchanges have been preserved in The Logos Archive at the Logos Study Center.

17. Ibid.

I am coming to where each of us is, and we need to see whether we know what is clear. When we see all of this that has happened and continues to happen—the refusal to engage with clarity—we need to say, 'Oh, maybe it could happen to me.'

A common response in the last few years is a slanderous claim that we are a cult. Some who left the church say that they were a member of a cult, which means they were not using their reason, therefore they have an excuse. It is a kind of spiritual suicide; they are not using their reason, and they are committing spiritual murder by speaking that word—cult—instead of engaging in discussion. These persons present themselves as believers—Reformed believers. Where is the reasoning in this?

I have had three graduate students in philosophy all depart at the same point. One said, 'I cannot know that *a* is *a* because I may have an incorrigible memory lapse. Yet it is probably true.'[18] Another one left saying, 'Reason is not transcendental and authoritative; there is not anything authoritative.' A third one said, 'We cannot know that God is not both eternal and not eternal at the same time in the same respect, except through Scripture; we cannot know that by reason.' These are graduate students in philosophy denying reason to get around a certain responsibility.

Then we have had philosophers whom we have debated at a local research university, claiming 'being from non-being is like a chicken from an egg.' No, a chicken and an egg are both in the category of being. Instead, a chicken and an egg from non-being is like being from non-being. Some have put it up on their website that the ontological argument (there must be something eternal[19]) is bogus because when applied to cherry cheesecake, it does not work. The opposite of 'some cherry cheesecake is eternal' is 'no cherry cheesecake is eternal.' So, all cherry cheesecake came from—what? Non-being? No, all cherry cheesecake would have come from non-cherry cheesecake, which is

---

18. This is a form of fallibilism. If there is no rational basis for certainty (re: *a* is *a*), there is no rational basis for certainty about anything, including probability. Appeal to incorrigible memory lapses, held consistently, is a universal solvent and constitutes a self-referentially absurd consequence, leading to the loss of thought and meaning—nihilism. No one can hold/live nihilism consistently.

19. Gangadean, *Philosophical Foundation*, 61–65; Gangadean, *History of Philosophy*, 40–44; Gangadean, "Paper No. 3: The Principle of Clarity," in *The Logos Papers*, 15–20.

different from non-being.[20] Slipped on the banana peel, right at the door. Paul says these persons boast of themselves: **"their thinking became futile and their foolish hearts were darkened. Although they claimed to be wise, they became fools"** (vv. 21b–22).

Another philosopher was saying that Christ cannot be both infinite and finite at the same time, and that He cannot be both God and man. He said that reason cannot grasp it, we have to explain it some other way, through "transcategorical reasoning," which will try to dismiss ordinary reasoning. Rather than saying that Christ is not both God and man at the same time *in the same respect*—in His human nature, He is finite, and in His divine nature, He is infinite. The infinite includes the finite, though the finite does not include the infinite.[21] People do all kinds of sleight of hand to get around the idea of clarity and inexcusability, and therefore sin, the wrath of God, and the need for the gospel.

Avoiding showing what is clear has come down in the history of theology and philosophy. Some have affirmed what is called the *sensus divinitatis*.[22] Avoidance of showing what is clear through common sense realism was done at Princeton, it was done in the Declaration of Independence,[23] and it is done in Reformed epistemology[24]—they do not engage with clarity and inexcusability. In the history of philosophy, it was done by Plato and Aristotle. It was done by Augustine and Aquinas.

---

20. This counterargument is a parody, drawing on Gaunilo of Marmoutier—a contemporary critic of Anselm—who used a *reductio ad absurdum* in response to Anselm's formulation of the ontological argument. He proposed the notion of a "perfect island," arguing that if Anselm's reasoning were valid, then one could define into existence the greatest conceivable island simply by imagining it. Since such an outcome is clearly absurd, Gaunilo contended that the ontological argument's logical structure must be flawed. This cherry cheesecake counterargument implies, by parallel, that, therefore, some cherry cheesecake is eternal. An argument is sound if it is valid (the premises logically support the conclusion) and the premises are true. The form might be valid, but the last premise here—"all cherry cheesecake came into being from non-being"—is not accurate; it is not written correctly. It should say, "All cherry cheesecake came into being from non-cherry cheesecake," which is a non-debatable point since it entails being.

21. Gangadean, *History of Philosophy*, 108–110; Gangadean, *Philosophical Foundation*, 28–31.

22. Gangadean, *Philosophical Foundation*, 32–33; Gangadean, *History of Philosophy*, 127–130; Gangadean, "Paper No. 70: Sources of Fideism," 369–377; "Paper No. 120: Contra Voluntarism," in *The Logos Papers*, 611–647.

23. Gangadean, "Paper No. 20: Christianity, Philosophy, and Public Education," in *The Logos Papers*, 127–133.

24. Gangadean, *History of Philosophy*, 175–179; Gangadean, *Philosophical Foundation*, 24, 49–50.

It was done by Hume and Kant, Hegel and Marx, Darwin and Freud, and today, Hawking. Stephen Hawking has said, 'We don't need God; being can come from non-being and there may be many universes, all of them popping into being from non-being.' And I suppose if it can happen one time, it can happen innumerable times. This may qualify him as a science fiction writer, but I think even fiction has to be more believable than that. **"Although they claimed to be wise, they became fools."** One must deny reason to avoid seeing what is clear. We find that this is done by Christians and by non-Christians. What should we say about the world religions and other belief systems: Hinduism, Buddhism, Islam, Confucianism, Daoism, Shamanism, Zoroastrianism, Mormonism, Mysticism, and Existentialism? Where are they in relation to clarity and inexcusability? They are not even close.

What about the divisions within the Church? Attention is not being paid to the historically cumulative insight resulting from much discussion—where reason is operating. We have failed to see what is clear, we have held on to what is not true, and the wrath of God is upon us. We may not be seeing what is clear because we are thinking, 'Jesus will come soon and rapture us out of this place.' Think on. Every one must be asked where they stand on the doctrine of clarity and inexcusability. No one is to be exempt from it. If they have not engaged with it to see what is clear, then they need to be called to engage.[25]

THE NEED TO REPENT OF ROOT SIN:
Not Seeking, Not Understanding, and Not Doing What Is Right

Sin is defined in Scripture in a number of ways, and it is defined from general revelation as well: it is an act contrary to one's nature as a thinking being. We neglect, avoid, resist, and deny reason, and the natural result is meaninglessness, boredom, and guilt. We put ourselves in the place of God to determine good and evil by believing "You shall be like God."[26] In verse 23, Paul says they **"exchanged the glory of the immortal God for images made to look like a mortal man and birds and animals and reptiles."** They are blurring the distinction between the Creator and the

---

25. Gangadean, *Philosophical Foundation*, 293–309.

26. *Genesis 3:5.*

creature, as against saying that God's invisible qualities are plain, and we should not blur the distinction. What should we do with the divisions within theism, between Judaism, Christianity, and Islam? Should we say, like some Muslims, 'Do not question, if you question, we will kill you'? Or should we say, like some Reformed Christians or Jews, 'I'm chosen; I do not need to give a reason'? What should we say about the divisions within Christianity and the divisions within Protestantism? Where is the attention to clarity and excusability that will enable us to get through all of these divisions? Where are we? All of these other divisions, which are grounded in a misconception about God, go back to this point: God's nature is clearly revealed. That is how all of these divisions connect.

There is a denial of the doctrine of clarity and inexcusability, which is the source of understanding sin—root sin. Sin is described in the Scriptures, in this very letter, as not seeking, not understanding, and not doing what is right.[27] Sin is described as not understanding because of not seeking. When we repent, we have to repent of our failure to understand because we are not seeking diligently; we have to repent of our misconceptions about God. It says, **"but became vain in their imaginations, and their foolish heart was darkened"** (v. 21b KJV). If you try to unpack what it is to have this vain thinking, this futile thinking, we will see there are contradictions in our thinking and pointlessness in our thinking that comes up because of our not seeking and understanding who God is. We do not even know we are in this condition, because our minds are darkened.

In this condition, we **"claimed to be wise,"** we say, 'I think I know.' We fail to know what we should know, and then we claim to know what we do not, in fact, know, and cannot know, because it is false. You cannot *know* what is false. It is like saying that man is entirely material and has evolved by chance, which involves saying that the mind and the brain are one and the same thing, which involves saying a neural impulse is a mental image. It is saying a neural impulse is not a cause of, but is the same as, a mental image. It involves saying *a* is *non-a*, which is a violation of the laws of thought. Perhaps one might say, 'We don't have to get *that* precise about it, can't we just be *roughly* there?' We will see that Scripture does call us to know *pointedly*. Not seeking and not

---

27. *Romans 3:10–11.*

understanding results in no righteousness. That is how it is described in Romans 3, which is quoting passages from two Psalms: 14:1–3 and 53:1–3. We need to repent of not seeking, not understanding, and not doing what is right. We need to repent of failing to know what is clear, and we are to avoid making excuses for ourselves.

If We Know What Is Clear, We Can Show What Is Clear

How can we know if we have repented? I would say that this is how we know: *If we know what is clear, we can show what is clear.* That is, we can show (1) the content of the knowledge of God from general revelation, and (2) the inexcusability of unbelief—we can show that unbelief is contrary to reason. I want to make a point. I would not have thought I needed to make this point, but it seems that I do. What we mean by 'know' is *justified, true belief.*[28] Knowledge is not just having a belief, and it is not just that the belief is true, but you have justification for it. You have a rational justification for it so that others can see it and work through it. If you are going to take thoughts captive, if you are going to demolish arguments and pretensions that raise themselves up against the knowledge of God,[29] you have to show it. You cannot say that the nonbeliever is without excuse when you cannot show how he is without excuse. That is why I said inexcusability is connected with the unbelief that we hold. It is by understanding, not just by declaration.

A Call to Repentance and Maturity: Diligently Seek to Know

In 2 Corinthians 10:5, Paul says, "We demolish arguments and every pretension that sets itself up against the knowledge of God." Even Reformed epistemology, which tries to avoid the idea of justification, speaks about losing your *prima facie* warrant.[30] You need to be able to show that unbelief is contrary to reason. You need to be able to show that unbelief is without excuse versus warranted belief. So, where are you? Have you truly repented for failing to see what is clear? Can you

---

28. Gangadean, "Paper No. 72: What Is Knowledge? (Concise Version)," 381–383; "Paper No. 73: What Is Knowledge? (Expanded Version)," in *The Logos Papers,* 385–390; Gangadean, *Philosophical Foundation,* 49–51.

29. *2 Corinthians 10:5.*

30. Gangadean, *History of Philosophy,* 175–177.

show what is clear? If you cannot show what is clear, then you need to bring forth fruit in keeping with repentance. You should be able to show it, and if not, you would have to say, 'I do not yet know what is clear.' You may need to add, 'I need to suffer under the curse to overcome my self-justification, my self-deception, and to seek diligently to get the foundation in place.' Even after that, since it will be a matter of degree, 'I need to suffer to grow to maturity.'

Paul speaks about clarity and inexcusability as the basis for sin. We need to ask ourselves, where are we in relation to seeing what is clear, the eternal power and divine nature of God? Can we show this the way the nonbeliever is supposed to know it? If we cannot, we are not yet mature in our faith, and we need to have teaching that will bring us to maturity. You need to apply yourself because the Scripture speaks about diligently seeking God. He is the rewarder of those who diligently seek,[31] and Scripture says, "No one seeks, no one understands, no one does what is right."[32]

THE WRATH/JUSTICE OF GOD ON ROOT SIN

Given Up to Meaninglessness, Boredom, and Guilt

The wrath of God is spoken of in the remainder of this chapter, starting with Romans 1:21. **"For although they knew God, they neither glorified him as God nor gave thanks to him, but their thinking became futile and their foolish hearts were darkened."** That is the wrath of God coming. Thinking becomes futile, and a person does not even see it because the heart has been darkened. They are not willing to come into the light, they do not want to come to the discussion, and they do all sorts of things to avoid it, but, ultimately, it cannot be avoided because "the light shines in the darkness, but the darkness has not understood it" (Jn. 1:5).

Another level of being given up to the wrath of God is: **"Although they claimed to be wise, they became fools"** (v. 22). I have mentioned a number of instances where people claim to know things that they do not know. They make claims such as, 'Only Presbyterian ordination

---

31. *Hebrews 11:6.*

32. *Romans 3:10–12.*

is lawful;' such as, 'Being can come from non-being;' such as, 'It is self-evident that God exists,' rather than showing how His existence is understood from the things that are made. We think we know when we do not, we make claims, and we simply show ourselves to be foolish. We shut our eyes and turn off the light in order not to see. How can someone go along and say, 'I cannot know that *a* is *a* because of an incorrigible memory lapse'? How can they want to continue to speak? These are graduate students in philosophy. They were here in this congregation. They are those who have left and have turned around and used the 'cult' word. I just heard that word used two days ago. That is where we end up. That is the direction in which we head when we do not get established in clarity and inexcusability. We end up making many other slanderous and self-referentially absurd claims.

Here are some of the things that happen when we do not have clarity and inexcusability in place. In verse 23, Paul says we "**exchanged the glory of the immortal God for images made to look like a mortal man and birds and animals and reptiles.**" That is, we exchange the glory of the infinite, eternal, and unchangeable God—who is spirit—for images of created things. This is blurring the distinction between the Creator and the creature. Remember Satan's lie to Adam—"you shall be like God"—and Adam's falling for that lie.[33] The heart is not only darkened, but we go another step down in misconceiving of God in holding these images. The wrath of God is revealed further by giving us up to sexual impurity: "**Therefore God gave them over in the sinful desires of their hearts to sexual impurity for the degrading of their bodies with one another**" (v. 24). Then we go another step down: "**They exchanged the truth of God for a lie, and worshiped and served created things rather than the Creator**" (v. 25a). And we go another step down:

> Because of this, God gave them over to shameful lusts. Even their women exchanged natural relations for unnatural ones. In the same way the men also abandoned natural relations with women and were inflamed with lust for one another. Men committed indecent acts with other men, and received in themselves the due penalty for their perversion (vv. 26–27).

---

33. *Genesis 3:5.*

In boredom, we give ourselves to excess and perversion. With that comes abortion and the killing of millions of babies. This is the fruit sin that comes out of the root. *All* sin comes out of this root of failing to see what is clear, for which we are without excuse. *All* sin, across the board and throughout history, comes out of this root.

Descent Into Full Moral Decay and Cultural Collapse

We go down another level: "**Furthermore, since they did not think it worthwhile to retain the knowledge of God . . .**" (v. 28a). They wanted to get rid of all the vestiges of God, including prayer in the public school (the idea of public school was a problem to begin with).[34] "**He gave them over to a depraved mind, to do what ought not to be done**" (v. 28b). He gave them over to a worthless mind. If it is not worthwhile to retain the knowledge of God, then they will have a worthless mind. What happens out of that worthless mind? "**They have become filled with every kind of wickedness, evil, greed and depravity. They are full of envy, murder, strife, deceit and malice. They are gossips, slanderers, God-haters, insolent, arrogant and boastful.**" This is what comes out of not holding to clarity and inexcusability. "**They invent ways of doing evil; they disobey their parents**" (vv. 29–30). Interestingly, disobeying parents is thrown in at that late stage in the process. "**They are senseless, faithless, heartless, ruthless**" (v. 31). That is how Paul describes the depravity. This is the depravity as it progresses. The cup is filled up, as it was in the days of Noah. He says, "**Although they know God's righteous decree that those who do such things deserve death, they not only continue to do these very things but also approve of those who practice them**" (v. 32). When the cup is filled up, it is time to be cut off by death. The culture, in accumulated apostasy, will collapse in judgment. It is time to turn off the lights; it is time to end it. This is the context in which the gospel is needed and must be heard. This is where it begins: in understanding sin and death and repentance of sin.

A Brief Overview of What Follows

Paul goes on in Romans 2 to speak about those who are in the Church—"covenant people," called Jews back then, or today, all those

---

34. Gangadean, *Philosophical Foundation*, 227–229.

who have the covenant sign of baptism on them—and those who are not. Those in the Church are no better than those who are not. In this gospel that Paul preaches, he is going to give the history of this gospel going back through Abraham to Adam—after he establishes the need for the gospel. Then he is going to speak in Romans 6–8 about sanctification and the deliverance from the power of sin. In Romans 9–11, he is going to speak about God's faithfulness concerning the promise made to Israel. Romans 12–16 will apply this gospel to all of life, and will close with greetings to the believers that are in Rome—very personal, concerned greetings. This is the gospel according to St. Paul. This is where he begins—with sin and death, and the wrath of God being revealed. In this context, we can have the ability to hear the gospel. All the fruit sin in the world goes back to this root sin.

3

GOD JUDGES ACCORDING TO THE LIGHT GIVEN

Covenant Blessings and the Law Written on the Heart

1994

Romans 2

¹You, therefore, have no excuse, you who pass judgment on someone else, for at whatever point you judge the other, you are condemning yourself, because you who pass judgment do the same things. ²Now we know that God's judgment against those who do such things is based on truth. ³So when you, a mere man, pass judgment on them and yet do the same things, do you think you will escape God's judgment? ⁴Or do you show contempt for the riches of his kindness, tolerance and patience, not realizing that God's kindness leads you toward repentance?

⁵But because of your stubbornness and your unrepentant heart, you are storing up wrath against yourself for the day of God's wrath, when his righteous judgment will be revealed. ⁶God "will give to each person according to what he has done." ⁷To those who by persistence in doing good seek glory, honor and immortality, he will give eternal life. ⁸But for those who are self-seeking and who reject the truth and follow evil, there will be wrath and anger. ⁹There will be trouble and distress for every human being who does evil: first for the Jew, then for the Gentile; ¹⁰but glory, honor and peace for everyone who does good: first for the Jew, then for the Gentile. ¹¹For God does not show favoritism.

¹²All who sin apart from the law will also perish apart from the law, and all who sin under the law will be judged by the law. ¹³For it is not those who hear the law who are righteous in God's sight, but it is those who obey the law who will be declared righteous. ¹⁴(Indeed, when Gentiles, who do not have the law, do by nature things required by the law, they are a law for themselves, even though they do not have the law, ¹⁵since they show that the requirements of the law are written on their hearts, their consciences also bearing witness, and their thoughts now accusing, now even defending them.) ¹⁶This will take place on the day when God will judge men's secrets through Jesus Christ, as my gospel declares.

¹⁷Now you, if you call yourself a Jew; if you rely on the law and brag about your relationship to God; ¹⁸if you know his will and approve of what is superior because you are instructed by the law; ¹⁹if you are convinced that you are a guide for the blind, a light for those who are in the dark, ²⁰an instructor of the foolish, a teacher of infants, because you have in the law the embodiment of knowledge and truth—²¹you, then, who teach others, do you not teach yourself? You who preach against stealing, do you steal? ²²You who say that people should not commit adultery, do you commit adultery? You who abhor idols, do you rob temples? ²³You who brag about the law, do you dishonor God by breaking the law? ²⁴As it is written: "God's name is blasphemed among the Gentiles because of you."

²⁵Circumcision has value if you observe the law, but if you break the law, you have become as though you had not been circumcised. ²⁶If those who are not circumcised keep the law's requirements, will they not be regarded as though they were circumcised? ²⁷The one who is not circumcised physically and yet obeys the law will condemn you who, even though you have the written code and circumcision, are a lawbreaker.

²⁸A man is not a Jew if he is only one outwardly, nor is circumcision merely outward and physical. ²⁹No, a man is a Jew if he is one inwardly; and circumcision is circumcision of the heart, by the Spirit, not by the written code. Such a man's praise is not from men, but from God.

REVIEW: ROMANS 1:16–32

IN ROMANS 1, WE SAW THAT PAUL WAS CONCERNED about preaching the gospel to those in Rome. He is "not ashamed of the gospel, because it is the power of God that brings salvation to everyone who believes . . . For in the gospel a righteousness from God is revealed" (Rom. 1:16a, 17a). That righteousness from God is the answer to the wrath of God that is "being revealed from heaven against all the godlessness and wickedness of men who suppress the truth by their wickedness" (Rom. 1:18). We saw that the result of this suppression of the truth that is given in clear general revelation is to be given over to the depravity of our hearts to do those things that are unbecoming, those things that are wicked, those things that are vile. We know that this wickedness deserves death, that is, we may go so far in our wickedness so as to be cut off by death, which is the end of the call to repentance. There is no call to repentance beyond physical death. But people "not only continue to do these very things but also approve of those who practice them" (Rom. 1:32b).

ALL ARE WITHOUT EXCUSE:
General and Special Revelation, Root and Fruit Sin

Those Who Appear Sinless and So Judge Others: They Too Are Without Excuse

At the beginning of Romans 2, Paul says that there are some who do not approve of the obvious wickedness that is done. Romans 2 is concerned with those who do not approve of the wicked practices of men. These persons, too, come under that Word in Romans 1:18: "The wrath of God is being revealed from heaven against *all* the godlessness and wickedness of men who suppress the truth by their wickedness."[1] What we have here is a contrast between those who are given to open forms of wickedness—because of their godlessness and failure to know God—and those who do not approve of those open forms of wickedness. Those who do not approve condemn those who do, but nevertheless, they are also godless. They, too, fail to know God, fail to seek God, fail to know clear general revelation. Paul says, "**You, therefore, have no excuse, you who pass judgment on someone else, for at whatever point you judge the other, you are condemning yourself, because you who pass judgment do the same things**" (v. 1). Some approve of open forms of wickedness, and some heartily disapprove and condemn it. Both those who do open forms of wickedness and those who do not still come short of the glory of God; they fail to seek. Those who condemn outward forms of wickedness, but themselves fail to know God as they

---

1. Emphasis added.

should, bring judgment on themselves by condemning others. Those who condemn the *fruit* but do not recognize the *root* in themselves bring God's judgment on themselves. He says, **"For at whatever point you judge the other, you are condemning yourself, because you who pass judgment do the same things."** Those who pass judgment do the same thing at the root, though not in outward form.

God Judges Based on Truth

We, therefore, have the inclination, the strong tendency, to rush into making outward judgments and not make *true* judgments. We condemn others for fruit sin and we excuse root sin in ourselves. But God's judgment is not like our judgment. Verse 2 says, **"Now we know that God's judgment against those who do such things is based on truth."** Those who do what things? It is those things for which His wrath comes upon them. We must keep clearly in mind the difference between the failure to seek and understand God as He has revealed Himself, and the secondary sins to which men are given over to. We must make that distinction. When Paul says, **"do the same things,"** he is referring to that for which the wrath comes. The wrath comes not for the secondary sin; the wrath comes for the primary sin. The wrath did not come upon mankind because Adam was engaged in fruit sins of open wickedness; the wrath came upon mankind because Adam failed to seek God. This is where *many* stumble. They look at the outward, obvious expressions of sin and fail to see the root of sin. But God's judgment against those who do such things is based on truth. That is, God does not look merely at the fruit sin that many are given over to. God is bringing His wrath because men are not seeing His clear revelation. That is the point at which we **"do the same things"**—we fail to see His clear revelation. It is certain that God's wrath "is being revealed from heaven against all the godlessness and wickedness of men who suppress the truth by their wickedness" (Rom. 1:18).

"For since the creation of the world God's invisible qualities—his eternal power and divine nature—have been clearly seen, being understood from what has been made, so that men are without excuse" (Rom. 1:20). Men are without excuse for failing to see clear general revelation. On that basis, the wrath comes. They are given over to the desires of their hearts as a result of their depravity, their failure to know God. We see two things from verse 2. First, God's judgment is based on the *real* case, on what the situation truly is. God's judgment is not based on outward appearances by which we may fool ourselves, but on the real situation. Second, just as God's judgment comes on those who fail to seek Him and know Him, and they are given over to the depravity of their hearts, so God's judgment will come on those who have not yet had these outward expressions of depravity, but who nevertheless fail to know Him. God's judgment is based on truth.

Privileges of Special Revelation: Do Not Exempt from Judgment, but Intensify It If Rejected

Some have privileges and think that because of these privileges, they will somehow be exempt from God's judgment—the judgment that comes on those who fail to see God and seek God as He has revealed Himself. In verses 3–5 we are told,

> So when you, a mere man, pass judgment on them and yet do the same things, do you think you will escape God's judgment? Or do you show contempt for the riches of his kindness, tolerance and patience, not realizing that God's kindness leads you toward repentance? But because of your stubbornness and your unrepentant heart, you are storing up wrath against yourself for the day of God's wrath, when his righteous judgment will be revealed.

The kindness of God here, and later on in the passage, regards those who have special revelation and the benefits of it, immediately or culturally, and who do not improve by virtue of having this special revelation. This is **"the riches of his kindness,"** which He has brought to man—His Word in His redemptive revelation. God has been tolerant and patient, and it is because of the special revelation present that men have been kept from some of the outward forms of expression of depravity; yet, they are not seeking and not knowing God as He has revealed Himself clearly.

This is where we can look at the condition of those who have special revelation, whether it is the Church under the Old Testament or the Church in the New Testament, and ask whether those who have that revelation have sought God and come to know God in all that whereby

He makes Himself known.[2] We have the forgiveness of sin, on the part of God, coming in special revelation against this original sin, which is the root of all sin, and we do not repent of that original sin.[3] In doing so, we **"show contempt for the riches of his kindness"** (v. 4a). When He came to us in special revelation, in Scripture, and we did not come to repent of our original sin, that is to **"show contempt for the riches of his kindness."** That is to show contempt for God's **"tolerance and patience."** God has been waiting and calling us, not only through natural evil, but through the Scripture itself. Because God did not bring judgment on us—in the sense that we have not been given over to the depravity of our hearts—we have taken that kindness of God for granted. We have taken it as meaning, 'God *approves* of our way.' We do not realize that **"God's kindness leads you toward repentance"** (v. 4b). That kindness, in the special revelation coming to us, should all the more lead us to repentance, but it has not. We have deceived ourselves and come to think we are okay before God.

There has been stubbornness in us, a self-centeredness where we will not give up our self-life, and a resistance to this call to know God and glorify Him. Though we have been called to repent, we have not done so. We hear the Word of God again and again, but without understanding. And by continuing to hear it while blocking it out due to our lack of understanding, we are storing up wrath for ourselves. This will be revealed on the day of God's wrath when His righteous judgment is made known. It is not the case that we have this additional kindness of God and can neglect it, and yet think we can go on as if everything is okay. In fact, we are storing up wrath for ourselves when we do not hear God's Word and repent at the basic level.

As we go through this chapter, we will see, very much so, that this idea of the basic level is *critical*. We will come to the outward and the inward, the surface and the depth, when we come to the specific application of circumcision. We see it in Romans 1, where the wrath begins. We see it in Adam, where the wrath begins. We see it also in Romans 3, when Paul says, "There is no one righteous, not even one;

---

2. Gangadean, *The Westminster Catechisms*, 100.

3. *Romans 3:10–11*; *Psalm 14:2–3, 53:1–3*; Gangadean, *The Biblical Worldview*, 177–195, 46–52; Gangadean, "Paper No. 103: The Noetic Effect of Sin," 531–538; "Paper No. 146: The Biblical Worldview (Part VI)," in *The Logos Papers*, 741–745; Gangadean, *The Westminster Confession*, 99–110.

there is no one who understands, no one who seeks God" (Rom. 3:10–11). That is where sin begins, and instead of looking at its root, at its depth, and dealing with it there, we bypass this basic level. That is the sense in which there has been stubbornness and unrepentance, and the wrath is being stored up.

God Will Give to Each According to What He Has Done

So there is judgment because of our judging. We have God's judgment, which is based on truth. Our privileges do not exempt us from judgment, but if we reject our privileges, it intensifies our judgment. The judgment comes upon those who have special revelation and yet disregard it. God's judgment is that He **"will give to each person according to what he has done"** (v. 6). In verses 6–8, we see that it is not those who *say* that are regarded as obedient, but those who actually *do*, and this difference between saying and doing is a prominent theme in this chapter. We have to look at whether we have actually repented, or whether we *say* we have repented. We have to look at whether we are, in repenting, turning away from that root sin, or whether we are still negligent and letting that continue. Many in the Church profess to believe, but when it comes to showing that they understand God's clear revelation, they cannot show it. That means that there has not been repentance at the root level—the basic level.

That is why Scripture says that **"God 'will give to each person according to what he has done.' To those who by persistence in doing good seek glory, honor and immortality, he will give eternal life"** (vv. 6–7). Those who have repented and have truly sought the Lord, to know Him, to make Him known, to glorify Him; they will have eternal life. They will have the knowledge of God.[4] But for those who are self-seeking—affirming themselves, putting themselves forward, and protecting themselves in pride—who reject the truth and refuse to know God as He has revealed Himself, despite repeated calls to do so, and who instead follow what is evil, disregarding His general revelation, there will be wrath and anger. **"But for those who are self-seeking and who reject the truth and follow evil, there will be wrath and anger"** (v. 8). God's

---

4. Gangadean, *Philosophical Foundation*, 171–177, 208–211; Gangadean, *The Biblical Worldview*, 109–124; Gangadean, *The Westminster Catechisms*, 109–111, 321–325; Gangadean, *On Natural and Revealed Theology*, 33–39, 127–139.

judgment is not on the basis of what we *profess*; God's judgment is on the basis of what we *do*. There is an inherent relationship between our failure to repent and the wrath—being given over to go our own way.

God Judges All Who Do Evil: There Is No Favoritism with God

God judges not only according to what we do—as against what we profess—but He judges *all* who do evil; there is no favoritism with God. Paul says, "**There will be trouble and distress for *every* human being who does evil: first for the Jew, then for the Gentile; but glory, honor and peace for everyone who does good: first for the Jew, then for the Gentile. For God does not show favoritism**" (vv. 9–11).[5] We might translate "Jew," in the New Testament, as those who have special revelation. In the Old Testament, the Israelites thought that they had a certain special relation to God through Abraham, that they stood in special relation to God through circumcision, the sign of the covenant, but that is not what stands. What stands is whether we see a real change within, producing fruit. So God judges *all* and there is no favoritism. It would be unworthy of us to think that God will judge other men who fail to know Him as He has revealed Himself, and somehow, because we are in this group,[6] or we have this tradition, or we have some privilege, and we do not do some of those outward forms of depravity, that we will be exempt. It just does not work that way. God's judgment is according to truth—the real situation. He judges according to our works; He judges all and there is no favoritism with Him.

We Are Judged According to the Light That We Have

"**All who sin apart from the law will also perish apart from the law, and all who sin under the law will be judged by the law**" (v. 12). Here is a case where both special revelation and general revelation are spoken of. There is general revelation for all men, and special revelation for some. "**All who sin apart from the law**"—apart from the law given in

---

5. Emphasis added.

6. This sermon series was delivered before Westminster Fellowship became a church (2000). Pastor Gangadean made numerous efforts to rejoin the Reformed Presbyterian Church of North America (RPCNA), but by 1999, it became evident that a new ministry needed to be established. A detailed history of Westminster Fellowship will be published after the completion of all other planned publications.

special revelation—"will also perish apart from the law, and all who sin under the law will be judged by the law." "For it is not those who *hear* the law who are righteous in God's sight, but it is those who *obey* the law who will be declared righteous" (v. 13).[7] We are judged according to whatever light we have. It is not those who merely hear who are righteous in God's sight. Particularly with regard to special revelation, there are those who sit every Lord's Day and hear the Word of God yet fail to put it into practice. It is not those who hear it, but those who obey it, who will be declared righteous. Jesus said, "My mother and brothers are those who hear God's word and put it into practice" (Lk. 8:21). We may flatter ourselves that we do obey, but what we may be doing is merely surface obedience. That is not what God has called us for. God is not the kind of holy God who will be satisfied with surface level, outward obedience of the letter and not the spirit. Clearly, we are taught in Scripture that if the original sin teaches us anything, it is that God judges the root sin, and it is by His judging the root sin that we see men are given over to the fruit.

God's judgment is according to the light that we have. Those who hear and do not do are not the ones who are righteous, but those who obey the law will be declared righteous. Paul says, "**Indeed, when Gentiles, who do not have the law, do by nature things required by the law, they are a law for themselves, even though they do not have the law**" (v. 14). Clearly the distinction here is between the law from special revelation and the law from general revelation. "**They show that the requirements of the law are written on their hearts, their consciences also bearing witness, and their thoughts now accusing, now even defending them**" (v. 15). Those who do not have the law as given in Scripture, but have the law written on their hearts,[8] have to respond to that law. They respond by condemning others, accusing others, and excusing themselves. Those who sin apart from the law and accuse others and excuse themselves will be judged. There are intellectuals in the academic world who accuse others and excuse themselves. There are religious leaders in the various religions of the world who accuse others and excuse themselves. They have general revelation; if they

---

7. *Emphasis added.*

8. Gangadean, *Philosophical Foundation*, 171–284; Gangadean, *History of Philosophy*, 61–69; Gangadean, *The Westminster Catechisms*, 215–267; Gangadean, *The Westminster Confession*, 207–221; Gangadean, *On Natural and Revealed Theology*, 127–139, 166–178.

accuse others and excuse themselves, they will be condemned *apart from the law*. Those who have the Scriptures who accuse others, excuse themselves, and fail to repent at the basic level, will be judged *by* the law. "**For God does not show favoritism**" (v. 11).

Our Secrets Are Judged by Jesus Christ

God judges all according to their works, and this judgment "**will take place on the day when God judges men's secrets through Jesus Christ, as my gospel declares**" (v. 16). It is not only our outward behavior that is judged, but our inward behavior, so to speak—what is going on in our thoughts—that will be judged. Our secrets will be judged, which is certainly getting to the inner, not just the things that are outwardly observable. We will be judged by Jesus Christ, the One who was given to us in mercy and special revelation, but whom we fail to honor by true repentance. This One who we rejected was offered in grace and mercy. That is the One who will judge the secrets of our hearts. We may be in the purest church in the world, yet we may be in that church merely outwardly. We may even speak the doctrine to others, but we may speak it without understanding—outwardly. God does not judge the outward. God judges according to what we really do, our innermost thoughts, our secrets, and the judgment is through Jesus Christ.

We have reaffirmed, in verses 1–16, God's righteous judgment. This picks up from Romans 1:18: "The wrath of God is being revealed from heaven against *all* the godlessness and wickedness of men who suppress the truth by their wickedness."[9] *All* forms of it. *All* those who have the clear revelation of God and yet have failed to see it, seek it, understand it, know it, and make it known. Particularly those who do not have the outward forms of depravity, but have an inward depravity—lack of the knowledge of God.

---

9. Emphasis added.

THE NEED FOR TRUE INWARD REPENTANCE

We Can Come Outwardly to God Without True Repentance of Our Former Way

Paul makes an explicit application to the Jews, and we can say this application is to all those who outwardly come to God, who outwardly profess the name of God, but inwardly are not there. "**Now you, if you call yourself a Jew; if you rely on the law and brag about your relationship to God; if you know his will and approve of what is superior because you are instructed by the law . . .**" (vv. 17–18). This was one of the boasts by the Jews then, that they had the Scriptures, and we find Christians boasting in the same way today. They say, 'We have the Scriptures.' They make much of having the Scripture and say, 'You need the Scripture, you must have it.' But they who do such things do not acknowledge the clarity of general revelation[10] and do not give themselves to seek and to know that revelation. We see the reality of this in the Church today. Similarly, you can understand how those in Old Testament times had the Scriptures, and they believed that having the Scriptures set them apart. However, they had not paid attention to the Scriptures or to general revelation.

There are many today who, like the Jews then, have the Scriptures and have turned the meaning of the Scriptures inside out and interpret it on a surface level. A lot of literalism[11] takes place in looking for outward deliverance—by the Rapture or by dying and going to heaven—rather than seeking the knowledge of God. The Jews were similar. They were looking for a Messiah who would deliver them from Rome—an outward deliverance. We may boast about our relationship to God in terms of our tradition, or we may boast about special revelation and the law, but we can come outwardly to God without true repentance of our former ways. We find that people often reinterpret the Scriptures that they hear in light of their former ways, so as to nullify its meaning. Sometimes, those who are from conservative Christian background traditions integrate

---

10. Gangadean, "Paper No. 102: The Clarity of General Revelation," 527–529; "Paper No. 41: What Is Clear About God," 225–229; "Paper No. 112: Why General Revelation Is Basic in the Christian Worldview," in *The Logos Papers*, 583–585; Gangadean, *On Natural and Revealed Theology*, 213–222; Gangadean, *The Epistle to the Hebrews*, 255–271.

11. Gangadean, *On Natural and Revealed Theology*, 18–26; Gangadean, "Paper No. 15: Hermeneutics," in *The Logos Papers*, 91–101; Gangadean, *The Westminster Confession*, 41–46.

the Word of God into their old way of thinking and then nullify the meaning of it.[12] What is done now with the Scriptures was also done then. It is possible to come outwardly to God. We may even come outwardly professing the true doctrine about clear general revelation and the use of reason, and we may agree to and profess these things but fail to truly repent, inwardly. We can come to God outwardly without true repentance of our former ways. We have to *reject* our tradition, which was vain, empty, and did not bring us to the knowledge of God. The Church, for hundreds of years, has been pursuing its traditions and has not been making progress in the knowledge of God. God is calling us to not just come to Him outwardly, but come to Him truly.

We Can Teach the Word of God Without Ourselves Being Taught by It

Paul says,

> If you know his will and approve of what is superior because you are instructed by the law; if you are convinced that you are a guide for the blind, a light for those who are in the dark, an instructor of the foolish, a teacher of infants, because you have in the law the embodiment of knowledge and truth . . . (vv. 18–20).

This is speaking about knowing His will in an outward sense. So we can teach the very words of God and yet need to be taught ourselves. We can teach the letter of the law rather than the spirit of the law. We can outwardly observe the Sabbath without understanding its true significance.[13] We can go for the literal without the true meaning. We can focus on the *fruit* sin and not the *root* sin.

Knowledge Without Understanding Does Not Sanctify but Increases Our Guilt

Paul continues, "You, then, who teach others, do you not teach yourself? You who preach against stealing, do you steal? You who say that people should not commit adultery, do you commit adultery? You

---

12. Gangadean, "Paper No. 64: Aaron's Rod," in *The Logos Papers*, 341–352.

13. Gangadean, *The Biblical Worldview*, 125–146; Gangadean, *The Westminster Confession*, 241–244; Gangadean, *The Westminster Catechisms*, 241–245.

who abhor idols, do you rob temples?" (vv. 21–22). We can teach that we "**should not commit adultery**" in the obvious, outward forms of adultery, but we may continue in our *spiritual* adultery by failing to seek God above all and loving the world instead. Scripture says, "You adulterous people, don't you know that friendship with the world is hatred toward God?" (Jas. 4:4a). We may condemn the outward fruit of actual, physical adultery and not see the root of the adultery. We say others should not steal but we may steal by failing to develop our talent in service to others.[14] Uncritically, we may say that the outward form is the obvious, pure, real, true form. We may say that the surface, outward meaning is the true meaning. It is not. That surface meaning comes out of the root. So, "**You, then, who teach others, do you not teach yourself?**" (v. 21a). We teach a kind of outward observance of the Sabbath; we teach about not stealing, adultery, and murder, and yet in its true essence, we continue to do the same thing. God's judgment is according to the truth. It is not what we say but what we do. It is possible to have knowledge without understanding. We can have knowledge at the grammatical level,[15] in that we speak knowledge in outward form, but that does not sanctify us; rather, it increases our guilt objectively. "**You, then, who teach others, do you not teach yourself?**" It is possible to have knowledge and to teach others, yet lack understanding of the meaning in order to be taught by it ourselves. We preach against stealing and we steal. This knowledge without understanding, knowledge of the surface level of things without understanding its meaning, does not sanctify us (in that we continue to do it), and it rather increases our guilt.

The Outward Without the Inward Is Especially Offensive to God and Man

"**You who brag about the law, do you dishonor God by breaking the law?**" (v. 23). It is dishonoring to God to speak that word with our mouth and think we are teachers of babes when we do not understand its root meaning and we continue to break the law at the root level. Not only is it dishonoring to God and displeasing to God and offensive to

---

14. Gangadean, *Philosophical Foundation*, 255–265.

15. The Logos Foundation, *Grammar Catechisms: Philosophical, Theological, and Historical Foundations* (Phoenix: Logos Papers Press, 2023), xiv–xvi; Dorothy Sayers, *The Lost Tools of Learning* (Grand Rapids, MI: CrossReach Publications, 2016).

God, but it is offensive to men. Paul says, "**As it is written: 'God's name is blasphemed among the Gentiles because of you'**" (v. 24). This type of surface living—the outward without the inward at the root—produces a life that is offensive to nonbelievers and causes nonbelievers to blaspheme the name of God. And so we, who should be in a place to honor God, are not doing so.

The Outward Is Nullified by the Lack of Inward Reality

In verses 25 and 26, we see that the outward is nullified by the lack of inward reality. "**Circumcision has value if you observe the law**" (v. 25a); circumcision is the outward sign, but the observance of the law is the true, inward reality—having a new heart.[16] Circumcision and outward profession have value if you have the inward reality. "**But if you break the law, you have become as though you had not been circumcised**" (v. 25b). The sign without the reality is of no significance, but if the reality is there, the sign has some significance. "**If those who are not circumcised keep the law's requirements, will they not be regarded as though they were circumcised?**" (v. 26). It is the reversal. If one has the outward but not the inward, it is of no value. If one does not have the outward but has the inward, they are regarded as truly circumcised—the reality is what counts.

Those Who Obey Without Circumcision Condemn Those Who Do Not Obey

The uncircumcised, who obey the law and are regarded as truly circumcised, will condemn those who have the outward sign but do not obey the law. Verse 27 says, "**The one who is not circumcised physically and yet obeys the law will condemn you who, even though you have the written code and circumcision, are a lawbreaker.**" Jesus said in Matthew 12:41–42:

> The men of Nineveh will stand up at the judgment with this generation and condemn it; for they repented at the preaching of Jonah, and now one greater than Jonah is here. The Queen of the South

---

16. Gangadean, *The Westminster Confession*, 143–148; Gangadean, *The Westminster Catechisms*, 191–192; Gangadean, *The Epistle to the Hebrews*, 306–309.

will rise at the judgment with this generation and condemn it; for she came from the ends of the earth to listen to Solomon's wisdom, and now one greater than Solomon is here.

This is the sense in which the uncircumcised, who seek and hear, will rise up in judgment against those who have the greater light and do not give heed to it.

A Man Is Not a Jew If He Is One Outwardly: Circumcision Is of the Heart

Paul says, "A man is not a Jew if he is only one outwardly" (v. 28a). This point that we are making about the outward and the inward, the surface and the root, comes out explicitly here:

> A man is not a Jew if he is only one outwardly, nor is circumcision merely outward and physical. No, a man is a Jew if he is one inwardly; and circumcision is circumcision of the heart, by the Spirit, not by the written code. Such a man's praise is not from men, but from God (vv. 28–29).

We see clearly here the point that has been made all along, that it is not the outward reality; it is not the surface that counts. It is not those who condemn others, but are themselves doing what they condemn; it is not those who say they would *like* to do it; it is not those who teach others to do it, but themselves do not do it; it is not these who are righteous. It is possible to declare to others the teaching about the clarity of general revelation without oneself actually engaging one's mind to see and understand it. Declaring and affirming something without actual seeing and understanding is not what is called for. Romans 3 includes in the definition of sin that there is *none* who understand.[17] To teach people about the knowledge of God filling the earth rather than going to heaven, and not giving oneself to actually develop and grow in that knowledge, is outward only. God calls us to recognize what true repentance is—at the root—and to live according to that repentance. God calls us to know that the wrath of God is upon *all* who fail to have this knowledge of God. We should not flatter ourselves because we do

---

17. *Romans 3:10–11.*

not have the outward forms of depravity—and yet have the depravity of the lack of the knowledge of God—that we somehow will be exempt from the judgment of God.

God has given to us Jesus Christ. We come to Christ by acknowledging our sin: our failure to see and know God given in clear general revelation. Those who would try to come without acknowledging their sin, or merely acknowledge outwardly, are not exempt from the wrath of God. Those who continue in this and do not make progress in this knowledge of God are not exempt from the wrath of God. But those who do truly come, through Jesus Christ, acknowledging their sin and seeking God and growing in the knowledge of God, are the ones who will have blessing and eternal life.

4

SIN IN THE CHURCH
God's Justice to All

2013

Romans 1–2

INTRODUCTION AND REVIEW

The Gospel in Genesis: First Mention (*Protoevangelium*)

BEFORE GOING ON TO ROMANS 2, WE WILL REVIEW Romans 1. Paul's focus is on the gospel. More explicitly, it is on the proclamation of the gospel. In Greek, *kerygma* is the proclamation of good news. We are to remember that the gospel was first mentioned in Genesis 3:15. There is a certain law of *first mention*, just as when the Sabbath is first mentioned in Genesis 2:1. The first mention should guide us in our thinking. In Genesis 3:15, we are told that God will put enmity between the serpent and the woman, between the seed of the serpent and the seed of the woman, and "he," singular, the seed of the woman, "will crush your head, and you will strike his heel" (Gen. 3:15b). In this we see a spiritual war: "I will put enmity" (Gen. 3:15a). It is spiritual and not physical: "For our struggle is not against flesh and blood, but against rulers, against the authorities, against the powers of this dark world and against spiritual forces of evil in the heavenly realms" (Eph. 6:12). More explicitly, the spiritual war is between belief and unbelief; that is how the enmity is established.

Man was seduced to Satan's side by believing the lie, and God will not allow that alliance to stand. He will put enmity between the serpent and the woman by bringing the woman to know the truth and by bringing the seed of the woman to know the truth. So there is a spiritual war that is going to go on through the ages, through those who believe and those who do not believe. Those who believe the lie of Satan are the seed of the serpent, children of the devil, because they believe the word of their father.[1] Those who believe the truth are the children of God. It is an asymmetrical war, and one will overcome the other. One will crush the head of the other by demolishing arguments raised up against the knowledge of God.[2] The other will not fight by truth and the light of reason but will do otherwise in every way.[3] Unbelievers may make a show of using reason and seeking truth, but they cannot, and they will eventually resort to force, as we see in the case of Cain and Abel, the persecution of the prophets through the centuries, and the killing of our Lord Jesus Christ.

The good news is the promise that good will overcome evil. We should not take that for granted. Heman the Ezrahite, in Psalm 88, shows how there are times when believers are brought so low that they are counted as sheep for the slaughter. They can hardly make sense of how this condition of theirs will glorify God, and yet we have to hold on to the promise that good will overcome evil, and have hope as an anchor for the soul.[4]

Paul says several things about this gospel. It is of old, from the beginning, through the prophets, and has come down to him. He has been called, set aside for the proclamation, and is desiring to proclaim the gospel. He has the obligation to preach this gospel. He desires to go to Rome, but he has been hindered from going, and so, he writes this letter. Interestingly enough, this letter has lasted. Paul endured much perplexity about being prevented from going to Rome, and he wrote this letter because he could not go. This letter not only went to Rome, but through Rome, has gone to the whole world. We see how God triumphs through His people, and this letter has come down to us today.

---

1. *John 8:44.*

2. *2 Corinthians 10:5.*

3. *The Contradictoriness of Sin,* Surrendra Gangadean.

4. *Hebrews 6:19;* Gangadean, *The Epistle to the Hebrews,* 83–98.

The Gospel Is the Power of God Unto Salvation

In Romans 1, Paul says he is not ashamed of this gospel **"because it is the power of God for the salvation to everyone who believes"** (1:16). It has the power to save through belief. By way of analogy, it is as if the power is there in the outlets in the wall, and you need to plug into it to get connected, and belief is what connects you. To continue the analogy, it is as if there is a rheostat on the electric wire that is plugged in, and it can be on *dim*—just barely coming through. You need to increase that flow, through understanding, to get the power of the truth into you, the truth of who God is. This truth is transformative, as we are transformed into that same glory as we behold the glory of God. **"It is the power of God unto salvation."**[5] This salvation is not only in the beginning, in terms of forgiveness through justification, but it is continuing through sanctification. There is justifying faith and there is sanctifying faith—to deliver us from the penalty and the power of sin.

Paul Warns Us Not to Preach Another Gospel

It is interesting that Paul says he is not ashamed of this gospel. He says in Philippians that he has been sent for the defense of the gospel.[6] The gospel is the comprehensive Word given from Genesis 3:15. In Galatians, Paul speaks about the Judaizers, we might call them, who were subverting and perverting the gospel.[7] He greatly denounces anyone who would preach another gospel: Let him be *anathema*.[8] Elsewhere, he uses the term *anathema maranatha*.[9] The Lord is coming in judgment if you do not repent of subverting and perverting the gospel. Judgment takes place throughout history, and often, that is what the word *judgment* is referring to in Scripture. Judgment will also certainly take place at the end of history in the Last Judgment. Paul warns us about preaching another gospel.

---

5. KJV.

6. *Philippians 1:16.*

7. *Galatians 1:6–10.*

8. *Galatians 1:9* KJV.

9. *1 Corinthians 16:22* KJV.

Paul Establishes Clarity, Inexcusability, and the Need for Redemption

Paul is not ashamed of the gospel, and I should confess with my mouth before you, that I am not ashamed of *this* gospel—I am not ashamed of this gospel that Paul preaches and proclaims. But I am more than slightly embarrassed by what comes short of this gospel. I do not want to be identified with what comes short of this gospel, and the greater part of Christendom does not connect with this gospel. It is interesting that Paul says, "**I am not ashamed of the gospel**" (1:16a). This gospel begins with establishing the condition of man and the *need* for salvation. Paul speaks of the reality of sin and death throughout this entire chapter, all the way, fully—from root sin to fruit sin, in all of its fullness and breadth, that brings about judgment when the cup of iniquity is filled. There is sin, there is death, and Paul outlines how sin works. It begins with the root sin of not seeking and not understanding what is clear about God.

Progression in Unbelief: From Root Sin to Fruit Sin

We have three stages of how sin unfolds: First, men *suppress* the truth (Rom. 1:18); they suppress the truth of general revelation. Second, they *change* the truth of special revelation; they are covenant breakers. Third, they do not have any care about the truth. Their minds have become *reprobate.* They do not care about the truth, knowing the truth, or proof of the truth—they *do not care.* Their minds have become worthless and reprobate. Mankind descends into the pit by digging themselves into it more and more through the years, decades, and centuries.

First Stage: Men Suppress the Truth of Clear General Revelation

All sin begins with not seeking and not understanding. What is clear about the invisible God is known through the things that are made— the visible creation. Particularly, what is clear is the eternality, the immortality, and the unchangeability of God, and men changed that to be like corruptible man. It is the sin in the Garden: "you will be like God, knowing good and evil" (Gen. 3:5b). The lie says that there is an essential likeness between you and God in knowing good and evil. There is a radical distinction between the infinite, eternal Creator and the finite, temporal creation—that distinction was blurred. Paul's description of sin applies all the way back to the beginning and all the way through history. It is clear: **"God's invisible qualities—his eternal power and divine nature—have been clearly seen, being understood from what has been made, so that men are without excuse"** (1:20b).

All in the Church who fail to reckon with the doctrine of clarity and inexcusability, all who merely give lip service to this doctrine, all who have not repented of this sin and brought forth fruit in keeping with repentance are going to be spoken to in Romans 2. This is the root sin. In every situation, we must ask: does this person begin with, understand, and affirm clarity and inexcusability? When the question is put that way, you see how many people have not heard or thought about it and do not seem to care much about it. We see again and again that many pious Christians are not connecting with clarity and inexcusability, and seem to disregard it, and persist in their way, and may oppose those who seek to pursue and hold on to clarity and inexcusability—root sin and the death that comes from it. *All* sin comes from this root, categorically, without any qualification whatsoever. This is a strong, universal, unqualified statement. All sin comes out of this root sin of failing to seek and understand what is clear about God: **"his eternal power and divine nature."**

There is a process of progression into unbelief. **"For although they knew God, they neither glorified him as God nor gave thanks to him"** (1:21a). Man's chief end is to glorify God—many confess this, but they do not go on to say, in all that whereby he makes himself known, in all of his works of creation and providence.[10] That statement is used, but it is emptied of meaning. It is meaning*less*, and that is precisely the spiritual death that is present—meaning*less*ness. **"They neither glorified him as God"**—this is a central truth—**"nor gave thanks to him."** They take His creation for granted. Psalm 100 is about giving thanks to Him and blessing His name because He has made us and endowed us with every good that we have. The progression in unbelief takes place in several stages.

They knew and did not glorify God in the sense that Adam knew and did not glorify God—he departed. He was left to himself and turned away. Or they knew, in the sense that they had a clear revelation, and

---

10. *The Shorter Catechism Questions 1, 101; Westminster Confession of Faith 4.1, 5.1.*

they disregarded that revelation. When we do not aim at the goal of glorifying God, and we do not give thanks to Him for the many ways in which He has revealed Himself, the thinking becomes "futile," purposeless, empty, and contradictory. Futile and vain—"their foolish hearts were darkened" (1:21b). They do not even recognize how their thinking has become contradictory and purposeless.

Verse 22 says, "Although they claimed to be wise, they became fools." This is another step downward. They claim to know, and say others do not know, when they themselves are the ones who do not know. They have not seen what is clear. They are trying to go on without a foundation in place, without the cornerstone in place. They claim to be wise, and in claiming to be wise and to be teachers of others, they become fools. A fool is one who is ridiculous and is seen as ridiculous by those who have eyes to see. When they profess to be wise, they should be laughed to scorn, dismissed, and they should be ashamed. That is part of what it means to say, "they became fools." It invites ridicule because the person has become *ridiculous*, claiming to be wise when they do not know what is clear. They "exchanged the glory of the immortal God for images made to look like a mortal man and birds and animals and reptiles" (1:23). The eternal, unchanging God is made to look like the temporal, changeable creature. Notice how it descends: mortal man, birds, animals, reptiles, or creeping things—it descends to the lowest level.

That is the first cluster, not seeking and not understanding which leads to vain thinking, darkened hearts, claiming to be wise and becoming fools, and changing the glory of God. In this condition, the first layer of judgment comes in. "Therefore God gave them over in the sinful desires of their hearts to sexual impurity for the degrading of their bodies with one another" (1:24). From very early on in this descent, the most common, frequent way in which we turn aside is to sexual impurity—indulging our natural desires, especially when they become inflamed with boredom, through sex separated from love. Time and again, this sin, sexual impurity, is first on the list.

Second Stage: They Change the Truth of Special Revelation

Then they descend further: "they exchanged the truth of God for a lie" (1:25a). As I was thinking about this, I believe this stage concerns special revelation. The first stage concerns general revelation: "**from what has been made**" (1:20). Here, they "**exchanged the truth of God for a lie, and worshiped and served created things rather than the Creator—who is forever praised. Amen**" (1:25). They want to get away from God by changing the truth of God. Cain changed the truth about the coats of skin, brought the offering without blood, and then could not understand why he was rejected, though he had been warned and called back. People, time and again, change the truth of God into a lie. Jesus said in Mark 7:9, "You have a fine way of setting aside the commands of God in order to observe your own traditions!" This is what the Jews were doing. They emptied the Word of God and *reversed* it. What was intended in one way becomes the opposite. Christ pointed out how the Corban (a gift devoted to God) was used to undermine honoring father and mother. So, they made the Word of God of no effect.[11] Nonbelievers fight against Scripture as well as believers. There is a progression in this; it is not each and every one descending in this way, but nonbelievers, over time, corporately and collectively, go in this direction. As a consequence, God gave them up to shameful lust—*vile* affections. Paul speaks again of the sexual impurity:

> **Even their women exchanged natural sexual relations for unnatural ones. In the same way the men also abandoned natural relations with women and were inflamed with lust for one another. Men committed indecent acts with other men, and received in themselves the due penalty for their perversion** (1:26b–27).

It is not politically correct to oppose such acts; it is even being established by law and required to be taught. It is taken as a badge of enlightenment to say that nothing should be spoken against this way of life. It has been building up to this in recent history and is now being accepted in the churches. These types of marriages are being performed in the churches. The churches have justified it; they "**exchanged the truth of God for a lie**" (1:25a). This is a further descent from root sin.

---

11. *Mark 7:10–13.*

Third Stage: The Reprobate Mind—No Care for the Truth

Then they descend further: "**Furthermore, since they did not think it worthwhile to retain the knowledge of God, he gave them over to a depraved mind, to do what ought not to be done**" (1:28). God gave them over to a depraved, reprobate, worth*less* mind—a mind that is wasted. We hear echoes of this worthlessness in the Socratic dictum: the unexamined life is not worth living.[12] We have a mind, and if we do not use it, it is worth*less*; it is good for nothing. One is not concerned about *knowing* the truth; one is concerned about simply *expressing* what they believe to be true, especially if they 'feel it deeply.' The feelings become the standard of the truth and not the Word of God. He gave them over to a mind that is without the concern for truth, knowledge, or proof. Think about this: nonbelievers, who fail to see what is clear, descend to a place where they *do not care* about the truth or knowledge. It is out of this state of mind that people come to God. The question is, when they come to God out of this state, do they come with repentance of root sin, which is what caused the descent into this state? Or do they attempt to slide in without dealing with repentance of root sin?

"**They have become filled with every kind of wickedness, evil, greed and depravity**" (1:29a). This is a general statement. Notice the word *filled* and the words *with every kind*—this has a depth and breadth to it. The depth is below all the breadth. This is the doctrine of the fullness of sin. This condition has occurred repeatedly in history, and when it occurs, judgment comes. The first example of this judgment is the Flood: "Then the LORD saw that the wickedness of man was great in the earth, and that every intent of the thoughts of his heart was only evil continually" (Gen. 6:5 NKJV); "Now the earth was corrupt in God's sight and was full of violence" (Gen. 6:11). This judgment occurred again at Babel. This is the pattern that has occurred again and again in history, and again and again, God judges. There is truth in the revelation of creation, and there is also truth in the revelation of providence, which can be known by all human beings, to see that God rules, starting with the existence of natural evil. It is not just natural; it is natural *evil*. Paul specifies all the kinds of evil, and the question is, can you think of any that he has left out, any law that is not referred to here?

---

12. Plato, *Apology*, trans. G. M. A. Grube, in *Plato: Five Dialogues*, 2nd ed., rev. John M. Cooper (Indianapolis: Hackett, 2002), 38a.

They have become filled with every kind of wickedness, evil, greed and depravity. They are full of envy, murder, strife, deceit and malice. They are gossips, slanderers, God-haters, insolent, arrogant and boastful; they invent ways of doing evil; they disobey their parents; they are senseless, faithless, heartless, ruthless. Although they know God's righteous decree that those who do such things deserve death, they not only continue to do these very things but also approve of those who practice them (1:29b–32).

This is the corruption that comes from sin. This is sin coming fully, the spiritual death that comes with sin, and the physical death that comes to cut off sin. That is what is being said here when Paul says, "**I am not ashamed of the gospel, because it is the power of God for the salvation to everyone who believes**" (1:16a). Man needs salvation. We have abundant proof throughout history of this pattern of sin and death and judgment that has occurred again and again and again—unless you are totally oblivious to history, as if the world just began when you became conscious of it and exists insofar as you are conscious of it. We should be mindful of God's revelation in the patterns of history.

I have come to see that what is said in verse 31 is not so much a greater depth; it is more like a summary addition of all these things that have been listed. "**They are senseless, faithless, heartless, ruthless**" (1:31). They are *senseless*: without understanding in terms of general revelation. They are *faithless*: covenant breakers in terms of special revelation—they change the truth of God into a lie. They are *heartless*: without natural affection. They are *ruthless*: implacable. That is the summation of all that has been said. What happens from here?

"**Although they know God's righteous decree that those who do such things deserve death . . .**" (1:32a). This is referring to what goes on in history: God's judgment. They deserve to be cut off. "**They not only continue to do these very things but also approve of those who practice them**" (1:32b). This is a widespread, cultural practice. We are talking about the fullness of sin in this way: the cup is full, and it is time to be cut off. How is it that they know God's righteous judgment? If they have eyes to see, they have a clear revelation that God has judged in history. What has happened to the civilizations that have gone before? If you accept that God exists at all, would you say that God does not judge at all in history? Would you be a deist and say God has forgotten, He does not care, God is indifferent? Will you go back to denying essential things about God, God's unchangeable nature? Do you think it is consistent with the goodness of God to have created the world with natural evil? Do you think God is indifferent, that He can be changeable like a human being? Or do you believe that God created the world very good because He—by His nature/essence—is unquestionably morally good, infinitely good, and unchangeably good? Remember the summary of the *could–would–must–did* argument:[13]

> If God is all powerful, He *could* create a world without evil.
>
> If God is all good, He *would* create a world without evil.
>
> If God could and would, He *must* have created a world without evil.
>
> If God could, would, and must, then He *did* create a world without evil.

Some may say that these are just words. No, they are not just words, they are words expressing ideas, and the question is, are those ideas true? If you say, 'I don't know, and I don't care,' there you have the reprobate mind—not concerned with knowledge, proof, or truth. That is a frightening place to be.

We have this revelation in history of God's righteous judgment. We can pay attention to it or not. They deserve to be cut off. They have become worthless and counterproductive. In the days of Noah, they deserved to be cut off. The world became full of corruption and violence.[14] Remember what happened in those days: "The sons of God saw that the daughters of men were beautiful, and they married any of them they chose" (Gen. 6:2). There was a natural physical attraction, "they married any of them they chose," and they lost their testimony. For the mind without God, it is all about sex. The mind without meaning is bored and tries to fulfill the desires and get some titillation. This happened during the 60s revolution; there is nothing new under the sun. The 60s revolution has happened time and again throughout history. Do not think there is anything really new here. This is the condition of man. Man needs salvation.

---

13. Gangadean, *The Westminster Confession*, 14–18; Gangadean, *On Natural and Revealed Theology*, 179–193.

14. *Genesis 6:11.*

NO EXEMPTION:
The Same Failure in Believer and Nonbeliever

Judging Others While Not Repenting of Our Root Sin

"You, therefore, have no excuse, you who pass judgment on someone else, for at whatever point you judge the other, you are condemning yourself, because you who pass judgment do the same things" (2:1). What are the *same things*? They are failing to seek and understand what is clear. When you came to God, did you repent of that failure? Did you repent of root sin or did you slide by and just try to deal with fruit sin? Did you bring forth fruit in keeping with repentance? Did you acknowledge that you did not see what is clear, like everyone else, and that deserves death? God shows no favoritism. That is the sense of "**you who pass judgment do the same things.**" It is the very same thing described in Romans 1. If we are not able to see what is clear and show what is clear, then we have not repented of root sin. When we make judgments on others who have root sin, and we are unrepentant of our own, we will not escape judgment. Do not think that God is going to hold a nonbeliever responsible for failing to see what is clear, but that He is going to wink and nod at the believer and say, 'Come on in!' God is not a respecter of persons. How can we justify that belief? Is that what we are secretly thinking in our heart? That we can judge a nonbeliever for their root sin, and all the while, we are unrepentant of our own root sin? Believers have the same failure as nonbelievers, and Paul is going to address this.

Abusing God's Kindness, Forbearance, and Patience: Storing Up Wrath

You, therefore, have no excuse, you who pass judgment on someone else, for at whatever point you judge another, you are condemning yourself, because you who pass judgment do the same things. Now we know that God's judgment against those who do such things is based on truth. So when you, a mere man, pass judgment on them and yet do the same things, do you think you will escape God's judgment? (2:1–3).

You who believe that God judges, do you think that you will escape His judgment? **"Or do you show contempt for the riches of his kindness, tolerance and patience, not realizing that God's kindness leads you toward repentance?"** (2:4). God still wants us to repent of root sin, and He has been waiting long. God has been patient, and we show contempt for the riches of His kindness, tolerance, and patience. Because God does not lower the *boom* on us for our failure to repent right away, as believers, we think we are okay. We are not okay. We are storing up wrath: **"But because of your stubbornness and your unrepentant heart, you are storing up wrath against yourself for the day of God's wrath, when his righteous judgment will be revealed"** (2:5). Judgment will come. Do you not realize that **"God's kindness leads you toward repentance?"** God has been witnessing through others and through history. Perhaps your paths crossed in one way or another with Historic Christianity. Or you may confront others who believe differently and understand the Scripture differently, but it does not bother you. Perhaps you have made it incidental. You have chosen the parts of Scripture that you think are important, and you have set aside other things. You may not realize that you have set aside the cornerstone. But you are not even concerned about building, so who cares about a cornerstone? We are stubborn.

An Impartial Judge: God Does Not, Cannot, and Will Not Show Favoritism

> But because of your stubbornness and your unrepentant heart, you are storing up wrath against yourself for the day of God's wrath, when his righteous judgment will be revealed. God "will repay each person according to what he has done" (2:5–6).

God is not a respecter of persons. **"To those who by persistence in doing good seek glory, honor and immortality, he will give eternal life. But for those who are self-seeking and who reject the truth and follow evil, there will be wrath and anger"** (2:7–8). Remember, these are believers who are not repenting of root sin and are going about proclaiming this other gospel. This other gospel includes the belief that 'Jesus is coming soon to rapture us out of here,' and that if He does not, 'We will die and go to heaven and get the fullness of joy.' They may say, 'What is the big deal? We are covered! The Scripture says we are covered in the blood of the Lamb. What sanctification?' We excuse ourselves and dismiss the need for repentance of root sin by appealing to false hope and false doctrine.

God will judge according to our deeds, and Christians who do repent will bring forth fruit in keeping with repentance.[15] **"There will be trouble and distress for every human being who does evil: first for the Jew, then for the Gentile"** (2:9). Today, we might translate "Jew" as covenant believers. The Gentiles are those who are not connected with the covenant whatsoever. Notice, believers, or those who have the sign of the covenant, are not exempt; Paul says, **"first for the Jew, then for the Gentile; but glory, honor and peace for everyone who does good: first for the Jew, then for the Gentile. For God does not show favoritism"** (2:9b–11). God is not changeable like a man. The whole universe will be screaming out against God if there is the least iota of favoritism. 'Wait a minute, you can't do that! Is this what your infinite justice amounts to? Is this what your righteousness is? Is this what your salvation is? Is this the glory of your justice and mercy?' God does not show favoritism; He does not, cannot, and will not.

ALL MEN HAVE THE LAW OF GOD: JEW AND GENTILE

"All who sin apart from the law will also perish apart from the law, and all who sin under the law will be judged by the law" (2:12). Believers have the law, you might say, the Word of God, or the Torah. We can speak of the Torah in a narrow sense or a broader sense: (1) The Ten Commandments, (2) the five books of Moses, (3) the entire Old Testament, or (4) the Rabbi as an embodiment of the Torah in his entire way of life. The word *Torah* has been used in these ways. The law may be used in a narrow sense or in a broad sense. When the law is used in a narrow sense, the law is misapplied. This was a point of contention between Christ and the teachers of the law.[16] But we see that the Scripture continually centers on the broader, deeper sense. So some who have had the law given in special revelation will be judged

---

15. *Luke 3:8.*

16. Gangadean, *The Gospel of Matthew,* 39–114, 217–233, 277–328.

by that law, and those who do not have the law given in special revelation will be judged apart from that law by general revelation. Paul addresses this in verse 13.

Gentiles Have the Law Through General Revelation

Paul says, "**For it is not those who hear the law who are righteous in God's sight, but it is those who obey the law who will be declared righteous**" (2:13). This passage is speaking about hearing the law that is given in special revelation. You may come to church every Lord's Day, you hear the preaching, and you feel good about yourself. The question to ask yourself is, 'Do I go out and do it?' Or maybe the law is not being preached in the church, or something distorted is being preached. Paul speaks about those who have the law and those who do not, and he shows that the Gentiles have the law, too. "**Indeed, when Gentiles, who do not have the law, do by nature things required by the law, they are a law for themselves, even though they do not have the law, since they show that the requirements of the law are written on their hearts**" (2:14–15a). They show the law is written in their innermost being, in their nature, in the way they are structured, the way they are made by God. It is written on their hearts. "**Their consciences also bearing witness, and their thoughts now accusing, now even defending them**" (2:15b). Moses said in Deuteronomy 30:11–14:

> Now what I am commanding you today is not too difficult for you or beyond your reach. It is not up in heaven, so that you have to ask, "Who will ascend into heaven to get it and proclaim it to us so we may obey it?" Nor is it beyond the sea, so that you have to ask, "Who will cross the sea to get it and proclaim it to us so we may obey it?" No, the word is very near you; it is in your mouth and in your heart so you may obey it.

Just think about the words that you use and look at your very being: "it is in your mouth and in your heart." You are born human; you are not born an animal. You are born as a child needing to be taught and under authority. You are born of a sexual union between one man and one woman. You make value judgments, and not all things have the same value. There is equality in human nature, and equals are to be treated equally. Truth is necessary and sufficient for justice: the truth, the whole truth, and nothing but the truth. We distinguish between relevant truth, things that are public, and things that are private. We can know from our nature what the good is, and that cannot be taken from us. We do not have to be covetous about other things that are not the good because the good is inalienable.[17] It is near you, in your mouth, and in your heart. So all have the law, some from general revelation, some from special revelation.

Jews/Believers Have the Law from General and Special Revelation

Paul heightens the contrast. He says, **"Now you, if you call yourself a Jew . . ."** (2:17a). This can be translated, 'If you call yourself a believer . . .' I trust that this equation is understood, that Paul is not just speaking about the Jews as against the Christians. We cannot say that this does not apply to us. This should be clear; perhaps it is not even worth addressing. He continues, **"If you rely on the law and brag about your relationship to God . . ."** (2:17b). Do we rely on Scripture, or brag about our relationship with God? Do we say, 'I know the Lord because I have Him in my heart. I asked Him into my heart'? He continues, **"If you know his will and approve of what is superior because you are instructed by the law . . ."** (2:18). In other words, do we think we are superior because we have the Scripture? Do we think, 'We have Scripture, and these others do not have Scripture'? Without affirming that they have clear general revelation, we may just emphasize that they do not have Scripture. Do we say, 'Those who have Scripture are better off than those who do not have Scripture'? Notice he says, **"If you are convinced that you are a guide for the blind, a light for those who are in the dark, an instructor of the foolish, a teacher infants, because you have in the law the embodiment of knowledge and truth . . ."** (2:19–20). Do we believe that we are guides because we have the form of it, or the essence of it, in the Scripture? One might say, 'I do not know the law from general revelation, but I have the Ten Commandments, so I know.' We may know what the Ten Commandments say without seeking, meditating on them day and night, and crying out to God. We believe we have the status of those who know. Remember, Paul

---

17. Gangadean, *Philosophical Foundation*, 208–211.

says, "**Although they claimed to be wise, they became fools**" (1:22). There is a foolishness in thinking we know when we do not know—the ridiculousness of it. Instead, we are to take the humble position: 'I have sinned, I have not repented, I need to go through the process of repenting and bringing forth fruit in keeping with repentance.' Only then can we go and instruct others. Christians are eager to go out and instruct others without first repenting of root sin. They want to teach without first having been taught.

A CONTRAST:
Outward and Inward, Sign and Reality

Professing but Not Practicing: Teaching Others Without Being Teachable Ourselves

Paul begins to address the problem of saying one thing and doing another; speaking about the law and not obeying it. "**You, then, who teach others, do you not teach yourself?**" (2:21a). Are you teachable? When others come with a different view of Scripture, especially if they come with the work of the pastor-teachers through Historic Christianity, are you paying attention? You may say, 'Yes, I'm Reformed. I go to a Reformed Church.' Yes, but are you *Doxologically* Reformed,[18] or are you, in a kind of self-centered way, Soteriologically Reformed? Have you paid attention to and thought about what the Westminster Confession says—all that it says?[19] You can outwardly connect with the Reformed faith on different levels, but not be instructed in it. Maybe others have come to you and talked with you about it over and over, and you may have been in the church for many, many, many years, but you have not really gotten that first basic piece in place: repentance of failing to see what is clear.

Do you teach yourself? You want others to be taught by you, but do you teach yourself and are you willing to be taught? There is inconsistency, a kind of hypocrisy, in wanting to teach but not be taught. "**You who preach against stealing, do you steal?**" (2:21b). There is a continual contrast being made between the outward and the inward: between

---

18. Gangadean, *The Westminster Confession*, xxix–xxxii, 347–348; Gangadean, "Paper No. 115: Doxological Christianity," in *The Logos Papers*, 595–596.

19. *The Westminster Confession*, Surrendra Gangadean.

outwardly stealing and inwardly stealing; being outwardly circumcised and inwardly circumcised; the outward observance of the Sabbath but not the inward reality of the Sabbath; the outward form of no adultery but not the inward form of no adultery. This is a pattern. It came up in the Sermon on the Mount.[20] It came up with the rich young ruler: "'All these I have kept,' the young man said. 'What do I still lack?' Jesus answered, 'If you want to be perfect, go, sell your possessions and give to the poor, and you will have treasure in heaven. Then come, follow me'" (Matt. 19:20–21). The Lord exposed the young ruler's covetousness, where his heart was, and what his view of the good was. Jesus said, "'Love the Lord your God with all your heart and with all your soul and with all your mind.' This is the first and greatest commandment" (Matt. 22:37–38). Jesus exposes that the surface, outward, apparent keeping of the law, in the letter of the law, in the minimal, outward, legal sense, is there, but the inward is not there.

There is a pattern of wanting to teach others but not being teachable. We say not to steal, and yet, we ourselves steal. We steal because we do not work with our talent for dominion for the knowledge of God. It is hardly on the radar. We live off the work of others who have done the work of dominion, and we are not contributing. Stealing is the failure to develop one's talent in pursuit of the good in service to others. It is the same with adultery: **"You who say that people should not commit adultery, do you commit adultery?"** (2:22a). A person could really, really strain this. One could define adultery, physical adultery, in the narrowest sense of the term, and then do everything short of that definition. That is one way. There is also spiritual adultery, where one does not get physically involved with another person, but they are looking at pornography. Or one could say, 'Do not touch, just look and lust but do not touch. Follow the letter of the law.' James said, "Adulterers and adulteresses! Do you not know that friendship with the world is enmity with God?" (Jas. 4:4a NKJV). 1 John 2:15 says, "Do not love the world or anything in the world. If anyone loves the world, the love of the Father is not in him." This is worldliness. The whole basic picture in Hosea is that of adultery, prostitution, serving God for what you can get, and if you do not get it from God, you get it from Baal. **"You who say that people should not commit adultery,**

---

20. Gangadean, *The Gospel of Matthew,* 39–114.

do you commit adultery?" (2:22a). The question is about adultery in any of those senses just mentioned.

"You who abhor idols, do you rob temples?" (2:22b). Do you commit sacrilege? Do you violate what is sacred? Some persons are dead set against gross, outward, physical idolatry and will cut off your head for it. A lot of people's heads were cut off in India by the Muslim rulers for gross idolatry. Question: Do you reject Christ and His atoning work, yet profess to believe in God? Is that a distortion of who God is? Is that idolatry, a misconception of God?[21] You who hate idolatry, do you engage in idolatry? All the divisions within Christendom go back to divisions based on distortions about God.[22] Are you concerned about these distortions and divisions? Through the Word of God, Paul is able to seek out and expose the condition of the human heart without God and its condition of being desperately wicked—in self-deception and self-justification. He exposes it, not for the sake of exposing it, but for the sake of calling to repentance. The gospel, through faith—the true gospel—is the power of God unto salvation.[23]

All of the hypocrisy that Paul has just named has caused God's name to be dishonored. In verse 24, he says, **"As it is written: 'God's name is blasphemed among the Gentiles because of you.'"** Isaiah 52:5, Ezekiel 36:20–23, and Micah 3:9–12 speak about how God's name is blasphemed because of covenant people. We take the name of God in vain and cause men to speak evil about God when we should be bringing honor to God. If we say that these people are persecuting us, and that they do not know and understand, we need to examine ourselves first. If we recognize and become concerned about the divisions among us, it would be a big step in the restoration of bringing honor to God's name.

Circumcision and Baptism: Sign and Reality

The tendency is to focus on the outward and not the inward, and Paul addresses that now concerning circumcision. He is speaking about sign and reality; those who go by the sign without the reality.

---

21. Gangadean, *Philosophical Foundation*, 191–192; Gangadean, *The Westminster Confession*, 21–27, 37–41, 67–69, 129–130, 236–238; Gangadean, "Paper No. 91: Christianity and Islam," in *The Logos Papers*, 479–484.

22. Gangadean, *Philosophical Foundation*, 185–198.

23. *Romans 1:16.*

Circumcision has value if you observe the law, but if you break the law, you have become as though you had not been circumcised. If those who are not circumcised keep the law's requirements, will they not be regarded as though they were circumcised? The one who is not circumcised physically and yet obeys the law will condemn you who, even though you have the written code and circumcision, are a lawbreaker (2:25–27).

They do not have the reality that is signified, they have emptied it of meaning. They have made circumcision meaningless although they engage in it. "**A man is not a Jew**"—a believer—"**if he is only one outwardly, nor is circumcision merely outward and physical**" (2:28). You cannot make it more explicit than this. We tend to focus on the outward and the visible rather than seeing that the physical reveals the spiritual. The same pattern of thinking in failing to connect the visible creation with the invisible Creator is going on here. He says, "**No, a man is a Jew if he is one inwardly; and circumcision is circumcision of the heart, by the Spirit, not by the written code**"—the letter of the law. "**Such a man's praise is not from men, but from God**" (2:29). Behind all of this is the tendency to want to appear good outwardly, but not have the reality inwardly. We want the praise of men, not the praise of God. Man looks outwardly; God looks inwardly, at the heart. The heart is where a lot of the concern for the outward/visible arises. God is not a respecter of persons. We do need to come to God according to the Word of the gospel, as Paul has declared to us in Romans 1 and 2.

5

ROOT SIN AND THE GOSPEL METHOD OF JUSTIFICATION

All Have Sinned and Fall Short of the Glory of God

1994

Romans 3

¹What advantage, then, is there in being a Jew, or what value is there in circumcision? ²Much in every way! First of all, they have been entrusted with the very words of God. ³What if some did not have faith? Will their lack of faith nullify God's faithfulness? ⁴Not at all! Let God be true, and every man a liar. As it is written:

"So that you may be proved right when you speak
    and prevail when you judge."

⁵But if our unrighteousness brings out God's righteousness more clearly, what shall we say? That God is unjust in bringing his wrath on us? (I am using a human argument.) ⁶Certainly not! If that were so, how could God judge the world? ⁷Someone might argue, "If my falsehood enhances God's truthfulness and so increases his glory, why am I still condemned as a sinner?" ⁸Why not say—as we are being slanderously reported as saying and as some claim that we say—"Let us do evil that good may result"? Their condemnation is deserved.

⁹What shall we conclude then? Are we any better? Not at all! We have already made the charge that Jews and Gentiles alike are all under sin. ¹⁰As it is written:

"There is no one righteous, not even one;

[11]there is no one who understands,

no one who seeks God.

[12]All have turned away,

they have together become worthless;

there is no one who does good,

not even one."

[13]"Their throats are open graves;

their tongues practice deceit."

"The poison of vipers is on their lips."

[14]"Their mouths are full of cursing and bitterness."

[15]"Their feet are swift to shed blood;

[16]ruin and misery mark their ways,

[17]and the way of peace they do not know."
[18]"There is no fear of God before their eyes."

[19]Now we know that whatever the law says, it says to those who are under the law, so that every mouth may be silenced and the whole world held accountable to God. [20]Therefore no one will be declared righteous in his sight by observing the law; rather, through the law we become conscious of sin.

[21]But now a righteousness from God, apart from law, has been made known, to which the Law and the Prophets testify. [22]This righteousness from God comes through faith in Jesus Christ to all who believe. There is no difference, [23]for all have sinned and fall short of the glory of God, [24]and are justified freely by his grace through the redemption that came by Christ Jesus. [25]God presented him as a sacrifice of atonement, through faith in his blood. He did this to demonstrate his justice, because in his forbearance he had left the sins committed beforehand unpunished—[26]he did it to demonstrate his justice at the present time, so as to be just and the one who justifies those who have faith in Jesus.

[27]Where, then, is boasting? It is excluded. On what principle? On that of observing the law? No, but on that of faith. [28]For we maintain that a man is justified by faith apart from observing the law. [29]Is God the God of Jews only? Is he not the God of Gentiles too? Yes, of Gentiles too, [30]since there is only one God, who will justify the circumcised by faith and the

uncircumcised through that same faith. ³¹Do we, then, nullify the law by this faith? Not at all! Rather, we uphold the law.

INTRODUCTION

PAUL DOES THREE THINGS IN ROMANS 3. First, in verses 1–8, he is responding to Jewish objections to his reasoning in Romans 2, which concluded that both Jews and Gentiles equally come short. Second, in verses 9–20, he confirms his doctrine that all have come short from Scripture and formally draws out the conclusion that he has been making. He says, **"Therefore no one will be declared righteous in his sight by observing the law; rather, through the law we become conscious of sin"** (v. 20). Third, in verses 21–31, Paul sets forth the gospel method of justification.

RESPONSES TO JEWISH OBJECTIONS

First Objection: There Is No Advantage for the Covenant People Who Have Special Revelation

Let us look at the first eight verses. **"What advantage, then, is there in being a Jew, or what value is there in circumcision?"** (v. 1). Circumcision was a particular element that marked out the Jew from the Gentile. It was circumcision that was thought to be that which was essential for salvation. Since they had practiced circumcision, they thought this was the basis of entry into salvation. Paul shows that the Jews, who had the Scripture, did not give heed to it but came short of it, and are therefore equally under condemnation. He said in Romans 2,

> You, then, who teach others, do you not teach yourself? You who preach against stealing, do you steal? You who say that people should not commit adultery, do you commit adultery? You who abhor idols, do you rob temples? You who boast in the law, do you dishonor God by breaking the law? As it is written: "God's name is blasphemed among the Gentiles because of you" (Rom. 2:21–24).

The question is, what advantage then is there for those who are Jews, those who are Christians, those who are covenant people? That is the broader sense of the question. Here, Paul explicitly addresses the Jews, but the question is broader. What advantage is there for the covenant people who have special revelation? That is understood, in Paul's mind, as an objection to the claim that all come short. He said that both those who have general revelation and those who have Scripture come short. So the response is: 'What is the advantage of having Scripture, then?' That is the idea of the argument in this objection. Many Christians say things like, 'We have the Scriptures; we have baptism.'

First Response: Much in Every Way, If Made Use Of

Paul says that there is an advantage: "**Much in every way! First of all, they have been entrusted with the very words of God**" (v. 2). So he is admitting that there is an advantage to those who have Scripture; they have "**the very words of God.**" But whether there was an advantage for *them*, whether they took advantage of this privilege, was another matter. He is not saying that there is no difference between general and special revelation and everyone is equally the same. He says that those who have special revelation have an advantage: they have "**the very words of God.**" But having an advantage does not mean making use of that advantage.

Response to the Second Objection: Does Unfaithfulness by Some Nullify God's Faithfulness?

Paul responds to that initial objection and then addresses a second objection. "**What if some did not have faith? Will their lack of faith nullify God's faithfulness?**" (v. 3). God will still be faithful. Granted, as "believers," we have not always had faith, but our lack of faithfulness does not nullify God's faithfulness according to His promise *in* the covenant. We are still in, we are still safe, because our unfaithfulness does not nullify the faithfulness of God. This is the second point he is making. What if some did not have faith? Will their lack of faith nullify God's faithfulness? Paul says, "**Not at all!**" (v. 4a). We cannot call into question God's faithfulness. To call into question God's faithfulness is to call into question the existence of God. He says simply, "**Not at all! Let God be true, and every man a liar**" (v. 4a). Do not, in any line of reasoning, raise an objection that goes so far as to question the very nature of God. When you question God's nature, you have gone too far. In order to defend themselves, they raise the question: 'Well, if we don't have an advantage that actually ensues in our salvation, then God is not faithful!' Obviously, God is faithful, so you cannot reason that way—stay away from that line of reasoning. "Let God be true, and every man a liar." We should be careful about crossing that line. Paul says, "As it is written: 'So that you may be proved right when you speak and prevail when you judge'" (v. 4b). Never justify yourself at the cost of blaming God. Adam certainly did so in the Garden: "The woman you put here with me—she gave me some fruit from the tree, and I ate it" (Gen. 3:12). We cannot justify ourselves in that way. "Let God be true, and every man a liar." When it comes down to it, we cannot question the justice, goodness, and mercy of God. But if we justify God and not ourselves, then we will be proved right in our words and prevail in judging. So, to blame God is not a way out of the problem for those who have Scripture and do not take advantage of it.

Third Objection: Since Sin Furthers the Glory of God, Then We Are Exempt from Judgment

Paul anticipates another objection: "But if our unrighteousness brings out God's righteousness more clearly, what shall we say?" (v. 5). In other words, an objection might be framed this way: 'Our sin does not really mean that we are outside of the blessing of God, this is just God's way of further showing His glory.' But Paul rejects that reasoning: "If our unrighteousness brings out God's righteousness more clearly, what shall we say? That God is unjust in bringing his wrath on us? (I am using a human argument.) Certainly not!" (vv. 5–6a).

Third Response: The Principle of Exemption Is False

We cannot use the argument that somehow, because our unrighteousness serves God's purpose and plan of manifesting His glory, we are exempt from judgment. Paul draws out the implications of that reasoning: "Certainly not! If that were so, how could God judge the world?" (v. 6). We cannot exempt ourselves from God's universal principle of judgment. We cannot say, 'If we sin in the same way that the Gentiles sin, our sin somehow shows God's glory all the more and we will be exempt from His judgment while the Gentiles will be punished.' This is not true. And to think that God would be unjust by bringing His wrath upon us; that cannot be true. He says, "**If that were so, how could God judge the world?**"

If the Principle of Exemption Were True, God Could Not Judge Any

If God is going to exempt you, when you sin in the same way as the Gentiles do, then God cannot judge the Gentiles, either. God's principle of judgment holds the same for *all* men. "**Someone might argue, 'If my falsehood enhances God's truthfulness and so increases his glory, why am I still condemned as a sinner?'**" (v. 7).

Reductio Argument: The Principle of Exemption Implies 'Let Us Do Evil That Good May Result'

Paul draws out the implication of this: "**Why not say—as we are being slanderously reported as saying and as some claim that we say—'Let us do evil that good may result'?**" (v. 8a). That is the line of reason that follows. If you think you will be exempt from judgment because somehow our sin furthers the glory of God, then you might as well "**do evil that good may result.**" That is *reductio ad absurdum*. He is showing that at no point can you break through what is a clear moral teaching: We cannot in *any sense* do evil that good may come. He simply says, "**Their condemnation is deserved**" (v. 8b).

BELIEF IN GOD ENTAILS REPENTANCE AND FAITH IN CHRIST:
Repentance of Root Sin

Let us go back and see just how it is that those who are covenant children, who have had the mark of the covenant, who have been raised in the faith, have no advantage over the Gentiles. We saw this in Romans 1; the sin for which God's wrath is upon the Gentiles is that they had clear general revelation, and they did not acknowledge it. Has the Church acknowledged the clarity of general revelation? Some people have said, 'I have always believed in God. All my life, I have believed in God. I just did not believe in Jesus Christ.' Well, is that so? Did that person really believe in God, then? Some people would say to themselves that they have always believed in God, but we would say that if you believe in God, you *would* believe in Jesus Christ. Otherwise, you are believing in a god of your own imagination. You are believing in a god who is not infinitely just and holy and concerned about sin. Those who have said this deceive themselves on this point.

Let us back up a little. Of what sin did you repent when you came to Christ? And what is it that led to that sin? Very seldom would you hear that it is the sin of failing to believe in God, who has clearly revealed Himself. If we have not come to God and repented of that sin, if we think that somehow we have done justice to general revelation and that all we need is special revelation, we are missing the point. In other words, we think that we ought to repent of fruit sin rather than root sin, and this calls into question whether we have truly repented. Justification comes *after* conversion. Conversion involves repentance from acts that lead to death, and having faith in God, specifically, in Christ.[1] If we have not gone through a true and proper conversion, on what basis can it be said that we are justified? Can it be said that we are justified simply by saying, 'Well, I believe in Christ and His promised salvation'? When we look at that line of reasoning, we see that that salvation is no different from the Buddha's salvation: 'I believe in Amitābha Buddha, and I call upon his name sincerely, and when I die, I will go to the lotus heaven with Amitābha Buddha, and there, enjoy paradise forever.' What is the difference between that gospel and the Christian gospel? Is the eternal life that Christ came to give us merely escape from natural evil in heaven, or is it the deliverance from moral evil, which is a failure to see and know God? Did Christ "come that they may have life, and have it to the full" (Jn. 10:10b)? The sin for which Adam was condemned (and all humanity was condemned because of him) was his failure to see God in clear general revelation. He failed to see the most basic things about God.[2] He believed the lie of the devil, and he outwardly did what was forbidden.

If the Gentiles fail to see God, and they are condemned, do we believe that we, who gloss over this in the name of 'faith'—failing to repent of not seeing the clear general revelation—will escape? That is the line of argument I think Paul is using. If we sin at the root level, in the same way that the Gentiles sin, and think God's judgment will come

---

1. *Hebrews 6:1.*
2. Gangadean, *The Biblical Worldview*, 37–54, 159–195.

upon the Gentiles, do we believe that God will judge by some other principle and exempt us? We must come through repentance of our sin and faith in Jesus Christ in order to be justified. If we do not repent of sin and simply have 'faith,' is that how we are justified—by 'faith' apart from repentance? Can there be faith apart from repentance of sin? There are those who argue the advantage of Scripture without engaging their minds with the purpose of God in creation and redemption—to know God in all that whereby He makes Himself known, in all of His works of creation and providence.[3] If, after many years of professing faith, they remain in the same position of disregard for the revelation of God, they are in a very tenuous position. Notice, we say *tenuous*; we are not saying they are not believers. However, the truth of the matter is that the faith by which we are justified is shown in fruit—an actual life in which we are overcoming root sin. If we overcome fruit sin and clean up our lives outwardly but are not overcoming root sin, it raises a question.

The Jews were able to overcome a lot of the fruit sin. The Church is able to overcome a lot of the fruit sin, but where is the progress in overcoming the root sin? We have to ask ourselves, "**What advantage, then, is there in being a Jew**" (v. 1a), or for the one who has special revelation? They have the advantage: "**Much in every way!**" (v. 2a). But if we do not make use of that advantage, it will only mean greater condemnation for us. We cannot try to slide around it through various kinds of reasoning when this Word is brought to us. Paul responds: "**Their condemnation is deserved**" (v. 8b). Remember, Paul is speaking about the covenant people. We should not be so presumptuous as to think that it would happen to the covenant people *then*, and not happen to the covenant people *now*. We cannot, by some external connection with Christ, God, the gospel, and the marks of that connection, think that we genuinely have faith. Paul said, "A man is a Jew if he is one inwardly; and circumcision is circumcision of the heart, by the Spirit, not by the written code" (Rom. 2:29). It is not one who is repentant outwardly of some external sin, but one who is repentant *inwardly*, at the root. This is how Paul began his declaration of the gospel to the Romans: "I am not ashamed of the gospel, because it is the power of God for the salvation of everyone who believes: first for the Jew, then

---

3. Gangadean, *The Westminster Catechisms*, 100.

for the Gentile" (Rom. 1:16). He is wrestling with the deeper issues of sin and death, and righteousness and life.

CONFIRMING THIS DOCTRINE FROM SCRIPTURE:
Jews and Gentiles Alike Are Under Sin

In the second section, Paul confirms the doctrine, from the Scripture, that all men have sinned and come short, and he draws out the formal implications. **"What shall we conclude then? Are we any better? Not at all!"** (v. 9a). Some have said, 'We have had the Scripture, and we have had it for centuries!' And somehow we think that by this, we are better. Some may say that their father, or grandfather, or great-grandfather was a priest, or a pastor, or a rabbi. They say, 'We have had the Scripture in this rich tradition for centuries, and we are better off. We have an inside edge on the gospel,' and they think they can be teachers to others. Tradition is *not* the gospel, whether it is Jewish tradition, Christian tradition, or any other tradition. What shall we conclude then? Are we any better? Are we better than them? Paul says, **"Not at all! We have already made the charge that Jews and Gentiles alike are all under sin"** (v. 9b).

Biblical Definition of Sin: Not Seeking, Not Understanding, and Not Doing What Is Right

Paul gives the central, scriptural definition of sin: **"As it is written: 'There is no one righteous, not even one; there is no one who understands, no one who seeks God'"** (vv. 10–11). This is his declaration of the essence of sin. Notice how this declaration covers all three aspects of our being: knowledge, holiness, and righteousness.[4] Righteousness is the third aspect of our being. It is in the outward act: doing what is right. When Adam ate the fruit, he failed to do what was right; he did what was wrong in the outward act. But behind that outward act, Paul says, **"there is no one who understands"** (v. 11a). God is holding man accountable for understanding. And behind that understanding, he says, there is **"no one who seeks God"** (v. 11b). Because the revela-

---

4. Surrendra Gangadean, *The Unity of the Church: That They May Be One That the World May Believe* (Phoenix: Logos Papers Press, 2024), 72–73, 134–136, 247–248, 275, 287–289; Gangadean, *The Contradictoriness of Sin,* 37–52.

tion of God is clear, if men were seeking God at all, in the least, they would have seen the revelation and would have understood. What was the sin for which our first parents were condemned? It was believing, 'You shall not surely die,' implying that God is not infinite, eternal, and unchanging in truth. They disregarded what was said by God; they disbelieved, and in disbelieving, they denied the character of God. What else did they believe? "You will be like God, knowing good and evil" (Gen. 3:5b). The absolute difference between the Creator and the creature was blurred. God created and determined the nature of things. God determined good and evil by determining the nature of things. We are finite; we cannot determine the nature of things; we cannot create. How, then, can we be like God and know good and evil the way God knows good and evil? When we deny the basics—that God is infinite, and we are finite—then we see that there is no one who seeks God, no one who understands, no one who does what is right.

The Consequence of Sin Is Death

"All have turned away, they have together become worthless" (v. 12a). There is a close connection between the knowledge of God, our devotion to God, our seeking of God, our piety, and our morals. A person may, for a while, by common grace, not give themselves over to outward expressions of moral depravity. But when they have that depravity and the lack of knowledge of God in them—"there is no one who understands"—they soon become worthless. They deny the image of God in them. "All have turned away, they have together become worthless." Notice the universality of it—this is the condition of *all* men. Someone could be brought up in a covenant home, hear the Word year-in and year-out, and somehow, let it slide by. "There is no one who does good, not even one" (v. 12b). The sins of our mouths—our words—are what is spoken of here: "Their throats are open graves" (v. 13a). An open grave is not something that we expect; we stumble and fall in. By what comes out of our mouths, our throats, we can create that kind of trap for men by misleading them through lack of understanding. Sometimes, this is done very much in the name of piety. Some are interested in seeing your soul saved so that you go to heaven—those who preach the second coming of Christ as coming at any moment and preach about the Rapture out of this world. Premillennial dispensationalism is false doctrine,[5] and it is blocking people from pursuing the knowledge of God; it becomes a trap. Jesus spoke about this: "You are like white-washed tombs, which look beautiful on the outside but on the inside are full of dead men's bones and everything unclean" (Matt. 23:27b). This doctrine has caused stumbling for many. Instead of speaking the doctrine of spiritual death, we put judgment off into the future as a physical hell or lake of fire out there, and we deny the inherent justice of God and cause many to stumble.[6] Our throats are like open graves.

"Their tongues practice deceit" (v. 13a). When arguments are presented against these false doctrines, it is seen that there is subterfuge going on, even to the point of trying to deny reason itself in order to get out of responding. How is this done? Well, it is said that these doctrines are believed 'by faith.' There is appeal to the "burning in the bosom" in order to hold the absurd doctrine that God is somehow eternal and finite, as Mormons do. They appeal to the burning in the bosom and the 'pious' appeal to faith to get out of responding: "Their tongues practice deceit." If you press back on these appeals, those holding false doctrines will counter-attack and say evil and slanderous things about you: "The poison of vipers is on their lips" (v. 13b). If you press even further, you will see: "their mouths are full of cursing and bitterness" (v. 14). We can get very close to the gospel and not understand. Remember what Jesus said: those who kill you will think they do God's service.[7] It was the religious establishment who, in the name of God, brought condemnation on Jesus. We should not be presumptuous about standing in the covenant—not only in the sins of our mouths but in our actions, too. "Their feet are swift to shed blood; ruin and misery mark their ways, and the way of peace they do not know. There is no fear of God before their eyes" (vv. 15–18). Some may even, in the name of David the king, appeal to the Branch Davidian—not just the Texas group,[8] but others, too—and say, 'David defended himself by the sword; we should defend ourselves by the

5. Surrendra Gangadean, *The Book of Revelation: What Must Soon Take Place—Doxological Post-millennialism* (Phoenix: Logos Papers Press, forthcoming); Gangadean, *On Natural and Revealed Theology*, 229–238; Gangadean, *The Gospel of Matthew*, 387–425.

6. Gangadean, *Philosophical Foundation*, 195–197; Gangadean, *The Epistle to the Hebrews*, 357–371.

7. *John 16:2.*

8. In reference to the 1993 siege at the Branch Davidian compound in Waco, Texas.

sword and take up the sword to slay and kill.' This has been done in the name of Christ. Once we stray from knowing God as He truly is, we can go into a lot of these distortions, perversions, and corruptions.

"Ruin and misery mark their ways, and the way of peace they do not know. There is no fear of God before their eyes" (vv. 16–18). There is not an awareness of what sin really is and what death is, and so the connection between sin and death is not seen, even as in the Garden. In the Garden, there was a denial of the connection between sin and death; the serpent said, "You will not surely die" (Gen. 3:4a). A denial of the connection between sin and death continually surfaces. It inevitably surfaces when we fail to see sin for what it is, and we fail to see that the consequence of sin is death. In denying the connection between sin and death, we fail to have the fear of the Lord, which is the beginning of knowledge, by which we seek Him and come to know Him.

Conclusion of the Argument: The Jews Do Not Have Preeminence Over the Gentiles

Paul draws out the formal conclusion of his argument after supporting it from Scripture.

> Now we know that whatever the law says, it says to those who are under the law, so that every mouth may be silenced and the whole world held accountable to God. Therefore no one will be declared righteous in his sight by the works of the law; rather, through the law we become conscious of sin (vv. 19–20).

The Scripture, in many places, affirms the universality of sin:[9] "There is no one righteous, not even one; there is no one who understands, no one who seeks God. All have turned away, they have together become worthless; there is no one who does good, not even one" (vv. 10b–12). He supports this point by the Scripture, and now he is saying, "Whatever the law says, it says to those who are under the law, so that every mouth may be silenced and the whole world held accountable to God." No one will be declared righteous by observing the law.

Many people establish their own legal righteousness through outward acts, consider themselves righteous, and then say, 'I am righteous, and

---

9. *Psalms 14:1–3, 53:1–3; Ecclesiastes 7:20.*

therefore, I am godly.' That is not the righteousness that God looks for. Legalistic righteousness, in terms of outward acts and lifestyle, does not measure up to the righteousness of God. We cannot, from those outward forms of righteousness, conclude that we have faith. **"No one will be declared righteous in his sight by observing the law; rather, through the law, we become conscious of sin"** (v. 20). What Paul does is establish the purpose of the law, which was not to convert, which was not to justify, which was not to sanctify, but it was to *convict* us of sin. **"Through the law, we become conscious of sin."** When we understand the law and what it truly says, we begin to see clearly, and measure ourselves against God's standard of righteousness, and then we see how we come short.

Paul has established that all have come short. Those who have general revelation and those who have special revelation have all come short, and we need to be justified. He sets forth the gospel method of justification in the last section. In this section, Paul speaks about the *nature* of the gospel—that it is not by works but by faith; the *ground* of the gospel—Christ's propitiating sacrifice; the *object* of the gospel—to display God's perfection in a particular way; and the *result* of this gospel—the humbling of men, showing that God is the God of all men, and the upholding of the law.

THE GOSPEL METHOD OF JUSTIFICATION

The Nature of the Gospel: Repentance of Root Sin and Faith in Christ

"But now a righteousness from God, apart from law, has been made known, to which the Law and the Prophets testify. This righteousness from God comes through faith in Jesus Christ to all who believe" (vv. 21–22a). In contrast to a righteousness which is on the basis of our works, which are inadequate before God, which may appear to us to be adequate because of our false, legalistic standards, Paul says, **"This righteousness from God comes through faith in Jesus Christ to all who believe"** (v. 22a). This righteousness is given to Jew and Gentile; those with special revelation—a long tradition of it—and those without. He says, **"There is no difference, for all have sinned and fall short of the**

glory of God" (vv. 22b–23). Notice how Paul speaks about sin here. We *all* come short of the glory of God.

How significant was coming short of the glory of God, even in a man who has been justified by faith? Is it enough to lose your children, to lose your wealth, to lose your health, that you might continue to grow in that knowledge of God, as Job did? How much more, with the first beginnings of the gospel, when those who profess to be Christians can articulate some of the first truths about God as infinite and eternal? We have come short of the glory of God. "**There is no difference, for all have sinned and fall short of the glory of God, and are justified freely by his grace through the redemption that came by Christ Jesus**" (vv. 22b–24). Notice, it is not by works but by faith, and that faith is one that understands sin as coming short of the glory of God. We cannot separate faith in Christ from repentance of sin. The sin we repent of has to be the sin of coming short of the glory of God at the most basic level—the root level of sin. We come short at the fruit level, which is a third or fourth level; we can speak of those levels, but that is not the critical point where we come short. We are talking about coming short at the root level. If you come short at the basic level, you also come short at these other levels.

The Ground of the Gospel: Vicarious Atonement—*Solus Christus*

If we understand what sin is, repent of it, and see Jesus Christ as the One who bore God's wrath for us, then we can have a true understanding of who Christ is and have faith in Him. We "**are justified freely by his grace through the redemption that came by Christ Jesus**" (v. 24). The ground of this gospel of justification is not only by faith, but it is faith *in* Christ as a propitiatory sacrifice. Christ bore, in our place, what we deserve for our sin. Christ was cut off from God; He was forsaken of God—that is what our sin deserves.[10] Our sin deserves being forsaken of God forever because we have forsaken God.

When we look upon Christ, we are looking at one who is not just hanging on the cross and dying, but one who is smitten of God, afflicted, and forsaken of God.[11] Two other persons were dying on crosses beside

---

10. Gangadean, *The Gospel of Matthew*, 483–498.

11. *Isaiah 53:4; Psalm 22:1.*

Jesus. Their mere outward act of death had no significance for us. Because Christ was sinless, and yet forsaken, He is the propitiation for our sins. All "**are justified freely by his grace through the redemption that came by Christ Jesus**" (v. 24). God is holy, God is just, and it is through Christ, in this sense, that we come to God. That is the ground of the gospel.

The Object of the Gospel: The Divine Perfection in God's Justice and Mercy

The object of this gospel is stated in verse 25: "**God presented him as a sacrifice of atonement, through faith in his blood. He did this to demonstrate his justice, because in his forbearance he had left the sins committed beforehand unpunished.**" Christ paid the penalty for all those who lived before Christ. The animal sacrifices did not take away sin; they merely pointed toward Christ. God did this "**to demonstrate his justice at the present time, so as to be just and the one who justifies those who have faith in Jesus**" (v. 26). Here is where the divine perfection shows forth—in showing how God can be both just and merciful to man in sin. In this verse, Paul says, "**so as to be just and the one who justifies those who have faith in Jesus**" (v. 26b). There is justice and mercy, and both of them are simultaneously in Jesus Christ. The object of this gospel of salvation is to demonstrate God's divine perfection: God is both just and merciful, and one does not overcome the other.[12]

The Result of the Gospel: Eliminates Boasting, Shows It Is for All Men, and Confirms the Law

The result of this gospel method of justification, first of all, eliminates all boasting. It humbles all men before God: "**Where, then, is boasting? It is excluded. On what principle? On that of observing the law? No, but on that of faith. For we maintain that a man is justified by faith apart from observing the law**" (vv. 27–28). We are not justified by anything we do; there is not anything in which we can boast. It is wholly God's work in Christ. God imparts the work of redemption to

---

12. Gangadean, *Philosophical Foundation*, 191–194; Gangadean, *The Westminster Confession*, 21–27, 37–41, 67–69, 129–130, 236–238.

us through the work of the Holy Spirit regenerating our hearts. One of the results is that no one may boast.

A second result is to show that God is the God of all men: "**Is God the God of Jews only? Is he not the God of Gentiles too? Yes, of Gentiles too, since there is only one God, who will justify the circumcised by faith and the uncircumcised through that same faith**" (vv. 29–30). There is a tendency to think we are special, that we are favorites of God, and that God is not concerned for all men. When God called Abraham, He called him with a promise that blessing would come to all the families of the earth.[13] While the attention is concentrated on Abraham and his line, the purpose of the promise was always for all men. The gospel method of justification by faith for all men shows that God is the God of all men; He does not have favorites.

The third result is that this method of justification confirms the law. In the last verse, Paul says, "**Do we, then, nullify the law by this faith? Not at all! Rather, we uphold the law**" (v. 31). The law is upheld because the requirements of the law must be met, and they can only be met through Christ. In Christ's death, the perfect righteousness that God requires of us by the law has been met. The law is not set aside by faith; rather, the requirements of the law are confirmed in this method of justification.

---

13. *Genesis 15.*

6

CONFIRMATION OF THE DOCTRINE OF JUSTIFICATION

The Necessity, Manner, Means, and Content of Justification by Faith

1994

Romans 4

[1]What then shall we say that Abraham, our forefather, discovered in this matter? [2]If, in fact, Abraham was justified by works, he had something to boast about—but not before God. [3]What does the Scripture say? "Abraham believed God, and it was credited to him as righteousness."

[4]Now when a man works, his wages are not credited to him as a gift, but as an obligation. [5]However, to the man who does not work but trusts God who justifies the wicked, his faith is credited as righteousness. [6]David says the same thing when he speaks of the blessedness of the man to whom God credits righteousness apart from works:

[7]"Blessed are they

whose transgressions are forgiven,

whose sins are covered.

[8]Blessed is the man
whose sin the LORD will never count against him."

[9]Is this blessedness only for the circumcised, or also for the uncircumcised? We have been saying that Abraham's faith was credited to him as righteousness. [10]Under what circumstances was it credited? Was it after

he was circumcised, or before? It was not after, but before! [11]And he received the sign of circumcision, a seal of the righteousness that he had by faith while he was still uncircumcised. So then, he is the father of all who believe but have not been circumcised, in order that righteousness might be credited to them. [12]And he is also the father of the circumcised who not only are circumcised but who also walk in the footsteps of the faith that our father Abraham had before he was circumcised.

[13]It was not through law that Abraham and his offspring received the promise that he would be heir of the world, but through the righteousness that comes by faith. [14]For if those who live by law are heirs, faith has no value and the promise is worthless, [15]because law brings wrath. And where there is no law there is no transgression.

[16]Therefore, the promise comes by faith, so that it may be by grace and may be guaranteed to all Abraham's offspring—not only to those who are of the law but also to those who are of the faith of Abraham. He is the father of us all. [17]As it is written: "I have made you a father of many nations." He is our father in the sight of God, in whom he believed—the God who gives life to the dead and calls things that are not as though they were.

[18]Against all hope, Abraham in hope believed and so became the father of many nations, just as it had been said to him, "So shall your offspring be." [19]Without weakening in his faith, he faced the fact that his body was as good as dead—since he was about a hundred years old—and that Sarah's womb was also dead. [20]Yet he did not waver through unbelief regarding the promise of God, but was strengthened in his faith and gave glory to God, [21]being fully persuaded that God had power to do what he had promised. [22]This is why "it was credited to him as righteousness." [23]The words "it was credited to him" were written not for him alone, [24]but also for us, to whom God will credit righteousness—for us who believe in him who raised Jesus our Lord from the dead. [25]He was delivered over to death for our sins and was raised to life for our justification.

REVIEW

WE HAVE SEEN HOW PAUL IS NOT ASHAMED of the gospel because "it is the power of God that brings salvation to everyone who believes" (Rom. 1:16). We saw how "all have sinned and fall short of the glory of God" (Rom. 3:23). Those who have clear general revelation fail to see,[1] and the wrath of God comes upon man.[2] This wrath is revealed in the condition of our lives: the spiritual death that is in the hearts of men, and the various ways that all men struggle with God's call to repentance through the curse, culminating in physical death.[3] That is God's objective eternal wrath that comes upon men in sin. But those who have special revelation likewise fail to respond to clear general revelation, and "God does not show favoritism" (Rom. 2:11). We cannot expect those without special revelation to be judged on the basis of clear general revelation, and for ourselves, the covenant people, expect that we can minimize and disregard general revelation. God is not a respecter of persons.[4] In the beginning of Romans 3, we saw various excuses that might be made by those with special revelation, and in the last part of Romans 3, we saw how righteousness comes by faith through Jesus Christ.[5]

THE NEED FOR JUSTIFICATION

Origin of the Need: Our Nature as Rational/Moral

In Romans 4, we have a confirmation of the doctrine of justification in terms of what has happened historically, and we have an explication of the nature of the faith by which we are justified. There are several arguments in the first part to confirm the doctrine of justification. Just remember that this doctrine is something that no one in the whole world has come to understand on their own. This is something known only by Scripture.[6] Even after hearing it, we often miss it, misunderstand it, distort it, and resist it, so that this doctrine is not worked into our lives in a way that we understand justification and embrace sanctification. We find that we have to continually resist attempts to justify ourselves. Just as we had sin before coming to Christ, so sin remains even after coming to Christ. Our response to sin, before coming to Christ and after coming to Christ, is to justify ourselves rather than

---

1. *Romans 1:20.*

2. *Romans 1:18.*

3. *Romans 1:21–32.*

4. *Romans 2:11; Acts 10:34* KJV.

5. *Romans 3:21–31.*

6. Gangadean, *The Biblical Worldview,* vvii–xxii.

to *rest* in the justification of God. It is a self-justification that hinders repentance so that we cannot rest in the knowledge of our justification. There is an important sense in which that tendency to justify ourselves still continues.

We should see that the origin of the need for justification is in our very nature as rational beings. We must give a *reason* for what we do, and giving that reason is the first moral requirement. Our nature as rational, moral beings puts a demand upon us—that we *ought* to act rationally. Remember, when Adam failed to do so, shame came in. He was ashamed of himself when his deeds, or lack of righteousness, made it obvious where he was heading. That is how much, from within our very consciousness, we have the *need* to be justified. When we are ashamed, we try to justify ourselves by covering it, blaming someone else, and excusing ourselves.

Origin of the Need: God's Divine Nature as Holy and Just

The origin of the need for justification is in our nature as rational, moral beings, but it is not only there; it is in God's nature as holy and just. We cannot come near to God in our sin. If we come near to God in our sin, God will destroy us. If God comes near to us in our sin, we will destroy God. That is exactly what happened to Jesus Christ. When He came near to us in our sin, in our sin we destroyed Him on the cross. If we come near to God in our sin, He will destroy us—God is holy. We *must* have righteousness. God, being holy, cannot tolerate sin. He will flash out and flame out against sin. God is holy and just. So, the need for justification is in our nature and in God's nature.

Desperation of Our Need: Self-Justification Versus Repentance and Faith

This is not just any need; this is a need of the most desperate source. This is not just an intellectual exercise in understanding the need for justification. This is a desperate, moment-by-moment, excruciating, existential need to know justification. If we do not understand justification, we will slip into our ways of self-justification and avoid repentance and faith. If we are not doing God's will now, we have to justify ourselves for not doing His will. An awareness of our coming short comes to the fore by God working in our hearts, through the law of God, or it can come in connection with someone else bringing it to our attention. We have to justify our way of life and our choices continually. That is the sense in which we say it is a desperate, excruciating, existential condition we are in—moment-by-moment. If we are not growing in the knowledge of God, if we are stuck or stalled out, we have to justify ourselves. If we are not seeking God, we have to justify ourselves; the Word of God in man demands justification.[7]

Self-Deception and Self-Justification: Our Lives Before Man Versus God

Recall how this worked in the Garden of Eden; there was self-deception and a covering over.[8] Usually, the shame is felt when we are exposed before other human beings, so we cover ourselves to hide from other human beings. We do not think of our lives before God. We only think that we want to look good in the eyes of others. We want to be accepted and seem acceptable. We think that others are laying guilt trips on us and we do not see that it is the Word of God, the voice of God, that is coming to us, so we slough it off by self-deception. We often blame others. We are more concerned with what others think than what God thinks of us, so our hiding is really self-deception in hiding it from others. This is where we need to be honest. We talked about being honest earlier. We resist the call to repentance. Christians, in their sin, can and do operate this way. Remember David, how he covered over his sin. He then wrote, in Psalm 32, which we sang today, "Blessed is he whose transgression is forgiven, Whose sin is covered. Blessed is the man to whom the LORD does not impute iniquity."[9] We tend to try to cover our sin; we tend to deny our need for cleansing; we tend to deny the reality of suffering imposed by God; we tend to deny our need for sanctification. We do not come before God daily, acknowledging we need to grow and that we need to be cleansed of a lot of worldliness and the pursuit of our lust. We resist repentance. We are often unteachable in this way. There is a stubbornness in us. There is a pride in us. We often charge others with hypocrisy (and do

---

7. Gangadean, *The Gospel of Matthew*, xv–xxxiv.

8. Gangadean, *The Biblical Worldview*, 241–294.

9. *Psalm 32:1–2* NKJV.

not measure according to God's standard), and we find fault in others to keep from our own repentance. We are blind to our own sin and do not respond objectively to reason. If we are responding objectively to reason, we will do as the Lord spoke of in John 3:19–21:

> This is the verdict: Light has come into the world, but men loved darkness instead of light because their deeds were evil. Everyone who does evil hates the light, and will not come into the light for fear that his deeds will be exposed. But whoever lives by the truth comes into the light, so that it may be seen plainly that what he has done has been done through God.

This means that if we are responding objectively to reason, we will expose our full way of life to others. We will not try to hide it and cover over it, but we will respond to the reasons that are given. We come up with all kinds of reasons and rationalizations to resist the objective, compelling nature of reason. Many of our troubles in interpersonal relationships come from engaging with people's unwillingness to have their actions examined. We should be willing to have our actions exposed and examined to see whether they are being done according to God or if we are attempting to find some justification for it and resisting correction. So this need for justification is an excruciating, immediate, existential need—moment-by-moment—in our walk with God.

When Adam failed to walk this way, he, too, fell into self-deception and self-justification. We have to remember and acknowledge that natural evil in the world is God's call to us to be cleansed. If we respond appropriately, we will acknowledge our need for God's justification and cleansing. So, as we begin Romans 4, we should know that we need to be justified. All you have to do is press someone's button by bringing the law to bear on what they are doing, and you will see that out of the mouth will come a whole recording of what they have been saying to themselves to justify their way of life. Just push that button, and an automatic recording of self-deception and self-justification will come out. Our need for justification is a desperate need. That is why the Scripture says, "The heart is deceitful above all things, and desperately wicked; Who can know it?" (Jer. 17:9 NKJV). The heart holds on to that autonomy, that form of self-life.

FATHER ABRAHAM:
Justified by Faith, Not by Works

Abraham was justified by faith and not by works, and this is illustrated in Romans 4 as Paul's first argument.

First Argument: If by Works, One Could Boast

"What then shall we say that Abraham, our forefather, discovered in this matter? If, in fact, Abraham was justified by works, he had something to boast about—but not before God" (vv. 1–2). Paul argues from the nature of our condition as creatures before God—we *cannot* boast about anything. If justification was by works, we would have something to boast about. But being creatures, wholly dependent on God, we have nothing of which we can boast—all good is from God. So he says that justification is not by works.

This matter of boasting comes up time and again. In Romans 3:27, Paul says, "Where, then, is boasting? It is excluded. On what principle? On that of observing the law? No, but on that of faith." In Romans 11, we see the whole economy of God's work in the way in which He dealt with the Jews and Gentiles so that none can boast: "Do not boast over those branches. If you do, consider this: You do not support the root, but the root supports you" (Rom. 11:18). There is something in us that is inclined to boast. Paul says that boasting is absolutely out of place. It is out of place to say '*I* did this,' or '*I* contributed this much,' or to think that we are somehow better than others because the reason for the difference between us and others is *our* particular contribution. We boast rather than seeing that it is by God's grace. We provoke each other by our boasting, though we often do not recognize when we are boasting. Paul says, "If, in fact, Abraham was justified by works, he had something to boast about—but not before God" (v. 2). Justification is not by works; the gospel method of justification is not by works but by faith.

The second part of the proof for the first argument is that Paul confirms it with the Scripture. He says, "What does Scripture say? 'Abraham believed God, and it was credited to him as righteousness'" (v. 3). That he believed God is stated in Genesis 15, and I would like to draw attention to it because we should understand what this means.

After Abraham's battle and defeat of the kings and the blessing of Melchizedek, it is said, "After this, the word of the LORD came to Abram in a vision: 'Do not be afraid, Abram. I am your shield, your very great reward'" (Gen. 15:1). God Himself is our protector and our reward.

> But Abram said, "O Sovereign LORD, what can you give me since I remain childless and the one who will inherit my estate is Eliezer of Damascus?" And Abram said, "You have given me no children; so a servant in my household will be my heir." Then the word of the LORD came to him: "This man will not be your heir, but a son coming from your own body will be your heir." He took him outside and said, "Look up at the heavens and count the stars—if indeed you can count them." Then he said to him, "So shall your offspring be." Abram believed the LORD, and he credited it to him as righteousness (Gen. 15:2–6).

What is it that Abraham believed? He believed that his seed would be numerous like the stars in the sky. This promise is the same as the earlier promise: "In you all families of the earth shall be blessed" (Gen. 12:3b NKJV). He will be heir of the whole world. This is the promise that the earth will be filled with the knowledge of God.[10] This is the promise Abraham believed. Notice that the promise does not come in this sense: 'Someone is going to die for your sins.' It does not come that way; it comes positively, in terms of life: 'You have the fullness of life. Your seed will be like the stars in the sky. All the nations will come to you; all the nations will be blessed.' But there is an intimate connection between justification—your sin not being counted against you and having the righteousness of God—and the blessings and the life that come from justification. The promise is understood in terms of the life that comes from justification. I do not think there is any question about this. Genesis 15:2–6 does not talk about anyone dying for Abram, but God speaks about the fullness of life. We tend to break up that promise and say, 'Christ died for you, so when you die, you go to heaven,' rather than seeing that Christ has died for us to bring us into the fullness of life: Christ said, "I am come that they might have life, and that they might have it more abundantly" (Jn. 10:10b KJV).

---

10. *Isaiah 11:9; Habakkuk 2:14.*

This is the promise, and we must keep this in mind, because this is the very promise that we, too, must believe if we are going to be justified.

Second Argument: Not by Grace/Faith Plus Works

Paul continues to distinguish works and grace—that these are two different things. "Now when a man works, his wages are not credited to him as a gift, but as an obligation. However, to the one who does not work but trusts God who justifies the wicked, his faith is credited as righteousness" (vv. 4–5). You cannot have both; it is either a free gift or an obligation. You cannot combine works and grace. Trusting in God for the promise is not works. Faith credited as righteousness is not works. Paul picks up this line of thought and begins a second argument from another part of Scripture.

Paul argues that all of the passages in Scripture that speak about 'free forgiveness' confirm this doctrine of justification by faith. Paul continues, "David says the same thing when he speaks of the blessedness of the man to whom God credits righteousness apart from works" (v. 6). Notice how this truth comes out in David; it comes out uniquely—different from Abraham. What we are looking at is one concept of justification from many different angles. We should not restrict the doctrine of justification. David put it this way: "Blessed are those whose lawless deeds are forgiven, And whose sins are covered; Blessed is the man to whom the Lord shall not impute sin" (vv. 7–8 NKJV). On the basis of works, the sin will be imputed—counted against him. On the basis of faith, the sin will not be imputed. Notice the *double imputation* that is going on here. One is the imputation of righteousness to man, and the other is the imputation of sin, not to that individual, but to Christ who bears it.[11] Either way you want to take it, whichever side of justification you want to emphasize (and both go together), the forgiveness of sin means you are not under law. If you are under law, sin is not forgiven, but under grace, sin is forgiven. We believe the promise and God imputes that to us as righteousness—these are two sides of the same coin. Paul is establishing that the doctrine

---

11. Altogether, justification by faith alone entails triple imputation: (1) Adam's sin is imputed to all; (2) believers' sin is imputed to Christ; (3) Christ's righteousness is imputed to believers. Gangadean, *The Westminster Confession*, 149–151; Gangadean, *The Westminster Catechisms*, 196–197.

of justification by faith is a biblical doctrine. It is not something new that was introduced with Christ's coming, but it was there in Abraham and it was there in David.

Third Argument: One Way of Justification for All—Circumcision Is Not Necessary for Justification

This method of justification is for all persons. There is one and only one method of justification. Not only has Paul covered the view that it has been for all time, going all the way back to Abraham, and even beyond Abraham to Adam when God made the coats of skin,[12] but it is for all persons: Jews and Gentiles. The understanding of this doctrine was distorted in such a way that a major controversy in the early Church arose: unless you are circumcised, you cannot be saved.[13] Paul points out that there is *one* method—for all time and for all persons. He asks, **"Is this blessedness only for the circumcised, or also for the uncircumcised?"** (v. 9a). In other words, do you have to be circumcised to be saved? Or is it that those who were in circumcision are saved in one way, and the Gentiles are saved in another way? Neither of those possibilities are the case. **"We have been saying that Abraham's faith was credited to him as righteousness. Under what circumstances was it credited? Was it after he was circumcised, or before? It was not after, but before!"** (vv. 9b–10). The passage we read in Genesis 15:6, "Abram believed the LORD, and he credited it to him as righteousness," was some time before circumcision was given. At that time, it is said that it was credited to him as righteousness.

Paul says, **"And he received the sign of circumcision, a seal of the righteousness that he had by faith while he was still uncircumcised"** (v. 11a). He received the sign and the seal of the righteousness that he had by *faith*, and that faith was before he was circumcised. Circumcision was a seal of the faith that he already had. In the case of the adult, Abraham, the seal came after he had the faith.[14] His faith was actually, really there. In the case of infants, it is a sign of what God will do.

---

12. Gangadean, *The Biblical Worldview*, 295–309.

13. *Acts 15*; Gangadean, "Paper No. 16: The Historic Christian Faith," 103–114; "Paper No. 60: The Spiritual War (Part II)," in *The Logos Papers*, 329–330.

14. Gangadean, *The Westminster Confession*, 291–305; Gangadean, "Paper No. 140: Argument for Paedobaptism," in *The Logos Papers*, 703–704.

There is also some sense in which it is a sign for the child, because it is saying the promise belongs to them, also. But for the one who is an adult and receives it, it is a seal. The actuality of faith was in Abraham, so he was circumcised. The faith was before the sign of circumcision.

> So then, he is the father of all who believe but have not been circumcised, in order that righteousness might be credited to them. And he is then also the father of the circumcised who not only are circumcised but who also walk in the footsteps of the faith that our father Abraham had before he was circumcised (vv. 11b–12).

What had happened is that some persons had rested in the *sign* of circumcision as if that were the reality. It is possible to think that *we* did this. We take a means of grace and sanctification and turn it into a work by which we think we are established before God. The Catholic Church did this with the sacraments. This is something in the human heart that keeps recurring. Protestants might even make *faith* the basis of justification, rather than seeing that Christ's fulfillment of all righteousness and His death are the grounds for justification, and faith is the instrumental means by which we receive it. We are always trying to find something *we* did by which we can be accepted. That is why Scripture says, "For it is by grace you have been saved, through faith—and this not from yourselves, it is the gift of God—not by works, so that no one can boast" (Eph. 2:8–9). That was the word that got to me before my conversion. That specific word *boast*, because I realized I was boasting. The Lord used that to help to humble my heart before Him. I realized that as a creature, I had everything from God, and there was nothing for which I could boast. Though men may commend me for many things, there is no way in which I could take the praise—the praise goes to God. That was connected with recognizing that I was a creature before God. Even faith itself is a gift of God so that no one can boast.

Abraham is the father of all who believe. Notice that the physical is not the reality but the sign. The spiritual relationship is what a true child of Abraham is. The one who has the spiritual relationship of walking in faith is the one who is, in reality, a child of Abraham. But, in the minds of some, the physical connection is taken as somehow more real than the spiritual relation. There again is a confusion of the sign with the reality. It is said that Abraham is the father of all who believe, even those among the uncircumcised who believe—Abraham is the father of them, too.

Fourth Argument (A): Heir by Covenant Promise, Not the Law

Notice the word *promise*, which is prominent throughout these arguments: "It was not through law that Abraham and his offspring received the promise that he would be heir of the world" (v. 13a). Notice how the promise is put—it is not just to believe in Christ and be saved and be justified—the promise is: you will be "heir of the world." It has to do with all of life, the fullness of life that Christ will bring. That is the promise—the fullness of life that God has for us. It comes through Christ's death, but it is the fullness of life. Notice also the word *offspring* is singular, referring to Christ. "It was not through law that Abraham and his offspring received the promise that he would be heir of the world, but through the righteousness that comes by faith" (v. 13). In contrast to the law, there was a promise. If it is through law, there is no need to make a promise, but it came by a promise. There was a covenant made and a promise in that covenant. So, as a means of justification, the law is contrasted with the promise. Furthermore, Paul says in verse 14, "For if those who depend on the law are heirs, faith has no value and the promise is worthless." This is another side of the same point. If even one person in the world could justify himself and get to the inheritance, then the promise is worthless.

Fourth Argument (B): For the Law Brings Wrath, but by Faith and Grace, the Promise Is Guaranteed to All

Paul says, rather, that the "law brings wrath" (v. 15a). He is saying it is not by law, but by promise. If it is by law, then faith and promise are of no value—the law brings wrath. "And where there is no law there is no transgression" (v. 15b). I am unsure how to handle that passage. When we come to Romans 7, we might have a chance to open that further.[15]

We are going to see what the faith is by which the promise comes. Paul says in verse 16, "Therefore, the promise comes by faith, so that it may be by grace and may be guaranteed to all Abraham's offspring—not

---

15. Since The Logos Archives does not have the actual sermon on Romans 7, we do not have an explicit exposition by Pastor Gangadean on this point.

only to those who are of the law but also to those who are of the faith of Abraham." The way in which this promise is going to be guaranteed for all—that it will come about and that we will be co-heirs with Christ as He inherits all things—is by faith in Christ and the grace of God, not by the law. What is guaranteed by law is wrath, and what is guaranteed by grace and faith is the promise and the fullness of the blessing. It is not just the minimum of the blessing but the fullness of the blessing. **"He is the father of us all. As it is written: 'I have made you a father of many nations'"** (vv. 16b–17a). God is saying that He is the author of the promise, and He will accomplish it: 'I have made you; it will come about; look at the stars.' Another way of saying that He has made Abraham the father of many nations is: "In you all the families of the earth shall be blessed" (Gen. 12:3b NKJV). All the families will be blessed. We do not now see all the families blessed. Many families in Albania are not blessed, are they? So we hope to go there and bring this promise. **"He is our father in the sight of God, in whom he believed"** (v. 17b). So Abraham is our father if we believe in God and in God's promise as he believed in God and in God's promise.

FAITH—ITS MANNER, MEANS, AND CONTENT:
Facing the Full Reality of the Need for Life from Death to Inherit the Promise

How did Abraham believe in God's promise? Let us look at how we might believe. In the last part of verse 17 and through the end of the chapter, Paul speaks about the manner, means, and content of faith. What did Abraham believe when he believed in God?

Paul says that Abraham believed in **"the God who gives life to the dead and calls things that are not as though they were"** (v. 17b). Things that are not—the dead—are considered alive; He gives life to the dead. We will see a number of senses in which He gives life to the dead and the extent to which He gives life to the dead. Remember, the promise is not to be understood just individually—'myself'—but we are to be heirs of the world. The whole world is dead in trespasses and sins; we were dead in trespasses and sins—this is spiritual death. There was also a kind of deadness of Sarah's womb that Paul speaks about in the following verses. And when we die physically, in order to inherit the promise, we have to be raised from the dead. So, we are dead spiritually—the whole world is dead spiritually—there was deadness in Sarah's womb, and there is a need to be raised from the dead physically. Life from death, in these various senses, is what is needed for the promise to be fulfilled. He gives **"life to the dead."** We have to believe that promise, as Abraham believed. That is the faith that is credited as righteousness. God Himself works that faith in us.

In verse 18, Paul says, **"Against all hope, Abraham in hope believed . . ."** He did not believe in hope itself, he did not believe in faith itself, but having hope, he believed, and it was *against* all hope. **". . . and so became the father of many nations, just as it had been said to him, 'So shall your offspring be'"** (v. 18). There is a promise that God will raise the dead. As far as our own selves are concerned, there is no hope, but in God, there is hope. Each one of us has to express that faith in an immediate sense. For Abraham, the ultimate fulfillment of the promise to become heir of the world had to come in his own life, at that time, by believing that Sarah would have a child. The *ultimate* promise is connected with *immediate* steps in our lives. Later on, Abraham will have to offer Isaac as a burnt offering, and he will have to affirm that same faith.[16] And as Abraham is dying, he has to believe that God will raise him from the dead to possess the promise. The promise is not apart from the land; it is not apart from the creation; it is the earth that will be filled with the knowledge of God. If we are going to dwell in the new heavens and the new earth, we have to be raised from the dead. We may not think of it very much, but as we get older and as we approach death, we might have to struggle with the question, 'Do I really believe that I will be raised from the dead?' Job confessed, "And after my skin has been destroyed, yet in my flesh I will see God" (Job 19:26).

Abraham must have faith, not only ultimately, but transferred into his own immediate situation for the next step—for each step. The content of faith is the promise, and what is the promise? **"That he would be heir of the world"** (v. 13). Paul says, **"Without weakening in his faith, he faced the fact that his body was as good as dead—since he was about a hundred years old—and that Sarah's womb was also dead"** (v. 19). Notice **"his body was as good as dead,"** and **"Sarah's womb was also dead."** He believed in God, who gives life to the dead. That was the immediate situation he had to face. Notice he faced the fact; he did

---

16. *The Epistle to the Hebrews,* Surrendra Gangadean.

not flinch at it. He clearly and fully saw that he was powerless in his being to bring it about. God could have had Abraham have a child when he was 40 and Sarah was 30. God could have brought it about, but he waited, and he waited, and he waited, and he waited. 'Now that you are 100 years old, Abraham, and now that Sarah is 90 years old, and it is way beyond the time of childbearing, Sarah is going to have a baby.' We might think that when you are 40, 45, or maybe 50, it could be a little bit risky, but it might still be possible. But Abraham faced the fact that his body was dead, and Sarah's body was dead. He faced not only that reality, but full reality. The full reality is not just his powerlessness; he faced the reality of God's power. We often face reality in a very limited sense, without facing the full reality. It was a double aspect of reality that he had to face. He was powerless, and God had power: **"Yet he did not waver through unbelief regarding the promise of God, but was strengthened in his faith and gave glory to God, being fully persuaded that God had power to do what he had promised"** (vv. 20–21).

There is a contrast between man's powerlessness and God's power. The creature is wholly dependent on the Creator for every good, for every breath we draw. We are dependent on God for the next step. We are not just saying, 'Well, I just want the next step.' We are talking about becoming heirs of the world. Nothing less than that is the promise. Do people in the Church need to be taught this doctrine of what justification is, and what the promise is, and affirm them in order to be walking as God would have us to walk? Or are we going to give a truncated version of justification and try to be satisfied with that version? **"This is why 'it was credited to him as righteousness.' The words 'it was credited to him' were written not for him alone, but also for us, to whom God will credit righteousness"** (vv. 22–24a). We must believe as Abraham believed. We must believe in the same promise: **"the promise that he would be heir of the world."** We must believe in the same means: **"God who gives life to the dead."** When we go out and preach the gospel, we have to believe that it is God who quickens the dead and makes them spiritually alive. Otherwise, we will not go and preach the gospel. We will find all kinds of excuses and say, 'No one wants to believe,' and for 10, 15 years not preach the gospel. We have to believe in the God who gives life to the dead. Paul continues, **"God will credit righteousness—for us who believe in him** who raised Jesus our Lord from the dead" (v. 24b). We must believe that Jesus was truly raised from the dead.

In this portion of Scripture, there are five senses of resurrection: (1) from spiritual death to life in regeneration, (2) the general resurrection, (3) Sarah's womb, (4) Isaac's resurrection, and (5) Christ's resurrection. With the five senses, we can articulate how we must believe in God, who gives life to the dead. And in believing this, we must believe it with understanding. "He was delivered over to death for our sins" (v. 25a). We must believe, not just that He died, but that He died for our sins. For *my* sin—I have sinned; I deserve death. That is what I must believe. And He "was raised to life for our justification" (v. 25b). He was perfectly righteous. He was not left under the power of death. He was raised from the dead, He is seated at the right hand of God, and He will bring all the blessings of justification to bear.

If Christ were not raised from the dead, we would have no evidence that His sacrifice was acceptable. If He were not raised from the dead and seated at the right hand of God, He could not bring to pass the promise. In Revelation 5, it is asked, Who will open the seals? No one on earth had the power to open the seals. But the Lamb of God who died, the Lion of the tribe of Judah, the One who died and is now ruling, He is the One who can open the seals and rule through history to bring about the promise that God gave to Abraham, that he would be heir of the world. The gospel method of justification has always been for all men, by faith, who will be heirs of the world with Christ through God,[17] who raises the dead.

---

17. *Romans 8:17.*

—

7

GRACE ABOUNDING
The Benefits of Justification

2013

Romans 5

[1]Therefore, since we have been justified through faith, we have peace with God through our Lord Jesus Christ, [2]through whom we have gained access by faith into this grace in which we now stand. And we rejoice in the hope of the glory of God. [3]Not only so, but we also rejoice in our sufferings, because we know that suffering produces perseverance; [4]perseverance, character; and character, hope. [5]And hope does not disappoint us, because God has poured out his love into our hearts by the Holy Spirit, whom he has given us.

[6]You see, at just the right time, when we were still powerless, Christ died for the ungodly. [7]Very rarely will anyone die for a righteous man, though for a good man someone might possibly dare to die. [8]But God demonstrates his own love for us in this: While we were still sinners, Christ died for us.

[9]Since we have now been justified by his blood, how much more shall we be saved from God's wrath through him! [10]For if, when we were God's enemies, we were reconciled to him through the death of his Son, how much more, having been reconciled, shall we be saved through his life! [11]Not only is this so, but we also rejoice in God through our Lord Jesus Christ, through whom we have now received reconciliation.

[12]Therefore, just as sin entered the world through one man, and death through sin, and in this way death came to all men, because all sinned—

¹³for before the law was given, sin was in the world. But sin is not taken into account when there is no law. ¹⁴Nevertheless, death reigned from the time of Adam to the time of Moses, even over those who did not sin by breaking a command, as did Adam, who was a pattern of the one to come.

¹⁵But the gift is not like the trespass. For if the many died by the trespass of the one man, how much more did God's grace and the gift that came by the grace of the one man, Jesus Christ, overflow to the many! ¹⁶Again, the gift of God is not like the result of the one man's sin: The judgment followed one sin and brought condemnation, but the gift followed many trespasses and brought justification. ¹⁷For if, by the trespass of the one man, death reigned through that one man, how much more will those who receive God's abundant provision of grace and of the gift of righteousness reign in life through the one man, Jesus Christ.

¹⁸Consequently, just as the result of one trespass was condemnation for all men, so also the result of one act of righteousness was justification that brings life for all men. ¹⁹For just as through the disobedience of the one man the many were made sinners, so also through the obedience of the one man the many will be made righteous.

²⁰The law was added so that the trespass might increase. But where sin increased, grace increased all the more, ²¹so that, just as sin reigned in death, so also grace might reign through righteousness to bring eternal life through Jesus Christ our Lord.

REVIEW AND INTRODUCTION

Man's Condition: No One Is Righteous

"BUT WHERE SIN ABOUNDED, GRACE DID MUCH **more abound**" (v. 20b KJV). As we come to Romans 5, let us quickly review what we have gone over in Romans. Paul speaks in Romans 1 about man's condition of sin and death in the face of God's clear revelation. In Romans 2, we saw how the Church, the covenant people, those who profess belief in God, likewise come short. The covenant people were the Jewish people then, and it applies to the covenant people today, those baptized and raised in the church. Paul states that we, too, when we make judgments, come short.[1] In Romans 3:23, Paul says, "For all have sinned and fall short of the glory of God" and "There is none righteous, not even one" (Rom. 3:10). Sin is universal. Paul has well

---

1. *Romans 2:1–5.*

established the universality of our sin, and we see the struggle that we have in acknowledging the full reality of clarity and inexcusability. In the Church, we notice how others have sinned in terms of their fruit sin, but we have not acknowledged and dealt with the root sin of not seeking and understanding what is clear. We come short. We are all unrighteous. Righteousness does not come from us, in any way, and there is nothing we can do that is righteous.

Righteousness Is from God and Imputed Through Faith

In Romans 4, we explored several ways in which we seek to be righteous or to justify ourselves rather than be justified by God. We say that the existence and nature of God are unclear, or God does not exist, or we do not need God. We might try salvation by works, or that we are saved by grace plus works, or other combinations. We cannot justify ourselves. Righteousness is from God and God alone and is received through imputation by faith. Romans 4 speaks about Abraham's faith; he "did not waver at the promise of God" (Rom. 4:20a NKJV). He was "fully convinced that what He had promised He was also able to perform" (Rom. 4:21 NKJV). Abraham acknowledged not only God's existence but the promise and the hope. This was the faith of Abraham. He lived it and he demonstrated it, even in the offering up of his son Isaac. And in that offering up, he received the revelation of Christ,[2] who would be the Lamb of God to take away the sin of the world, who would be provided by God. On that basis, the blessing will come to all nations.

RESULTS AND BENEFITS OF JUSTIFICATION

Sanctification Through Suffering

In Romans 5, we begin to see the benefits of justification, and that is sanctification. Not only are we forgiven, but we are cleansed.[3] The promise that we profess, that he would be the heir of the world,[4] that all nations will be blessed,[5] and that the earth will be filled with the

---

2. *John 8:56.*

3. *1 John 1:9.*

4. *Romans 4:13.*

5. *Genesis 12:3, 18:18, 22:18.*

knowledge of God,[6] will come through Christ reigning through His people. That means the people must be prepared to do that work by which God is made known, as His glory fills the earth. They must be prepared to proclaim the gospel,[7] to give a reason for the hope that is in them,[8] to take thoughts captive that are raised up against the knowledge of God,[9] to observe all that Christ has commanded.[10] They must understand that grace does not set aside the law, grace establishes the law,[11] because grace is in Christ Jesus who kept the law in our place.[12] Mercy does not set aside justice; mercy affirms the requirements of justice. The requirements are met in Christ, not only by way of imputation as His righteousness is credited to us, but also in terms of actuality—we are to be transformed into His same image.

So then, what are the benefits of justification? **"Therefore, since we have been justified through faith . . ."** (v. 1a). Notice the past tense—Paul has established that point, that we need justification, and it is applied in God and comes in this way, exemplified in Abraham. **"Since we have been justified through faith . . ."** This is not the end of the story. It is the beginning of the story. This story goes back to the Garden, after God called man back the third time, the last time—the continuing call back through the curse. Adam and Eve were first called back through the inner conscience of shame, and they avoided the shame by covering up. They were called back the second time outwardly, through the question: "Where are you?" And Adam justified himself by blaming others. They were called back the third time through the curse and the promise, and Adam submitted to God and "named his wife Eve, because she would become the mother of all the living" (Gen. 3:20). Adam, in naming his wife Eve, committed to obeying and doing the work of dominion, even under the curse. Then God clothed them with coats of skin, signifying the covering of righteousness through the death of another. The doctrine of justification was there from the

---

6. *Habakkuk 2:14.*

7. *Mark 16:15.*

8. *1 Peter 3:15.*

9. *2 Corinthians 10:5.*

10. *Matthew 28:20.*

11. *Romans 3:31.*

12. *Matthew 5:17–20; Galatians 4:4–5; Romans 8:3–4.*

beginning; righteousness was imputed. We must keep in mind that Adam has been forgiven. Adam is not being punished for his sins, he is forgiven. Physical death is not punishment, it is a call back. Adam is expelled from the Garden to live under the curse of toil and strife, and old age, sickness, and death, that he might be cleansed from the sin of not seeking and not understanding—from the sin of turning aside. Adam, the finite creature, imagined that he could be like God, the infinite Creator, who determines good and evil by creation. Adam failed to understand the most basic things. Please also note how his failure affected his wife; following in her husband's footsteps in not seeking, she took the lead. In the name of wisdom, she partook in eating of the tree of the knowledge of good and evil, and Adam submitted to that. All of this is there in the story. All we need to do is pay attention.[13]

There is the sin of not seeking and not understanding, and there are the added elements of self-deception and self-justification. We see the many, many ways in which human beings try to justify themselves by all kinds of excuses, but Scripture says they are without excuse.[14] We are inexcusable, but that does not keep us from trying to excuse ourselves. Nevertheless, the light shines in the darkness, and the darkness cannot overcome it—the darkness cannot withstand the light.[15] If anyone would come into the light, and their excuses were brought into the light, it would be seen for what it is—a spider's web in which they are entangled.[16] So, having been justified, we are now sanctified. But "we have peace" as we go into that process "with God through our Lord Jesus Christ, through whom we have gained access by faith into this grace in which we now stand" (vv. 1b–2a). I think one of the reasons we have an inadequate sense of *sanctification* is because we have an inadequate sense of *justification*—because we have an inadequate sense of *sin*. We do not see the sin remaining that we need to be cleansed from; we have not repented of it as we should. We can and should repent of it in principle, and submit to the process of cleansing, because sin blinds us to sin. The very nature of sin is to distort everything, including what sin is, what the good is, and what good and evil are, and that evil

---

13. *The Biblical Worldview*, Surrendra Gangadean.

14. *Romans 1:20.*

15. *John 1:5.*

16. *John 3:20–21.*

remains in us.[17] We need to go through this process of sanctification by which we obtain the promise. Remember, Adam called his wife's name Eve. She will be the mother of all the living. He is going to submit to the process of cleansing and obey what God has said, to be fruitful and multiply and fill the earth and have dominion over it.[18] This obedience is in the context of "man's chief end is to glorify God;"[19] it is not separated from this goal.

Sanctification, Dominion, and Discipleship

How does having dominion connect with glorifying God?[20] Creation is revelation, and through the work of dominion, the earth is filled with the knowledge of God. This is to be understood in the context of the Sabbath—the work will be completed.[21] We will complete the work of dominion through which the earth will be filled with the knowledge of God, even under the condition of sin. Abraham "did not waver at the promise of God" (Rom. 4:20a NKJV). The promise was not that he was going to die and go to heaven; the promise was that he would be the heir of all the earth,[22] and in him all nations will be blessed.[23] That involves being discipled as Jesus said: go and make disciples of all the nations.[24] Discipleship of the whole earth is going to happen. Adam was the figure of the One to come. Christ will *undo* what Adam did and *do* what Adam failed to do. Christ is going to have a people through whom He will subdue the earth and fill the earth with the glory of God, except now—after the Fall—His work is enlarged because it includes sin. Sin is not to have dominion over us; we are to overcome. Again and again, Scripture speaks about overcoming our struggle against sin.

---

17. *Gangadean, The Westminster Confession, 369–376.*

18. *Genesis 1:28.*

19. Gangadean, *The Westminster Catechisms,* 109–111.

20. Gangadean, *The Westminster Catechisms,* 321–325; Gangadean, *On Natural and Revealed Theology,* 9–32; Gangadean, "Paper No. 106: The Good and Heaven," 547–556; "Paper No. 117: Knowing and Making God Known," in *The Logos Papers,* 599–601; Gangadean, *The Biblical Worldview,* 109–124.

21. Gangadean, *The Biblical Worldview,* 125–146.

22. *Romans 4:13.*

23. *Genesis 12:3, 18:18, 22:18.*

24. *Matthew 28:19.*

We are to take the thoughts captive within ourselves as they rise up, as the self-life attempts to compromise, bargain, and make allowance for itself. Giving in to the self-life is not consistent with the holiness of God.

Standing by Grace: Sufficient for Justification, Sanctification, and the Unity of the Church

"**Therefore, since we have been justified through faith, we have peace with God through our Lord Jesus Christ, through whom we have gained access by faith into this grace in which we now stand.**" (vv. 1–2a). We are standing by grace. This grace is sufficient to deal with the sin remaining. The grace of God is sufficient, not only for forgiving our sins, but also for cleansing us from our sin. Through the curse, and through the fiery trials that come, the grace of God is sufficient for our sanctification. Paul argues that it is more than sufficient: "**Where sin increased, grace increased all the more**" (v. 20b). It is not merely equality of sin and grace, but something *greater* is coming now because of grace. That includes having a Church that is united in the truth by His Word and Spirit; it involves knowing the truth and the work of the pastor-teachers through Church history. We believe this accumulated insight is most highly summed up to date in the *Westminster Confession of Faith* and the *Larger and Shorter Catechisms*.[25] Grace abounding includes the need to go further since the time of those works. We need to respond to the challenges of the last 350+ years, take those thoughts captive, and not be the tail of the culture but be the head,[26] that they might be one that the world might believe.[27] We have to think that somehow, in the midst of all of this division, that grace is sufficient, we will overcome, we will not waver at the promises of God, and we will believe that God is able to bring about what He has promised—this is the faith of Abraham.[28] This faith gets us to the completion of the work

---

25. *The Westminster Confession*, Surrendra Gangadean; *The Westminster Catechisms*, Surrendra Gangadean.

26. *Deuteronomy 28:13*.

27. *John 17:21; The Unity of the Church*, Surrendra Gangadean.

28. Gangadean, *The Epistle to the Hebrews*, 167–201; Gangadean, "Paper No. 49: Eschatology (FAQ)," 271–274; "Paper No. 104: Eschatology (Twelve Points)," 539–544; "Paper No. 118: Eschatology (Seven Points)," 603–607; "Paper No. 119: Pauline Eschatology," in *The Logos Papers*, 609–610.

because it forces us to look at the root sin underneath. There is grace to forgive in justification, and there is grace to cleanse in sanctification.

Joy in the Hope of the Glory of God: Rejoice in Suffering

The joy of the hope of the glory of God leads us to rejoice in suffering. **"And we rejoice in the hope of the glory of God. Not only so, but we also rejoice in our sufferings"** (vv. 2b–3a). Not only do we suffer, but we rejoice in our sufferings. These are the trials we face—*tribulations* is used in the King James Version, and *afflictions* is yet another term. These are also described as fiery trials of every kind:[29] toil in providing a sufficient livelihood, strife in our relationships, increasing old age, sickness, and death. **"Not only so, but we also rejoice in our sufferings, because we know . . ."** We *know*—how strong should we make the word *know*? How strong is it for you? Do you *know*? Or do you say, 'Well, the Bible says it, so I believe it, but I don't really think I could show it—I don't understand it'? If we *know*, that is one of the ways in which we can rejoice. If we have seen through the problem of evil, understanding what evil is and how the cleansing is working, if we have that kind of knowledge, we will rejoice. If we do not have that kind of knowledge, we can be brought to it, more and more, through the use of ordinary means. We must make use of ordinary means through the work of the pastor-teachers, summed up in history, in the historically cumulative insight. We are not going to get that joy apart from having the foundation laid in our lives.[30] Do you think the Holy Spirit is going to work through all of the events in Church history, starting with the Council of Jerusalem, and then give up and start again? God is wise; He does nothing in vain; nothing is wasted. Even the scraps after the feeding of the five thousand, Jesus told them to gather, saying, "Let nothing be wasted" (Jn. 6:12b).

We rejoice in our sufferings because we understand God's wisdom and purpose. This is more than just enduring. Paul speaks in Galatians about the fruit of the Spirit: love, joy, peace, and longsuffering. He speaks in 1 Corinthians about faith, hope, and love. And now, he speaks again about love, joy, and peace: **"We have *peace* with God through**

---

29. *James 1:2–4.*

30. Gangadean, *The Epistle to the Hebrews*, 253–369.

our Lord Jesus Christ" (v. 1b), "we *rejoice* in the hope of the glory of God" (v. 2b), and "God has poured out his *love* into our hearts by the Holy Spirit, whom he has given us" (v. 5b).[31] The Holy Spirit works in bringing his people into all truth, sanctifying them through the truth.[32]

Through suffering, worked out in our lives, we persevere in hope. "And we rejoice in the hope of the glory of God. Not only so, but we also glory in our sufferings, because we know that suffering produces perseverance; perseverance, character; and character, hope" (vv. 2b–4). Out of suffering comes patience, and patience produces character. The term *character*, in Greek, is *dokimē*, which means *experiential proof*. We come to know in a way that we had not known before—we *know*. As we persevere and endure, we come to see what we had not seen before, as Job said, "Now my eye sees you. Therefore I abhor myself, and repent in dust and ashes" (Job 42:5b–6 NKJV). Job came to this through perseverance,[33] thinking he was going to die every day, wishing he was never born, believing God had forsaken him. But we are to persevere in hope. Paul said of Jesus, "For the joy set before him he endured the cross" (Heb. 12:2).

God is working in us so that He can bring about the promise. God is working in us so that He can bring us to possess the land. Coming out of Egypt, we did not have to do much; we just picked up our belongings, observed the Passover blood, and walked out—this typifies justification. Coming into the land, we have to fight—this typifies sanctification. Instead of saying, 'There are giants in the land,'[34] we go in and fight; we possess the land and have dominion. In sanctification, there is a fierce fight going on. God enables us by the Word and Spirit to overcome, persevere, and have proof. When we see how God works in our lives, then we can have hope. 'If God can work in me, He can work in anybody.' God does not disappoint; we see the love of God as He works to bring us to that knowledge. God is working by love. We may have thought He did not love us, that He had forsaken us, or hated us. There are many, many, many ways we doubt the love of God, but as we come through the trials, we say, 'Yes, Lord, you were

---

31. Emphasis added.
32. *John 16:13, 17:17.*
33. *James 5:11.*
34. *Numbers 13:33.*

there; you had not forsaken me.' Sometimes it feels like a kick in the gut, and I know what that feels like, but God is there. He is working in us to bring us to the place to help us see His love in a greater way, and all in the context of bringing us to glory.[35]

"**We rejoice in the hope of the glory of God**" (v. 2b). The hope in verse 5 is connected with the hope in verse 2, and the hope in verse 2 is connected with the glory of God, which is connected with faith and the promise made to Abraham, who did not waver at the promise of God.[36] All nations will be blessed, and the earth will be filled with the knowledge of His glory. God is working in us to that end. "**And hope does not disappoint us, because God has poured out his love into our hearts by the Holy Spirit, whom he has given us**" (v. 5). The Holy Spirit works with the Word. We are brought to see the Word, and we are brought to see the truth of God. After the suffering, then the glory—the glory revealed. The suffering is not worth comparing with the glory that is revealed.[37] We begin to see God in a new way, as Job did. The need to suffer before the glory is revealed is a life principle: "Ought not the Christ to have suffered these things and to enter into His glory?" (Lk. 24:26 NKJV). First, the sin has to be worked through to bring in the truth of the glory of God. We have to tear down first before we build up. The Holy Spirit, working *by* and *through* the Word of God, brings us to see the love of God as we had not seen before.

Christ Died for the Ungodly: Grace Abounding

Now, the idea of grace abounding begins to be opened up.[38] It is seen in the particulars of the way Christ died for us. "**You see, at just the right time, when we were still powerless, Christ died for the ungodly**" (v. 6). We were completely powerless; it is not that Christ came and we were doing our best and making an effort; we were powerless. He died for the ungodly. Paul explains further, "**Very rarely will anyone die for a righteous man**" (v. 7a). A righteous man seems to be someone who is at least outwardly righteous, living a good life, not a down-and-outer. In

---

35. *Hebrews 2:10.*

36. Gangadean, "Paper No. 128: Abraham's Faith," 665–666; "Paper No. 129: Faith and Reason in the Life of Abraham" in *The Logos Papers,* 667–669.

37. *Romans 8:18; 2 Corinthians 4:17.*

38. *Romans 5:20.*

other words, very rarely will anyone sacrifice to help a person living an 'upright life,' someone outwardly righteous. "**Though for a good man someone might possibly dare to die**" (v. 7b). A good man seems to be beyond a righteous man. For a good man, someone might possibly dare to die, or to give their life. Someone might possibly sacrifice their life for a good man. But now we come to see, through our sanctification, what is shown objectively in verse 8—the greatness of God's love: "**But God demonstrates his own love for us in this: While we were still sinners, Christ died for us.**" *Demonstrate* is a strong epistemic word in terms of *proving*. God proves His love in a way that we cannot doubt if we are paying attention. "**While we were still sinners, Christ died for us.**" He died for us while we were *enemies* to God.

Sometimes, we hear of Christians becoming martyrs and praying for those who are persecuting them. Stephen prayed, "Lord, do not hold this sin against them" (Acts 7:60). Jesus prayed, "Father, forgive them; for they know not what they do" (Lk. 23:34a KJV). Richard Wurmbrand was being tormented, and he prayed for his tormentors.[39] In this, we see a death or suffering that is for those who are enemies. So we see that when we were in such a vile state of opposition, Christ died for us. It humbles us; it breaks our hearts. And then we are moved by that to consider, as Christ has loved us, we are to love others, and the spirit of retaliation subsides. We see how Christ loved us when we were yet sinners and enemies in our minds.

Reconciled Through His Death—Saved Through His Life!

Paul continues in verse 9: "**Since we have now been justified by his blood, how much more shall we be saved from God's wrath through him!**" Notice, "**saved from God's wrath.**" There is wrath in the lives of the people of God where there is sin. In Romans 7, we will see the expression from Paul: "this body of death" (Rom. 7:24b). There is an inherent connection between sin and death. This is in the Church— the splitting up of the Church, the weakness of the Church, and the

---

39. "It was in prison that we found the hope of salvation for the Communists. It was there that we developed a sense of responsibility for them. It was in being tortured by them that we learned to love them. A flower, if you bruise it under your feet, rewards you by giving you its perfume. Likewise, Christians, tortured by the Communists, rewarded their torturers by love." Richard Wurmbrand, *Tortured for Christ* (Bartlesville, OK: Voice of the Martyrs, 2013), 43.

blasphemy that comes against the name of God instead of praise to the name of God because of sin remaining in the Church. There is judgment in this, as Jesus says in Matthew: "If the salt loses its saltiness, how can it be made salty again? It is no longer good for anything, except to be thrown out and trampled by men" (Matt. 5:13b). The Church, again and again, has been brought under judgment in nations where it has not been salt and light. This salvation from the wrath of God does not refer to the wrath of God in the final judgment, but it refers to the wrath of God manifested in history.

When we send our children off to college, and they come under non-Christian teaching, and they leave the faith, that is *wrath*. Listen up—teach your children diligently.[40] Obey the law, deal with the problem of false authorities, deal with the problem of totalitarian states, enlarge their conception of the world in light of foundational truth. Do not just pick up the pieces and think, in zeal, that you are doing a good work. Deal with the causes: the false prophet and the false teachings. Sacrifice—in practical ways—is never a substitute for obedience—by knowing the truth and putting it into practice. Sacrifice without addressing root causes is zeal without knowledge.

We will be saved in this life. Having been justified and seen the love of God and the way it comes, we have reason to hope that we will be saved. Paul will develop this right up to the end of Romans when he says that nothing in all creation will be able to separate us from the love of God that is revealed in Christ Jesus our Lord.[41] Nothing, no affliction of any kind, will be able to separate us from the love of God. This truth is going to crest at that point in Romans 8. All things work together for good.[42] This is grace abounding, even when we are as sheep being led to the slaughter. Over and against the jihadists, who blow themselves up and blow others up, we have Christians suffering in their witness, willing to suffer unto death for the name of Christ. That is our answer. It is not that we are afraid to die; we will die as faithful witnesses to Christ, and we will not shrink back, even from

---

40. *Deuteronomy 6:6–9.*

41. *Romans 8:39.*

42. *Romans 8:28.*

death. "Even on through death itself, our constant guide is He."[43] **"For if, while we were God's enemies, we were reconciled to him through the death of his Son, how much more, having been reconciled, shall we be saved through his life!"** (v. 10). To be saved through His life is the salvation of sanctification. That aspect of salvation will happen; God will bring it about. We may think it is impossible, but as we go through the trials, persevere and endure, and come to proof in the experience, we see the love of God.

God's love has been demonstrated, and we can hope and rejoice: **"Not only is this so, but we also rejoice in God through our Lord Jesus Christ, through whom we have now received reconciliation"** (v. 11). If we have justification, we can have hope for sanctification: **"How much more, having been reconciled, shall we be saved through his life!"** (v. 10b). We have proof—in the justification, in the forgiveness, with repentance—that we will be sanctified, assuming that our repentance is from root sin. Root sin is not just failing to see what is clear, but the layers of self-deception and self-justification that go with it. If we repent of root sin, then we can embrace our sanctification in the curse as a merciful call back. I suspect that the reason why the Church has such a difficult time understanding the curse as a call back is because they do not see that it is not just a call back from sin, but from self-deception and self-justification. We might say, 'So much suffering, Lord? Could you not accomplish sanctification in some other way?' This is another aspect of the problem of evil.[44]

THE DOCTRINE OF IMPUTATION
SHOWN BY ILLUSTRATION:
Covenant of Works in Adam and Covenant of Grace in Christ

Paul makes the comparison between the covenant of works made with Adam and the covenant of grace. Grace abounds in the covenant of grace. This is particularly redemptive grace. It is not the case that redemptive grace was present in the covenant of works since there was no need for

---

43. *Psalm 48:14, 48B, The Book of Psalms for Singing* (Pittsburgh: The Board of Education and Publication, Reformed Presbyterian Church of North America, 1998).

44. Gangadean, "Paper No. 147: The Biblical Worldview (Part VII)," in *The Logos Papers,* 747–757.

redemption, but there was grace in the first covenant. How so? It is a voluntary condescension on the part of God to bless man, to raise him to a state of constant relationship with Himself, as in a marriage.[45] That is why we have the parallel in Genesis 2 between the covenant God made with Adam and the covenant of marriage, the invisible revealed in the visible, which is the theme throughout Scripture. There was grace in that covenant of works with Adam, which was to raise him to a new height to walk with God. So we would not say that was redemptive grace, but it was grace in that it was an act of condescension on the part of God to establish man in a permanent relationship with Himself. Adam turned away from that grace. "**Therefore, just as sin entered the world through one man, and death through sin . . .**" (v. 12a). This affirms the covenant representation in Adam and the reality of sin and death. Adam was the representative. "**Sin entered the world through one man, and death through sin, and in this way death came to all men, because all sinned**" (v. 12). Now, we speak about both spiritual death and physical death, and the wages of sin is spiritual death.[46] But I think that here, Paul is speaking about the physical death that was passed on—physical death was not there in the beginning. Natural evil, the curse, was not original; God created the world very good.[47] Natural evil is due to moral evil; it is due to sin. Physical death came into the world as a call back because of sin. Natural evil is a call back from sin.

> **And in this way death came to all men, because all sinned—for before the law was given, sin was in the world. But sin is not taken into account when there is no law. Nevertheless, death reigned from the time of Adam to the time of Moses, even over those who did not sin by breaking a command, as did Adam, who was a pattern of the one to come** (vv. 12b–14).

There are a lot of things here to be sorted out and worked through. What does this mean: "**even over those who did not sin by breaking a command, as did Adam**"? Adam was given a specific command in the covenant of works: do not eat of the tree in the middle of the Garden.

---

45. Gangadean, *The Biblical Worldview*, 147–158; Gangadean, *The Westminster Confession*, 111–120.

46. *Romans 6:23; Ephesians 2:1.*

47. Gangadean, *The Biblical Worldview*, xxvi.

That is in addition to the moral law that was written on his heart. Adam was called to obey the law written on his heart from the beginning. But Adam sinned in a particular way, and as the representative, his sin affected all of us. Interestingly, the sin of eating the forbidden fruit revealed his sin in breaking the first commandment: to know and acknowledge God to be the only true God and our God and worship and glorify Him accordingly.[48] When Adam and the woman believed the lie that "you will be like God, knowing good and evil" (Gen. 3:5), it showed their deficiency in understanding the nature of God, the nature of man, and the nature of good and evil. Believing that lie showed their deficiency in understanding how good and evil come about, how God knows good and evil, and how man knows it.

The law is given to Moses by way of special revelation, and the law has a purpose. The law was added because of transgression, to make sin more exceedingly sinful, and to raise our consciousness, in our fallen state, about sin.[49] Paul, in Romans 7:9, says, "For I was alive without the law once: but when the commandment came, sin revived, and I died."[50] Romans 5:20 says, **"The law was added so that the trespass might increase."** That is, that the *awareness* of trespass might increase. So we are going along, and then someone brings God's standard to our attention, and the self-life becomes active and resistant to that standard and begins to justify itself and say all kinds of false things. All you have to do is have someone to say to you, 'Do not do it.' It is as if you are driving along, unaware, speeding, then the police lights flash in your eyes, and you begin the justificatory process. 'They should have had a speed limit sign there, they should have warned us,' and so it goes. The law entered, sin revived, and I died. The law stirs up all kinds of opposition in us. That is the condition in which **"where sin increased, grace increased all the more"** (v. 20b). He said, **"For before the law was given, sin was in the world. But sin is not taken into account when there is no law"** (v. 13). Sin was in the world from the Garden, it was not dealt with, and its effects accumulated and resulted in the Flood. Sin was in the world, and God judged after the Flood, reduced man's lifespan from 950 years to 70 years, and increased the curse.

---

48. Gangadean, *The Westminster Catechisms*, 229–232.

49. *Galatians 3:19; Romans 7:13, 7.*

50. KJV.

God intensified the curse after Babel. Sin was in the world, and God was dealing with it, but as the law came in, light increased, and God dealt with it more severely. Especially as we have the work of the Holy Spirit in Church history, and we are ignoring it, the fifth commandment bears more heavily upon us.[51] We may not give attention to the work of the pastor-teachers and honor our fathers and mothers in the faith that way, but God does not hold them guiltless who take His name in vain. He visits the iniquity of the fathers upon the children to the third and fourth generation.[52] As sin, subjectively in our awareness, increases, the wrath of God comes if we do not repent.

"Death reigned from the time of Adam to the time of Moses" (v. 14a), but he says, **"The gift is not like the trespass"** (v. 15a). Paul begins to compare Adam and the covenant of works with Christ and the covenant of grace and the greater blessing that there is in Christ. **"The gift is not like the trespass."** The covenant of grace goes further. The gift came from one man to the many: **"For if the many died by the trespass of the one man, how much more did God's grace and the gift that came by the grace of the one man, Jesus Christ, overflow to the many!"** (v. 15b). How does it overflow to the many? There was one actual sin in Adam that brought about the Fall. In the grace of God, the gift that came by Jesus covers many actual sins of many people.

> The judgment followed one sin and brought condemnation, but the gift followed many trespasses and brought justification. For if, by the trespass of the one man, death reigned through that one man, how much more will those who receive God's abundant provision of grace and of the gift of righteousness reign in life through the one man, Jesus Christ. Consequently, just as the result of one trespass was condemnation for all men, so also the result of one act of righteousness was justification that brings life for all men. For just as through the disobedience of the one man the many were made sinners, so also through the obedience of the one man the many will be made righteous (vv. 16b–19).

If we try to measure this gift simply quantitatively, we will find difficulty. We may ask the question, 'Then why isn't everyone saved?' There

---

51. Gangadean, *Philosophical Foundation*, 221–229.

52. *Exodus 20:7, 5.*

is some other sense in which we are to understand this. We might see this in verse 20 when he says, **"The law was added so that the trespass might increase. But where sin increased, grace increased all the more."** Earlier, in Romans 3:5–7, Paul says,

> But if our unrighteousness brings out God's righteousness more clearly, what shall we say? That God is unjust in bringing his wrath on us? (I am using a human argument.) Certainly not! If that were so, how could God judge the world? Someone might argue, "If my falsehood enhances God's truthfulness and so increases his glory, why am I still condemned as a sinner?"

Through the sin of a person, even though that person may not benefit, the truth of God abounds more. That is the qualitative sense. The truth abounds more through our falsehood. Our sin causes the truth to shine forth. Just as there is a subjective sense of awareness of sin increasing, so the awareness of God's truth is increasing. As we wrestle with and overcome our sin and the lie connected with our sin, God's truth abounds more to His praise and glory, and that revelation is for the many.

We are building on what is said in Romans 3 and 5 about how this grace may abound. There are at least these two senses in which grace abounds. First, it covers many sins, and second, the sin of one causes the grace of God to be revealed more clearly, more fully, and that benefits many. We can say then, that according to Scripture, not everyone is saved, but the promise given to Abraham that all nations will be blessed, and that the promise will come about, remains true, and all the more true in connection with sin and grace abounding.

We have the love of God shown in the way Christ died for us when we were still sinners.[53] Many sins are covered in Christ's justification, not just one. The truth abounds through our sin to His glory and benefits many. For all of these reasons, we can believe in the love and grace of God, that God will bring about what is promised, and as Abraham believed, we can rejoice in the hope of the glory of God. God is working lovingly to bring about His purpose on earth, which is that the earth will be filled with the knowledge of His glory as the waters cover the sea.[54]

---

53. *Romans 5:8.*
54. *Isaiah 11:9; Habakkuk 2:14.*

8

OUR UNION WITH CHRIST IN DEATH AND LIFE

The Relation Between Regeneration, Justification, and Sanctification

1994

Romans 6

[1]What shall we say, then? Shall we go on sinning so that grace may increase? [2]By no means! We died to sin; how can we live in it any longer? [3]Or don't you know that all of us who were baptized into Christ Jesus were baptized into his death? [4]We were therefore buried with him through baptism into death in order that, just as Christ was raised from the dead through the glory of the Father, we too may live a new life.

[5]If we have been united with him like this in his death, we will certainly also be united with him in his resurrection. [6]For we know that our old self was crucified with him so that the body of sin might be done away with, that we should no longer be slaves to sin—[7]because anyone who has died has been freed from sin.

[8]Now if we died with Christ, we believe that we will also live with him. [9]For we know that since Christ was raised from the dead, he cannot die again; death no longer has mastery over him. [10]The death he died, he died to sin once for all; but the life he lives, he lives to God.

[11]In the same way, count yourselves dead to sin but alive to God in Christ Jesus. [12]Therefore do not let sin reign in your mortal body so that you obey its evil desires. [13]Do not offer the parts of your body to sin, as instruments

of wickedness, but rather offer yourselves to God, as those who have been brought from death to life; and offer the parts of your body to him as instruments of righteousness. [14]For sin shall not be your master, because you are not under law, but under grace.

[15]What then? Shall we sin because we are not under law but under grace? By no means! [16]Don't you know that when you offer yourselves to someone to obey him as slaves, you are slaves to the one whom you obey—whether you are slaves to sin, which leads to death, or to obedience, which leads to righteousness? [17]But thanks be to God that, though you used to be slaves to sin, you wholeheartedly obeyed the form of teaching to which you were entrusted. [18]You have been set free from sin and have become slaves to righteousness.

[19]I put this in human terms because you are weak in your natural selves. Just as you used to offer the parts of your body in slavery to impurity and to ever-increasing wickedness, so now offer them in slavery to righteousness leading to holiness. [20]When you were slaves to sin, you were free from the control of righteousness. [21]What benefit did you reap at that time from the things you are now ashamed of? Those things result in death! [22]But now that you have been set free from sin and have become slaves to God, the benefit you reap leads to holiness, and the result is eternal life. [23]For the wages of sin is death, but the gift of God is eternal life in Christ Jesus our Lord.

INTRODUCTION:
Wild Inferences Reveal Misunderstandings

IN THE CLOSING WORDS OF ROMANS 5, PAUL SAYS, "But where sin abounded, grace did much more abound" (Rom. 5:20b KJV). Continuing that thought, he begins Romans 6 in this way: "**What shall we say, then? Shall we go on sinning so that grace may increase?**" (v. 1). This is a thought that has often occurred and still occurs. There are people today who debate the issue between what is called *faith salvation* and *lordship salvation*. That is a debate that is going on strongly in the evangelical community. John MacArthur is on one side of the debate, affirming lordship salvation,[1] and on the other are those who affirm faith

---

1. Lordship Salvation asserts that saving faith necessitates repentance, submission to Christ's lordship, and evidence of obedience. It teaches that faith and repentance are inseparable, emphasizing transformation and discipleship as essential fruits of salvation. Genuine faith produces ongoing sanctification and good works, reflecting Christ's authority over a believer's

salvation and say, 'All you have to do is have faith to be saved.' Behind faith salvation is a faulty understanding of what it means to be saved, and out of that faulty understanding comes the wild inference that we do not have to obey the law. They say, 'You are adding a burden; this is contrary to the doctrine of justification. We can be saved even though we do not obey.' Many who profess to be Christians have thought that since we are freely forgiven by Christ, that is all we need, because when we die, on the basis of the forgiveness of Christ, we will go to heaven. Therefore, there is not much effort made to apply oneself to obey the Word of God. We are talking about a real problem in this sermon, not something manufactured.

Some believers have come to think of salvation in terms of pardon from the penalty for sin, and that this pardon extends to the consequences of sin. In other words, we can be saved, continue under the power of sin, and we will suffer no consequences. Behind this wild inference, there is a faulty understanding of the relation between the *penalty* of sin and the *power* of sin. Some seem to suggest that you can have the penalty removed but not have the power removed—the power of sin that holds us. To put it in another way, it raises the question of the relation between justification (freedom from the penalty) and sanctification (freedom from the power), and whether justification is sufficient for sanctification.

The *Ordo Salutis*: Misunderstood, Distorted, and Denied

The larger context behind the faulty understanding of justification and sanctification is the specific denial of each step in the process of salvation. Every single step in the order of salvation (*ordo salutis*)[2] has been misunderstood and distorted. (1) Being foreknown by God, *chosen* by God, has been denied. (2) Being predestinated according to His purpose and His plan, to be conformed to the image of Christ, has been denied. Both the choosing and the planning of salvation have been distorted. (3) The effectual calling—regeneration—has been denied or taken out of order. (4) Justification has been taken out of order and sometimes put after

---

life. Assurance of salvation arises from both faith and the observable transformation, rejecting any notion of passive belief.

2. Gangadean, *The Westminster Confession,* 143–206; Gangadean, *The Westminster Catechisms,* 191–207.

sanctification; that is, we are justified on the basis of our actual holiness, not on the basis of Christ's righteousness imputed to our account. The Roman Catholic Church has made that error. There are also some who say that you can be justified but not progress much in sanctification. That is the doctrine of the carnal Christian. Many churches seem to revel in that, and they seem to magnify the grace of God while living the carnal life. That is the spirit in which Paul is saying, **"What shall we say, then? Shall we go on sinning so that grace may increase?"** (v. 1). In addition, (5) glorification has been denied by saying that when we die, we are not fully perfected, but we go through purgatory for a long time. There is not one single doctrine, there is not one single step in the *ordo salutis*, that has not been misunderstood, denied, and inverted. Such is the power of the deceitfulness of the human heart.

REVIEW AND CONTEXT

In Romans 6, we are particularly looking at the relation between regeneration, justification, and sanctification. *Regeneration* is the reality pointed to by baptism; it speaks of our union with Christ. *Justification* is done by the imputation of Christ's righteousness on our behalf. *Sanctification* entails that we should no longer live in sin after we have been justified. We need to see the connection between the three. The *ordo salutis* consists of the doctrines that were worked out during the Reformation. Hundreds of thousands gave their lives for this doctrine—for holding to the right soteriology and breaking with the teaching of Rome. This is not, historically, a light matter.

In Romans 1–3, we see that Paul establishes the universality of sin and death, and that we are under the power of sin and death. In Romans 1:18–32, Paul shows that we have failed to see what is clear about God in general revelation and that God gives us up to go our way into the darkness of our minds and corruptions of our hearts. In Romans 2, Paul establishes that we have the law of God written in our hearts; we have the law of God given to us by special revelation, and we neglect the law. Furthermore, Paul establishes that no one has special privilege; all are treated in the same way before God; all have sinned and come short of the glory of God. He concludes in Romans 3:21–24:

But now a righteousness from God, apart from law, has been made known, to which the Law and the Prophets testify. This righteousness from God comes through faith in Jesus Christ to all who believe. There is no difference, for all have sinned and fall short of the glory of God, and are justified freely by his grace through the redemption that came by Christ Jesus.

It is on the basis of *His* righteousness that we are accepted. In Romans 4, Paul shows that this method of justification is not something new; it goes back to Abraham. Abraham was justified by faith. Remember, we spoke about the existential character of justification: by our very nature, by being rational, we need justification. Justification is one of the most terrible needs in our lives. If we do not know and do not have Christ's justification, we will justify ourselves in our sin and excuse our sin and our way of life.

We saw self-justification in Adam; he blamed God and blamed others rather than taking responsibility.[3] We see that this is very widespread in our society. We blame others by saying things like, 'I am a victim,' or 'It is my mother's fault,' or 'I was abused as a child, that is why I am so bad.' The excuses border on the ridiculous. Someone has said, 'I have this problem because someone took away my ice cream cone when I was seven.' We have men blaming women and women blaming men for their problems. All of this is according to the same spirit of *self*-justification. People do not take responsibility, and they justify themselves before God.[4] We need a justification from God most desperately. At the end of Romans 3 and in Romans 4, Paul says that this justification is done by imputation of righteousness, and this is the way it was from Abraham. Then, in Romans 5:18–19, Paul says that this is the way justification was applied from the time of Adam:

Consequently, just as the result of one trespass was condemnation for all men, so also the result of one act of righteousness was justification that brings life for all men. For just as through the disobedience of the one man the many were made sinners, so also through the obedience of the one man the many will be made righteous.

---

3. Gangadean, *The Biblical Worldview*, 259–273.

4. Gangadean, *Philosophical Foundation*, 231–243.

This is not something new coming up in what is sometimes called "new covenant teaching"—a teaching that claims this is a new teaching, beginning with Christ in the New Testament and not before. This is not so. This has been present since the Garden.[5]

CONTINUE IN SIN THAT GRACE MAY ABOUND?
Understanding the Nature of Salvation from Sin

Paul is now moving from the doctrine of justification to the doctrine of sanctification. We are justified once and for all, at a particular moment in time, in connection with our believing. Notice that I said in connection with, not on the basis of, our believing. It is by faith that we receive this righteousness. That *by which* we receive justification does not *originate* the justification received. So faith is not a special work that we do in order to be justified. We are justified by faith, which means that faith is the instrumental basis by which we receive that justification and not a special work of ours. Human beings have a tendency to turn something we do into a means of justification. Whether it is baptism, circumcision, or faith, it reflects the self-life that we want to hold on to and say that we, by ourselves, have our own standing before God. "For it is by grace you have been saved, through faith—and this not from yourselves, it is the gift of God—not by works, so that no one can boast" (Eph. 2:8–9). It was that word *boast* that particularly penetrated the cloud of pride that had surrounded me, and God used that to bring conviction of sin in my heart at the time of my conversion.[6]

Dead to Sin: Buried with Christ in His Death

"What shall we say, then? Shall we go on sinning so that grace may increase? By no means!" (vv. 1–2a). 'God forbid! Absolutely not! How could you possibly think such a thing?' That is the answer. That is so absurd; it is a contradiction. It is like speaking about a good-bad man or a live-dead person. Paul responds by exclamation because it is a patent absurdity, yet the person who was saying it did not notice the absurdity. "By no means! We died to sin; how can we live in it any

---

5. Gangadean, *The Biblical Worldview*, 295–309.

6. Gangadean, *On Natural and Revealed Theology*, xv–xvi.

longer?" (v. 2). In other words, if we are dead to sin, it has no more hold over us. Have you ever seen a dead person? Are they responsive to anything in this life? No, they are dead. If they are touched or poked, it does not bother them, they are dead. For we who are dead to sin, **"how can we live in it any longer?"** So the person saying, 'Let us sin that grace may abound' misunderstands the nature of salvation.

Paul goes on to say, **"Or don't you know that all of us who were baptized into Christ Jesus were baptized into his death?"** (v. 3). He said, **"Don't you know that . . . ?"** That is what baptism signifies. Baptism signifies our union with Christ in His death and His resurrection.[7] And just as Christ, on the basis of sin being imputed to Him, dies, and by death, is freed from the burden and the power of sin because he paid the penalty, so on the basis of our union with Christ, we die to sin. Remember, Paul said in Romans 5:18, "Just as the result of one trespass was condemnation for all men, so also the result of one act of righteousness was justification that brings life for all men." And he echoes this in 1 Corinthians 15:22: "For as in Adam all die, so in Christ all will be made alive." As in Adam all die—those who are united to Adam by natural descent, the unrighteousness of Adam imputed to us—so those who are united to Christ are united to Him in His death, His burial, His resurrection, His ascension, and His being seated at the right hand of God. We are seated with Christ in the heavenly places.[8] This truth needs to be emphasized: our union with Christ, particularly that we are united with Him in His death. **"Or don't you know that all of us who were baptized into Christ Jesus were baptized into his death?"** (v. 3). When Paul says, **"We died to sin,"** he is speaking about it in connection with baptism.

Alive in Christ: Raised with Christ to New Life

Paul is not just speaking about baptism as an external *rite* but in terms of what baptism signifies. Baptism signifies our *union* with Christ. Another way of putting it is that it signifies our regeneration—our being made alive. We were dead in our trespasses and sins, or rather, we were living in trespasses and sins; we were living a life of sin, which

---

7. Gangadean, *The Westminster Confession*, 143–148, 299–305.

8. *Ephesians 2:6.*

had to be cut off. When we were regenerated and made alive, that old self had to be cut off; we cannot have both at the same time, so the life of sin is cut off when we are regenerated in Christ. The old life ends where the new life begins. So there is an actual change in our nature, in the core of our being, in our hearts, where we receive a new heart. Circumcision in the Old Testament and baptism in the New Testament signify regeneration—having a new heart. We are to circumcise our heart and not our flesh.[9] We cannot have a new heart and the old heart in the same respect at the same time.

Conflict Between the Old and the New Heart

We will see later on that there is a new heart and an old heart; a new nature and an old nature, but not in the same respect at the same time. At the core of our being, there is one or the other—either life or death. At the core of our being, there is newness of life—death is no longer at the core of our being. There is a continued conflict, throughout life, between that new living center and the old nature that remains, and that is precisely what sanctification is about. We will see that we are not to allow that old way of life—the way of death—to remain in us. So when it is said, 'Let us sin that grace may abound,' there is not an understanding that at the core of our being, we are brought to life. That life will war against and push out the remaining old nature. That is the process of sanctification.

Regeneration Precedes Conversion and Justification

"We were therefore buried with him through baptism into death in order that, just as Christ was raised from the dead through the glory of the Father, we too may live a new life" (v. 4). So at this point, baptism introduces the notion of union with Christ, and it introduces the notion of regeneration. Therefore, we must bring regeneration into the picture to understand how regeneration, justification, and sanctification connect. Regeneration occurs *before* justification. It is on the basis of regeneration that, being made alive, we have a conviction of sin and an awareness of death. As we are made alive, we become aware of the effects of death—the emptiness of our lives that is due to our sin,

---

9. *Colossians 2:11; Romans 2:25–29.*

our not believing in God, and our not knowing and acknowledging God. So we repent of our sin and have faith in Jesus Christ, which is conversion. Regeneration comes first, then conversion, which involves repentance toward God and faith in our Lord Jesus Christ. And through that faith in our Lord Jesus Christ, the righteousness of God is imputed to us—the righteousness of Christ—and it is on that basis that we are justified. So there is regeneration, conviction, and conversion before we are justified that we need to keep in mind, and that is what Paul is referring to here when he speaks about being baptized into Christ, being united with Christ, and being dead to sin.

If we back up and understand the nature of regeneration—how regeneration leads to justification, and how justification leads to sanctification—we will see how absurd it is for a person to say, "**Let us sin that grace may abound.**" It is always true, before and after conversion, that sin is accompanied by death. There is an inherent connection between sin and death.[10] We cannot sin and not have death abound. Where sin abounded, death abounded—but grace did much more abound, much more than sin and death, to deliver us from sin and death. There is something greater than both sin and death: the grace of Christ.

Raised to Life for *Life*

Paul continues explaining the idea of our union with Christ: "**We were therefore buried with him through baptism into death in order that, just as Christ was raised from the dead through the glory of the Father, we too may live a new life**" (v. 4). We are not only united with Him in His death but united with Him in His resurrection. We did not come to Christ simply to die in sin. If we were simply to die in sin, we would remain under the power of sin. We came to Christ for *life*. So we are not only united with Him in His dying to sin, but we are united to Him in His being raised from the dead, and so we will live with Him, and we cannot live in newness of life and continue sinning. We will have opportunity in the weeks, months, and years ahead to encounter Christians who emphasize the forgiveness of God but show little or no regard for the cleansing from sin, little or no regard for the

---

10. Gangadean, *The Biblical Worldview*, 37–54, 177–195; Gangadean, "Paper No. 146: The Biblical Worldview (Part VI)," in *The Logos Papers*, 741–745; Gangadean, *The Westminster Catechisms*, 144–152; Gangadean, *The Westminster Confession*, 99–110, 369–376.

sanctification process, little or no regard for learning to live by the law of God, little or no regard for discipleship. You will find that struggle in your own life. You may fall back and say, 'I am forgiven, and when I die, I will go to heaven.' If that is the case, you will need to come back to some of the teachings in Romans 5–6 to be reminded.

Regeneration Breaks the Power of Sin

"If we have been united with him like this in his death, we will certainly also be united with him in his resurrection" (v. 5). If we die with Him, we live with Him. So we that are dead die to sin, we cannot live in it any longer, and we go on to a new life. He continues this thought: "For we know that our old self was crucified with him so that the body of sin might be done away with, that we should no longer be slaves to sin—because anyone who has died has been set free from sin" (vv. 6–7). The power of sin is broken when there is regeneration. Sin does not have its power over us any longer. Regeneration is simultaneously the killing off of the old nature and the implanting of the new nature. We are not simply left in that state—death is being replaced by life. Just as life is replaced by death, and there is nothing in between, so death to the old nature is replaced by the life of the new nature. So we were buried with Him, and we are raised with Him. As a result of dying with Him, our old self was crucified with Him so that the body of sin might become powerless.

By Grace, We Must Crucify the Sin That Remains

One of the ways in which difficulty comes in is when we think that the old nature has been crucified, and that is the end of it. That is not true; it is not the end of it. We have to, by the grace of God, crucify "the flesh with the affections and lusts" (Gal. 5:24b KJV). What we can say is that the vital center has been killed, but the operation of sin is still in our members.[11] To use another metaphor: there were some Japanese soldiers who did not realize that World War II was over; they were held up in caves somewhere. The central command had been destroyed, but word had not yet gotten out to the others in the field that the war was over. They were putting up resistance, fighting to the

---

11. *Romans 7:23* KJV.

death. These guys knew it was a life-or-death struggle—it was them or us—and they were going to fight, each last man, to the death. But they did not know that the war was over. It is in this same sense that Satan is defeated by the resurrection of Christ, but he continues to fight—though it is an absolute loss. Not only is this true of Satan and his host, but it is also true of sin remaining in our members. That is the sense in which you can say the decisive battle has occurred, but we still have a cleaning-up operation to engage in. **"For we know that our old self was crucified with him so that the body of sin might be done away with, that we should no longer be slaves to sin—because anyone who has died has been set free from sin"** (vv. 6–7).

Forever Living Unto God—Consistently with the Truth

In Romans 6:8–10, Paul emphasizes being alive in Christ.

> **Now if we died with Christ, we believe that we will also live with him. For we know that since Christ was raised from the dead, he cannot die again; death no longer has mastery over him. The death he died, he died to sin once for all; but the life he lives, he lives to God.**

Just as Christ died once and lives unto God, so we die once in Him, and we will live—and continue to live, and will forever live—unto God. We will not go through that death again. Regeneration is a one-time operation. Coming to life, at the core, is a one-time operation, and that life is going to spread and increase until all sin is removed.

So, knowing this truth—that we are united with Christ in His death, that baptism signifies that union with Him and points to the regeneration we have in Him, and that death has occurred to the old nature at its core—let us live accordingly. Many people live without understanding what has really happened to them in Christ. Many live as if they have chosen God, not as if God is the one who has chosen them. They need to be instructed—even though they think they have chosen God—that it is true, as a matter of fact, that God has chosen them. God is sovereign in grace. Paul is calling us back to recognize that truth and, in recognizing it, to live more consistently. That is what is going on in Romans 6:11: **"In the same way, count yourselves dead to sin but alive to God in Christ Jesus."** Live more consciously and consistently with the truth. Understand what faith really is. Faith is not something in contrast to reason and understanding—faith is based on understanding. Live consistent with the truth. There are many truths in Scripture that we do not recognize, though we are alive to God and dead to sin. The Lord explains the reality of our situation to us. If we rely only on our surface consciousness of things, we will not understand what is going on in our nature. We have to think deeply to understand what is going on in our nature—not merely what is surfacing in our consciousness.

Do Not Let Sin Reign

In Romans 6:12, Paul says, "**Therefore do not let sin reign in your mortal body so that you obey its evil desires.**" Because the power is broken, do not let it reign. Particularly, do not think that you are in the same place now, as a believer, as you were before—with respect to lusts, with respect to the struggles that are going on. We do not have to yield to sin and say, 'Sin reigned in us before, it is the same now, and there is nothing to be done.' It may feel that way to you, but it is not. You are being encouraged—by the true explanation of the fact—to resist this remaining sin, because we are not under the power of sin as we once were.

Romans 6:14 says, "**For sin shall no longer be your master, because you are not under the law, but under grace.**" We are not merely under the law as something that we must live by in our own strength and ability, but we have the grace of God working in us to sanctify us. Paul says, "**Do not offer any part of yourself to sin, as an instrument of wickedness, but rather offer yourselves to God, as those who have been brought from death to life; and offer the parts of your body to him as instruments of righteousness**" (v. 13). We are not to offer or yield our members to sin, whether it is through our eyes or through our mouth, or some other part of the body through which we characteristically sin. Do not offer it up and use our lives in that way. Paul tells the Ephesians, "And be not drunk with wine, wherein is excess; but be filled with the Spirit" (Eph. 5:18 KJV). Do not hang around with winebibbers, but put yourself in the Word and be filled with the Word of Christ and let the Spirit of God dwell in you richly through His Word.[12] We do not have to yield, because we have a new power working in us. We have new resources in us.

"**Shall we go on sinning so that grace may increase?**" (v. 1). Paul answers this objection against justification—this misunderstanding—by speaking about the nature of things. By nature, we are dead to sin in Christ because of our union with Him in regeneration. That which is in us—this life in us—displaces death, and sin cannot reign in us. It remains in us, but we are not to yield ourselves in this way to sin.

CONTINUE IN SIN THAT GRACE MAY ABOUND?
Understanding the Effect of Sin—Sin Leads to Death, Not Grace

The Penalty of Sin Is the Power of Sin

In the second part of this chapter, Paul speaks about the application of why we should not go on sinning. Having spoken about the *nature* of things, he now speaks about the *fruit* of things. He asks the question, "**What then? Shall we sin because we are not under the law but under grace?**" (v. 15). This question is the same as "**Shall we go on sinning so that grace may increase?**" (v. 1). Verse 15 picks up from the last part of verse 14: "**You are not under the law, but under grace.**" Paul asks the same question and answers it again. He says that it is not only true that the penalty of sin is broken, but the power of sin is also broken, because the penalty is inherent in sin. The penalty is the power: it is impossible to sin—to fail to use our mind to seek God—and yet avoid the inherent consequences of death: meaninglessness, boredom, and guilt. It is impossible. So the penalty of sin is its inherent effect, and that inherent effect is its power. We cannot have the penalty removed and the power continue. We cannot have justification, where the penalty is removed, and somehow the power continues. It cannot be that Christ has forgiven the penalty of sin, and we continue under the power of sin. We cannot have life as Christ intends it for us if the power of sin remains. That is why Jesus says, "I have come that they may have life, and that they may have it more abundantly" (Jn. 10:10b NKJV).

---

12. *Colossians 3:16.*

Either Slaves to Sin or to Righteousness

Paul is saying that it is not only true that we are dead to sin, but if we continue in sin, the only result will be death. That is why Paul ends this section by saying, **"For the wages of sin is death, but the gift of God is eternal life in Christ Jesus our Lord"** (v. 23). Do you want to have death? He explains the psychology of this section. Let us read it through and see what he is saying. **"Don't you know that when you offer yourselves to someone to obey him as slaves, you are slaves of the one whom you obey—whether you are slaves to sin, which leads to death, or to obedience, which leads to righteousness?"** (v. 16). One way or the other, we are going to be slaves. Paul uses slavery as a figure of speech because of our weakness. One way or the other, we will be mastered by that which is in us. Either sin reigning in us will be the master, or righteousness reigning in us will be the master. When we become believers, there are some things we just cannot do because we are believers. A lot of things we will still do—and they are wrong—but there are some things we cannot do. We cannot curse Christ. We cannot call Christ a curse. We may go out and commit adultery and fall in sin in that way, but no Christian can call Christ a curse. That is one thing we cannot do at the basic level. In that sense, there is something in us that will not let us do that—we would rather die, be beaten up, and be thrown under a semi than call Christ a curse. And so life increases. It will come to the point where we cannot commit adultery. We would rather be shot through the heart seven times than commit adultery. In that sense, the new nature is master of us, and we are a slave. Just as the old nature of sin mastered us when we were a slave, the new nature is mastering us.

Paul says in Romans 6:17: **"But thanks be to God that, though you used to be slaves to sin, you wholeheartedly obeyed the form of teaching to which you were entrusted."** Though in one case or the other, it is slavery, it is not equal, because when we become Christians, we *wholeheartedly* yield obedience. It is not that we were reluctant sinners before we were believers, but sin involves a denial of our nature, and in that sense, it is not wholehearted. When we come to Christ, obedience involves a uniting of our nature, and it is wholehearted. **"You have been set free from sin and have become slaves to righteousness"** (v. 18). Both sin and righteousness exercise rule in us, and we may be mastered by either. In the case of sin, the mastery is foreign to our nature, but in the case of righteousness, the mastery is *according* to our nature, and so it is wholehearted—it is from the heart.

"I put this in human terms because you are weak in your natural selves. Just as you used to offer the parts of your body in slavery to impurity and to ever-increasing wickedness, so now offer them in slavery to righteousness leading to holiness" (v. 19). When we were slaves to sin, we were free from the control of righteousness. We want to be free, but we cannot be free in that sense. In one sense, we are always free—in the sense of being responsible. If we sin, wanting to sin, we are free; and if we obey, wanting to obey, we are free.[13] In one very basic sense, we are always free. In another sense, Paul is saying we are either going to be a slave to righteousness or a slave to sin. Some people might want to say, 'Nobody is going to tell me what to do; I'm going to adopt a middle ground between good and evil, between Christ and sin. I'm not yet ready to go with Christ, but I do not particularly want to go with sin.' Have you ever heard of that situation? These persons are trying to carve out a middle ground where they are 'their own boss,' but that never happens. There is nothing in between life and death; there is nothing in between good and evil. We simply deceive ourselves because we are looking at it subjectively.

Ever-Increasing Joy in the Lord Versus Pleasure in Sin

We want to be alive, and we mistake that intense emotion and feeling of pleasure for being alive. That is not the way it works. That intense emotion may be manic-depressive—up quickly and down deeply—as opposed to something gradually building, building, and building through all the days of your life. The joy of the Lord is not just a quick fix; the joy of the Lord is something that is ever-increasing as a result of the fruit of the Spirit. We tend to translate joy into a particular intense experience of pleasure, but that is not the way it works. We say, 'I want to feel deeply; I want to feel it now,' and since pleasure is taken as a sign of life, we are taking the appearance for the reality—and this is how sin deceives us again and again. We seek for lust; it promises life, but it produces death.

---

13. Gangadean, *Philosophical Foundation,* 66; Gangadean, *History of Philosophy,* 113–114, 153–154.

There is pleasure in sin for a season. All of popular culture sings about fleeting desires. People feel intensely this romantic view of love. They think they are so intensely alive at that time—when they are floating at the edges of an affair, and the emotions are increasing. It gives an intense pleasure for a while, but it does not last, unlike the joy of God, which ever increases. If you walk in that way and think that you are in the middle ground between life and death, where you appear to be having life—it is not true.

Acknowledging Shame Versus Self-Deception and Self-Justification

"**When you were slaves to sin, you were free from the control of righteousness. What benefit did you reap at that time from the things you are now ashamed of?**" (vv. 20–21a). When we were engaged in sin, we were not ashamed—but as we look back on it, we are ashamed of it. Those who trust in the Lord and live by His Word will never be ashamed.[14] He continues, "**Those things result in death!**" (v. 21b). We are ashamed of it now. By God's grace, we are willing to acknowledge the shame instead of covering it up and blaming someone else, as Adam did in self-deception and self-justification.[15] It is death, and when we experience it as shame, we try to avoid it. Paul is saying that the only thing that results if we continue in sin is that it produces death. You might deceive yourself about it, but it is there—and sooner or later, it will come out. "**But now that you have been set free from sin and have become slaves of God, the benefit you reap leads to holiness, and the result is eternal life. For the wages of sin is death, but the gift of God is eternal life in Christ Jesus our Lord**" (vv. 22–23). This is the way God has made it.

Conclusion: We Need to Be Cleansed from Sin

Two arguments are given against the position that we should continue sinning that grace may abound. First, by *nature*, it cannot be so, because those who are dead to sin cannot go on sinning. Those who are alive unto God cannot go on sinning. Second, from the *effects*: sin leads to

---

14. *Romans 10:11* KJV.
15. Gangadean, *The Biblical Worldview,* 259–273.

death. We are ashamed of our sin. You may deceive yourself about it for a while, but that deception will be ripped open, and you will have to go deeper and deeper into deception to continue deceiving yourself. Sin leads to death; we are ashamed of death—it was worthless, it had no benefit, it deceived you. So there is no point in continuing in sin that grace may abound. By nature and by effect, it makes no sense whatsoever to say that we should sin that grace may abound. So Paul finishes responding to this objection that justification means we are free to sin. It does not. Sin remains, and we need to be cleansed from sin.

9

SANCTIFICATION

The Spiritual War Within the Believer

2025

Romans 7

EDITOR'S NOTE

The sermon audio recording on Romans 7 is not currently in the possession of The Logos Foundation Editorial Board. We have used the existing hand-written outline and content from other sermons and writings to formulate a brief exposition of the central theological ideas of this chapter. Romans 7 continues the argument that began in Romans 5, explaining the benefits that follow from our reconciliation by grace through Christ's atoning death and its extension to the whole of creation and triumph over every opposition, as explained in Romans 8.

Romans 7 addresses a crucial element of sanctification by describing the spiritual war in believers—between the old and new nature, between belief and remaining unbelief, and between the self-life operating under the covenant of works and the new self under the covenant of grace. It describes the subjective side of sanctification, bringing into focus the continual, agonizing, savage, and irreconcilable nature of this war.

THE TWO COVENANTS: WORKS AND GRACE

In Christ: Dead to the Law of Works, Bound to Him by Grace

Paul begins by addressing the legal principle that the law has authority over a person only as long as they live. He uses marriage as an analogy: a woman is bound to her husband as long as he is alive, but when he dies, she is released from the law of marriage.[1] Similarly, believers were once bound to the covenant of works under Adam, but through Christ's death, we have died to that old covenant and belong to Christ under the covenant of grace.

This transition is not merely a change of external status in justification; it is a deep transformation in sanctification—from imputed righteousness to actual righteousness. We were united to Adam in the covenant of works; the fruit of that union was sin and death. But in Christ, we have been joined to the One who was raised from the dead, so that we might bear fruit to God.[2] This is more than forensic justification;[3] it is a real participation in the life and rule of Christ. What happens once in justification is distinct from what is ongoing in sanctification. Forgiveness is not the same as cleansing,[4] but both together constitute the salvation that is in Christ under the covenant of grace.

The Content and Covenantal Context of the Law

Paul contrasts the old realities of those in Adam versus the new realities of those in Christ. **"For when we were controlled by the sinful nature, the sinful passions aroused by the law were at work in our bodies, so that we bore fruit for death"** (v. 5). Under the covenant of works, the law functions not as a means of righteousness but as an instrument that exposes and provokes sin. The law has always been, and will always be, the standard and rule for life. The law does not change, though the context does—from the covenant of works, where we are required

---

1. *Romans 7:1–3.*

2. *Romans 7:4.*

3. Forensic justification is the act by which God, as Judge, declares the sinner righteous solely on the basis of the righteousness of Christ imputed to them through faith. It is a legal judgment, not a change in the moral condition of the person, and rests entirely on the sufficiency of Christ's atonement and obedience, rather than any work or merit of the individual.

4. *1 John 1:9; John 17:17.*

to obey in order to be accepted, to the covenant of grace, where we are accepted in Christ's righteousness and then enabled to obey. This distinction between *content* and *context* is crucial. The law itself remains holy, but under the covenant of works in Adam, it becomes a curse rather than a guide to life. There is no tension between law and grace. The law shows us our need for grace; in turn, grace enables us to keep the law. Law leads us to grace, and grace leads us to law. The law and grace are in harmony. Thus, we must not abstract law and grace from the covenantal context.

The law itself is not the covenant; the covenant of works was established through Adam, our covenant representative. But now, through Christ, our new covenant head, we have entered a new and better covenant.[5] This is why Paul writes, "**But now, by dying to what once bound us, we have been released from the law so that we serve in the new way of the Spirit, and not in the old way of the written code**" (v. 6). The problem is not the law itself; the problem is our relationship to it outside of Christ. The law provides several uses for the believer: it is a rule of life to inform us of our duty and the will of God; it further directs and binds us to obedience; it shows us our true condition; it cultivates hatred against sin; and it raises awareness of our need for Christ. The law also restrains the corruption of the believer and manifests God's approbation and blessing upon obedience. Sanctification is by grace through faith, not through the law. If we attempt to overcome sin by law-keeping, we will only arouse sin further.[6] But if we walk by the Spirit, under grace, the law is fulfilled through faith in Christ.[7]

The Covenant of Grace: Justification and Sanctification

In Christ, believers enter a new covenant—the covenant of grace. The Mosaic laws were given for a specific redemptive purpose: they pointed to the fulfillment of the covenant of works in Christ, but they were never the means of salvation. The believer, having been freed from the covenant of works, is bound to Christ by grace.

---

5. Gangadean, *The Epistle to the Hebrews*, 99–148.

6. *Romans 7:5.*

7. *WCF 19.6.*

The covenant of grace includes the distinction between justification and sanctification, and between imputed and actual righteousness. Properly understanding these distinctions was at the heart of the Reformation. The medieval church blurred the lines between justification and sanctification, teaching that righteousness is infused rather than imputed. Luther struggled with this, realizing that if righteousness is something infused into the believer through sacraments, then sin could nullify it—leaving the believer in a constant state of uncertainty. Instead, Scripture teaches that righteousness is imputed by faith in Christ, and sanctification follows as a work of the Spirit cleansing us from sin.[8] Salvation is not merely about forgiveness but also cleansing. We are not just *declared* righteous but are being *made* righteous. The means of this transformation is not the law but the Spirit enabling us to obey the law under the covenant of grace.

Bondage to Sin Under the Covenant of Works: The Law Distorted and Grace Turned into Works

The moral law is permanent and perpetual because it is grounded in human nature.[9] Under the covenant of works, the law is distorted, and we are enslaved to sin. The old nature, inherited from Adam, continues to operate under the covenant of works—even in those who profess faith. Those outside of Christ, and those in whom the old nature is dominant, will take the very teachings of grace, transform them into works, and—because they cannot live by them—excuse themselves, justify themselves, and reject the teachings of grace. This was the case for many in the Old Testament, where the teachings of grace were turned into works. They reinterpreted circumcision, Passover, and the Day of Atonement—each meant to point to grace—and made them into works. The old nature operates under the old covenant of works and reacts in opposition to the covenant of grace. The old nature cannot grasp grace and always defaults to a works-based righteousness. This is why believers must be watchful: the old nature still struggles for dominance, waging war against the new nature that operates under grace.

---

8. *Romans 8:1–4.*

9. Gangadean, *The Westminster Confession*, 208–210.

THE IRRECONCILABLE WAR WITHIN:
The Struggle Between the Old and New Natures

The Law Exposes but Cannot Empower

The law is not the cause of sin but reveals sin and death.[10] Paul says, **"I was alive apart from law; but when the commandment came, sin sprang to life and I died"** (v. 9). Under the covenant of works, the law condemns. As a rule of life, it shows what is good but cannot produce holiness nor empower us to fulfill the law. Sin distorts, condemns, and awakens opposition to God's commands.

The Subjective Side of Sanctification: The Ongoing Reality of Indwelling Sin

Paul describes the ongoing war *within* believers. Even though we are justified, sin still remains. There is an inseparable connection between sin and death. Though death no longer reigns in us, Paul acknowledges that it still remains in our members.[11] This war is not merely a surface struggle but a continual war—a savage war, an irreconcilable war. Paul does not suggest this is rooted in a weakness of will (*akrasia*),[12] as though

---

10. *Romans 7:7.*

11. *Romans 7:17.*

12. The problem of *akrasia*—knowingly doing evil—has its roots in ancient philosophy over the relationship between reason and the will. Socrates and Plato argued against *akrasia*, claiming that all wrongdoing is the result of ignorance; to know the good is to do the good (*Protagoras* 351b–358d; *Gorgias* 466a–468e; *Meno* 77b–78b; *Republic IV*, 439e–441e; *Apology* 25d–26a). Aristotle departed from their understanding and defended *akrasia*, arguing that one can act against reason due to weakness of will (*Nicomachean Ethics*, VII. 1–10). This anthropological dispute carried forward into theology, where the question of whether the will or the intellect holds primacy became central. Voluntarism, the view that the will has primacy over the intellect, gained momentum, especially in the medieval period with Duns Scotus and William of Ockham, who emphasized the supremacy of the will in moral action. In Reformed theology, the problem of *akrasia* is grounded in the understanding of the triune personality in man and the noetic effect of sin. Cornelius Van Til argues in *Christian Apologetics* that fallen humanity suppresses the truth it knows: "Men in general are, therefore, truth-suppressors. But they are first of all truth-possessors, or truth-knowers, who have, by sinning, become truth-suppressors" (Van Til, *Christian Apologetics*, 2003, 103). R.C. Sproul similarly maintains in *Essential Truths of the Christian Faith* that unbelief is not due to a lack of knowledge but to moral rebellion: "Unbelief is judged by Jesus not as an intellectual error but as a hostile act of prejudice against God Himself" (Sproul, *Essential Truths*, 1992, 35). This long-standing dispute has significantly shaped theological conceptions of human nature, rationality, sin, apologetics, and moral responsibility.

he merely lacks effort or discipline. Instead, he speaks of a war between the law of God in his mind and the law of sin in his members—a conflict that exposes the ongoing presence of sin in the life of the believer at the root level, at the level of unbelief, accompanied by self-deception and self-justification. This is a war that can only be overcome by the grace of God, by the power of the Spirit, by the renewing of the mind, and by the crucifying of the flesh daily.

Paul declares, **"We know that the law is spiritual; but I am unspiritual, sold as a slave to sin"** (v. 14). This is not a denial of justification but an admission that, in his flesh, sin still operates. He is not speaking as one who is under condemnation but as one who experiences the daily reality of indwelling sin. This is why he continues, **"I do not understand what I do. For what I want to do I do not do, but what I hate I do"** (v. 15). He recognizes that even though his mind delights in God's law, his actions do not always align. The battle is existentially strenuous, frustrating, and perplexing. Paul describes the deceptive nature of sin: **"For sin, seizing the opportunity afforded by the commandment, deceived me, and through the commandment put me to death"** (v. 11). The law is not the problem; the law is **"holy, righteous and good"** (v. 12b). But sin, when confronted by the law, reacts with rebellion. This is how the self-life is manifest—when God commands, sin within us resists, deceives, and rises in opposition. The self-life asserts itself in autonomy, 'I will do what I want. No one can tell me otherwise.' When the law says, **"Do not covet"** (v. 7b), sin seizes the opportunity and produces covetous desires.[13] The commandment, which was meant to bring life, instead brings death, because it exposes the power of indwelling sin.

Paul continues, **"As it is, it is no longer I myself who do it, but it is sin living in me"** (v. 17). This does not mean he denies personal responsibility, but rather that he recognizes his new nature in Christ is at war with the old nature inherited from Adam. Two principles are at work within him—the law of God in his mind and the law of sin in his flesh. These two laws are constantly at odds, leaving him unable to carry out his deepest desires for righteousness. **"For I have the desire to do what is good, but I cannot carry it out"** (v. 18b).

---

13. *Romans 7:7–8.*

This battle has been described as *akrasia*, or weakness of will—knowing what is right but failing to do it. But the issue here is not merely willpower; it is a spiritual war between two opposing natures. Paul says, **"When I want to do good, evil is right there with me"** (v. 21b). He delights in God's law in his inner being,[14] yet he sees another law at work, making him a prisoner of sin's influence.[15] This is why renewing the mind is so critical. It enables us to overcome the remaining unbelief—Paul later commands in Romans 12:2, "Do not conform any longer to the pattern of this world, but be transformed by the renewing of your mind."

Greater Dependence on the Spirit of God for Victory

The struggle described in Romans 7 is not simply about outward behavior but about how the believer relates to the law under grace. Those outside of Christ take the law and twist it into a system of works-based righteousness. Likewise, believers, if they are not careful, can fall into the old mindset of legalism—thinking that their standing before God depends on their performance. This is why Paul reminds us, "Where sin increased, grace increased all the more" (Rom. 5:20b). Grace does not remove the struggle but does change the outcome. This war within the believer is why sanctification is by faith and not by works. If we attempt to overcome sin by our own efforts, we will experience greater frustration. But if we trust in God's grace, we will find victory. Paul cries out in desperation, **"What a wretched man I am! Who will rescue me from this body of death?"** (v. 24). His answer follows immediately: **"Thanks be to God—through Jesus Christ our Lord!"** (v. 25a). This struggle points forward to Romans 8:1, where Paul declares that "there is now no condemnation for those who are in Christ Jesus." The believer's confidence is not in their ability to win the battle but in Christ's victory over sin and death. The presence of this internal war should not lead to despair but to greater dependence on the Spirit of God. This is why, even in the midst of struggle, we can be sure: "For it is by grace you have been saved, through faith—and this not from yourselves, it is the gift of God—not by works, so that no one can boast" (Eph. 2:8–9). It

---

14. *Romans 7:22.*

15. *Romans 7:23.*

is through faith—the understanding of the truth. The answer to the war within is not more effort but more faith—faith in Christ's finished work and the sanctifying power of the Holy Spirit.

The Objective and Subjective Nature of the Conflict

The conflict between the two natures is to be understood objectively and subjectively:

Objectively, the conflict is in all aspects of the triune personality. The conflict is *within* knowledge, *within* holiness, and *within* righteousness. We are divided against ourselves and within each of the aspects of our triune personality. These divisions become manifest in our actions—not doing. The conflict is not between knowledge and holiness, but *within* knowledge and holiness, and expressed through unrighteousness. Unrighteousness—not doing—is expressive of prior divisions within knowledge and within holiness: **"I do not understand what I do. For what I want to do I do not do, but what I hate I do"** (v. 15).

Subjectively, we are more or less conscious and consistent—and we should be more conscious and consistent. This happens through the trials of faith, by which we come to know and overcome the sin that remains. You may be aware of the belief that is in you, but not the unbelief that remains—as Peter was not aware. Peter confessed, "You are the Christ, the Son of the living God" (Matt. 16:16b), yet he failed to see that Christ must suffer and die.[16] Because of our sin (lack of seeking), the understanding, devotion, and righteousness that we have is, at times, insufficient to overcome the unbelief, lack of devotion, and unrighteousness that remains. While we may **"delight in God's law"** (v. 22b), there is another law at work, which is **"waging war against the law of my mind and making me a prisoner of the law of sin at work within my members"** (v. 23b).

CONCLUSION:
The Law of God in My Mind Versus the Law of Sin in My Flesh

Paul ultimately distinguishes between the law of God—understood by grace and trust in Christ—and the law of sin, which operates in the

---

16. *Matthew 16:21-23.*

flesh, leading to works and self-reliance. Either belief or unbelief is at the core of man. Over time, what is at the core will assert itself and ultimately prevail. The subjective struggle of the Spirit against the flesh within a person is the spiritual war in the believer—sanctification. We are no longer under the law as a covenant of works but under grace. This is our assurance: we can trust in God, not only in justification but also in sanctification, and ultimately in every trial and circumstance. Our hope is not in self-discipline, law-keeping, or moral striving—it is in Christ alone, through faith alone, by grace alone.

10

THE FULL EXTENT OF SALVATION

Overcoming by the Law of the Spirit of Life—In Every Way

1994

Romans 8:1–27

¹Therefore, there is now no condemnation for those who are in Christ Jesus, ²because through Christ Jesus the law of the Spirit of life set me free from the law of sin and death. ³For what the law was powerless to do in that it was weakened by the sinful nature, God did by sending his own Son in the likeness of sinful man to be a sin offering. And so he condemned sin in sinful man, ⁴in order that the righteous requirements of the law might be fully met in us, who do not live according to the sinful nature but according to the Spirit.

⁵Those who live according to the sinful nature have their minds set on what that nature desires; but those who live in accordance with the Spirit have their minds set on what the Spirit desires. ⁶The mind of sinful man is death, but the mind controlled by the Spirit is life and peace; ⁷the sinful mind is hostile to God. It does not submit to God's law, nor can it do so. ⁸Those controlled by the sinful nature cannot please God.

⁹You, however, are controlled not by the sinful nature but by the Spirit, if the Spirit of God lives in you. And if anyone does not have the Spirit of Christ, he does not belong to Christ. ¹⁰But if Christ is in you, your body is dead because of sin, yet your spirit is alive because of righteousness. ¹¹And if the Spirit of him who raised Jesus from the dead is living in you, he who raised Christ from the dead will also give life to your mortal bodies through his Spirit, who lives in you.

[12]Therefore, brothers, we have an obligation—but it is not to the sinful nature, to live according to it. [13]For if you live according to the sinful nature, you will die; but if by the Spirit you put to death the misdeeds of the body, you will live, [14]because those who are led by the Spirit of God are sons of God. [15]For you did not receive a spirit that makes you a slave again to fear, but you received the Spirit of sonship. And by him we cry, "Abba, Father." [16]The Spirit himself testifies with our spirit that we are God's children. [17]Now if we are children, then we are heirs—heirs of God and co-heirs with Christ, if indeed we share in his sufferings in order that we may also share in his glory.

[18]I consider that our present sufferings are not worth comparing with the glory that will be revealed in us. [19]The creation waits in eager expectation for the sons of God to be revealed. [20]For the creation was subjected to frustration, not by its own choice, but by the will of the one who subjected it, in hope [21]that the creation itself will be liberated from its bondage to decay and brought into the glorious freedom of the children of God. [22]We know that the whole creation has been groaning as in the pains of childbirth right up to the present time. [23]Not only so, but we ourselves, who have the firstfruits of the Spirit, groan inwardly as we wait eagerly for our adoption as sons, the redemption of our bodies. [24]For in this hope we were saved. But hope that is seen is no hope at all. Who hopes for what he already has? [25]But if we hope for what we do not yet have, we wait for it patiently.

[26]In the same way, the Spirit helps us in our weakness. We do not know what we ought to pray for, but the Spirit himself intercedes for us with groans that words cannot express.

[27]And he who searches our hearts knows the mind of the Spirit, because the Spirit intercedes for the saints in accordance with God's will.

REVIEW

IN ROMANS 7, WE SAW THAT WE DIED TO THE LAW, as a covenant of works, in Christ, who represented us in terms of the requirements of that covenant of works God made with Adam. Adam did not obey, and Christ was cut off in order to *undo* the sin of Adam. Christ cried out to His Father, "My God, my God, why have you forsaken me?" (Matt. 27:46b) as He approached His death. Christ was raised and ascended into heaven; He sat at the right hand of God, and from there, He sent the Spirit. He fulfilled the requirements of the law—both in the punishment and in the obedience required. We are now dead to the covenant of works under Adam and alive to God through Christ in a new covenant. We can use the marriage analogy to understand: a marriage ends when death occurs, and we are free to marry another. By original generation, we are united to Adam; by the covenant of grace through adoption, we are united to Christ. We see that, though sin remains in us and we do not do the things we would,[1] yet we have the supply of grace in Christ Jesus our Lord, by which we increasingly overcome sin.

TWO COVENANTS—TWO PRINCIPLES:
The Law of the Spirit of Life Sets Us Free from the Law of Sin and Death

In Romans 8, Paul summarizes what he has been saying about God's way of justifying and receiving us. "Therefore, there is now no condemnation for those who are in Christ Jesus" (v. 1). In that first covenant of works, we had condemnation. But because of Christ's perfect obedience, we have been taken out of the covenant of works and brought into the covenant of grace. Now, there is no condemnation; rather than condemnation, there is life, because we have been placed in a new covenant of grace. Christ fulfilled the covenant of works, and the proof of the fulfillment is that He has been raised from the dead, He is seated at the right hand of God, and He has sent the Holy Spirit. Instead of condemnation, we have, in its place, life. "Because through Christ Jesus the law of the Spirit of life set me free from the law of sin and death" (v. 2). In that expression, "the law of the Spirit of life set me free from the law of sin and death," we have the two covenants represented. The new covenant—the covenant of grace—is the covenant sealed to us and put into effect by the Spirit of God. The result of that new covenant is life. The law of the Spirit of life does not refer to the Ten Commandments, *per se*, but to the new covenant—the covenant of grace—put into effect where sin abounded. When Adam sinned and covered up his sin, there was sin abounding in his cover-up, and even there, God brought the promise of salvation through Christ.[2] God then continued that call to repentance upon us by imposing the curse of toil

---

1. *Romans 7:15.*

2. Gangadean, *The Biblical Worldview,* 295–309.

and strife, and old age, sickness, and death. The curse and the promise work together for our salvation.[3] Paul is going to make the point that none of these sufferings will separate us from the love of God; rather, we are more than conquerors through suffering.[4] This is part of the new covenant. **"The law of the Spirit of life set me free from the law of sin and death"** (v. 2).

No Condemnation—But Security: Life in Place of Death

The remainder of this chapter is concerned with showing how there is no condemnation; rather, there is security. Paul shows the many ways in which we are secured in Christ. We are sealed in this new covenant because Christ has perfectly accomplished the work of redemption, and in showing how there is no condemnation but security, Paul shows how there is life in place of death. Wherever there was death, life will come; it has come and will continue to come. That is the main theme that is shown in Romans 8. All of this is summed up in the first two verses: **"Therefore, there is now no condemnation for those who are in Christ Jesus, because through Christ Jesus the law of the Spirit of life set me free from the law of sin and death"** (vv. 1–2). That is the summary. Remember, Adam was told in the Garden, "In the day that you eat of it you shall surely die" (Gen. 2:17b NKJV). There was sin and death as part of the covenant of works, but now, in this new covenant of grace, the Spirit is in us to enable us to obey—we have life and life to the fullest.[5]

Obedience by the Power of the Spirit

Paul explains how it is that there is no condemnation in verse 3: **"For what the law was powerless to do because it was weakened by the sinful nature . . ."** Remember, we said the moral law is written in our hearts and the moral law is given in the Ten Commandments.[6] The problem

---

3. Gangadean, *The Biblical Worldview,* 275–294.

4. *Romans 8:37–39.*

5. *John 10:10.*

6. Gangadean, *Philosophical Foundation,* 171–284; Gangadean, *History of Philosophy,* 61–69; Gangadean, *The Westminster Catechisms,* 215–267; Gangadean, *The Westminster Confession,* 207–221; Gangadean, *On Natural and Revealed Theology,* 127–139, 166–178.

is not with the law; "the law is holy, righteous and good" (Rom. 7:12b). The way in which we were related to the law in the covenant of works was the problem. We failed in Adam, and because of his failure, and the weakness of our sinful nature, we cannot function by the law in the covenant of works. The law was powerless, but it is not that the law is ineffective. The law is powerful in the sense that it produces conviction of sin. Paul said, "Once I was alive apart from the law; but when the commandment came, sin sprang to life and I died" (Rom. 7:9), but it is powerless to make us obedient. It is the Spirit working, in the most intimate way, in the very core of our being, that makes us obedient to the law of God. The Spirit is the one that makes us delight in the law of God: **"For what the law was powerless to do in that it was weakened by the sinful nature, God did by sending his own Son in the likeness of sinful man to be a sin offering. And so he condemned sin in sinful man"** (v. 3). There is now no condemnation, because Christ has come. He, representing us, bore that condemnation, and therefore, there is no condemnation—but only for those who are in Christ Jesus.

Christ Bore the Penalty and Perfectly Obeyed the Law

God condemns sin in sinful man but does so **"in order that the righteous requirement of the law might be fully met in us"** (v. 4a). Not only did He condemn sin, but He fulfilled all righteousness. Christ perfectly obeyed in every way, so He was raised from the dead, and we were raised in Him because He has perfectly fulfilled the righteousness of the law. There is no condemnation—both because Christ bore the penalty for sin, and because His perfect righteousness is accounted to us. In both ways, there is no condemnation to those who are in Christ Jesus. There should not be any hint of condemnation in our thinking. Christ died, He bore away our sins in dying, and He fully and perfectly obeyed. In Him, His righteousness is imputed to us. **"Therefore, there is now no condemnation"** (v. 1a). Nothing can shake the finished work of Christ on the cross. Nothing can shake His perfect righteousness.

The Ruling Principle: Life According to the Spirit

"Therefore, there is now no condemnation for those who are in Christ Jesus" (v. 1)—for those **"who do not live according to the sinful nature but according to the Spirit"** (v. 4b). That is how we *know* we are in

Christ Jesus: we are no longer living according to that sinful nature. We are not saying the sinful nature is not there, remaining in us; the remnants of that nature is in us, but we are not controlled by the sinful nature. It is no longer the ruling principle in our lives, because we have been made alive in Christ. That new principle of life is the ruling principle. However much it may conflict with the old nature and succumb at times, the principle of life is there, remains there, and continues alive—and that which is alive grows, and that which grows pushes back the death that is in us. This is so **"that the righteous requirement of the law might be fully met in us"**—we, **"who do not live according to the sinful nature but according to the Spirit"** (v. 4). That is the great work of our Lord Jesus Christ. His very name, Christ, means *Anointed One* in Greek and *Messiah* in Hebrew. The Holy Spirit anoints Christ, and that Spirit by which He is anointed flows down on us. Remember the oil that is poured on Aaron's head; it flows down his beard, down to the very edge of his garment.[7] So, in Christ, we have the Holy Spirit. In Acts 1:4, Jesus said to wait in Jerusalem until the Spirit comes, and the Spirit came in His fullness on the Day of Pentecost. He was present before, but He came in His fullness to enable us to be witnesses to the ends of the earth.

THE TWO WAYS AND THE WORD OF GOD:
Autonomy, Hostility, and Death Versus Submission, Peace, and Life

In verses 5–8, Paul contrasts the way of the new covenant and the way of the old covenant. And please do not identify the new covenant simply with the New Testament; the new covenant is to be identified with the covenant of grace in contrast to the covenant of works made with Adam. The Old Testament is the old administration of the covenant of grace. The New Testament is the new administration of the covenant of grace.[8] **"Those who live according to the sinful nature have their minds set on what that nature desires"** (v. 5a). Paul is contrasting the two ways: the covenant of works—the sinful nature leading to death— and the covenant of grace—the way of the Spirit in us, leading to life.

---

7. *Psalm 133:2.*

8. Gangadean, *The Westminster Confession,* 111–120.

Those who live according to the sinful nature are still operating under the covenant of works. The sinful nature leading to death is man living independently of God, as man in Adam, determining good and evil for himself. That is the sinful nature: it is the autonomous man, living apart from God, determining good and evil for himself.

"Those who live according to the sinful nature have their minds set on what that nature desires; but those who live in accordance with the Spirit have their minds set on what the Spirit desires" (v. 5). There are desires that surface in us when we think of ourselves apart from God—independent of God, as if we were God. Whatever desires come about in our thinking of ourselves apart from God is what we seek to please. We seek whatever happens to please us—whatever floats up to our consciousness that we desire—whether it is a relationship, or a thing, or a place. These desires, thought of apart from God's purpose, apart from the goal that God has set before us, are where the sinful nature sets its mind and heart. "But those who live in accordance with the Spirit have their minds set on what the Spirit desires" (v. 5b). Now the Spirit has given to us the Word of God. The Scripture speaks about the Ten Commandments as that Word, the summary of what God requires.[9] So those who live in accordance with the Spirit have their minds set on what the Spirit desires—and what the Spirit desires is what is given to us in the Word, the law of God. Those who live in accordance with the Spirit delight in that law. We have the contrast between man's desire as he thinks of himself apart from God, and the desire of that new nature, which is recreated in us by the Spirit. In that new nature, we are brought to acknowledge the Word of God in all of life. Paul is contrasting these two ways.

"The mind of sinful man is death, but the mind controlled by the Spirit is life and peace" (v. 6). He speaks of the way of the law of the Spirit of life, which brings us life and peace. The sinful nature under the covenant of works brings death, because "the sinful mind is hostile to God. It does not submit to God's law, nor can it do so" (v. 7). Those controlled by the sinful nature cannot please God. The sinful mind is hostile because we have set ourselves in a position that God has reserved for Himself—we have put ourselves in the place of God. So when God comes to us, as He did to Adam in the Garden,

---

9. Gangadean, *The Westminster Catechisms*, 215–225.

we will have fear, hostility, and defensiveness; we will accuse God and clear ourselves. The remnants of the sinful nature remain in us. That old, fallen, Edenic nature; the autonomous man putting himself in the place of God—that mind is hostile to God. It is not neutral; it is hostile. We are against God; we resist God. There is an active opposition. Whatever reminds man of God, he cannot stand; he wants to blot it out. He wants to blot out even the reminder of his autonomous rebellion against God. That is the sinful nature. That is the mind that is hostile to God, and it certainly does not submit to God's law. It is autonomous: *auto-nomos*—where we are a law unto ourselves. The term *nomos* refers to law, *auto* meaning self. Autonomous man is a law unto himself; he does whatever he pleases. God may do whatever He pleases because He is God—and being infinitely good, wise, just, and holy, He is pleased to do what is good, wise, just, and holy. But we cannot put ourselves in the place of God to do whatever we please, apart from God.

"The sinful mind is hostile to God. It does not submit to God's law, nor can it do so" (v. 7). The law of God is always directing us toward God. And when we put ourselves in the place of God, we cannot submit to God's law. Those controlled by the sinful nature cannot please God. That whole way of life that controlled us before we came to Christ was not pleasing to God and cannot be pleasing to God. Paul says, **"Those controlled by the sinful nature cannot please God"** (v. 8). The autonomous life cannot please God. When man is a law unto himself, when man is the determiner of good and evil, when man has eaten of the tree of the knowledge of good and evil, which means to determine good and evil for oneself apart from God, man cannot be pleasing to God. God cannot delight in falsehood. God cannot delight in all the uncleanness that grows out of falsehood, which sometimes grows to the point of vileness; God cannot be pleased by that way of life. **"The law of the Spirit of life set me free from the law of sin and death"** (v. 2)—death which comes from the sinful nature operating under the covenant of works.

THE SPIRIT BRINGS LIFE TO OUR
SPIRITS AND OUR BODIES:
Regeneration, Ruling, and Resurrection

"You, however, are controlled not by the sinful nature but by the Spirit, if the Spirit of God lives in you" (v. 9a). When the Spirit of God comes to live in us, He takes a ruling position; He regenerates us, first of all, brings us back to life, and He rules in us, in that new life. The Spirit becomes controlling. It is not just that the new life is there and somehow, left to itself, it succeeds. Even that new life can only succeed as the Spirit of God enables it. That is why Paul says, "**You, however, are controlled not by the sinful nature but by the Spirit, if the Spirit of God lives in you**" (v. 9a). It is the Spirit who regenerates us, lives in us, and upholds that new life. Remember, it was the upholding of that life that made the difference between continuing in righteousness or not. When God left Adam to himself, without a fallen nature, Adam turned away. We must have that upholding of the Spirit of God in us to enable us to be obedient. "**And if anyone does not have the Spirit of Christ, he does not belong to Christ**" (v. 9b). If we acknowledge Christ, we do so by the Spirit, and so we belong to Christ, and the Spirit will be in us.

"**But if Christ is in you, your body is dead because of sin, yet your spirit is alive because of righteousness**" (v. 10). Look at some of the benefits that come to us because of this new covenant. When Paul says, "**your body is dead because of sin**" (v. 10a), some have thought this to be the old nature merely. But I think in this context, it needs to be understood as the physical body. Your body is dead because of sin; that is, you will die physically because of sin, the sin that remains in us. God uses physical death that remains in our body as a call back to repentance to enable us to grow in righteousness. "**But if Christ is in you, your body is dead because of sin, yet your spirit is alive because of righteousness**" (v. 10b). Though our bodies will die, this law of the Spirit of life gives life in our spirit, because He enables us to obey the Word of God, and that life grows and grows as He enables us to obey His Word. So our spirit is no longer dead, and there is the benefit of justification, the law of the Spirit of life. We should not consider, though our bodies die, that our spirits are not alive. He says, "**And if the Spirit of him who raised Jesus from the dead is living in you, he who raised**

Christ from the dead will also give life to your mortal bodies through his Spirit who lives in you" (v. 11). That is why we think this passage requires us to think of it as a physical body. He "will also give life to your mortal bodies through his Spirit, who lives in you" (v. 11). So yes, the body will die, but that body will be raised from the dead by the Spirit. Here is the law of the Spirit of life, bringing life where there was once death. It brings life in our spirit now, which is increasing, and life in that our bodies will be raised from the dead. This is the blessing of the covenant of grace.

THE SPIRIT-EMPOWERED OBLIGATION:
Putting to Death the Old Way by the Life-Giving Understanding of the Word

In light of the life-giving power of the Spirit, Paul says, "Therefore, brothers, we have an obligation—but it is not to the sinful nature, to live according to it. For if you live according to the sinful nature, you will die, but if by the Spirit you put to death the misdeeds of the body, you will live" (vv. 12–13). These two ways are mutually exclusive. The more one increases, the more the other must decrease. If we live by the sinful nature, it will result in death, but if we live by the Spirit, this will require us to "put to death the misdeeds of the body." As it says in Galatians 5:24, "Those who belong to Christ Jesus have crucified the sinful nature with its passions and desires." We crucify those passions and desires by the Spirit, as the Spirit enables us to have *new* desires, in Christ. The Spirit enables us not only to know what we ought to do, but the Spirit enables us to see God. And in seeing God, we are transformed into His image, and we are enabled, in seeing God, with a new desire, to set aside the old desire. And in denying the old desire, we put to death, or crucify, the remnants of that old nature.

We have an obligation not to live by the remnants of the sinful nature that remains, but to live by the Spirit, and living by the Spirit requires us to put to death that old desire. Think about the many habits, thoughts, attitudes, and desires that come from our past and our particular tradition, and how these still continue in us. Then, think about the desire to live by the Word of God and to take every thought captive.[10] All those old beliefs and the desires connected with them are to be put to death. That is why it says later on in Romans, "I beseech you therefore, brethren, by the mercies of God, that you present your bodies a living sacrifice, holy, acceptable to God, which is your reasonable service. And do not be conformed to this world, but be transformed by the renewing of your mind" (Rom. 12:1–2a NKJV). The 'world,' for each one of us, is our particular background. And not just our background, but our individual patterns, our individual psychology, and the things that we lived by before we were brought to Christ and made to live by His Word. All those things that we trusted in must be put away.

So Paul says, "**But if by the Spirit you put to death the misdeeds of the body, you will live**" (v. 13b). We cannot put to death what remains of the old nature apart from being empowered by the Holy Spirit. If we try to do self-reform, it will not work, but if enabled by the Spirit to understand God's Word and obey it, we can put to death that old way of life. It is that old way of life that is a source of all the tensions in our lives. If you have tension in your life, tension with others, you can trace it back to the old nature, living by the old patterns, and that is what has to be put to death. You may say, 'I've known this way for so long; it is so near and dear to me; I cherish it; it is the darling of my heart; it has served me so well.' No, it did not serve you well. It produced death in you apart from Christ. We have to *crucify* this 'little darling of our hearts' that we are so fond of. We have to crucify many of those longings that we have developed apart from the Word of God, things that made us feel good about ourselves apart from Christ. There is great beauty in the way of the Lord, and there is great beauty and strength in holiness. But that beauty in holiness is not the same as worldly beauty. We need to put that aside.

We have an obligation always to reject the old nature. There will be a lot of renewal that needs to happen. It will feel, to the old nature, like a crucifixion. And that is exactly what it is. You have to recognize it for what it is and cast it out. King Saul did not kill Agag when God sent Saul to fight against that nation, but he spared him. Saul was easy on the old nature. There was something in Agag that Saul connected with in himself, and Saul could not deal with it in himself, therefore,

---

10. *2 Corinthians 10:4–5.*

he could not deal with Agag. But when Agag was brought to Samuel, Samuel put Agag to death.[11] We have an obligation to live by the Spirit and, in doing so, put to death the misdeeds of the body.

"**Because those who are led by the Spirit of God are sons of God**" (v. 14). Being led by the Spirit of God is not some mystical leading; the Spirit of God leads and enables us to understand His Word more and more, to make applications of His Word, to discern circumstances, to make godly judgments in those circumstances, and have a sense of peace in those circumstances. One of the privileges that is ours because of this new covenant of life is that we have the Spirit, and having the Spirit, we are sons of God, and we have the privilege of sonship.

THE SPIRIT AND PRIVILEGE OF SONSHIP:
From Slaves to Children to Heirs

The Root of Our Fear

Having the Spirit of God and the privilege of sonship is contrasted in verse 15 with being a slave. "**For you did not receive a spirit that makes you a slave again to fear**" (v. 15a). Remember, when God came to Adam, Adam hid himself from God because he was afraid. Whenever we are walking in the flesh, and the Word of God comes to us, or someone who would speak the Word of God comes to us, we feel that fear. That is how the flesh naturally responds. We have to discern whether that fear comes from our old sinful nature because we are yielding to that sinful nature. We should not have that fear if we are walking in God. We should not affirm our fear by saying to ourselves that we should not feel afraid, and then reject the Word of God. Rather, we should say that we should not feel afraid, and then put aside our sinful nature and all that the sinful nature is holding on to that makes us feel afraid. Many of us who are tuned in to the feelings—and not the cause of the feeling—will feel that fear, and will think, rightly, that we should not have that fear. But by not understanding the cause of the fear, we will deal with the fear improperly. We often deal with it by rejecting the Word of God, or rejecting the person speaking that Word, rather than seeing that the fear is coming out of our old sinful nature and we need

---

11. *1 Samuel 15.*

to put to death the sinful nature. That is where a lot of the war comes. You might reject, or put to death, so to speak, the one speaking the Word of God, or you might put to death the old sinful nature out of which this fear is coming. We have to learn, by the Spirit of God, to put to death those things in us that seem so close, so much a part of our intimate, interior life.

Enabled to See God as Our Father

"For you did not receive a spirit that makes you a slave again to fear, but you received the Spirit of sonship. And by him we cry, 'Abba, Father'" (v. 15). The fact that we can speak to God and come to God and call Him our Father is because the Spirit is in us and working in us. We cannot take it for granted that we can just come to God and call Him our Father. Our Creator is one thing, but our Father—that is a very close, intimate, personal relationship. By what right can we come before the Creator of heaven and earth and say, 'You are our Father'? The fact that we are His creatures does not simply make Him our Father. By Him, by the Spirit, we cry, **"'Abba, Father.' The Spirit himself testifies with our spirit that we are God's children"** (v. 16). So there is an internal working of the Spirit of God within us that enables us to see that God is our Father.

Inheriting All the Graces of Christ

Here are further blessings of being sons and having no condemnation, but rather, life. **"Now if we are children, then we are heirs—heirs of God and co-heirs with Christ"** (v. 17a). I do not have much money to pass on to my children. I have a spiritual heritage to pass on to my children, but that is because it has been given to me by Christ. All who are in Christ will have an inheritance directly from God. That spiritual inheritance does not come to God's grandchildren; God has no grandchildren; He has only children. That inheritance comes from God through Christ because He is the Son, and we are adopted in Him; we are co-heirs with Christ. He is going to inherit everything, the whole universe, and we are heirs with Him. The property that we have now, that we think we can pass on, is *nothing* compared with the grand inheritance that is ours in Christ. All things are ours in Christ.

We not only inherit the creation, but most of all, we inherit all the graces of Christ that are given to His people. All of you are given, by God's grace, to me, and we are given to each other in this way. Now, that is a great blessing. There may be trouble right now because sin remains in us, but we will possess, in Christ, the glory of God's grace in each of us. God's inheritance is in His people, and that is forever. We may not always get along with one another now quite the way we should, but we can trust that by God's grace, it will improve, and we will have that inheritance. So we are heirs with Christ.

Christ brings about the fullness of His inheritance through His work on the cross. Christ continues to suffer in His union with us, with the members of His body. **"Now if we are children, then we are heirs—heirs of God and co-heirs with Christ, if indeed we share in his sufferings in order that we may also share in his glory"** (v. 17). That is the way we come into the fullness of His inheritance. Paul says we are to fill up in ourselves the sufferings of Jesus Christ.[12] As we, in His name, go out to speak the Word, we suffer. We sometimes suffer contempt and insult from others and sometimes deprivation in the process of doing His work. That is the sufferings of Christ. If we share in the suffering, we shall also share in the glory.

THE HOPE OF THE FULLNESS OF SALVATION:
The Removal of All Sin and All Its Effects

Paul opens up this sharing of suffering in verse 18: **"I consider that our present sufferings are not worth comparing with the glory that will be revealed in us."** Then he tells us something of the extent of the glory that will be revealed in us.

> **The creation waits in eager expectation for the sons of God to be revealed. For the creation was subjected to frustration, not by its own choice, but by the will of the one who subjected it, in hope that the creation itself will be liberated from its bondage to decay and brought into the glorious freedom of the children of God** (vv. 19–21).

---

12. *Colossians 1:24.*

"The creation waits in eager expectation for the sons of God to be revealed." As we come into the fullness of our sonship, into mature sonship, as we deal with the sin remaining in us and in the world, the bondage to which the creation was subjected, the curse on the ground and on the creatures, will be removed. We have seen this teaching in many other places. Isaiah says that the wolf will lie down with the lamb when the earth is filled with the knowledge of God as the waters cover the sea.[13] That is part of our inheritance. We are not going to inherit a world that is under a curse any longer. We will inherit a world that is liberated from the curse in every way. The creation is waiting on us. The birds and the fish and the beasts are waiting on us. The trees, plants, and flowers are waiting on us, the people of God, to deal with moral evil so that natural evil may be removed. That is part of what we will inherit; we are going to inherit a creation where the curse is removed. There is an intimate connection between what we do and the creation being liberated.

> We know that the whole creation has been groaning as in the pains of childbirth right up to the present time. Not only so, but we ourselves, who have the firstfruits of the Spirit, groan inwardly as we wait eagerly for our adoption as sons, the redemption of our bodies (vv. 22–23).

Our adoption will be completed when our bodies are raised from the dead. That will be the completion of the work of redemption. We have this hope. Life is promised. The law of the Spirit of life will extend to removing all the effects of sin in creation, and it will extend to removing death in our bodies, and we have this hope. "For in this hope we were saved" (v. 24a). We have this hope fixed in our minds; we have this hope as a helmet of salvation. We dare not forget this hope that God is going to bring about the fullness of His salvation in the earth being filled with the knowledge of God and all the curse being lifted and death itself being removed. In this hope, we are saved. We are not saved in the hope of just dying and going to heaven. That is not the hope that is spoken of here. It is the hope that the *creation* will be liberated from bondage, and our bodies will be raised from the dead

---

13. *Isaiah 11:6–9.*

as a consummation of the removal of sin and its effects. It is this hope that we have, as a helmet of salvation, that saves us. It does not save us in the sense of justification, but it brings us more and more fully into the completion of the work. **"But hope that is seen is no hope at all. Who hopes for what he already has? But if we hope for what we do not yet have, we wait for it patiently"** (vv. 24b–25). We have this hope in us. By this hope, we are saved. That is, by this hope and the endurance that comes by this hope, we persevere in the work, are enabled to do the work, and complete the work. In the same way, the Spirit helps us in our weakness. How far does this work of the Spirit of life work? It works in the depth of our innermost being.

LONGING FOR THIS FULLNESS:
The Spirit Enables Our Prayers Through Groans

"In the same way, the Spirit helps us in our weakness. We do not know what we ought to pray for, but the Spirit himself intercedes for us with groans that words cannot express" (v. 26). These are not groanings of the Spirit but something produced by the Spirit as the Spirit works in us. We do not sometimes know what to pray for in particular, but the Spirit works in us to create new desires and new longings, and these new longings come to expression as a groaning—a waiting for the fullness of redemption. We are longing for fullness. The One who searches the hearts of men, the only One who can, God, sees these longings deep within us, produced in us by the Spirit. It is those longings that God hears in our prayers, and He answers. Can you get any deeper in terms of the working of the Spirit? The Spirit helps us in our weaknesses. We do not know what we ought to pray, but the Spirit Himself intercedes for us with groans that words cannot express. **"And he who searches our hearts knows the mind of the Spirit, because the Spirit intercedes for the saints in accordance with God's will"** (v. 27). The Spirit of life is working in us according to the new covenant. I think perhaps we should pause; I do not think we can rush through the remainder of the chapter. Let us turn to Psalm 139A.[14] God searches us and knows us.

---

14. *The Book of Psalms for Singing.*

11

Christ's Victory and Ours
Crossing the Finish Line

2011

Romans 8:28–39

28And we know that in all things God works for the good of those who love him, who have been called according to his purpose. 29For those God foreknew he also predestined to be conformed to the likeness of his Son, that he might be the firstborn among many brothers. 30And those he predestined, he also called; those he called, he also justified; those he justified, he also glorified.

31What, then, shall we say in response to this? If God is for us, who can be against us? 32He who did not spare his own Son, but gave him up for us all—how will he not also, along with him, graciously give us all things? 33Who will bring any charge against those whom God has chosen? It is God who justifies. 34Who is he that condemns? Christ Jesus, who died—more than that, who was raised to life—is at the right hand of God and is also interceding for us. 35Who shall separate us from the love of Christ? Shall trouble or hardship or persecution or famine or nakedness or danger or sword? 36As it is written:

"For your sake we face death all day long;
   we are considered as sheep to be slaughtered."

37No, in all these things we are more than conquerors through him who loved us. 38For I am convinced that neither death nor life, neither angels nor demons, neither the present nor the future, nor any powers, 39neither height nor depth, nor anything else in all creation, will be able to separate us from the love of God that is in Christ Jesus our Lord.

INTRODUCTION

OUR FOCUS TODAY IS CONNECTING CHRIST'S victory and ours. While we speak about Christ's victory in the past, our victory is in the present. While we sometimes speak of Christ's victory as connected to the resurrection, our victory is also certainly connected to it. But I want to clarify something in the message today concerning that victory. It is not quite where we tend to locate it. A mislocation of the victory can have serious, if not disastrous, consequences for us.

HOPE AND VICTORY VERSUS SHAME

In connection with victory, there is hope. And we hope that we will overcome. Hope stands in contrast to shame. So, while hope is connected to victory, it is also contrasted with shame. Keep in mind the Scripture Reading we just read: **"In all these things we are more than conquerors through him who loved us"** (v. 37). *There* is the theme of victory. In Romans 5:5, the point is made concerning hope: "And hope does not disappoint us, because God has poured out his love into our hearts by the Holy Spirit, whom he has given us." In Romans 10:11, it is written: "As the Scripture says, 'Anyone who trusts in him will never be put to shame.'" In reflecting on these passages, we are trying to make the connection between hope and victory and hope versus shame. In 1 Peter 2:6, this point is made again: "See, I lay a stone in Zion, a chosen and precious cornerstone, and the one who trusts in him will never be put to shame." The disaster that comes is when our hope is not located properly. A slight change in the location of that hope can make the difference between shame and victory. So, we want to speak about Christ's victory—and ours.

Deliverance *in* Our Trials Versus Deliverance *from* Our Trials

Where I am going with this is to make the distinction between deliverance *in* our trials versus deliverance *from* our trials. This deliverance is connected with the resurrection life of Christ. The Call to Worship referred to these words: "to him who overcomes, I will give the right to sit with me on my throne, just as I overcame and sat down with my Father on his throne" (Rev. 3:21). Christ has overcome and is seated on his Father's throne. As we overcome, we are seated with Christ on the throne. That overcoming is connected with the resurrection life.

To be delivered in our trials requires us to endure—to *persevere*. Jesus said, "But he who endures to the end will be saved" (Matt. 10:22b NKJV). Of Christ, it is said that "he endured the cross, scorning its shame, and sat down at the right hand of the throne of God" (Heb. 12:2b). Paul, in 2 Corinthians 11:23–28, speaks of his endurance through many trials. And he speaks again of his afflictions in 2 Timothy: "What persecutions I endured" (2 Tim. 3:11 KJV).

I am going to look at Christ's affliction, Christ's endurance, and Christ's completion of the work. Then I am going to look at Paul's afflictions, Paul's endurance, and Paul's completion of the work. And then we are going to look at our afflictions, our endurance, and our completion of the work. So first, Christ's affliction and completion of the work of redemption.

CHRIST'S FINISH LINE:
"It Is Finished"

This week, I had the opportunity to speak about Christ's arrest, trial, crucifixion, burial, and then His resurrection, ascension, and session at the right hand of God. I gave some attention to Christ's death on the cross—His words and the sequence of those words—and I tried to order them, and paid close attention to some of the details about that.

I am looking now particularly at the words recorded in John 19:28–30.

> Later, knowing that all was now completed, and so that the Scripture would be fulfilled, Jesus said, "I am thirsty." A jar of wine vinegar was there, so they soaked a sponge in it, put the sponge on a stalk of the hyssop plant, and lifted it to Jesus' lips. When he had received the drink, Jesus said, "It is finished." With that, he bowed his head and gave up his spirit.

Very likely, the first words of Jesus on the cross were His prayer for His tormentors: "Father, forgive them; for they know not what they do" (Lk. 23:34a KJV). Probably in connection with that prayer, the thief on the cross saw, and heard, and turned. He spoke to Christ, saying, "Jesus, remember me when you come into your kingdom" (Lk. 23:42b). At first both thieves were reviling Him, but something happened, and one of them turned. Then Jesus, in concern for the thief, said, "I tell you the truth, today you will be with me in paradise" (Lk. 23:43b). Then, between the next two statements, Jesus turned to his mother and said, "Dear woman, here is your son," and to John, "Here is your mother" (Jn. 19:26b, 27a). Then Jesus cried out: "My God, my God, why have you forsaken me?" (Matt. 27:46b). After this, "knowing that all was now completed, and so that the Scripture would be fulfilled, Jesus said, 'I am thirsty'" (Jn. 19:28). The Scripture being fulfilled here is this: "They put gall in my food and gave me vinegar for my thirst" (Ps. 69:21). They gave Him the vinegar, and when that had happened, then He said, "It is finished" (Jn. 19:30a). It was at that point, I believe, that Christ crossed the finish line—when He said, "It is finished"—in that final sequence of events as He hung on the cross. And then it says, "With that, he bowed his head and gave up his spirit" (Jn. 19:30b). There is one other reference that was spoken. He said, "Father, into your hands I commit my spirit" (Lk. 23:46a). These were His last words on the cross. Though He had cried out, "Why have you forsaken me?" (Matt. 27:46b), in the midst of that cry, He affirmed His faith by saying, "My God, my God." He affirmed His relationship to God—not merely "my God," but my Father[1]—and He committed His spirit to Him.

Jesus Triumphed Over the Principalities and Powers on the Cross

There are some details we should bring into further focus. It was in connection with His death, at this point, that Scripture records the event that the veil of the temple was torn in two, from top to bottom. This is mentioned in Matthew, Mark, and Luke.[2] Twice, it is emphasized that the veil was torn "from top to bottom," showing that the old order was completed. Sin had been atoned for. The way into the Most Holy Place had been opened. God Himself opened the way, and He signified that by rending the veil—the symbol of separation—in two. That is why we say it was *at that time* the work was completed. It was at that time—at the ninth hour, around three o'clock in the afternoon—that these events

---

1. *Luke 23:26.*
2. *Matthew 27:51; Mark 15:38; Luke 23:45.*

occurred.[3] From the sixth to the ninth hour, darkness covered the land.[4] When the veil was torn, there was an earthquake. The rocks were split, and many tombs broke open. The bodies of holy people who had died were raised to life.[5] It was at that time that the centurion saw and felt the earthquake. It was at that time that the dead came forth. It was at that time that the work was finished. It was at that time that the victory was accomplished. Jesus triumphed over the principalities and powers on the cross—not when He rose from the grave. Colossians 2:15 says, "And having disarmed the powers and authorities, he made a public spectacle of them, triumphing over them by the cross." All the things that stood against us—all the regulations and ordinances—were nailed with Him to the cross.[6]

Jesus Humbled Himself Unto Death

Paul said of Jesus that "he humbled himself and became obedient to death—even death on a cross! *Therefore* God exalted him to the highest place and gave him the name that is above every name" (Phil. 2:8b–9).[7] The exaltation was because He had accomplished that obedience, even to death on the cross.

Now Is the Crisis of This World[8]

As He approached the cross, Jesus said, "Now is the time for judgment on this world; now the prince of this world will be driven out" (Jn. 12:31). The crisis of this world was upon Him. It was on the cross that this triumph occurred. He was raised because He had been obedient. He was raised because He had triumphed.

---

3. *Matthew 27:46, 50.*

4. *Luke 23:44.*

5. *Matthew 27:51–52.*

6. *Colossians 2:14.*

7. Emphasis added.

8. Gangadean, *The Gospel of Matthew,* 329–347.

Jesus Was Hated Without a Cause

Jesus said, "They hated me without reason" (Jn. 15:25b). The world, the kingdom of this world, the kingdom of darkness, and the prince of this world—"the spirit who is now at work in those who are disobedient" (Eph. 2:2b)—oppose Him still. This opposition works through the lie and the falsehood—ever since the Garden of Eden, even until now. In John 3:19–20, Jesus said, "This is the verdict: Light has come into the world, but men loved darkness instead of light because their deeds were evil. Everyone who does evil hates the light, and will not come into the light for fear that his deeds will be exposed."

John 1:4–5 says, "In him was life, and that life was the light of all mankind. The light shines in the darkness, and the darkness has not overcome it." *There* is that victory that is spoken of. He continued to hold to that truth and exemplified it in His life—the truth of who God is, that He is to be obeyed even unto death. That light—that very light—shines in all of us. And the darkness cannot overcome it. It *has not* overcome it. It *will not* overcome it.

"I Have Overcome the World"

Jesus said in John 16:33, "In this world you will have trouble. But take heart! I have overcome the world." He is victorious over it, and He was victorious on the cross. So Jesus crossed that finish line when He said, "It is finished" (Jn. 19:30). And the context and the particular sequence of what He said confirms it. When He said those words, He had accomplished the work.

PAUL'S FINISH LINE:
Fought the Good Fight, Kept the Faith, and Finished the Race

Paul also saw this finish line to be crossed. In 2 Timothy 4:6, seeing his death draw near, he said, "For I am already being poured out like a drink offering, and the time has come for my departure." Remember the drink offerings, and look at Paul's application of it here. These are the words of the apostle. What words are going through his mind? What is he thinking? These are his words: "I have fought the good fight, I have finished the race, I have kept the faith" (2 Tim. 4:7). He anticipates what is to come. In connection with his finishing, he says,

"Now there is in store for me the crown of righteousness, which the Lord, the righteous Judge, will award to me on that day—and not only to me, but also to all who have longed for his appearing" (2 Tim. 4:8). Jesus said, "But he who endures to the end will be saved" (Matt. 10:22b NKJV). Paul had gone through much—a *great* deal. Even at that moment, he was in chains. We will speak about what Paul went through and how he endured all things. He said, I have endured all things.[9] There is a race. There is a finish line. You know the difference between not reaching the finish line and reaching the finish line. And you know when you reach it, you can say, 'It is finished.' There is very *definitely* a finish line. There is very definitely a finishing. As Jesus said, "It is finished" (Jn. 19:30), so Paul is saying, "I have finished the race, I have kept the faith" (2 Tim. 4:7b).

There are many things that would tear at us—things that seek to rip us apart as we go through life. I must say, the tearing increases as you go along. It does not get easier. There were many moments when Paul could have been torn apart—many places where he could have turned back. That tearing could have led to troubling thoughts: 'Perhaps I am forsaken. Where is the love of God?' But Paul did not doubt the love of God. He said, "I have kept the faith." Jesus said, "But he who endures to the end will be saved" (Matt. 10:22b NKJV).

Paul in Chains: The Word of God Is Not Bound

Paul was in chains, but he said, "God's word is not chained" (2 Tim. 2:9b). It was while he was in chains that he did his most fruitful work. It was while he was in chains that he wrote many of his letters.[10] What endures is the Word of God. Paul saw this. Instead of thinking he would be delivered *from* his chains, Paul was delivered *in* his chains.

There is something about this Word of God. It seems so light, so ephemeral—almost like something that the wind could blow away. Yet of this Word it is said, "The grass withers and the flowers fall, but the word of our God endures forever" (Is. 40:8). Jesus spoke of this in a

---

9. *2 Timothy 2:10* KJV.

10. Reformed scholars generally agree that Ephesians, Philippians, Colossians, and Philemon were written during Paul's first Roman imprisonment (A.D. 60–62), while 2 Timothy was written during a later imprisonment shortly before his death (A.D. 64–67), though it is not typically grouped with the Prison Epistles.

very special way. When pronouncing judgment on the house of Israel, He said, "Look, your house is left to you desolate" (Matt. 23:38). He also said, "That the blood of all the prophets which was shed from the foundation of the world may be required of this generation, from the blood of Abel to the blood of Zechariah . . . Yes, I say to you, it shall be required" (Lk. 11:50–51 NKJV). That Word of God is not merely repeated; it is *cumulative*. And it is passed down. Each generation is responsible for what has been said before, what has been added, and what has been passed on. So all of that cumulative understanding was being required of that generation, Jesus said. That is the Word of God that endures. That is the Word of God spoken of by Paul. It is the same Word spoken of when it is said, "They overcame him by the blood of the Lamb and by the word of their testimony" (Rev. 12:11a). It is spoken of as "the word of God and the testimony of Jesus Christ" (Rev. 1:2b). That Word is the means by which we overcome. We keep the faith. We fight the good fight, to the end, testifying to the truth of God—the Word of God that has come down to us, accumulated from the Garden of Eden to the present day. And we should say that it has not stopped with the Book of Revelation—in the sense that the Scripture is completed and not to be added to, but the work of the Holy Spirit in enabling us to understand the things of the Word of God, spoken through Christ and all the prophets, continues. Jesus said, "But when he, the Spirit of truth, comes, he will guide you into all truth" (Jn. 16:13a).[11] That is what it means to fight the good fight, to finish the race, to keep the faith.

Running with Perseverance While Endangered Every Hour and Dying Daily

Paul was very aware of the conflict, and he spoke of it in 1 Corinthians 15:30–32 in connection with the resurrection:

> And as for us, why do we endanger ourselves every hour? I die every day—I mean that, brothers—just as surely as I glory over you in Christ Jesus our Lord. If I fought wild beasts in Ephesus for merely human reasons, what have I gained? If the dead are not raised, "Let us eat and drink, for tomorrow we die."

11. Gangadean, *The Westminster Confession*, xix–xxix, 349–351.

Paul is saying: the conflict is *every hour*. He says, "I die every day." This is not something occasional; it is *every day*. It is connected with taking up our cross *daily* and following Him.[12]

Paul speaks of his sufferings again in 2 Corinthians 11:23–26. Though reluctant to boast, he lists his afflictions:

> I have worked much harder, been in prison more frequently, been flogged more severely, and been exposed to death again and again. Five times I received from the Jews the forty lashes minus one. Three times I was beaten with rods, once I was stoned, three times I was shipwrecked, I spent a night and a day in the open sea, I have been constantly on the move. I have been in danger from rivers, in danger from bandits, in danger from my own countrymen, in danger from Gentiles; in danger in the city, in danger in the country, in danger at sea; and in danger from false brothers."

Every hour. Daily. Paul said, "I endured all things."[13] This is what it means to run with perseverance the race set before us.[14]

Always Bearing the Dying of the Lord Jesus, That His Life May Also Be Revealed in Our Body

In 2 Corinthians 4, Paul gives us this reflection: "We are hard pressed on every side, but not crushed; perplexed, but not in despair; persecuted, but not abandoned; struck down, but not destroyed. We always carry around in our body the death of Jesus, so that the life of Jesus may also be revealed in our body" (2 Cor. 4:8–10). There is the resurrection life. As Paul faces danger every hour, dying daily, he is *always* carrying around in his body the dying of the Lord Jesus, so that the life of Jesus may be revealed. "Because we know that the one who raised the Lord Jesus from the dead will also raise us with Jesus and present us with you in his presence" (2 Cor. 4:14). Paul's answer to this daily dying, every hour being in danger, is to find the resurrection life of Christ at work in him.

---

12. *Luke 9:23; Matthew 16:24; Mark 8:34.*

13. *2 Timothy 2:10* KJV.

14. *Hebrews 12:1.*

Do Not Be Ashamed: Partake in Christ's Afflictions

Paul understood that others might see him in his weakness and affliction and despise him. They despised Jesus as He hung on the cross, but He did not hide his face from mocking and spitting.[15] He "endured the cross, scorning its shame" (Heb. 12:2). Mocking and spitting is the way of the world—He overcame the world. And the means by which He overcomes the world is through faith. "This is the victory that has overcome the world, even our faith" (1 Jn. 5:4b).

In 2 Timothy, Paul says, "So do not be ashamed to testify about our Lord, or ashamed of me his prisoner. But join with me in suffering for the gospel, by the power of God, who has saved us" (2 Tim. 1:8–9a). There is a sense that when someone is suffering, it is easy for that person to think they are forsaken by God. And when someone is suffering, it is even easier for others to think he is forsaken. If a person becomes aware of what others are thinking, and gives it any credence, they may feel ashamed to speak the gospel. If we adopt that worldly point of view, we might say: 'Where is God? How can I speak of God when I am in this condition?' Paul is aware that Timothy might be thinking such things. So he said, "Do not be ashamed to testify about our Lord," and—notice—to testify "in suffering." These are related. One may testify without suffering, but here, Paul says, "Join with me in suffering for the gospel." We have to see this the way the Lord sees it, instead of being to our shame. Our suffering, in Christ, is not to be viewed as something to be ashamed of. I want to be careful, but it may rather be viewed as an *honor* to suffer in this way for Christ.

In last week's sermon, *The Will of God*,[16] we spoke about passive obedience and active obedience.[17] We pointed out that it is through the passive obedience of Christ that we are redeemed—that our sin is paid for. And so, sometimes we may not be actively suffering in the cause of Christ, but we are in Christ, and we are suffering, and we are obedient to Christ in that suffering. We are not to be ashamed, nor are we to shrink back from partaking in His afflictions.

---

15. *Isaiah 50:6.*

16. This sermon has not yet been published. The title and date have been included for historical record-keeping. *The Will of God* was preached on April 17, 2011.

17. Gangadean, *The Westminster Confession*, 127–128.

I Am Not Ashamed: I Know Whom I Have Believed

In 2 Timothy 1:10–12, Paul exhorts us to not be ashamed.

> But it has now been revealed through the appearing of our Savior, Christ Jesus, who has destroyed death and has brought life and immortality to light through the gospel. And of this gospel I was appointed a herald and an apostle and a teacher. That is why I am suffering as I am. *Yet* I am not ashamed, because I know whom I have believed, and am convinced that he is able to guard what I have entrusted to him for that day.[18]

Paul Desired to Be Conformed to the Death of Jesus

Paul wanted to be conformed to the death of Jesus; He wanted to know Him, and "the fellowship of His sufferings, being conformed to His death, if, by any means, I may attain to the resurrection from the dead" (Phil. 3:10a–11 NKJV). We should not minimize the affliction or Paul's subjective state. He said, "We stand in jeopardy every hour . . . I die daily" (1 Cor. 15:30b, 31b NKJV). How is Paul dealing with this? In 2 Corinthians 1:8–11, Paul explains:

> We do not want you to be uninformed, brothers, about the hardships we suffered in the province of Asia. We were under great pressure, far beyond our ability to endure, so that we despaired even of life. Indeed, in our hearts we felt the sentence of death. But this happened that we might not rely on ourselves but on God, who raises the dead. He has delivered us from such a deadly peril, and he will deliver us. On him we have set our hope that he will continue to deliver us, as you help us by your prayers.

We sometimes think God will not allow us to be tempted above what we can bear, so how is Paul saying this—"far beyond our ability to endure"? He said, "so that we despaired even of life." What if you met Paul at that moment, when he despaired even of life? What would you say to him? How would you comfort him? What would you think? It had reached that point. It is real—"the sentence of death." And it is equally real that there is the resurrection life.

---

18. Emphasis added.

OUR FINISH LINE:
Reigning with Christ as Heirs in the Kingdom

We may be tempted to think that with all of this, 'God will somehow, at the last minute, spare us, and deliver us from death.' Somewhere in the back of our minds, we may think that. We say we hope in God who raises the dead—but hope for what? This is the first question I asked at the beginning of the message. Let us then continue thinking about this by looking at our finish line. We saw Christ's finish line—it was as He hung on the cross and said, "It is finished" (Jn. 19:30). And what happened? The veil was torn in two, the rocks were split open, and the bodies of many holy people who had died came out of their tombs.[19] Paul said, "I have fought the good fight, I have finished the race, I have kept the faith" (2 Tim. 4:7). And what was Paul anticipating? What was Jesus anticipating as He hung on the cross? That somehow God would now remove Him from the cross and save Him from death? That would be a travesty of the faith. Was Paul expecting that God would now deliver him *from* death? He did not. He expected to be delivered *in* death.

To Him That Overcomes

As we heard in the Call to Worship: "To him who overcomes, I will give the right to sit with me on my throne, just as I overcame and sat down with my Father on his throne" (Rev. 3:21). Christ overcame, and He was seated. 1 John 5:4 says, "This is the victory that has overcome the world, even our faith." Romans 8:24 says, "We are saved by hope."[20] So what is this hope, and how does it connect with faith?

Nothing Can Separate Us from the Love of Christ

Let us now go to the text we read in Romans 8. What I want to focus on in this passage is that Paul says, "No . . ." And he says this in connection with what he had just asked: "**Who shall separate us from the love of Christ? Shall trouble or hardship or persecution or famine or nakedness or danger or sword?**" (v. 35). And whatever else you

---

19. *Matthew 27:51–52.*
20. KJV.

might imagine—any new category you might wish to add—if these are not sufficient, try to come up with something else. Paul's answer is emphatic: nothing in heaven or on earth "**will be able to separate us from the love of God that is in Christ Jesus our Lord**" (v. 39b). He continues: "**As it is written: 'For your sake we face death all day long; we are considered as sheep to be slaughtered'**" (v. 36). And as sheep, we are slaughtered. Then he says, "**No, in all these things we are more than conquerors through him who loved us**" (v. 37). *In all these things*—in "**trouble or hardship or persecution or famine or nakedness or danger or sword**"—Paul declares victory. Many of God's people have been slaughtered throughout history. Many of the saints. That is why the psalmist says, "We are considered as sheep to be slaughtered" (Ps. 44:22b).

I Will Fear No Evil, for Thou Art with Me

We have often sung Psalm 23. We know how we have been moved by this psalm, and how we have applied it. "Surely goodness and love will follow me all the days of my life, and I will dwell in the house of the LORD forever" (Ps. 23:6). This is true. But it also says, "Even though I walk through the valley of the shadow of death, I will fear no evil" (Ps. 23:4a). That is true. And it is not the case that halfway through that valley, we escape and do not die. We are going to die. And if we are living in Christ, we will die in Christ. How will we die in Christ? Will we die in the faith, not doubting the love of God in anything that comes to pass, but persevering to the end and keeping the faith—never doubting that love? I would say that is what it means for a Christian to die in dignity: to die, whatever the affliction, without doubting the love of God.[21]

Paul went through this. Our Lord Jesus went through this. He said, "Father, into your hands I commit my spirit" (Lk. 23:46a). Though He cried out earlier, "Why have you forsaken me?" (Matt. 27:46b), He continued on beyond that, to the point where He said, "It is finished" (Jn. 19:30), and then, "Father, into your hands I commit my spirit." There is no sense of any doubt in the mind of our Lord Jesus when He uttered those words. He is affirming the truth of what we read in

---

21. Gangadean, *On Natural and Revealed Theology,* 67–70.

Romans 8:38–39: that nothing separates us from the love of God. Nothing Paul mentioned—nor anything we can imagine. Paul intends to be all-encompassing in the strongest conceivable sense. He writes,

> For I am convinced that neither death nor life, neither angels nor demons, neither the present nor the future, nor any powers, neither height nor depth, nor anything else in all creation, will be able to separate us from the love of God that is in Christ Jesus our Lord.

The saints in Revelation "did not love their lives so much as to shrink from death" (Rev. 12:11b). Jesus exhorts the churches, "Be faithful, even to the point of death, and I will give you the crown of life" (Rev. 2:10b). And Revelation 20:4 says, "I saw the souls of those who had been beheaded because of their testimony for Jesus and because of the word of God." The enduring, eternal Word. Those are the ones who testified even in suffering—because of "the word of God and the testimony of Jesus Christ" (Rev. 1:2b).

And here, if I may, a poetic expression of hope—not the Word of God, but a human effort to speak of hope:

> "Hope" is the thing with feathers -
> That perches in the soul -
> And sings the tune without the words -
> And never stops - at all -
>
> And sweetest - in the Gale - is heard -
> And sore must be the storm -
> That could abash the little Bird
> That kept so many warm -
>
> I've heard it in the chillest land -
> And on the strangest Sea -
> Yet - never - in Extremity,
> It asked a crumb - of Me.[22]

Hope—in the Word of God.

---

22. Emily Dickinson, "'Hope' is the thing with feathers," in *The Complete Poems of Emily Dickinson*, ed. Thomas H. Johnson (Boston: Little, Brown, 1960), 254.

Believers Lived and Reigned with Him for a Thousand Years

I saw thrones on which were seated those who had been given authority to judge. And I saw the souls of those who had been beheaded because of their testimony for Jesus and because of the word of God. They had not worshiped the beast or his image and had not received his mark on their foreheads or their hands. They came to life and reigned with Christ a thousand years (Rev. 20:4).

"Blessed and holy are those who have part in the first resurrection. The second death has no power over them, but they will be priests of God and of Christ and will reign with him for a thousand years" (Rev. 20:6). These are the believers—those who have been raised from the dead spiritually.[23] The second death has no power over them. It is *all* believers through the ages. They reign with Christ, even when they are being killed. Christ triumphed over the powers on the cross. Paul said, **"In all these things we are more than conquerors"** (v. 37). And Christ said, "To him who overcomes, I will give the right to sit with me on my throne" (Rev. 3:21a).

"This is the victory that overcomes the world, even our faith" (1 Jn. 5:4b).

---

23. Gangadean, *The Westminster Confession*, 143–148; Gangadean, *The Westminster Catechisms*, 191–192; Gangadean, *The Epistle to the Hebrews*, 306–309.

12

THE SOVEREIGNTY OF GOD AS CREATOR AND REDEEMER
Free to Give or Withhold Mercy

1994

Romans 9

¹I speak the truth in Christ—I am not lying, my conscience confirms it in the Holy Spirit—²I have great sorrow and unceasing anguish in my heart. ³For I could wish that I myself were cursed and cut off from Christ for the sake of my brothers, those of my own race, ⁴the people of Israel. Theirs is the adoption as sons; theirs the divine glory, the covenants, the receiving of the law, the temple worship and the promises. ⁵Theirs are the patriarchs, and from them is traced the human ancestry of Christ, who is God over all, forever praised! Amen.

⁶It is not as though God's word had failed. For not all who are descended from Israel are Israel. ⁷Nor because they are his descendants are they all Abraham's children. On the contrary, "It is through Isaac that your offspring will be reckoned." ⁸In other words, it is not the natural children who are God's children, but it is the children of the promise who are regarded as Abraham's offspring. ⁹For this was how the promise was stated: "At the appointed time I will return, and Sarah will have a son."

¹⁰Not only that, but Rebekah's children had one and the same father, our father Isaac. ¹¹Yet, before the twins were born or had done anything good or bad—in order that God's purpose in election might stand: ¹²not by works but by him who calls—she was told, "The older will serve the younger." ¹³Just as it is written: "Jacob I loved, but Esau I hated."

¹⁴What then shall we say? Is God unjust? Not at all! ¹⁵For he says to Moses,

"I will have mercy on whom I have mercy,
    and I will have compassion on whom I have compassion."

¹⁶It does not, therefore, depend on man's desire or effort, but on God's mercy. ¹⁷For the Scripture says to Pharaoh: "I raised you up for this very purpose, that I might display my power in you and that my name might be proclaimed in all the earth." ¹⁸Therefore God has mercy on whom he wants to have mercy, and he hardens whom he wants to harden.

¹⁹One of you will say to me: "Then why does God still blame us? For who resists his will?" ²⁰But who are you, O man, to talk back to God? "Shall what is formed say to him who formed it, 'Why did you make me like this?'" ²¹Does not the potter have the right to make out of the same lump of clay some pottery for noble purposes and some for common use?

²²What if God, choosing to show his wrath and make his power known, bore with great patience the objects of his wrath—prepared for destruction? ²³What if he did this to make the riches of his glory known to the objects of his mercy, whom he prepared in advance for glory—²⁴even us, whom he also called, not only from the Jews but also from the Gentiles? ²⁵As he says in Hosea:

"I will call them 'my people' who are not my people;
    and I will call her 'my loved one' who is not my loved one,"

²⁶and,

"It will happen that in the very place where it was said to them,

    'You are not my people,'
    they will be called 'sons of the living God.'"

²⁷Isaiah cries out concerning Israel:

"Though the number of the Israelites be like the sand by the sea,

    only the remnant will be saved.

²⁸For the Lord will carry out
    his sentence on earth with speed and finality."

²⁹It is just as Isaiah said previously:

"Unless the Lord Almighty

    had left us descendants,

we would have become like Sodom,
    we would have been like Gomorrah."

[30]What then shall we say? That the Gentiles, who did not pursue righteousness, have obtained it, a righteousness that is by faith; [31]but Israel, who pursued a law of righteousness, has not attained it. [32]Why not? Because they pursued it not by faith but as if it were by works. They stumbled over the "stumbling stone." [33]As it is written:

"See, I lay in Zion a stone that causes men to stumble
　and a rock that makes them fall,
　and the one who trusts in him will never be put to shame."

SORROW FOR THOSE WHO DO NOT BELIEVE:
The Covenant People

IN ROMANS 9, WE ARE LOOKING AT THE DOCTRINE of the unconditional election of God. We are looking at it in the context of the promise made in Romans 8: "For those God foreknew he also predestined to be conformed to the image of his Son" (Rom. 8:29a). We are also looking at this doctrine of unconditional election and its application to the people of God—the covenant people under the old covenant. Paul is anticipating speaking about something very painful. It is painful to those about whom Paul is speaking, and it is painful to Paul himself. He wants his hearers to know that this subject is, indeed, very distressing. Paul speaks and assures his hearers that the condition of his heart is one of **"great sorrow and unceasing anguish"** (v. 2). Paul assures them that this really is so: **"I speak the truth in Christ"** (v. 1a). Paul is calling Christ as his witness. **"I am not lying, my conscience confirms it through the Holy Spirit"** (v. 1b). Paul is giving the greatest assurance of his own heart's condition as he prepares to deal with this subject of how God's predestination and promise operate in the context of the covenant people of the Old Testament.

"I have great sorrow and unceasing anguish in my heart" (v. 2). It is appropriate that when we speak, we are aware of the feelings that the subject will bring about in the hearers, and that we should seek to address the subject in the most sensitive, delicate, and loving manner possible. Paul does this by saying, 'I want you to know how I feel about this.' Paul's feelings are of **"great sorrow and unceasing anguish,"** which is not something incompatible with the joy of the Lord and the peace of God. It is possible to be so concerned about those to whom the promise of God has come, who are showing no evidence of responding truly to that promise, that we might have this feeling of great sorrow and unceasing anguish, while still finding comfort in God's purpose.

Further, Paul states that he would do anything possible to see a change brought about: **"For I could wish that I myself were cursed and cut off from Christ for the sake of my brothers, those of my own race"** (v. 3). This sorrow and anguish is translated into a desire to do anything possible within moral limits. He says, hypothetically, **"For I could wish that I myself were cursed and cut off from Christ for the sake of my brothers, those of my own race"**—if that were possible. He is not saying he wishes to do evil that good may come about. Paul wishes to become unholy in being cut off, because no one is cut off that is not unholy. Perhaps he is conceiving of what Christ experienced when He was cut off for His people, but Paul cannot be in that position, either. Paul cannot wish himself to be cut off and to be made unholy for the sake of others because that is incompatible with his standing before God. But neither can Paul wish himself cut off as if he could die in their place, because Christ has done that, and Paul, as a sinner, cannot do that. But it does say something of Paul's heart, just as it was revealed of Moses when he feared that the people would be cut off for their sin of worshiping the golden calf. Moses prayed that they would be forgiven, then he prayed, "But if not, then blot me out of the book you have written" (Ex. 32:32b). This is to say that we should go to the greatest extent possible to see the reclamation, the recovery, the restoration, the renewal, the regeneration of those to whom God's promise has come.

Paul's desire is a mixture of two elements. It is not just kinship, though that certainly is a factor; he says, **"my brothers, those of my own race."** But then he adds, **"the people of Israel"** (v. 4a)—the people who are called by that name, whose ancestry goes back to Jacob, who, in seeking God, in wrestling with God, received the promise.[1] These are the people of Israel—those who have the covenant promise. We can take this concern of Paul to be for our family members and emphasize kinship only. We can take this to be for the people of Israel, and say we should all be praying and seeking the well-being of Israel. But I think both of those are combined, and there is a larger sense in which it may be applied. Praying for the people of Israel applies to all who are

---

1. *Genesis 32.*

members of the covenant, who are outwardly connected to the visible church—particularly covenant children who have been brought up in the church—who may not display evidence of regeneration or coming to Christ. So, both the element of kinship and the element of promise, in terms of being in the covenant, are combined. Our concern should ever be that those who have the promise given to them will indeed hear that Word, receive that promise, and come to the Lord.

Paul focuses on the people of God, at that time, who had that promise:

> **Theirs is the adoption to sons; theirs the divine glory, the covenants, the receiving of the law, the temple worship and the promises. Theirs are the patriarchs, and from them is traced the human ancestry of Christ, who is God over all, forever praised! Amen (vv. 4b–5).**

These promises belong to the people of Israel in a particular way. Paul enumerates the basis on which these promises came to them. They were the ones who were in the covenant, they continued in the covenant, and they preserved the covenant. The promises came to them, to their fathers, the Patriarchs. Christ was born of this human ancestry, but He is God, who is over all. We will later see that these promises come to the covenant people today.

GOD'S WORD HAS NOT FAILED:
The Promise Is According to the Spiritual Seed

Paul is concerned that the predestinating purposes of God, out of His love, would be properly understood. Concerning those to whom this promise came in the Old Testament but in whom it was not realized, Paul does not want this to be taken as a denial of God's predestinating purpose or His love. Paul says, **"It is not as though God's word had failed"** (v. 6a). Paul explains how it is that the Word has not failed: **"For not all who are descended from Israel are Israel. Nor because they are his descendants are they all Abraham's children"** (vv. 6b–7a). The promise, he is saying, is never made to merely natural descendants. The promise is made according to the spiritual seed. He makes a distinction between the natural seed and the spiritual seed. In the Epistle to the Galatians, Paul makes the same point:

Consider Abraham: "He believed God, and it was credited to him as righteousness." Understand, then, that those who believe are children of Abraham. Scripture foresaw that God would justify the Gentiles by faith, and announced the gospel in advance to Abraham: "All nations will be blessed through you." So those who have faith are blessed along with Abraham, the man of faith (Gal. 3:6–9).

Those who have faith, those who believe, are blessed along with Abraham, the father of the faithful. A distinction is being made between the natural seed and the seed that is by promise. **"For not all who are descended from Israel are Israel. Nor because they are his descendants are they all Abraham's children"** (vv. 6b–7a).

Paul gives an example of this, which you can see clearly. **"On the contrary, 'It is through Isaac that your offspring will be reckoned.' In other words, it is not the natural children who are God's children, but it is the children of the promise who are regarded as Abraham's offspring"** (vv. 7b–8). Both Ishmael and Isaac were children of Abraham, but the fulfillment of the promise came through the one who had faith, that is, through Isaac. Isaac himself was an illustration of this at his very birth—he was born not in the natural way, but as a result of a promise. So our children born in the natural way, the physical way, are not thereby inheritors of the promise. Scripture says that the true children are "children born not of natural descent, nor of human decision or a husband's will, but born of God" (Jn. 1:13). Paul says, **"It is the children of the promise who are regarded as Abraham's offspring. For this was how the promise was stated: 'At the appointed time I will return, and Sarah will have a son'"** (vv. 8b–9). God's Word has not failed. His predestination, in love, comes not to those who are the natural seed, but to those who are the spiritual seed. Remember the Jews had said to Jesus, "Abraham is our father."[2] It was often thought that just by having Abraham as their father, the promise was guaranteed to them. Jesus pointed out that if they were Abraham's children, they would not be doing what they were doing. Abraham was one who had faith. He did not and would not have opposed the Promised One.

Paul establishes, by making the distinction between the natural seed and the spiritual seed, that God's Word has not failed. However, there

---

2. *John 8:39.*

is a close connection between the natural and the spiritual seed. We should see how they are related. Ordinarily, one would expect that the natural seed would also be the spiritual seed. Ordinarily, one would expect that all members of the visible church would be true believers. We are not to separate the connection between the visible and the invisible Church. But we must make the point, at the same time, that being a member of the church, being baptized (or circumcised), partaking of the Lord's Supper (or of Passover), is not a guarantee of the inward reality. To partake outwardly is not identical to partaking inwardly. If one partakes outwardly, properly, it should *all the more* be an outward expression of an inward reality. But for those who would come and partake outwardly, without having the inward reality, they are eating and drinking judgment upon themselves.[3] The promise has always been to those who are born of God, those who have faith, and not merely those who are members of a community of believers.

JACOB VERSUS ESAU:
Election Is Unconditional

Paul makes a further point about natural and spiritual seed, and of election. He says, "**Not only that, but Rebekah's children had one and the same father, our father Isaac**" (v. 10). Some may think that in the case of Ishmael and Isaac, who had different mothers, the mother makes the difference. In traditional Jewish law, it is said that to be a Jew, one must be born not just of a Jewish father, but of a Jewish mother.[4] Paul is making the point that this is not the case, although it has been held historically in post-biblical Judaism. Clearly, we see in the case of Ruth the Moabitess that she was a woman without a Jewish mother. Paul is making the point that to say the physical connection guarantees the promise, whether the connection is through the father or the mother, is false. Paul uses the example of Rebecca:

---

3. *1 Corinthians 11:27–32.*

4. In traditional Jewish law (Halakha), Jewish identity is passed down through the mother. This matrilineal principle is based on *Talmud Kiddushin* 68b, which holds that a child is Jewish only if born to a Jewish mother, regardless of the father's status. This has remained the standard in Orthodox and Conservative Judaism.

> Not only that, but Rebekah's children had one and the same father, our father Isaac. Yet, before the twins were born or had done anything good or bad—in order that God's purpose in election might stand: not by works but by him who calls—she was told, "The older will serve the younger." Just as it is written: "Jacob I loved, but Esau I hated" (vv. 10–13).

In this case, the children had the same parents, father and mother, and not only that, but they were born at the same time; they were twins. **"Yet, before the twins were born . . ."** God told Rebecca not after the twins were born, but before they were born. And the explanation is explicitly given: before they **"had done anything good or bad—in order that God's purpose in election might stand . . ."** They had not done anything good or bad, but that does not mean that sinful depravity was not present, even from conception. We are saying that the election unto life is always out of those who are sinful. They had not done anything good or bad, but the natural disposition was present and would become manifest in due time.

Paul is establishing that this predestinating work, this election, is *unconditional*. Later on, we will see that this election is not unto merely outward privileges, such as being a church member, but it is unto eternal life. It is not of groups, it is of particular individuals. It is not on the basis of any works foreseen or done, it is unconditional. That is what we mean by *unconditional election*. The election is of particular individuals, unto eternal life, and it is unconditional in the sense that it does not regard work. It is not on the basis of works or by natural descent; it is not on the basis of anything one may do, like the partaking of sacraments; it is unconditional.[5] This doctrine is being taught here and applied in a way that shows that it does not negate the Word of God.

"The older will serve the younger" shows the position of privilege and honor that is bestowed upon Jacob. Even there, the reversal is seen—the firstborn is usually preferred. Esau was the firstborn, and that is bypassed here. **"Just as it is written: 'Jacob I loved . . .'"** God foreknew; He set His redeeming love upon Jacob; He did not set that love upon Esau. That is the sense in which it is said, **"Esau I hated."** There is a comparison; God's love is being set upon one and not set

---

5. Gangadean, "Paper No. 18: Salvation by Grace," in *The Logos Papers*, 119–122.

upon the other. That is why it says elsewhere, unless you hate your father and mother, you are not worthy of me.[6] In other words, we are not to love father and mother above God. There is to be no earthly human attachment of any sort whatsoever that comes before God—father or mother or son or daughter. In that sense, we speak about *hate*. It is, by comparison, loving one more than the other. "No man can serve two masters: for either he will hate the one, and love the other; or else he will hold to the one, and despise the other. Ye cannot serve God and mammon" (Matt. 6:24 KJV). They cannot both be served at the same time. We love one and hate the other. They cannot both occupy the same space. This is not what we might call a positive *hate*, but it is a hate in the sense of the absence of God's foreknowing love being set upon him. Those who do come to God should know that it is in the unmerited favor of His love that He set upon us. That is what the word *foreknew* means, not foreknew in terms of thinking about the future and seeing what we will do. Reformed translators all agree that this is the meaning of the word *foreknew*. Romans 8:29 says, "For those God foreknew he also predestined to be conformed to the likeness of his Son." He set His love upon them so that they would be conformed to the Son, Jesus Christ.

IS GOD UNJUST?
Not at All!—As Redeemer, God's Mercy Is Sovereign

The two most common objections to the doctrine of unconditional election are, first, that God is unjust, and second, that we are not responsible for unbelief.

"What then shall we say? Is God unjust? Not at all!" (v. 14). This is an exclamation. 'Absolutely not! How can the thought even enter your mind that God is unjust?' Apparently, this idea is missing something crucial. What is missing? There is a mixing up of justice with mercy. God is not unjust; God is merciful. There is a difference between justice and mercy. The difference is not between just and unjust. God is perfectly just, and God is perfectly merciful. The distinction here is not between just and unjust, but between justice and mercy. "**For he says to Moses, 'I will have mercy on whom I have mercy, and I**

---

6. *Luke 14:26.*

will have compassion on whom I have compassion'" (v. 15). We are all sinners, and by our sin, we are all condemned. If two persons are condemned, and God chooses to pardon one, that is not injustice on the part of God, but mercy. And it is not merely mercy, but it is *sovereign* mercy. "I will have mercy on whom I have mercy." If we want to object, the objection needs to be not that God is unjust, but that He ought not to be *sovereign* in His mercy, and that we can instruct God on whom He might have mercy, and that there is something outside of God that constrains His mercy. That is where the objection really needs to be centered. Of course, the question is, can God be sovereign in redemption? We will see that the question will come up against the sovereignty of God in general. Can God be sovereign in creation? We will see, both in the case of creation and in redemption, He not only can be sovereign, but He *must* be sovereign.

We will see that the second objection, about why God holds us responsible, also has to do with sovereignty. God is sovereign in creation in that He cannot consult the creature, who does not exist, and say, 'Shall I make you?' That is absurd. Neither can He consult the creature, who is dead in trespasses and sins,[7] who cannot hear and will not hear, because they have shut their eyes and ears, and say, 'Shall I redeem you?' In one case, the creature is nonexistent, and in the other case, the creature is dead and unable to hear. Because we have killed ourselves, we have destroyed ourselves by our sin, and the wages of sin is death,[8] we cannot hear. God is sovereign in both cases.

Paul emphasizes God's sovereignty by saying, negatively, "It does not, therefore, depend on man's desire or effort, but on God's mercy" (v. 16). In this, we understand, it is not that some are desiring and making an effort and are rejected. But rather, the very desiring and seeking depend on God's mercy. All those who do desire and seek will come to God, but it is said of men left to themselves in their sin: none seek God.[9] The clarity of general revelation is the basis of saying that no one seeks God. Because it is clear, if human beings do not see it, it is because they are not seeking. That is the true condition of all men in our fallen state.

---

7. *Ephesians 2:1.*

8. *Romans 6:23.*

9. *Romans 3:10–12.*

Double Predestination

"It does not, therefore, depend on man's desire or effort, but on God's mercy. For Scripture says to Pharaoh . . ." (vv. 16–17a). Notice, His sovereignty goes both ways. God is sovereign in bringing someone out of the state of sin and death and into life, and He is sovereign, therefore, on the other side, in leaving someone in that state of sin and death. God is not *making* them wicked, but *leaving* them in their wickedness and in spiritual death. God never makes anyone wicked, but God does make men righteous by regenerating, imputing righteousness to them, and working in their hearts to transform them and conform them to His Son, Jesus Christ.

On the negative side, Paul says,

> For Scripture says to Pharaoh: "I raised you up for this very purpose, that I might display my power in you and that my name might be proclaimed in all the earth." Therefore God has mercy on whom he wants to have mercy, and he hardens whom he wants to harden. (vv. 17–18).

This is the doctrine of *double* predestination. Some are predestined to remain in death in trespasses and sins, and some are predestined to life by being taken out of that state of sin and death. Notice how it worked in Pharaoh. The acts of mercy to call Pharaoh back to repentance, those *very* acts of mercy, are the very acts by which Pharaoh, left to himself, hardens himself against God. The Scripture says both that Pharaoh hardened his heart and that God hardened Pharaoh's heart.[10] In God sending that outward call to Pharaoh to call him back to repentance, God's special expressions of miracles, He is giving greater truth to Pharaoh. That is mercy. Yet God sending that truth outwardly, and leaving Pharaoh to himself, will mean that Pharaoh will harden himself. God hardens Pharaoh's heart by increasing objective revelation—truth—and forcing Pharaoh to respond to it. When we speak the Word of God to anyone, it will be either life unto life or death unto death. The very means under which some come to the Lord are the same means under

---

10. *Exodus 7:3, 13–14, 22–23; 8:15, 19, 32; 9:7, 12, 14, 34–35; 10:1, 20, 27; 11:10; 14:4–5, 8, 17.*

which some may harden themselves.[11] Pharaoh hardened his heart to avoid the truth. God sent him the truth and brought about the occasion—not the cause, but the occasion—for Pharaoh to harden his heart.

One Ultimate Purpose: To Display God's Glory—Perfect Justice and Mercy

We should note that the purpose of the display of God's sovereignty is one ultimate purpose: to display God's glory.[12] There is no higher purpose in the world, and that very purpose is operating in the display of God's sovereignty. He said to Pharaoh, "**I raised you up for this very purpose, that I might display my power in you and that my name might be proclaimed in all the earth**" (v. 17). We are to keep the ultimate purpose of God's glory in mind.

When God leaves men to go on in their sin, it is so that the perfection of His justice and His holiness might be displayed. When God brings men to Himself, it is so that the perfection of His mercy and His goodness might be displayed. Both of these are perfect. There is not the slightest tension between these two, at the deepest level, because the very act that is the greatest display of God's justice—the death of Christ—is the very same act that is the greatest display of His mercy. Christ bore our sins, and that is justice; *He* bore our sins, and that is mercy. There is perfect unity, within God, of justice and mercy.

WHY DOES GOD STILL BLAME US?

The second objection is that we are not to blame; that we are not responsible. "**One of you will say to me: 'Then why does God still blame us? For who resists his will?'**" (v. 19). Paul's response to this objection is twofold. First, he responds to the sentiment, the attitude, and the spirit of irreverence that would ever respond to God in this way. Second, he responds with an argument to address the content of the objection.

---

11. Gangadean, *The Westminster Confession*, 95–96.

12. Gangadean, *The Westminster Confession*, xxix–xxxii, 347–348; Gangadean, "Paper No. 115: Doxological Christianity," 595–596; "Paper No. 118: Eschatology (Seven Points)," in *The Logos Papers*, 603–607.

First Response: Who Are You to Question God's Justice and Goodness?

He says, "But who are you, O man, to talk back to God?" (v. 20a). We, as mere men, creatures wholly dependent on God, should never, at any time, ever call God's justice and goodness into question. It is blasphemous to do so. It is the very denial of who God is. If you ever think you have a reason to question God's justice and goodness, you are absolutely wrong—no ifs, ands, or buts. The fault does not lie with God. The fault lies somewhere else. Search more deeply, and you will find it. It is logically impossible that God could be unjust. It is logically impossible that God could be in error. Whenever we see that kind of thing swelling up within us, that is our human pride. We are justifying ourselves rather than receiving the justification God will provide us in Jesus Christ. That is exactly how the chapter ends, as to why Israel is rejected, because of that very thing—self-justification in pride.

Second Response (A): God Can and Must Be Sovereign

Having addressed the spirit of irreverence behind the questioning of God, Paul goes on to say, "Shall what is formed say to him who formed it, 'Why did you make me like this?' Does not the potter have the right to make out of the same lump of clay some pottery for noble purposes and some for common use?" (vv. 20b–21). Then He answers further: "What if God, choosing to show his wrath . . ." (v. 22a). God is sovereign in His creation, and God is sovereign in His redemption. God does not and cannot consult with a creature as to what He will do. God has the absolute right to make us or not to make us. God has the absolute right to make us in the particular way we are made, and all of us are made differently. We are made male and female. We are made with different gifts and different circumstances in our lives. All of these are part of God's sovereignty, which cannot be called into question. God can and must be sovereign in this way. We do not have any right to say of the same lump of clay, 'Why have you made me so?'

Second Response (B): Death Is Never Apart from Our Own Sin

There is another level to Paul's response. It is that we, as creatures, cannot call our natures into question. It is not that a person wants to be different and cannot be;[13] it is not that a person finds himself with a sinful nature and says, 'Lord, I don't want this sinful nature. Why did you give this to me? Please take it away.' No sinful creature ever thinks that and would never say that to God. And no redeemed creature ever says, 'Why did you have mercy on me? I don't want you to have mercy.' No sinful creature says, 'I wanted you to have mercy, and you didn't. Why did you do that to me?' It never happens that way on either side. So we cannot say, 'Why have you made me so?' The reason we are in a state of death is because of our own sin. In verse 22, Paul says, **"What if God, choosing to show his wrath and make his power known, bore with great patience the objects of his wrath—prepared for destruction?"** God, in patience, endured us in our sin. It is because of our sin that destruction comes; it is because of sin that death comes.

God's purpose is to display His justice and, likewise, His mercy. **"What if he did this to make the riches of his glory known to the objects of his mercy, whom he prepared in advance for glory—even us, whom he also called, not only from the Jews but also from the Gentiles?"** (vv. 23–24). We are blameworthy because we do have sin. The election anticipates the condition of sin, and we are elected out of fallen humanity unto redemption. When we go the way of death, it is not apart from our sin, but *always* in connection with our sin. We never have death apart from sin. It is we ourselves that sin; it is we ourselves that shut our eyes. God did not shut our eyes for us, we shut our own eyes. God did not hinder us from seeking, we are the ones who are not seeking.

AS THE SCRIPTURES FORESAW:
The Gentiles Included, the Israelites Excluded

Paul, in the early part of this chapter, makes the point that God has the right, as Creator and Redeemer, to be sovereign and have mercy on whom He will have mercy. Just as God is free to have mercy on Israel at one time, and there has been no objection to that show of mercy, so also God is free not to have mercy. Furthermore, the Scripture foresaw that when the Gentiles come in, at that time, there would be an exclusion of

---

13. Gangadean, *Philosophical Foundation*, 66, 154–156, 166–169; Gangadean, "Paper No. 97: Freedom and Predestination," in *The Logos Papers*, 509–510.

Israel, but that exclusion is never full, complete, or final. God's mercy will yet triumph in the redemption of all men. At the time, at the very beginning, a significant number of Jews came to Christ, but the larger part of the nation did not. Since then, a greater part of the nation has not come, but that is not complete. Scripture speaks about a remnant, and Paul will make reference to the remnant. It is not final; it is not that the Jews will never be restored. The inclusion of one, the Gentiles, in God's sovereign purpose for the display of His justice and mercy, meant the exclusion of another, but it will not be a final exclusion.

Not Just by Addition but by Substitution

First, Paul addresses the inclusion. **"As he says in Hosea: 'I will call them "my people" who are not my people; and I will call her "my loved one" who is not my loved one'"** (v. 25). If we understand how the Israelites have historically provoked the Holy One to anger, and aroused His jealousy by going after other gods, we can understand God's just dealing in provoking Israel by taking someone else to be His loved one. It was in connection with the persistence of Israel in going after the idols of the nations that God chose those very nations, who themselves were going after these idols, to make them His people. Because Israel was moving from a position of rejection of God to go to these idols, God chose the Gentiles, who were immersed in senseless idolatry, to bring them to Himself: **"I will call them 'my people' who are not my people."**

Sometimes, when we have a great privilege in God, we do not recognize it, and we are ungrateful for it. God takes that privilege away so that we might be humbled before Him, and that we might once again return to Him in gratitude. Never think of it as a light thing that we have the privilege of being in the covenant. Remember, we can be in the covenant in an external way. Children can be raised in the covenant but not have that internal life and faith in God. **"I will call them 'my people' who are not my people; and I will call her 'my loved one' who is not my loved one. It will happen that in the very place where it was said to them, 'You are not my people,' they will be called 'sons of the living God'"** (vv. 25–26). Here is the sovereignty of God in election. God is not bound by the natural, physical descent of any person. He is not bound by any work of man in the display of His mercy. **"Where** it was said to them, 'You are not my people,' they will be called 'sons of the living God.'" They will be children of God—those born of God.

A Remnant Will Remain

Second, Paul addresses the exclusion. "Isaiah cries out concerning Israel: 'Though the number of the Israelites be like the sand by the sea, only the remnant will be saved. For the Lord will carry out his sentence on earth with speed and finality'" (vv. 27–28). A remnant will remain. The Lord will carry this out with finality, at least at that time. A remnant will remain, not only at the time that the gospel went to the nations, but even in the days of Isaiah, when a small portion was then saved. "It is just as Isaiah said previously: 'Unless the Lord Almighty had left us descendants, we would have become like Sodom, we would have been like Gomorrah'" (v. 29).

Humbled Hearts

The difference in human beings does not depend on outward conditions such as birth or station; it depends fully upon God, who shows mercy. The difference between Israel and Sodom and Gomorrah is the grace and mercy of God. "There, but for the grace of God, go I."[14] All of this should humble our hearts in dealing with those who, at any time, do not have the mercy of God. We should always come with the attitude: there, but for the grace of God, go I. Everyone to whom we speak, who do not seem to have God's grace—there, but for the grace of God, go I. God uses His sovereign election to humble our hearts. The Scripture foresaw that this would occur, that one would be included and the other would be excluded; yet, there will come a time when all will be included.

WHY DID ISRAEL NOT ATTAIN RIGHTEOUSNESS?
Stumbling Over the Stumbling Stone

What then shall we say? That the Gentiles, who did not pursue righteousness, have obtained it, a righteousness that is by faith; but Israel, who pursued a law of righteousness, has not attained

---

14. Commonly attributed to John Bradford, a 16th-century Protestant Reformer.

it. Why not? Because they pursued it not by faith but as if it were by works (vv. 30–32a).

Paul connects this with the teaching earlier. We do not have righteousness on our own basis but by God alone. Even if in Adam we had righteousness, it would have been by God's grace sustaining us, and left to ourselves, we would turn away from God. Israel sought righteousness, but sought it in a way that would bring self-satisfaction, resting in one's own merit rather than resting solely on the merit of Christ. To seek righteousness in this way would raise up the creature above what it is, to some measure of independence from God, rather than seeing that we are creatures wholly dependent on God for our very being, for our continued existence, and for everything good that we do.

Israel sought righteousness in a way that disregarded the grace of God. We might say the real essence of the disregard for the grace of God was manifest when that grace was most fully shown. The One through whom that grace came was opposed to the point of being crucified. It shows what really is the significance of our self-life, what really is the significance of our self-righteousness, rather than having the righteousness that comes from God alone.

"They stumbled over the 'stumbling stone.' As it is written: 'See, I lay in Zion a stone that causes men to stumble and a rock that makes them fall, and the one who trusts in him will never be put to shame'" (vv. 32b–33). Israel was waiting for the Messiah, and yet, it was a messiah that they had conceived in unbelief—one they had conceived in error. We should never underestimate how powerful error is in blinding us, making us fail to see our true condition, and making us complacent because we fail to see our true condition. This is true not only of the covenant people of God then, but it is true of the covenant people of God today. There are many who are church members, whose dominant attitude is one of self-righteous legalism, seeking to merit by one's efforts the grace of God. Let us guard against this, understand our creatureliness, and acknowledge God's sovereignty in creation, election, and providence.

13

ZEAL FOR GOD WITHOUT KNOWLEDGE
The Way of Faith Is Available to All

1994

Romans 10

¹Brothers, my heart's desire and prayer to God for the Israelites is that they may be saved. ²For I can testify about them that they are zealous for God, but their zeal is not based on knowledge. ³Since they did not know the righteousness that comes from God and sought to establish their own, they did not submit to God's righteousness. ⁴Christ is the end of the law so that there may be righteousness for everyone who believes.

⁵Moses describes in this way the righteousness that is by the law: "The man who does these things will live by them." ⁶But the righteousness that is by faith says: "Do not say in your heart, 'Who will ascend into heaven?'" (that is, to bring Christ down) ⁷"or 'Who will descend into the deep?'" (that is, to bring Christ up from the dead). ⁸But what does it say? "The word is near you; it is in your mouth and in your heart," that is, the word of faith we are proclaiming: ⁹That if you confess with your mouth, "Jesus is Lord," and believe in your heart that God raised him from the dead, you will be saved. ¹⁰For it is with your heart that you believe and are justified, and it is with your mouth that you confess and are saved. ¹¹As the Scripture says, "Anyone who trusts in him will never be put to shame." ¹²For there is no difference between Jew and Gentile—the same Lord is Lord of all and richly blesses all who call on him, ¹³for, "Everyone who calls on the name of the Lord will be saved."

[14]How, then, can they call on the one they have not believed in? And how can they believe in the one of whom they have not heard? And how can they hear without someone preaching to them? [15]And how can they preach unless they are sent? As it is written, "How beautiful are the feet of those who bring good news!"

[16]But not all the Israelites accepted the good news. For Isaiah says, "Lord, who has believed our message?" [17]Consequently, faith comes from hearing the message, and the message is heard through the word of Christ. [18]But I ask: Did they not hear? Of course they did:

"Their voice has gone out into all the earth,
   their words to the ends of the world."

[19]Again I ask: Did Israel not understand? First, Moses says,

"I will make you envious by those who are not a nation;
   I will make you angry by a nation that has no understanding."

[20]And Isaiah boldly says,

"I was found by those who did not seek me;
   I revealed myself to those who did not ask for me."

[21]But concerning Israel he says,

"All day long I have held out my hands
   to a disobedient and obstinate people."

SUMMARY OVERVIEW OF ROMANS 1–9

Romans 1: Those with Clear General Revelation

IN ROMANS 1, PAUL SAYS THAT HE IS NOT ASHAMED of the gospel, "For in the gospel a righteousness from God is revealed" (Rom. 1:17a). Throughout the Epistle to the Romans, Paul is speaking about the gospel, and in the gospel, he is speaking about a righteousness that is from God, by the grace of God. Paul is speaking about the covenant of grace over and against the covenant of works made with Adam. Outside of Christ, we are all in that covenant of works made with Adam, and because Adam failed, we also, in Adam, failed.[1] And just as Adam failed to see God's clear general revelation, our failure is revealed in our

---

1. Gangadean, *The Biblical Worldview,* 147–158; *The Westminster Confession,* 111–120.

failure to see clear general revelation.[2] In that covenant with Adam, *none* are saved; all are perishing. We need righteousness, and we attain that righteousness by the covenant of grace, in which Christ pays the penalty that is due to us for our failure. Christ perfectly obeyed the law of God; His righteousness is imputed to our account, and we receive that righteousness by faith, by trusting in Him. On the basis of that righteousness—being regarded as righteous—God deals with us as righteous and sends His Spirit into our lives. That is the gospel Paul is preaching: "A righteousness from God is revealed, a righteousness that is by faith from first to last" (Rom. 1:17)—from the beginning, all the way through sanctification, to the point of glorification.[3] Righteousness comes to us by faith, by trusting in God, not trusting in ourselves, not trusting in our own works or our own effort, but by trusting in God, who will make us able and willing to do His will. "A righteousness that is by faith from first to last, just as it is written: 'The righteous will live by faith'" (Rom. 1:17b). We will have life by trusting in God.

In contrast, under the covenant of works, we are all in the condition of spiritual death. Paul describes that death: all men have the clear revelation of God, and those who have that clear general revelation— because of the sinful condition of their hearts, their disposition, their desire to do their own will—have turned away from it, suppressed it, and tried to justify themselves by saying, 'We cannot see how you can say there is a God.' That very sin carries within itself spiritual death. We cut ourselves off from God; we cut ourselves off from the Word of God in every form; we cut ourselves off from using reason at the basic level; we have suppressed the light in us, which is that by which we see and understand.[4] We are naturally in a state without meaning; our lives are empty. That is the condition of spiritual death that comes from not knowing and acknowledging God—that comes from sin.[5] That is death; that is the wrath of God. "The wrath of God is being revealed from

---

2. Gangadean, *The Biblical Worldview*, 159–176; Gangadean, "Paper No. 102: The Clarity of General Revelation," 527–529; "Paper No. 41: What Is Clear About God," 225–229; "Paper No. 112: Why General Revelation Is Basic in the Christian Worldview," in *The Logos Papers*, 583–585.

3. Gangadean, *The Westminster Confession*, 143–206; Gangadean, *The Westminster Catechisms*, 191–207.

4. *John 1:4.*

5. Gangadean, *The Westminster Confession*, 369–376.

heaven against all the godlessness and wickedness of men who suppress the truth by their wickedness" (Rom. 1:18). When we are in that state of death, we are given up to it, and we go into all the lusts that we try to satisfy to fill the emptiness in us.[6] As we learn to recognize death remaining in ourselves, and that at one time, we were under the power of death in the world, we will be able to appreciate the righteousness that comes by faith in Jesus Christ. Because only on the basis of that righteousness will we be accepted before God and have His blessing upon us. So Paul is speaking about this gospel—righteousness that is by faith. As we go all the way through the Epistle to the Romans, we see how Paul is defending this righteousness that is by faith rather than a righteousness by our own efforts, by our own works.

Romans 2: Those with Clear Special Revelation (in the Church)

Paul says that those with clear special revelation have come short of what God calls them to; they, too, have sinned. This was true in the Old Testament when Israel had a special revelation in the law, but they did not heed it. In the Church today, those who have that revelation do not heed it or hear it. So, both those who have general revelation and those who have special revelation fail to heed and live by the Word. It shows the sin nature and our need for righteousness.

Romans 3: All Have Sinned—No One Is Righteous by the Law; All Righteousness Is by Faith in Christ

Paul sums up that all have sinned: "For all have sinned and fall short of the glory of God" (Rom. 3:23). When he says, "all have sinned," he means those with general revelation and those with special revelation—at that time, Jews and Gentiles. The Jews were the Church in the Old Testament; they were the covenant people; they had the covenant blessings. The Church in the New Testament time likewise had the covenant blessings. But because they have it outwardly does not mean they have it inwardly. We should never profess outwardly what is not there inwardly, but because of self-deception, we do that sort of thing. "All have sinned," there is no one who is righteous by the law. All who have righteousness have it by faith in Christ. When Paul says "all," he

---

6. *Romans 1:21–32.*

is speaking about Jews and Gentiles—all men. In Romans 9–10, Paul emphasizes that all—Jews and Gentiles alike—have righteousness; it is not Jews only. So all have sinned, there are none righteous by the law, and all have righteousness by faith in Christ. There is one and only one way in which we can be accepted before God—by trusting God for His grace, the righteousness that comes to us through Christ, and all the blessings that come to us on the basis of His righteousness.

Romans 4: Abraham Was Justified by Faith Before Circumcision

Paul makes it abundantly clear that this way of salvation, righteousness by faith, was the way in which Abraham was saved. Abraham was justified before circumcision: "Abraham believed God, and it was credited to him as righteousness" (Rom. 4:3b). Abraham "believed God" in the sense of *trusting* in God. He trusted in what God would do for him, not what he himself would do. In doing so, Abraham became the father of all who believe—both those who are circumcised and those who are not—because he had this faith while he was still uncircumcised.

Romans 5: Where Sin Increased, Grace Increased All the More

Paul speaks about the blessings that come through justification by faith. We have peace with God, we have joy in God, and this is because "where sin increased, grace increased all the more" (Rom. 5:20b). This way of salvation not only goes back to Abraham, but it goes back to Adam, and not only does it go back to Adam and his one sin, but it *abounds* all the more. Christ's justification covers many sins of many people, not just one sin of one man. This way of righteousness, this covenant of grace, brings us blessings far greater than the effects that came through the failure of Adam.

Romans 6: If We Have Been Made Alive, We Cannot Go On Sinning

Paul explains that people misunderstand this way of righteousness, which is by trusting in God. They continually want to go back to the old way—the way of works, the way of trusting in ourselves, of achieving righteousness by ourselves, by something that we do. Some have perverted this gospel and said, "Shall we go on sinning so that grace may increase?" (Rom. 6:1b). Paul gives two objections to this: First, we have been made alive in Christ; therefore, we cannot go on sinning. No one who has been made alive in Christ will be satisfied with continuing in sin. Second, if we do go on sinning, that does not produce grace—that produces death. At the end of Romans 6, Paul says, "For the wages of sin is death, but the gift of God is eternal life in Christ Jesus our Lord" (Rom. 6:23). No one can abuse the way of righteousness, the way of grace.

Romans 7: We Died to the Law of Works Through Christ

Paul explains that we died to the law of works in Christ. I am underscoring this point—the law as a covenant of works. Remember this: everyone who is outside of Christ is regarded by God and treated by God as under the covenant of works, and they will have to obey in order to be righteous, and God is treating them on that basis. This is not just something that happened with Adam; it happened to Adam and continues for all those who are outside of Christ and, therefore, are *in* Adam.[7] Paul is saying that all who believe—whether we were in the covenant community outwardly or outside of that—all who believe in Christ have died to that old covenant. Remember the law of marriage:[8] because we have died in Christ, and Christ bore the penalty of the failure to live by that covenant, we have likewise died to that covenant. We are in a new covenant; we are in the covenant of grace.

We have a new nature in Christ that makes us desire to do the will of God. There is remaining in us, not in the core of our beings, but remaining in us, in our members, in the outward elements of our being, the old nature. And there is a war between the new nature and the old nature. The new nature is established in us by the Spirit of God through regeneration, and the old nature by imputation through Adam. The old nature is continually operating under the covenant of works, and the new nature is operating under the covenant of grace. Those outside of Christ, those in whom the old nature is dominant, will take the very teachings of grace, transform it into works, and because they

---

7. Gangadean, *The Westminster Confession*, 153–178.

8. *Romans 7:1–3.*

cannot live by it, they will excuse themselves, justify themselves, and reject the teachings of grace.

We have to see that there are remnants of the old nature in us and it is operating by the covenant of works. Some will take circumcision and make it into a work and say we are saved by circumcision.[9] They will take Passover, which speaks of grace, and turn it into a work. They will take the Day of Atonement, which speaks of grace, and turn it into a work. They will take the very law of God and turn it into something we have to work to keep in order to be saved. That is how the old nature operates; it still operates under that old covenant of works and it is reacting to the covenant of grace. We have to be careful. There is, in us, a way in which we can slip from that new nature of faith and trust in Christ. There is a struggle between the old and new natures constantly in us, and one is seeking to dominate. "I do not understand what I do. For what I want to do I do not do, but what I hate I do" (Rom. 7:15). There are times when we are not being watchful, we are left to ourselves, and that old nature is struggling against the new nature to get the upper hand. We may begin to think about life in God as something that we have to work for in order to achieve, rather than trusting in God and receiving the benefit of His work in us. We have to watch ourselves so that we do not slip from this righteousness that is by faith from first to last.

We have to watch that we are trusting in God all the way—in all of our circumstances, in all the trials that we are having in our lives—as we go through the process of sanctification. Everyone in this room is facing trials of various kinds. We have to watch that we do not forget to trust in God, and that, on the basis of trust, we will be saved. We are to trust not only initially, to be justified, but also to be sanctified and delivered in terms of external circumstances—it is on the basis of trusting in God. Watch out for that old nature; it will change the significance of the means of grace, making it a matter of works—something we have to do by ourselves, in our own strength, rather than by trusting in God.

In every trial that we face—every circumstance, every difficulty—we can respond in that old nature and think of it as a matter of works, where we have to work it out ourselves in order to overcome. Or we

---

9. *Acts 15*; Gangadean, "Paper No. 16: The Historic Christian Faith," 103–114; "Paper No. 60: The Spiritual War (Part II)," in *The Logos Papers*, 329–330.

can respond by trusting in God—that God is going to work all things together for good. The one response is trusting in ourselves and in our own works; the other is trusting in God, in the love of God, and in His promise to work all things together for good. Do you find yourselves slipping back and forth between these two—between trusting in God and, at times, forgetting? In our personal relationships, in our work, and in all our circumstances? That is the war that is going on. It reflects the old nature in us and the two covenants: the covenant of works and the covenant of grace. We are not any longer under the law as a covenant of works; we are under grace. We can trust in God for His grace.

Romans 8: The Full Extent of Salvation

Paul says, "Therefore, there is now no condemnation for those who are in Christ Jesus" (Rom. 8:1). When trials come our way, we are not to take these trials as punishment for something wrong that we have done. Trials come as part of God's loving care for us as His children, to conform us to Jesus Christ: "There is now no condemnation for those who are in Christ Jesus." We should never experience that spirit of condemnation if we are trusting in God. We are freed from condemnation; we have the joyous liberty of the children of God. It is our very Heavenly Father who is dealing with us. Toward the end of Romans 8, Paul speaks about all the sufferings we may go through. "There is now no condemnation for those who are in Christ Jesus." Not only that, but by the Spirit that Christ has given us, we are able to put to death, deny, say no to, and cancel out—more and more—the remnants of the old nature. As we put the old nature to death, we increasingly grow in grace in the knowledge of God. Not only that, but we increasingly receive all the benefits that come in the whole of the creation, which is groaning under the curse.[10] As we, the people of God, trust in God and obey more and more, we will find that the creation will eventually be delivered from the curse. That is part of the blessing of the covenant of grace. Christ's work will bring the removal of all sin and all the effects of sin—including natural evil, which is God's way of calling us back to Himself—as we repent more and more. From this, we can conclude that nothing can "separate us from the love of God that is in Christ

---

10. *Romans 8:22.*

Jesus our Lord" (Rom. 8:39b). Nothing can separate the believer from the love of God that is in Christ Jesus. We rest in God, who loves us. We trust in God. In all the difficulties, all the anguish of heart that each of us experiences from day to day—in all the trials with health, relationships, and work—none of these separate us from God's love. God is working in all of these trials to bring us to Himself and conform us to our Lord Jesus Christ.[11]

Romans 9: The Promise Is to Abraham's Spiritual Seed

Romans 9, which we covered last time, says that true believers are not cut off. They are not separated from the love of God in Christ. But those who are externally connected—those who have special revelation and are relating to it externally, particularly relating to it in the old nature and turning it into a covenant of works, something to be justified by—do not inherit the blessing. The promise is to those who believe, to all who believe, whether Jew or Gentile, whether those with special revelation or those without. The promise is to Abraham's spiritual seed. Who are those who are Abraham's seed? Those whom God has chosen. In contrast to Ishmael, Isaac is chosen; in contrast to Esau, Jacob is chosen. It is the election of God by which we come to believe. God is neither unjust in showing mercy sovereignly, nor are we excused. "Then why does God still blame us? For who is able to resist his will?" (Rom. 9:19b). We have sin, and because of our sin, we perish. God has said that He would call the Gentiles, who have not sought, though they had general revelation. God has said in the prophecy that He would do so.[12] God has said He would reject those who reject His way; He would reject those who do not put their trust in Christ but who put their trust in their own righteousness. Those who put their trust in their own righteousness—whether outside of the law or in the context of special revelation—will be rejected. But all who believe and trust in God through Christ will receive the blessing.

---

11. *Romans 8:29.*

12. *Romans 9:24–26.*

ZEAL FOR GOD WITHOUT KNOWLEDGE:
Failure to Understand God, Sin, and the Way of Righteousness

In Romans 10, Paul continues to address the calling of the Gentiles and the rejection of those people who possess the covenant. He says, **"Brothers, my heart's desire and prayer to God for the Israelites is that they may be saved"** (v. 1). Paul, in dealing with a most sensitive and painful subject, assures those who hear him what his desire is. His heart's desire and prayer is that they may be saved. Paul is explaining that true believers are never cut off, but those who outwardly profess, not truly believing, are cut off. He explains how this has happened in the case of Israel. **"For I can testify about them that they are zealous for God"** (v. 2a); he acknowledges their zeal, but he acknowledges how that comes short: **"but their zeal is not based on knowledge"** (v. 2b). They did not understand who God is and the holiness of God. They did not understand their own heart condition, and they did not understand the way of righteousness. In this, we see the sense in which we can have zeal without knowledge. They are zealous to have righteousness, but they do not understand the perfect righteousness of God, nor do they understand God's infinite justice and holiness. They do not understand that God cannot be satisfied by the mere outward observances of the law, and they do not understand that the law is much deeper than we have made it out to be.

Bringing Death Upon Death

Remember, our Lord Jesus said, "Unless your righteousness surpasses that of the Pharisees and the teachers of the law, you will certainly not enter the kingdom of heaven" (Matt. 5:20). "You give a tenth of your spices—mint, dill and cumin. But you have neglected the more important matters of the law—justice, mercy and faithfulness" (Matt. 23:23). In that sense, there is a misunderstanding of the law and what it requires because of a misunderstanding of God's nature, His holiness, and the depth of righteousness He calls us to, and a misunderstanding of their own heart condition. The true condition of the heart was revealed when the righteousness of God came, and He was crucified. He was rejected. There was a zeal without knowledge. Paul is not denying their zeal, but Jesus said, "A time is coming when anyone who kills you will think he is offering a service to God" (Jn. 16:2b). It shows how important it is that we do have knowledge and that zeal without knowledge is by no means sufficient. Zeal without knowledge could be very deadly, deadly to oneself, and deadly to others who truly believe. That is the condition of men who do not know God and who are seeking to establish their own righteousness. It does not come anywhere close to the righteousness that God requires. That is a condition of men in the covenant of works, where they try to establish righteousness by their own effort. Human beings who are dead in trespasses and sins, but have the covenant outwardly, try to understand that covenant and act according to it in their fallen condition. They have zeal without knowledge and bring further death upon themselves.

The Heart Distorts the Grace of God

"Since they did not know the righteousness that comes from God and sought to establish their own, they did not submit to God's righteousness" (v. 3). They were exceedingly zealous for the law as it was interpreted through the traditions. When anyone would seek to change anything in the law, they were very upset. Remember, Paul said he was exceedingly zealous for the law,[13] but he did not understand what the law required.[14] Those who would try to say that you have to be circumcised to be saved are making circumcision an absolute necessity of works for salvation. They say that this is something you must do, as if this work itself will merit salvation.[15] We see the Catholic Church trusting in the sacraments in this way. They say that you must have these sacraments in order to be saved, and apart from the sacraments, you cannot be saved. There is something in the human heart, whether in the Church in the Old Testament or in the New Testament, that will distort the grace of God. They transform the very instruments, the sacraments that speak of grace, into works, and bring condemnation on themselves. **"Since they did not know the righteousness that comes from God and sought to establish their own, they did not submit to God's righteousness."** They did not submit to God's righteousness. Go

---

13. *Galatians 1:14; Philippians 3:4–6.*

14. *1 Timothy 1:13.*

15. *Acts 15.*

all the way back to Romans 1:17: "For in the gospel a righteousness from God is revealed, a righteousness that is by faith from first to last, just as it is written: 'The righteous will live by faith.'" We are called to trust in God, not only for justification, but also for sanctification.

In Christ We Have Perfect Righteousness

"**Christ is the end of the law so that there may be righteousness for everyone who believes**" (v. 4). Christ has fulfilled the law; He has completed redemption. It is in Christ that we have perfect righteousness. Christ is the One who perfectly obeyed. He was examined for three years, beginning with the temptation in the wilderness—beginning with a fast. After 40 days, Jesus was tempted to exercise His power independently of God. He was tempted to think that saving His life is what is good. Jesus responded, "Man shall not live on bread alone" (Matt. 4:4). That is the righteousness that God requires. Jesus saw clearly. Jesus was tempted to presume on the grace of God: "Throw yourself down. For it is written: 'He will command his angels concerning you'" (Matt. 4:6). Jesus knew not to tempt the Lord God. He knew not to put God to the test. Jesus was called to use those means that God has ordained and not go beyond those means and presume on God's grace. Jesus was called to compromise His way in order to achieve what was good: "Bow down and worship me" (Matt. 4:9). In other words, 'I will give you the ends by some other means.' Jesus knew He should not make any compromise. That temptation continued all the way to the end when people said, 'Do something spectacular as you hang on the cross, come down, and we will believe you.'[16] Christ was not going to approach this in His own way. He endured the cross, despising the shame, and sat down at the right hand of the Father.[17] That is the righteousness that God requires of us. When He was slandered, accused, spit upon, and mistreated, He did not complain. Christ was not resentful; He did not rail, but He committed Himself into the hands of the faithful Creator. That is the righteousness that God requires of us. That is why Christ "**is the end of the law so that there may be righteousness for everyone who believes**" (v. 4). If anyone thinks that their righteousness

---

16. *Matthew 27:42.*

17. *Hebrews 12:2.*

can measure up to the righteousness of God, or if anyone thinks they can come before God, that God does not require righteousness, or if anyone thinks that they can have righteousness apart from trusting in Christ, God will deal with us on the basis of our righteousness, which is as filthy rags.[18] There is no acceptance outside of Christ. God is holy, God is just. We are thankful to God for His grace to us in Christ.

THE TWO WAYS OF RIGHTEOUSNESS:
By Obedience or by Faith

No Obedience, Therefore No Life

Moses describes the two ways of righteousness. **"Moses describes in this way the righteousness that is by the law: 'The man who does these things will live by them'"** (v. 5). If you obey, you will have life, and the one who does these things will have life by obedience, but no one has obeyed, so no one can have life by that law. All of us have sinned and come short, not just in the small things, but in the big things. At the very beginning, in Romans 1, Paul says that we have general revelation, and men have turned away from it. Persistence in unbelief brings the wrath of God on men, and they are given up more and more.[19] Even within the Church, we see how much we compromise God's Word. Look at all the divisions within the Church; look at all attempts made to speak to others, and to other branches of the Church who truly believe, and yet there are struggles when discussing basic things.[20] Would we be saved by our own righteousness? We have no righteousness by which we can be saved.

The Word Is Near You: Believing and Confessing the Lordship of Christ

"But the righteousness that is by faith says: 'Do not say in your heart, "Who will ascend into heaven?" (that is, to bring Christ down) or "Who will descend into the deep?" (that is, to bring Christ up from the

---

18. *Isaiah 64:6.*

19. *Romans 1:21–32.*

20. This statement refers to his lifelong attempt to engage in discussion regarding basic things with believers in other churches and those discussions not bearing much fruit.

dead)'" (vv. 6–7). We do not have to go far and wide and do anything spectacular to have this righteousness that is by faith. Who can **"bring Christ down"**? On what basis can we lay a claim to have Christ come down from heaven for us? On what basis can we bring Christ up from the dead since He bore away our sins? We cannot, but on the basis of *His* righteousness that *He* has done, He is raised from the dead. Jesus bore away our sins. We do not have to go far and wide. It is not far away, and it is not difficult. This is the way of righteousness: **"'The word is near you; it is in your mouth and in your heart,' that is, the word of faith that we are proclaiming"** (v. 8). How are we then saved by this way of righteousness? He says, **"If you confess with your mouth, 'Jesus is Lord,' and believe in your heart that God raised him from the dead, you will be saved"** (v. 9). That Word is near us, it is the Word we are proclaiming, and it is in your mouth and in your heart. This is where it occurs: if you believe in your heart that Jesus Christ is Lord, that He died for our sins, and God has raised Him from the dead because He is righteous. If you believe that in your heart and confess it with your mouth, you will be saved.

It is necessary, as a duty, to confess with our mouth. It is necessary, as a means through which we receive this salvation, to believe in our heart and to trust. **"For it is with your heart that you believe and are justified, and it is with your mouth that you confess and are saved"** (v. 10). We should be confessing with our mouths that Jesus Christ is Lord on the basis of that work done in our hearts. It is not that telling others about Jesus is necessary in order to be justified; we are not going to slip into that kind of 'works' religion. Many have thought that unless you go out and speak the Word of God, you will not be saved—in the sense of justified. But we say that in the process of growing in God, we will confess Him as Lord and Savior. The way in which we know that we have believed in our hearts is that we see the expression of that belief. One of the most basic, chief expressions, is that we confess it to others. This is one of the ways in which we know, and this is part of what God requires of us as believers in the way we live: to confess that Jesus Christ is Lord. That is, to confess the lordship of Christ in all of our lives. It does not matter what our particular calling is; it does not matter what our circumstances are. There are plenty of circumstances in which we are called to confess Christ. That is the way of righteousness. Believing in our hearts and confessing with our mouths that Jesus Christ is Lord. In that way, we find salvation. We find salvation not only in terms of justification but in terms of sanctification.

THE WAY OF FAITH IS AVAILABLE TO ALL:
God Is Lord of All

"As the Scripture says, 'Anyone who trusts in him will never be put to shame'" (v. 11). That was also said at the end of Romans 9: "And the one who trusts in him will never be put to shame."[21] Notice the sense in which we speak about righteousness that is by faith: it is by trusting in Him, by trusting in God for salvation, and trusting in God for deliverance in every circumstance. When we complain before God of our situation, and we are not trusting, we find God's deliverance comes, and it puts us to shame for not having trusted. When we try to work it out in our own strength, in our own way, by our own wisdom, we find that we come to naught; it is frustrated. "Anyone who trusts in him will never be put to shame." This way of salvation, by trusting, is something that is suitable to *all* men. It is not confined to time, place, and circumstance. It is this message that is to go to the ends of the earth.

"For there is no difference between Jew and Gentile" (v. 12a). There is no difference between those who have the covenant and those who do not. God is the Lord of all. He is not the God of those in the Church only. He is not the God of those who have the sign of the covenant on them only. He is not the God of those who are baptized or who are circumcised only. God is the Lord of all. He will save the Chinese in the very same way as He will save the Lutherans, the Baptists, the Presbyterians, the Jews, and anyone else. There is no difference between Jew and Gentile, between those who have the covenant and those who do not. "The same Lord is Lord of all and richly blesses all who call on him" (v. 12b). You can be a Jew and not call on the name of the Lord, and you can be a Gentile and call on the name of the Lord. Because you have the covenant outwardly does not mean you are calling on the name of the Lord, truly, from your heart. And those outside the covenant who call on the name of the Lord and trust in the Lord will be saved. This is the gospel method of salvation, the way of righteousness, by trusting the Lord, and it is spoken now to whom

---

21. *Romans 9:33.*

that salvation comes—it comes to *all* men. It is heightened in that it comes to all men. Those who would appear to have salvation, and are outwardly called but not from their hearts, do not really have it. And those who are not seeking the Lord, and are going along carelessly in sin and under the power of sin—God, who will bring the Word to them, will call them by His sovereign grace, and they will come.

BRINGING THE WORD OF CHRIST TO OTHERS:
Believing Requires Preaching—Ends Require Means

In order that men everywhere may hear this Word and come to the Lord, people must bring this Word; they must confess it. **"How, then, can they call on the one they have not believed in? And how can they believe in the one of whom they have not heard? And how can they hear without someone preaching to them? And how can anyone preach unless they are sent?"** (vv. 14–15a). Each step that is necessary for salvation is spoken of here. If they are going to believe, they must hear; if they hear, they must be preached to; if they are preached to, those who preach must be sent. God has sent us to go into all the world and preach the gospel and make disciples of all nations.[22] This is one of the ways we know that change has occurred in our hearts; we are aware of the grace that has come to us, and God's great goodness to us, and that the same goodness is for others. We will love our neighbors as ourselves,[23] and we will go, with the gospel, to others, as evidence that God has worked in our hearts. **"As it is written: 'How beautiful are the feet of those who bring good news!'"** (v. 15b).[24] We ourselves, our feet, will no longer be swift to go our own way, but be swift to go the way of the Lord. We are not going about seeking our own way and working out our own plan of salvation in the circumstances of this life.

---

22. *Matthew 28:19–20; Mark 16:15–20.*

23. *Mark 12:30–31.*

24. *Isaiah 57:2.*

NOT ALL WHO HEAR UNDERSTAND

It Is by Faith We Understand

We are told that though this Word comes, not all believe. Not all the Israelites accepted the good news, and not all to whom we come will accept, at least not initially. **"But not all the Israelites accepted the good news. For Isaiah says, 'Lord, who has believed our message?'"** (v. 16). The message did come, but people did not believe it. Faith comes from hearing the message, and the message is heard through the Word of Christ. But there is something more than hearing outwardly; there must be an understanding inwardly. **"Consequently, faith comes from hearing the message, and the message is heard through the word of Christ. But I ask: Did they not hear? Of course they did: 'Their voice has gone out into all the earth, their words to the ends of the world'"** (vv. 17–18). Paul is using a statement connected with general revelation, Psalm 19, to speak about the special revelation message also going out. That message went out, but those who heard it did not understand, because it was not mixed with faith. It is by faith we understand.[25] It was heard in some outward fashion only. Paul says, **"Again I ask: Did Israel not understand?"** (v. 19a). Israel did not understand. Those who have sat under the preaching for some time, not hearing, become hardened and do not understand.

Hardening Under the Very Means of Grace

As a result, the message went to others. **"First, Moses says, 'I will make you envious by those who are not a nation; I will make you angry by a nation that has no understanding'"** (v. 19b). The Gentiles had no understanding. The Jews, who had special revelation, had no understanding, but they professed to have understanding. God chose to bring those who had no understanding, and never professed to have understanding, to Himself. Remember the case of the Pharisee and the woman who anointed Jesus; the woman recognizes that she has no righteousness, while the Pharisee thinks he has righteousness of his own, and that becomes a block.[26] So God turns away from those

---

25. *Hebrews 11:3.*
26. *Luke 7:36–50.*

who turned away from Him. Not only did Moses say this, but Isaiah said this even more fully and clearly: **"Isaiah boldly says, 'I was found by those who did not seek me; I revealed myself to those who did not ask for me'"** (v. 20). So the message has been going to the ends of the earth. It has been going to Africa, it has been going to Asia, it has been going to Europe, it has been going to North America and South America, it has been going to the islands of the seas—to all those who have not sought for God. But those who had God's way of righteousness distorted its meaning and rejected it; they have not received it. **"But concerning Israel he says, 'All day long I have held out my hands to a disobedient and obstinate people'"** (v. 21). We have to be careful that we do not harden ourselves under the very means of grace, because of what has happened to the people of God under the Old Testament. God does not change. Notice the pain and poignancy of this: **"All day long I have held out my hands to a disobedient and obstinate people."**

Death in Turning Away, Life Through Trusting in Christ

The message of salvation will be taken from those nations that have turned away from it, and they will be left, for some time, in that state of darkness. We see places that were at one time prospering in the gospel now turning away from it, and we see them sinking into the mire, into the pit of sin and death. We see the gospel going to new parts of the world today—nations that have not heard it for centuries, and some that have never heard it before, are hearing it for the first time. God will call those persons through the preaching of the Word. Just as from Israel came the original preachers and the gospel went out, eventually, perhaps from the preachers that went out to China, India, Central Asia, and Africa, will come preachers who come to the United States, come to Europe, and bring that message of salvation to a land that had once heard but has turned away from it. We should realize that America turning away from the gospel involves *more* sin than Israel turning away, because there has been a whole history that has occurred. There has been a whole history of development of understanding in the Historic Christian Faith,[27] and we have turned away from it. We see our nation sinking into the mire. We are thinking about cultural

---

27. Gangadean, *The Westminster Confession*, xix–xxix, 349–351; Gangadean, "Paper No. 16: The Historic Christian Faith," in *The Logos Papers*, 103–114.

wars—it is the war for the gospel; the war concerning the two ways: life and death, the covenant of works and the covenant of grace. Life comes through trusting in God.

14

THE MYSTERY OF THE FULLNESS OF SALVATION

The Rejection of Israel Is Neither Total nor Final

1994

Romans 11

¹I ask then: Did God reject his people? By no means! I am an Israelite my-self, a descendant of Abraham, from the tribe of Benjamin. ²God did not reject his people, whom he foreknew. Don't you know what the Scripture says in the passage about Elijah—how he appealed to God against Israel: ³"Lord, they have killed your prophets and torn down your altars; I am the only one left, and they are trying to kill me"? ⁴And what was God's answer to him? "I have reserved for myself seven thousand who have not bowed the knee to Baal." ⁵So too, at the present time there is a remnant chosen by grace. ⁶And if by grace, then it is no longer by works; if it were, grace would no longer be grace.

⁷What then? What Israel sought so earnestly it did not obtain, but the elect did. The others were hardened, ⁸as it is written:

"God gave them a spirit of stupor,

   eyes that could not see

   and ears that could not hear,
to this very day."

⁹And David says:

"May their table become a snare and a trap,

a stumbling block and a retribution for them.

¹⁰May their eyes be darkened so they cannot see,
  and their backs be bent forever."

¹¹Again I ask: Did they stumble so as to fall beyond recovery? Not at all! Rather, because of their transgression, salvation has come to the Gentiles to make Israel envious. ¹²But if their transgression means riches for the world, and their loss means riches for the Gentiles, how much greater riches will their fullness bring!

¹³I am talking to you Gentiles. Inasmuch as I am the apostle to the Gentiles, I make much of my ministry ¹⁴in the hope that I may somehow arouse my own people to envy and save some of them. ¹⁵For if their rejection is the reconciliation of the world, what will their acceptance be but life from the dead? ¹⁶If the part of the dough offered as firstfruits is holy, then the whole batch is holy; if the root is holy, so are the branches.

¹⁷If some of the branches have been broken off, and you, though a wild olive shoot, have been grafted in among the others and now share in the nourishing sap from the olive root, ¹⁸do not boast over those branches. If you do, consider this: You do not support the root, but the root supports you. ¹⁹You will say then, "Branches were broken off so that I could be grafted in." ²⁰Granted. But they were broken off because of unbelief, and you stand by faith. Do not be arrogant, but be afraid. ²¹For if God did not spare the natural branches, he will not spare you either.

²²Consider therefore the kindness and sternness of God: sternness to those who fell, but kindness to you, provided that you continue in his kindness. Otherwise, you also will be cut off. ²³And if they do not persist in unbelief, they will be grafted in, for God is able to graft them in again. ²⁴After all, if you were cut out of an olive tree that is wild by nature, and contrary to nature were grafted into a cultivated olive tree, how much more readily will these, the natural branches, be grafted into their own olive tree!

²⁵I do not want you to be ignorant of this mystery, brothers, so that you may not be conceited: Israel has experienced a hardening in part until the full number of the Gentiles has come in. ²⁶And so all Israel will be saved, as it is written:

"The deliverer will come from Zion;

  he will turn godlessness away from Jacob.

²⁷And this is my covenant with them
  when I take away their sins."

²⁸As far as the gospel is concerned, they are enemies on your account; but as far as election is concerned, they are loved on account of the patriarchs, ²⁹for God's gifts and his call are irrevocable. ³⁰Just as you who were at one time disobedient to God have now received mercy as a result of their disobedience, ³¹so they too have now become disobedient in order that they too may now receive mercy as a result of God's mercy to you. ³²For God has bound all men over to disobedience so that he may have mercy on them all.

³³Oh, the depth of the riches of the wisdom and knowledge of God!

How unsearchable his judgments,

and his paths beyond tracing out!

³⁴"Who has known the mind of the Lord?

Or who has been his counselor?"

³⁵"Who has ever given to God,

that God should repay him?"

³⁶For from him and through him and for him are all things.
To him be the glory forever! Amen.

THE REJECTION OF ISRAEL IS NOT TOTAL

IN ROMANS 11, PAUL SPEAKS OF TWO THINGS. First, the rejection of Israel that he spoke of in Romans 9–10 is not total. Second, the rejection of Israel is not final. God's purpose in ordering the affairs of redemption in this way will bring praise, honor, and glory to God.

A Recurring Pattern: The Chosen Are Not Rejected

In verses 1–10, Paul explains that the rejection of Israel is not total. He says, **"I ask then: Did God reject his people? By no means!"** (v. 1a). God did not reject His people in the sense of being utterly rejected. What Paul has been saying should not be taken as the full, total, and final rejection of the people of Israel. Paul says emphatically, **"By no means!"** The chosen are not rejected. Those who had privileges but did not make use of them were rejected, but of that group, those who were chosen were not rejected. Also, Paul says that this pattern has been occurring in the past, even in the days of Elijah, but now it has occurred more fully in the days when Christ Himself was rejected.

Paul says, "I am an Israelite myself, a descendant of Abraham, from the tribe of Benjamin. God did not reject his people, whom he foreknew" (vv. 1b–2a). So Paul does speak about the rejection, but it is not total. Of that group, those who are foreknown are not rejected, and he—Paul the Apostle—is living proof. But it is not just one or two; there is a significant number who are not rejected. Paul explains this by appealing to the days of Elijah: "Don't you know what Scripture says in the passage about Elijah—how he appealed to God against Israel: 'Lord, they have killed your prophets and torn down your altars'" (vv. 2b–3a). Remember, this is the people who have had the privilege of the Word, but have not mixed it with faith/understanding, and that Word has no place within them. They have rejected those who brought the Word, including our Lord Jesus.

Elijah appealed to God against Israel: "Lord, they have killed your prophets and torn down your altars; I am the only one left, and they are trying to kill me" (v. 3). It appeared to Elijah, in his day, that he was the only one left. Elijah knew of no others. "And what was God's answer to him? 'I have reserved for myself seven thousand who have not bowed the knee to Baal.' So too, at the present time there is a remnant chosen by grace" (vv. 4–5). So, the rejection of Israel is not total. A remnant—those who were chosen—remains, and the remnant may be larger than we think, just as it was larger than Elijah thought. There were a significant number of Jews in the days of Christ who believed in Him. They may not have confessed Him publicly, but there was a significant number that did believe. So at that time, while the nation as a whole did not believe, and the privileges that belonged to the people as a whole were taken from them, there were still a significant number that believed.

Rejection Comes by Rejecting the Word of God

In answer to the question, "Did God reject his people?" Paul says, "By no means!" Those who were chosen believed. And as it was in the past, so it is now in the present. Except that now, just as the rejection of the Lord is more significant than the rejection of Elijah, so the rejection of those who reject the Lord is more significant. Notice that rejection is not something that occurs without any cause, but the rejection occurs upon their rejection of the Word of God and of the Word of God incarnate.

The Remnant: Under the Covenant of Grace in Christ

"So too, at the present time there is a remnant chosen by grace" (v. 5). One of the things to consider here is that it has always been by grace that people come to the Lord—by God's sovereign grace. It has never been by bloodline connection, and the belief that being born to covenant privileges gives a person an 'inside connection' is not true. Rather, having the privileges without making use of them is something that works against us.

"Chosen by grace" means chosen to the full privileges and blessings of God. It does not mean the 'outward national blessings' that Israel had, as some have tried to say. They were chosen by grace. That grace is the same blessing we receive by grace—it is no different.[1] Paul emphasizes this in light of what he has been saying before, that we are not under the covenant of works as in Adam, we are under the covenant of grace in Christ. He says, "And if by grace, then it is no longer by works; if it were, grace would no longer be grace" (v. 6). There is a radical distinction between these two covenants in terms of how we come to God: whether we come to God on the basis of our works or whether we come to God on the basis of His mercy to us in Christ; whether we come to God trusting in our own efforts to bring blessing, or whether we come trusting in Christ's work to bring us blessing.

The Covenant People Hardened: Mindless of the True Blessing—Zeal Without Knowledge

> What then? What Israel sought so earnestly it did not obtain, but the elect did. The others were hardened, as it is written: "God gave them a spirit of stupor, eyes so that they could not see and ears so that they could not hear, to this very day" (vv. 7–8).

Israel, or those who have the privileges of the covenant, those who have the privileges of the Word spoken, did not hear because they were not mindful, they were ignorant, they were mindless about what the true blessing was. That mindlessness, that ignorance, that failure to know what we should know, brings a judgment. It is a violation of the third

---

1. Gangadean, *The Westminster Confession*, 111–120.

commandment: taking the name of God in vain.[2] It is one thing to speak about Pharaoh being hardened. Pharaoh had general revelation, and he had the Word through Moses declared to him in signs, miracles, and wonders, but Pharaoh did not have the covenant privileges to begin with. It is one thing to see Pharaoh hardened; it is another thing to see those with the covenant privileges hardened; that is a dreadful thing. Those who hear the Word of God but do not take it to heart, those who hear the Word of God but do not put it into practice—this is the group of people that the Word of God is speaking of here.

As it was with Israel of old, so it is today; those who hear the Word of God and do not put it into practice will come under the same condition. "For God does not show favoritism" (Rom. 2:11). Those who reject His Word, reject His mercy, and affirm themselves under the covenant of works, are treated accordingly, are judged for their works, and are rejected. God cannot reject Pharaoh, who hardened himself to general revelation, and accept Israel, who hardened themselves to general revelation *and* special revelation. It is impossible for God to show favoritism; it would be a violation of His very nature.

When we hear the Word without giving heed, without paying attention, without seeking diligently, we are given up to the spirit of stupor.[3] It is as if our minds were drugged, turned off, asleep. We barely hear, but we do not understand; we see, but we do not perceive.[4] This is the condition that comes about when we hear the Word of God in vain. When we seek something other than God, when we seek the outward blessings of God and not God Himself, this is what happens to us. The concern must be for one thing and one thing only: to know Him, to possess Him.[5] Remember, Israel had a zeal, but it was not based on knowledge.[6] Paul says, **"What Israel sought so earnestly it did not obtain"** (v. 7a). What did they seek? Did they seek the knowledge of God so earnestly, or did they seek a righteousness of their own by the

---

2. Gangadean, *Philosophical Foundation*, 199–205; Gangadean, *The Westminster Catechisms*, 237–240.

3. Gangadean, "Paper No. 103: The Noetic Effect of Sin," in *The Logos Papers*, 531–538.

4. *Mark 4:12; Isaiah 6:9–10.*

5. Gangadean, *Philosophical Foundation*, 171–177, 208–211; Gangadean, *The Westminster Catechisms*, 109–111, 321–325; Gangadean, *On Natural and Revealed Theology*, 33–39, 127–139.

6. *Romans 10:2.*

law, under the covenant of works? You see how close we can come to seeking something less than God. That is why the Scripture says that none seek *Him*.[7] It does not say, 'None seek,' it says, 'None seek *Him*.' The first departure is with regard to the good, the knowledge of God, seeking Him. That is the ultimate departure. When we turn away from that, we turn to determining something else as good and evil, from ourselves, and because of this, judgment comes. Because we are not mindful of what life is, what the good is, we are given up to a spirit of stupor. When we do not pay attention to God's call to us to repent through toil and strife, and old age, sickness, and death, when we do not heed and continue to neglect the call to repentance, we are given up further to a spirit of stupor.

Blessings Taken for Granted Become a Curse

What happens, then, is that our blessings are turned to curses. Paul says in the next verse, **"And David says: 'May their table become a snare and a trap, a stumbling block and a retribution for them. May their eyes be darkened so they cannot see, and their backs be bent forever"** (vv. 9–10). When we boast and put our trust in the law and in the privileges that are given, rather than in God, that very boasting causes those privileges to become a snare for us and a trap. **"David says: 'May their table become a snare and a trap.'"**

Two things are going on in this section: First, if we have the Word of God without seeking Him, we become more and more dull in our minds, more and more turned off. That means every one of us here present, and every one of us who read the Word of God, will have the inherent darkening of our minds when we neglect it, take it for granted, and do not improve and use the privileges that we have. We become increasingly dull; we go into stupor. Second, when we, in zeal, boast about these privileges without really understanding and using them to the right and proper end, those privileges become a snare for us. So two things happen; one is not seeking, and the other is thinking we are seeking, making our boast in things other than God, and raising up the privileges to a position of idolatry, which becomes a curse to us. So then we are bowed down under the weight of this and perish.

---

7. *Psalms 14:1–3, 53:1–3; Romans 3:10–12.*

The realization that we can be neglectful, not seek the Lord, and be mindless under the preaching should cause us to be very careful and not take it for granted. God takes away the privileges from us. If we abuse those privileges and boast about them without understanding them, they can become a curse to us. It should cause us to walk in the fear of the Lord, to seek Him, and to ask for grace so that we can be mindful and not thoughtless. If it happened to Israel, it certainly can happen to us. Later on, Paul says we should fear the Lord, and that fear of the Lord is the beginning of wisdom.[8] We are to regard the means of grace the Lord has given us to grow and not fall under His wrath.

THE REJECTION OF ISRAEL IS NOT FINAL

Judged Under the Covenant of Works, Having Rejected Grace

Paul explains that the rejection of Israel is not final. **"Again I ask: Did they stumble so as to fall beyond recovery? Not at all!"** (v. 11a). Though Israel is rejected because Israel rejected the Word of the Lord, their rejection is not total, and it is not final. Paul is looking forward to a time when this rejection will be removed, and he explains how it is and why it is that the rejection will be removed. Paul says, **"Rather, because of their transgression, salvation has come to the Gentiles to make Israel envious"** (v. 11b). That is one of the effects of salvation coming to the Gentiles; it is not the purpose of it, but it is one of the effects. Remember, Israel rejecting the way of grace and rejecting the Word of the Lord requires, in turn, that Israel be rejected, because under the covenant of works, we are dealt with according to our works. They place themselves under the covenant of works when they reject the covenant of grace and reject trusting in the Lord for salvation.

Serving God's Purpose: Extending Salvation to All Families of the Earth

Israel's rejection serves God's purpose in that the privileges that belonged to Israel are extended to the Gentiles. In this sense, Paul says, **"Because of their transgression, salvation has come to the Gentiles."** It is taken from one and given to another. Jesus Himself had said, "For many are

---

8. *Romans 11:20–22.*

called, but few are chosen" (Matt. 22:14 KJV). The way, at that time, was very narrow; few there would be that find it.[9] Jesus said that many will come from the east and the west, and will take their places at the feast with Abraham, Isaac, and Jacob in the kingdom of heaven, but the sons of the kingdom will be thrown out.[10]

The rejection of Israel, in some ways, facilitated the salvation of the Gentiles. In this sense, it was a very difficult time, since the rejection was because of unbelief. It was very difficult, even for many of those Jews who had believed, to see that the Gentiles would come in. And when they were coming in—remember the first church council in Jerusalem in Acts 15—the Jews thought that the Gentiles would come in on the basis of the old way, through circumcision, through coming up to Jerusalem to worship, et cetera. The old pattern would not have facilitated the gospel extending beyond Jerusalem. The difficulty of accepting the Gentiles coming in extended even to those Jews who had believed. So it was because of unbelief, of failing to understand God's purpose originally in calling Abraham—that through him all the families of the earth would be blessed[11]—it was because of unbelief that they took it as a privilege for themselves only, making it very difficult to see that the gospel was to go out to all the nations. Remember, Peter had to have the vision of the sheet let down, and in the sheet were all kinds of animals, and Peter was rejecting and resistant, not seeing God's purpose to extend salvation to the Gentiles, even as the Jews had received salvation.[12] One and the same Lord is over all, and He saves all human beings in one and the same way.[13] This was a real struggle in the early Church.

For Israel's Good: Provoking to Envy That They Might Be Saved

"Salvation has come to the Gentiles to make Israel envious." The inclusion of the Gentiles is one of the purposes that was fulfilled in the rejection of Israel. The hope is, that by seeing how the Gentiles are receiving this privilege, Israel will come to realize what it had, and

---

9. *Matthew 7:13–14;* Gangadean, *The Gospel of Matthew,* 95–114.

10. *Matthew 8:11–12.*

11. *Genesis 22:18.*

12. *Acts 10.*

13. *Romans 10:11–13.*

through envy of the Gentiles, will come to embrace it. The purpose is not just to provoke Israel to envy and leave them in a state of envy, but to provoke them to envy to bring them to see what they truly had, so they might say, 'But that was really ours; that was for us!' Sometimes, we do not realize what we truly have until it is taken away and we see others possessing it. In that sense, the purpose was to provoke them to envy that they might be saved.

Greater Riches Brought by Israel's Fullness: The Completion of Redemption and the Resurrection from the Dead

Paul continues, **"But if their transgression means riches for the world, and their loss means riches for the Gentiles, how much greater riches will their fullness bring!"** (v. 12). I would like to read on in order to get a sense of what he means by the greater riches that their fullness will bring.

> **I am talking to you Gentiles. Inasmuch as I am the apostle to the Gentiles, I make much of my ministry in the hope that I may somehow arouse my own people to envy and save some of them. For if their rejection is the reconciliation of the world, what will their acceptance be but life from the dead?** (vv. 13–15).

There have been questions and discussions about this passage. The view that I believe is to be affirmed is that the Gentiles are being reconciled to God, so the reconciliation of Israel is not the reconciliation of the Gentiles; rather, the rejection of Israel is the reconciliation of the Gentiles. The fullness of Israel is not the reconciliation of the Gentiles. What is seen here is that when the Israelites come in, it will bring much greater riches than we have seen before. And what would the greater riches be? What will their acceptance be? It will be **"life from the dead."** Many interpreters have taken the position that this is referring to the resurrection, because with the coming in of Israel is the completion of the process of redemption and the ushering in of the final stage. I think this view seems to make sense here, unless someone wants to take a position that, somehow, there will be new blessings that will occur with the coming in of Israel. Notice that the coming in of Israel occurs *after* the fullness of the Gentiles. The anticipation here is that the Gentiles have been reconciled, and their full numbers have come in. We are talking about all the nations being converted to Christ. We are not talking about a certain number of Gentiles coming in, and then Israel coming in, and then the rest of the Gentiles coming in. That is incompatible with **"the reconciliation of the world,"** and incompatible with the idea of the fullness of the Gentiles coming in.[14] That is why I believe that what is to occur is the completion of the work of redemption and the bringing in of the final blessing: **"life from the dead."** I think that is referred to here as the **"much greater riches"** when Paul refers to it in the parallel phrase, **"life from the dead."**

Paul is anticipating that the rejection of Israel is not final. Their rejection brings salvation to the Gentiles and, through the Gentiles, salvation to Israel. We see later on in the passage that there is a pattern that God has used: just as God has been merciful to the Gentiles through Israel, so God will be merciful to Israel through the Gentiles.[15] The reason for this is so that no one would boast.[16] The idea seems to be that through the fullness of the Gentiles coming in, they will be instruments of God's mercy to Israel. So Israel's rejection is not final. Instead, the Gentiles coming in, followed by Israel, will usher in the fullness of the blessing that God has for us in the resurrection from the dead.

Paul argues further, **"If the part of the dough offered as firstfruits is holy, then the whole batch is holy; if the root is holy, so are the branches"** (v. 16). Commentators have said that this part of the dough refers to those Jews who have believed. It can certainly be taken as the Jews who believed at the time of Christ, or those Jews who believed throughout history, or it could be taken to mean the truth upon which the Gentiles also are blessed. **"If the root is holy, so are the branches."** Paul anticipates that the restoration will occur, and he affirms this in verse 25, which we will come to shortly.

The two reasons to say the rejection of Israel is not final are, first, that it brought blessing to the Gentiles. It was not a rejection for the sake of rejection, period, but it furthered God's purpose. Secondly, the Gentiles coming in, followed by Israel, will bring in the fullness of blessing that God has for us: **"life from the dead"** (v. 15b).

---

14. *Romans 11:25.*

15. *Romans 11:30–31.*

16. *Romans 11:18–20; Ephesians 2:8–9.*

Warning the Gentiles Against the "Pride of Grace"

Paul warns the Gentiles that they should be careful about having God's privileges and going in the direction of complacency and arrogance. It is the same thing for which Israel fell, and if Israel fell for that reason, they, too, will be cut off, and God can restore the *natural* branches. "**If some of the branches have been broken off, and you, though a wild olive shoot, have been grafted in among the others and now share in the nourishing sap from the olive root, do not boast over those branches**" (vv. 17–18a). The nourishing sap from the olive root is the blessing, the promise, the covenant that God gave to Israel. Paul is concerned that men will have the 'pride of grace.' Whether it be the 'pride of race' or the 'pride of grace,' we somehow turn the privileges that God gives us into an occasion for boasting. You may think that we are better off than some nation that is in darkness, or some tribe that is in darkness, but we are no better off in and of ourselves; it is wholly of God's grace. And so he says, "**Do not boast over those branches.**" Particularly here, it means do not boast over Israel. If Israel, at one time, thought of its privileges in such a way as to set herself up over and against the Gentiles, the Gentiles are not to do the same, because the same thing will happen to them. There is to be no boasting anywhere. It is all by grace, it is all by the mercy of God. Any time we slip in the least *iota* from recognizing it is all by grace, we are sliding down the road to disaster.

Paul continues, "**If you do, consider this: You do not support the root, but the root supports you. You will say then, 'Branches were broken off that I might be grafted in'**" (vv. 18b–19). This is a twisting of God's grace to exalt oneself. He answers, "**Granted. But they were broken off because of unbelief, and you stand by faith. Do not be arrogant, but be afraid**" (v. 20). Those who have the privileges and do not improve them, or twist the privileges of God in such a way as to boast about them, will be rejected. We should be afraid, lest pride arise in us, lest carelessness and casualness arise concerning the privileges that God has given us. "**Do not be arrogant, but be afraid. For if God did not spare the natural branches, he will not spare you either**" (vv. 20b–21). Out of this, we are to see God's kindness and God's sternness, God's mercy and God's justice. Just as God's mercy and justice is revealed in His leaving the Gentiles to go their way and being merciful to Israel, so too, in an even greater way, God's mercy and justice are seen in His rejecting those who have the covenant privileges but are casual and take it for granted. They might even treat it with contempt and twist it around to suit their own purposes of pride. God's justice and mercy is seen in His dealings.

"**Consider therefore the kindness and sternness of God: sternness to those who fell**"—those who have the covenant privileges but distorted it—"**but kindness to you, provided that you continue in his kindness**"—continue in His mercy; continue in understanding His mercy. "**Otherwise, you also will be cut off. And if they do not persist in unbelief, they will be grafted in**" (vv. 22–23a). God is not a respecter of persons.[17] Not only was it true when Israel had the blessing and it went also to the Gentiles, but if the Jews believe now, they will have that blessing.

> If they do not persist in unbelief, they will be grafted in, for God is able to graft them in again. After all, if you were cut out of an olive tree that is wild by nature, and contrary to nature were grafted into a cultivated olive tree, how much more readily will these, the natural branches, be grafted into their own olive tree! (vv. 23–24).

There is no room for boasting here. Paul is warning us, the Gentiles. There is a natural connection between the Israelites today and their forefathers; it is not a spiritual relation, but there is a natural relation, and in that sense, he speaks about how the natural branches will be grafted into their own olive tree. So the rejection of Israel is not total; those chosen, those whom God foreknew, are not rejected. And as it was in the past, so it is at present. Those who take God's Word for granted become increasingly mindless; they are given up to a duller and duller mind; they are in stupor. And those who boast in privileges and pride, those very privileges become a curse for them. The privileges prevent them from entering into the promise of God.

---

17. *Romans 2:11* KJV.

THE MYSTERY OF ISRAEL'S RESTORATION REVEALED:
To Show God's Sovereign Mercy Is
For All, That No One May Boast

God's justice and mercy is seen in His dealings, not only with the Gentiles, and bringing people out of the Gentiles to be saved, but in His dealing with the covenant people who are in unbelief. God's justice and mercy are seen in both cases. Paul explains to them that it is not only desirable that Israel will be restored, but it is the case that Israel will be restored. In verse 25, he says, **"I do not want you to be ignorant of this mystery, brothers, so that you may not be conceited: Israel has experienced a hardening in part until the full number of the Gentiles has come in."** That is why we anticipate that according to the promise, all nations will come to the Lord. When the nations have come to the Lord, when the full number of the Gentiles have come in, when the world has been reconciled, Israel, too, will be brought to the Lord. They will be brought to the Lord through the preaching of the Gentiles. This has been a mystery, something formerly hidden and now revealed,[18] and now made known more explicitly.

Paul says, **"And so all Israel will be saved, as it is written: 'The deliverer will come from Zion; he will turn godlessness away from Jacob. And this is my covenant with them when I take away their sins'"** (vv. 26–27). This is not just saying simply all the chosen of Israel will be saved; that is already known; that is taken for granted. The context here is that Israel as a whole will be saved after the fullness of the Gentiles has come in. The mystery is being revealed here to the people to avoid conceit. We are being warned in so many ways to be watchful against complacency, arrogance, conceit, and boasting. This is the root pride, that somehow, in ourselves, we are capable of achieving what is good. Paul explains that the purpose of this is so God's mercy may be to all men, over and against works, lest any man should boast.

> As far as the gospel is concerned, they are enemies on your account; but as far as election is concerned, they are loved on account of the patriarchs, for God's gifts and his call are irrevocable. Just as you who were at one time disobedient to God have now received mercy as a result of their disobedience, so they too have now be-

---

18. *Colossians 1:26* NKJV.

come disobedient in order that they too may now receive mercy as a result of God's mercy to you (vv. 28–31).

Consider this: God sovereignly chose Abraham and made His promise through Abraham. God left all the nations of the world to go their way, and He left them for almost 2,000 years to go their way. God, in His sovereign purpose, may do this. Now God has brought those nations to Himself and has let Israel go her way, the way He had let those nations go, and it has gone her way now for almost 2,000 years. Paul is anticipating that through the blessing to the nations, and through the mercy that has been shown to them, and through the preaching of the Word, Israel, too, will come to have the mercy of God. The Gentiles have nothing in which to boast, and the Jews have nothing in which to boast. "For God has bound all men over to disobedience so that he may have mercy on them all" (v. 32). So great is our propensity to boast, even in the privileges that God has given to us, which are totally by grace, that God works His purpose in this way and shows that all men are bound up to mercy.

FROM HIM, THROUGH HIM, AND
TO HIM ARE ALL THINGS:
To Him Be the Glory Forever! Amen.

The result of this is to bring praise to God. This is the doxology with which Paul closes:

Oh, the depth of the riches of the wisdom and knowledge of God!
  How unsearchable his judgments,
  and his paths beyond tracing out!
"Who has known the mind of the Lord?
  Or who has been his counselor?"
"Who has ever given to God,
  that God should repay him?"
For from him and through him and to him are all things.
  To him be the glory forever! Amen (vv. 33–36).

If we keep in mind how prone we are to boast, to think ourselves capable of something in ourselves, to see how we can turn the very means of grace into boasting, we will understand and appreciate the way God deals with all mankind. We will walk in the fear of the Lord, remembering that as God left the nations to go their way for thousands of years, since the call of Abraham and even before, so too He left the people who had privileges to go their way for thousands of years. So, neither those who have general revelation nor those who have special revelation can, in any way, boast before God, and we are all bound up to His mercy. We see that every good thing we have is from the Lord.

15

A LIVING SACRIFICE
Wholehearted Devotion to God

1994

Romans 12

[1]Therefore, I urge you, brothers, in view of God's mercy, to offer your bodies as living sacrifices, holy and pleasing to God—this is your spiritual act of worship. [2]Do not conform any longer to the pattern of this world, but be transformed by the renewing of your mind. Then you will be able to test and approve what God's will is—his good, pleasing and perfect will.

[3]For by the grace given me I say to every one of you: Do not think of yourself more highly than you ought, but rather think of yourself with sober judgment, in accordance with the measure of faith God has given you. [4]Just as each of us has one body with many members, and these members do not all have the same function, [5]so in Christ we who are many form one body, and each member belongs to all the others. [6]We have different gifts, according to the grace given us. If a man's gift is prophesying, let him use it in proportion to his faith. [7]If it is serving, let him serve; if it is teaching, let him teach; [8]if it is encouraging, let him encourage; if it is contributing to the needs of others, let him give generously; if it is leadership, let him govern diligently; if it is showing mercy, let him do it cheerfully.

[9]Love must be sincere. Hate what is evil; cling to what is good. [10]Be devoted to one another in brotherly love. Honor one another above yourselves. [11]Never be lacking in zeal, but keep your spiritual fervor, serving the Lord. [12]Be joyful in hope, patient in affliction, faithful in prayer. [13]Share with God's people who are in need. Practice hospitality.

[14]Bless those who persecute you; bless and do not curse. [15]Rejoice with those who rejoice; mourn with those who mourn. [16]Live in harmony with one another. Do not be proud, but be willing to associate with people of low position. Do not be conceited.

[17]Do not repay anyone evil for evil. Be careful to do what is right in the eyes of everybody. [18]If it is possible, as far as it depends on you, live at peace with everyone. [19]Do not take revenge, my friends, but leave room for God's wrath, for it is written: "It is mine to avenge; I will repay," says the Lord. [20]On the contrary:

"If your enemy is hungry, feed him;

   if he is thirsty, give him something to drink.
In doing this, you will heap burning coals on his head."

[21]Do not be overcome by evil, but overcome evil with good.

ROMANS 1–11:
From the Most Basic to Most Comprehensive

"THEREFORE, I URGE YOU, BROTHERS, IN VIEW of God's mercy, to offer your bodies as living sacrifices, holy and pleasing to God—this is your spiritual act of worship" (v. 1). When Paul says, "In view of God's mercy," that the brethren should offer themselves as living sacrifices, he is saying to us that it is necessary to know and understand God's mercy if we are going to give ourselves wholly to Him. To know what Paul is speaking about, we will look back at Romans 1–11.

In Romans 1–3, we saw how the wrath of God is on all men because God has given clear revelation of Himself in the way He has created the world,[1] yet all have turned away from that revelation. We saw how the law was given both to the Jews in special revelation, and to the Jews and Gentiles in general revelation, and men have turned from that revelation. We saw how Paul concluded that none seek God, no, not one.[2] What a condition we are in—as creatures, left to ourselves, we do not seek God. We realize that it is by God's grace only that we seek Him. By our own doing, we cannot come to God, and He has provided justification for us in Christ—forgiveness of sins. We do not have to spend so much of our time trying to justify ourselves

---

1. *Romans 1:18–20.*
2. *Romans 3:10–12.*

by blaming others and excusing ourselves in one way or another. So much of our life is spent that way. If we have eyes to see and hearts to understand, as we look about us, as we look at our own lives, we will see how self-deception and self-justification are present, and we will thank God for His mercy—that He has provided justification for us.

The way of justification is nothing that we could have anticipated, and God makes it clear that this is how it was from Abraham—this is how it was from Adam. Paul speaks about sanctification, that though we are forgiven, we still have the power of sin in us. All of us this week, all of us here now, are struggling in various ways with that process of sanctification. As we see how sin works death in us, we are so thankful that God has been merciful to us and brought us to Christ. We hope in Him that He will continue to show us mercy. We are not only thankful for God's work in us, but we long for God to work in others, whether in the Church or outside of the Church, whether believers or nonbelievers. We long for the mercy of God to come upon all.

We saw how God dealt with the Church under the old covenant and how they had the same promises of grace, yet how it is possible, even within the Church, for people to come short of that grace. The old nature is so deceitful that it would, even in the context of Scripture and the grace of God, turn that grace into something that we do, or something that we earn, rather than seeing our dependence on God. How subtle this sin is, how deceitful it is, and how people labor, over long periods of time, under the burden of sin and death. And so we are thankful that God has begun His work in us, and we trust Him to complete it. It is in view of this mercy that we say there is no hope for anything good outside of God, but we have *everything* promised to us, in the most secure way, in Christ. What is there left for us to do but to give ourselves wholly, to devote ourselves fully, in service to God? When we understand the reality of sin and death and God's mercy, righteousness, and life in Christ, that is the only thing left for us to do.

IN VIEW OF GOD'S MERCY

Living Sacrifices: A Reasonable and Pleasing Worship Before God

"In view of God's mercy . . ." We must keep this constantly in view, rehearsing it before ourselves every day as we meditate on the condition around us. "**I urge you brothers, in view of God's mercy, to offer your bodies as living sacrifices**" (v. 1a). This is in contrast to the sacrifices that were killed on the altar—our lives, our whole lives, are to be a sacrifice to God. "**This is your spiritual act of worship**" (v. 1b). The terms *spiritual* and *reasonable*[3] are used interchangeably in Scripture, and the root term is from *logos,* which refers to the idea of being reasonable. We should not separate the reasonable from the spiritual, as we see in this context. This worship is holy; it is devoted to God; it is an aroma that is sweet and well-pleasing to God. There are times when we smell fragrant blossoms, and sometimes the scent just lifts you; it is joyful. Our lives before God, devoted to Him, are in God's sight, in God's presence, a sweet aroma, well-pleasing to Him.

Do Not Be Conformed to This World: Giving Ourselves to God

We are not to be conformed to the pattern of this world. Paul says, "**Do not conform any longer to the pattern of this world, but be transformed by the renewing of your mind**" (v. 2a). Let us think about ways in which the world operates. We can see some gross ways, and our temptation may not only be in the gross ways, but in the subtle ways. There is, first of all, idolatry. Idolatry is the breaking of the first commandment: "You shall have no other gods before me" (Ex. 20:3). It is when we hope that through some *thing,* some *activity,* some *person,* we will receive what can come only from God.[4] It could be so many things: the comfort, the pleasure, and the security that we get in another person, a job, a recreational activity, and many other things. Anything that we seek to find comfort and security in apart from God

---

3. "I beseech you therefore, brethren, by the mercies of God, that ye present your bodies a living sacrifice, holy, acceptable unto God, which is your *reasonable* service" (Romans 12:1 KJV). Emphasis Added.

4. Gangadean, *Philosophical Foundation,* 171–183; Gangadean, *The Westminster Catechisms,* 229–232.

is idolatry; it is something put in the place of God—that is the way of the world. And we, as believers, are not exempt from that. We still have sin and find that sort of division in us. Paul tells the Corinthians, "Flee from idolatry" (1 Cor. 10:14b). This is not just fleeing from a gross form of an idol that we may bow down before, it is *anything* that we put in the place of God.

Think about the comforts, delights, and security we seek, whether we pursue them through something in the place of God or through God. If it is apart from God, God will blow on it, and it will wither away. That is the way of the world. We are to put that aside. **"Do not conform any longer to the pattern of this world"** (v. 2a). Sometimes, we put the seeking of these things first before God. Scripture says, "But seek first his kingdom and his righteousness, and all these things will be given to you as well" (Matt. 6:33). Many of us anticipate work, career, and education. We sometimes get educated first for a job and then consider our commitment to the Lord—that is a worldly way. Scripture says, "But seek first his kingdom and his righteousness, and all these things will be given to you as well." This includes what we eat and what we drink.[5] Paul says, "And having food and clothing, with these we shall be content" (1 Tim. 6:8 NKJV). We may have to depend on God each day for food and pray, "Give us today our daily bread" (Matt. 6:11). The lilies of the field and the birds of the air will reprimand us.[6] Jesus said, "The Son of Man has no place to lay His head" (Matt. 8:20). We do not advocate apostolic poverty as was done sometimes in the early church and the medieval period, but remember who is speaking—Paul, one who lived in this way before the Lord.

Jesus said, "But seek first his kingdom and his righteousness, and all these things will be given to you as well." We cannot reverse that order; we have to be careful about this, otherwise, we will be going the way of the world. When we worry, as against trusting, that is being worldly. Sometimes, in subtle ways, our very virtues, separated from the goal, manifest worldliness. You know how the liberals advocate compassion, but it is not defined in terms of the good.[7] Sometimes, we may hold

---

5. *Matthew 6:25–34.*

6. *Matthew 6:26–30.*

7. Gangadean, *Philosophical Foundation, 171–177, 208–211;* Gangadean, *The Westminster Catechisms, 109–111, 321–325;* Gangadean, *On Natural and Revealed Theology, 33–39, 127–139.*

up our sensitivity—being sensitive to others is a great ideal—but we are not sensitive to the deeper things that are going on in life that we ought to be aware of. We may hold up these virtues apart from the good and feel very secure and righteous in them, but that is not God's way; that is the way of the world.[8] Those are subtle ways, and we can easily be drawn into them. We could be neglecting to meditate on God's law day and night; we could follow the laws of the world and live by them, as if those things were fixed. We could be living in a worldly way instead of gearing our lives toward and preparing to teach all people all that Christ has commanded.[9] We could be accommodating these laws, living by them, taking them for granted, and settling down, instead of thinking about teaching God's Word. Do not be conformed to that worldly view; put it aside.

When we seek the praise of men more than the praise of God, that is where the element of pride comes in. We should be more concerned to please God, and sometimes we forget that and seek what is accepted by men. Remember, the Lord said, "For what is highly esteemed among men is an abomination in the sight of God" (Lk. 16:15b NKJV). Why should we seek to be accepted by such a false standard? We are not seeking to please our Lord, who loved us and gave Himself for us. If He died for us, surely we should be willing to die in His service, and to give ourselves to Him.

Be Transformed by the Renewing of Your Mind: An Ongoing Repentance

Paul says, "**I urge you . . . in view of God's mercy, to offer your bodies as living sacrifices, holy and pleasing to God**" (v. 1). In order to do this, we must not conform to the world, but be transformed: "**Do not conform any longer to the pattern of this world, but be transformed by the renewing of your mind**" (v. 2a). That involves change in our thinking; it is the *renewing* of our minds. That involves repentance—*metanoia*—a change of mind, a renewing of the mind. Instead of walking in the old way, we walk in the new way. This repentance is not only initial, but continual; it is ongoing. As we walk with the Lord day

---

8. Gangadean, *The Unity of the Church*, 135–141, 170–172, 241–242.

9. *Matthew 28:20.*

by day, we seek to put His Word into practice; we see how we come short, we confess our coming short as sin, we repent, we look to God for grace, and we go through a transforming process. It is the process of sanctification, and Jesus said, "Sanctify them by the truth; your word is truth" (Jn. 17:17). "Then you will know the truth, and the truth will set you free" (Jn. 8:32). That means we have to spend time reading the Word—no excuses. There are no excuses for not spending time in the Word. We hear the statement, "No excuses," regarding working out physically. But the Scripture says, "Physical training is of some value, but godliness has value for all things" (1 Tim. 4:8a). There are no excuses for not being in the Word. Not just in the spirit of *doing time*—'I did my time in the Word; I did my chapter today.' No, we need to really *be* in the Word. We need to ask the Lord, before coming to read the Word, to prepare us and speak to our hearts. After reading, throughout the day, we need to look to the Lord for the renewal of our minds by meditating on the Word. We need to gather with other believers where the Word is being opened up, where we can hear that Word, and not continually take in the world's unbelief in so many forms as it presents itself, as it tries to allure and appeal to us. If we are going to hear the Word of God, we have to put aside this other word. We are not to fill our minds with these worldly things, but we are to fill our minds with the Word of God, which has a bearing on every detail of life. We are to be prepared through the preaching and teaching of the Word and benefit from those who have gone before us. That is how our minds are transformed; that is how we are no longer conformed to this world. Do not be *conformed*, but be *transformed*. Do not be molded by the world, but be molded by God, in the image of Christ.

Approving God's Perfect Will: From Burden to Delight

It is *then*, as we are transformed more and more, that we are able to approve the will of God. **"Then you will be able to test and approve what God's will is—his good, pleasing and perfect will"** (v. 2b). In our worldly state, insofar as sin has its way in us, we find His will burdensome. Yet Jesus said, "Take my yoke upon you and learn from me, for I am gentle and humble in heart, and you will find rest for your souls. For my yoke is easy and my burden is light" (Matt. 11:29–30). How much anxiety do we have when we do not walk in His way?

Some things are *very clear.* Let me begin with an example of what is very clear about God's work: "Do not be unequally yoked together" (2 Cor. 6:14a NKJV). Some things are very clear; just obey, and more understanding will come.

As we are transformed, we will *approve* of God's will. We will say yes to it, and we will find ourselves delighting in it. It will be the **"good, pleasing and perfect will"** of God. It is perfect in the sense of complete, full, and total. We will stand in awe of how broad the law of God is, how deep, how intimate; it touches every detail of life. There is not a single situation where the law of God does not come to bear. We will understand this; we will find it pleasing; we will find it as bringing life; it will be good. That is how we will rejoice and delight in the law of God. God does not intend for the life of the believer to be just a grin-and-bear-it kind of thing. There are times when we cannot see clearly, and we may just have to endure for a time. But the kingdom of God is *righteousness, peace,* and *joy* in the Holy Ghost.[10] The fruit of the Spirit is love, joy, peace.[11] There is a joy that comes in fellowship with other believers, and the more we walk in the truth, the more complete our fellowship is, and the more complete our joy is. We will delight in the saints of God. We will see God working and preserving, upholding, and transforming lives. We will see a brother and sister in Christ, and our hearts will light up. That is, a brother or sister who is walking, not just hearing the Word of God, but who is doing it. It will be a delight to see them; it will be an encouragement.

MATURITY, FRUITFULNESS, UNITY, AND FULLNESS: Sober-minded Service According to Our Measure of Faith

As our hearts are transformed, we will approve the will of God and find delight. Paul brings this to bear in a very specific way in the following verses. This has to do with God's calling for each of us in the particular ability God has given us. In other words, Paul is moving from general to more specific. He says, **"For by the grace given me I say to every one of you: Do not think of yourself more highly than you ought, but rather think of yourself with sober judgment"** (v. 3a). Paul speaks

---

10. *Romans 14:17.*

11. *Galatians 5:22.*

about boasting to the Corinthians. He says, "I am out of my mind to talk like this" (2 Cor. 11:23), or in other versions, "I speak as if insane" (NASB), "I'm talking like a madman" (ESV), and "I speak as a fool" (KJV). We are to think of ourselves sanely—not as a madman. Anyone who thinks of themselves more highly than they ought is talking like a madman, as if he is insane. When we come to appraising ourselves, we must recognize that whatever gifts and abilities we have originate in and are sustained by God; they are from God.

By the grace given to him, Paul is able to exhort others not to think more highly of themselves than they ought. He says, "**But rather think of yourself with sober judgment, in accordance with the measure of faith God has given you**" (v. 3). The sense here seems to be that we are to minister according to the understanding of God in whatever particular area He has given each of us. We are to be ever-growing in the knowledge of God, but there is a particular area that God has given each of us. And in that area, according to our measure of faith, we are to serve.

First of all, Paul warns against pride when we go beyond our measure of faith, and then he warns against division. Those two—pride and division—go together. There is an underside to pride: those who have conceit and ambition because they have gifts that are more easily noticed than the gifts of others. Then, there are those whose gifts, like the liver, may not be as easily noticed as those of others. The liver is not noticed; when was the last time you heard anyone praise their liver? You could do without your right arm, perhaps do without one of your eyes, but not your liver; you cannot do without it. So, we should not view things just from outward appearance, but think with sober judgment—that is, sanely. I would rather give up my arm than my liver, because if I give up my liver, I'm gone! Yet, it is not in our custom to give thanks for our liver. Maybe we should start reminding ourselves, 'Lord, thank you for my liver.' I bring up the liver as a way to concretize it—as a metaphor, a symbol—to remind us.

Unity of Diversity: One Body, Many Parts

We are not to be lifted up in pride, go beyond our measure, or disregard others, and we are to be careful to maintain unity. This is the next point that Paul makes here, as he comes to speak about our diversity.

He says, "Just as each of us has one body with many members . . ." (v. 4a)—there is the *one* and the *many*. There is *unity of diversity*. That is precisely what unity is: many working together as one. "**Just as each of us has one body with many members, and these members do not all have the same function, so in Christ we who are many form one body**" (vv. 4–5a). The members do not have the same function, but they have the same goal. This verse is one expression of the famous problem that we have wrestled with throughout history: the problem of the *one* and the *many*.[12] God is *one* and *many*; He is diverse. There is one being and three persons. There is a *tri*-unity.[13] In so many ways, within our own being, within our bodies, there is one and many. The Church is one and many; we need to reckon with that. So, Paul brings that image before us and applies it to Christ. There is no question about it. This is not just true locally, in this congregation, but also in the larger body, and the universal body of Christ, stretching back in history. The Church is one body. It is one body not only stretching back in history, but also stretching forward, because what we do, God willing, others will inherit and build on. Our primary concern, perhaps, should be the more local body first, putting that into practice, and then the larger body of Christ and other believers with whom we come into contact. We need to appreciate the reality that there is one body.

Different Gifts for One Goal: That Christ Might Fill Everything in Every Way

"**We have different gifts, according to the grace given us**" (v. 6a). Paul specifies what these gifts are, and there are a number of questions that are to be raised in connection with this. Paul continues, "**If a man's gift is prophesying, let him use it in proportion to his faith. If it is serving, let him serve; if it is teaching, let him teach; if it is encouraging, let him encourage**" (vv. 7–8a). Various functions are noted: prophesying, serving, teaching, and encouraging. (Prophesying and teaching are not identical.) "**If it is encouraging, let him encourage; if it is contributing to the needs of others, let him give generously; if it is leadership, let him govern diligently; if it is showing mercy, let him do it cheerfully**"

---

12. Gangadean, *History of Philosophy*, 81–85.

13. Gangadean, *The Westminster Confession*, 56–60; Gangadean, *The Westminster Catechisms*, 123–125.

(v. 8). The question is raised, 'Is this just an exhaustive list of the gifts and graces of God?' We would say it has been understood variously. Some say that this is speaking of the offices in the church—those connected with teaching and those connected with serving—which are the office of elder and the office of deacon. I believe that it includes these offices but is not limited to them. These gifts and abilities are broader. If we understand who these gifts are from and what the goal is, we will see why we say that it is to be understood in a broader sense. This is important because as we seek the will of God, each of us has to ask, 'What is my gift?' If we define gifts in terms of the church and working in the church, then we have the problem of thinking, 'If I am not a Sunday school teacher, pastor, or missionary, then what am I? What do I do for my work?' There has been a tendency in the past to think of gifts only in terms of the church and to have everything concentrated in the church. But in doing so, we restrict and minimize the extent of Christ's work.

The opposite also happens. It has not been done often, but there is a danger on the part of those who broaden the gifts more generally to include secular activities, but the activities are separated from the goal. What happened in religiously liberal circles was a secularizing of the gospel in this way, in terms of broad areas of service. I think if we understand that Christ is to fill everything in every way,[14] that He is to fill the universe,[15] that He is to bring all the nations to Himself, all the families of the earth, we will see that the fullness of Christ includes everything. His work is to make God known and to fill the earth with the knowledge of His glory. If we understand fullness as the goal of the Christian life, we will see how we cannot restrict the gifts just to the church activities, and we cannot take the gifts outside of the church, separate them from the goal, and merely secularize it. If we understand fullness, we will see the gifts are working so that Christ might fill everything in every way. There is not one area of the world that has not been created by Christ. There is not one area of the world of which

14. *Ephesians 1:23.*

15. *Ephesians 4:10.*

the Lord does not say, 'This is mine!'[16] In every area of life, His glory is revealed and He will be honored. I challenge you to come up with even one area that seems to be disconnected from Christ.

We need to ask ourselves: what is God's will for my life? What is God's purpose for me? How am I to serve? Paul says, **"Each member belongs to all the others"** (v. 5b). He does not say, 'Each member belongs to each,' which tends to be egocentric, but **"each member belongs to all the others."** It is a whole; it is the work for the common good, for *the* good. You do not belong to yourself in the body of Christ. You belong to Christ and to all the other members. So the gift that God has given you, the grace that God has given you, is to be used to serve others. Elsewhere, it is said, "As each one has received a gift, minister it to one another, as good stewards of the manifold grace of God" (1 Pt. 4:10 NKJV). A good part of our lives is lived out in the area of our work. We have to connect with our gift, understand God's will, and learn to bring the Word of God to bear in that area of work. We are to be princes ruling with Christ. Part of that ruling involves teaching the Word of God; that is how Christ rules—by teaching. Jesus says, "All authority in heaven and on earth has been given to me. Therefore go and make disciples of all nations . . . teaching them to obey everything I have commanded you" (Matt. 28:18b–20a). We are to make disciples and teach all nations. As we learn to apply the Word of God in each particular area, and bring that understanding to others, we will be ruling with Christ. If we do not prepare ourselves, we will be a vessel not fit for honor. But if we prepare ourselves, give ourselves to opportunities, to the use of ordinary means, and are patient and diligent in them, we will prosper, grow, and be able to serve. We will be a vessel for honor. God intends His people to rule in the sense that He intends His people to take His Word and bring it to bear in every area of life. That is what it is to rule with Christ. As we said earlier, there is not one area for which Christ does not say, 'This is mine!'

---

16. This is a paraphrase of the famous quote by Abraham Kuyper, "There is not a square inch in the whole domain of our human existence over which Christ, who is Sovereign over all, does not cry: Mine!" James D. Bratt, ed., *Abraham Kuyper: A Centennial Reader* (Grand Rapids, MI: William B. Eerdmans, 1998), 461.

Discovering and Developing Our Gifts: Function, Order, and Pressing Forward in God

We have to learn the particular *fit* that we have to an area, and if we prepare ourselves, we will be able to do so. That is the sense in which we know the will of God and present ourselves in devoted sacrificial service to Him all our days.[17] We said it is not the *narrower* interpretation of the gifts, focused only within the church in the context of special revelation, but it is a *broader* interpretation of the gifts, connected with the kingdom of God in all the earth. It is not just a supernatural manifestation of gifts; it is natural, in the sense that it is created—so it is the way God has made us. Paul's abilities did not start at the time he was converted. Some of his abilities manifested *before* he was converted; he just turned in the opposite direction. God structures our gifts and abilities into the very way He has made us—our personality and our areas of sensitivity—and this operates from a very early age.

It is through our gifts and abilities that we learn to acknowledge God and to serve. There is not just a twofold distinction in terms of teaching and service. We say it is a threefold distinction: the prophetic, the priestly, and the kingly. We could suggest how the gifts listed might connect with these three areas. For instance, in terms of showing mercy, or in terms of exhorting—these are some of the priestly dimensions of teaching. Prophesying seems to be involved not just with the Scripture, the written Word of God, but with the prophetic work of bringing the Word of God to bear in all of life, including general revelation—opening that up, pushing further, and laying foundation.[18] That is a broader sense of prophesying—opening up the Word of God in all of life—not just the Word of God in special revelation, because God has created all things. John says, "He was in the world, and though the world was made through him, the world did not recognize him" (Jn. 1:10)—He, the Logos. Those who are involved in psychology and the other disciplines should be understanding the *logos* of that area, opening it up, and teaching and leading in that area. That is how we are called to rule in the kingdom of God.

God wants fruit. He wants fruit from our lives. Every branch that does not bear fruit, it is not really a branch, and He cuts it off. "He cuts

---

17. *Romans 12:1–2.*

18. *History of Philosophy,* Surrendra Gangadean.

off every branch in me that bears no fruit, while every branch that does bear fruit he prunes so that it will be even more fruitful" (Jn. 15:2). We may think, 'Oh, but that was such a beautiful branch. I loved it.' Off it goes, or it is pruned away that the branch might bear more fruit. Be prepared for the pruning and watch for it. God is glorified in our bearing much fruit—fruit that will remain.

This is the way that the promises and the mercy of God are manifested. Paul says, "For the earnest expectation of the creation eagerly waits for the revealing of the sons of God" (Rom. 8:19 NKJV), and he says, "We know that the whole creation has been groaning as in the pains of childbirth right up to the present time" (Rom. 8:22). We should be reminded that the whole creation is groaning, waiting for the appearance of the sons of God. When we complain that it is hot in Phoenix—it is sometimes 115 degrees—that is part of the groaning of the creation. Even nonbelievers have a sense of the relation between morality and the state of the culture—especially the morality of those in leadership.[19] Who are those in leadership? The Church—the light of the world, the salt of the earth, and the fruitfulness of the ground.

God's plan is full and complete in every way. In terms of devoting ourselves to God, Paul reminds us how we should be pursuing the kingdom of God in terms of our particular gifts and understanding the gifts. There is an order in the gifts, in terms of the prophetic, priestly, and kingly. The prophetic lays the foundation, and we are to build on it. The priest is to take that Word and work it into the lives of the believers. This is where exhortation comes in: we bring the Word in a way that connects with the feelings, the conscience, or the activity. Some are gifted in bringing the Word in this way, and we should be giving ourselves to learning how to do this. There is the gift of mercy connected with the ministry to the sick. As we continue to see the worsening of the healthcare system, Christians should be leading in finding ways to improve it by finding more merciful and compassionate ways to provide medical care. We should be striving to find more godly

---

19. In the sermon, Pastor Gangadean illustrates this point using the examples of Oedipus and King Arthur. In Sophocles' *Oedipus Tyrannus*, the plague afflicting Thebes is traced to the hidden guilt of its king: "You are the land's pollution" (Sophocles, *Oedipus Tyrannus*, line 350). Similarly, in Thomas Malory's *Le Morte d'Arthur*, the land of Logres becomes barren and cursed as Arthur's kingdom descends into moral corruption: "the realm of Logres began to waste" (*Le Morte d'Arthur*, Book XVII, Chapter 1).

ways of doing that work and not just finding a job in the system and holding on to it because we think we just need to make a living.

The Church must also recover the area of extending mercy to the poor apart from state-funded welfare. This, too, used to be primarily under the care of the Church in culture—where welfare is administered with responsibility. Believers should take over and run the healthcare and welfare systems according to godly principles. They should not exist in the hands of the government *per se*, or be left merely to financial motives by and large in the private sector. We are to think *grandly*, for our Lord is great! He rules over all. This is part of the preparation of sitting under a teaching ministry—to educate others to think, plan, dream, and work in this way. Dreaming, not in the sense of fantasizing, but in the sense that we work patiently, deliberately, devotedly, perseveringly, and wisely to bring this about. In five, ten, fifteen, and twenty years from now, we will see fruit borne and it will leave an example for others to follow. So when the Scriptures say, **"showing mercy"** (v. 8b), do not think in the minimum sense; think in the maximal sense, because it is our Lord whom we are serving.

If we remember the common goal and purpose of filling the earth with the knowledge of God, we will maintain the unity of the Spirit in the Church as we work towards the unity of the faith.[20] We should not, first of all, ask, 'What is my gift?' We should first ask, 'What is the goal?' As we deeply understand the goal of the knowledge of God, our gifts will become manifest. The vision of the goal naturally activates the gift; it makes us aware of it; it motivates and sustains the gift. As we develop our abilities in God, there will be a channel created for ministry. If we have to cut through rock, there will be a channel created for ministry. We cannot keep the goodness of God back; it will burst forth in this way when our gifts are developed. This is the sense in which you will find new ways, despite obstacles, because you are eager and moved by the love of God to spend nights scheming and planning to find a way forward by God's grace. As in the image of the climber looking for a toe-hole to get a little bit higher in the rock, you inch forward and find a way for that gift to be poured out—because you have to have it, or you will die! This is the way the Lord would have us press forward.

---

20. *The Unity of the Church,* Surrendra Gangadean.

THE OPERATION OF LOVE:
The Chief Virtue—Love Seeks the Good for Others

If we understand what the goal is, we will understand what the gift is. The vision of the good activates the gift, and the gift develops in ministry in pursuit of the good. Paul further discusses how it is to be worked out in love. Love is the chief virtue; it encompasses all other virtues. Love is a virtue; it is not the good, but seeks the good for others. Love is not the same as the good; we are not in love with love—we are in love with God, and we love the good. The means to the good is virtue, and love is a comprehensive virtue. Therefore, Paul speaks much about love in this passage.

"**Love must be sincere**" (v. 9a). We should not love as the world loves; the world speaks much about love, but it is not a true love because it is not directed towards the good. Paul says, "**Hate what is evil; cling to what is good**" (v. 9b). It is the good that we are to seek after, and we have to cling to it, grasp it, hold on to it, and not let it be taken from us. If we define love in terms of what is good, as God defines the good, then love will be sincere. If not, it will be something else, yet called by that name. We may say that it is love formally, but if love is not directed to what is truly good, it is not love. 'We love the world or we love God'—this is the same love, *formally* speaking. But what truly defines love—whether it is true love or not—is the object of our love. If our love is directed towards the world, it is not true love. If it is directed towards the good—eternal life, knowing and making God known—that is true love. "**Love must be sincere.**" There is a strong tendency in us to deceive ourselves about love. There is a lot of talk in the Christian community about love, but very little connection with the good. Their conception of the good is connected with many other virtues, but when we try to define those other virtues in terms of the ultimate, a blank is drawn.

"**Be devoted to one another in brotherly love**" (v. 10a). There is a lot of sin in us that alienates, and we rub each other the wrong way. We have to come to realize that God forgives our sin, and we must forgive one another. We must learn to bear with each other, see the good in each other that God has given, and be devoted to one another by helping each other develop that good. We cannot afford these tensions that weaken us; we must be devoted to one another in brotherly love and in forgiving one another. **"Honor one another above yourselves"** (v. 10b) in terms of realizing that God has given different gifts in different areas; we honor these persons. We are to recognize when others are excelling and should be in positions of leadership in a particular area. In that way, we honor one another more than ourselves in the particular areas of gifts and abilities that God has given.

"Never be lacking in zeal, but keep your spiritual fervor, serving the Lord" (v. 11). It is the Lord that we serve, and in serving the Lord, we should not give way to cynicism or hopelessness—that is the worldly way. For we hope in God, who is able to bring these things to pass, and in that hope, we can be fervent in zeal that continues to burn. It is when we lose hope that we begin to weaken. If our zeal is according to knowledge, it will bring hope.

"Be joyful in hope, patient in affliction, faithful in prayer" (v. 12). If we want to see the sincerity of love, it is expressed in this way. Love always hopes in God—not in another person, but in God. God can and does work through a person. But we know our nature—human nature—and, left to ourselves, we do not seek. But we can hope in God that He will bring about change. Trusting in God to work in a person will keep our hope going. That is love—patient in affliction, not cross, not fretful, faithful in prayer, always persevering.

"Share with the Lord's people who are in need. Practice hospitality" (v. 13). This is very concrete. We have to learn hospitality and put it into practice, knowing that we are contributing to others in the kingdom and building up the kingdom of God in that way. We need to ask God to help us discern opportunities and find ways to share and practice that hospitality.

"Bless those who persecute you; bless and do not curse" (v. 14). Our concern is for the good and for others' welfare. If we understand the nature of sin, we should not be surprised by sin. If we keep these things in mind, then we will not fall back on our default responses. When we start blasting instead of blessing, it is because our eyes are off the good and off God's purpose for us. We are to keep our eyes on the good and on God's purpose, and seek the good of the other.

"Rejoice with those who rejoice; mourn with those who mourn" (v. 15). We should be sympathetic with those who rejoice, sharing in their joy and rejoicing with them. And for those who mourn, we should mourn with them. Sometimes, we have to manifest that first and make contact with a person at the level of feeling. I am not advising that as a standard policy or expecting it from others, but sometimes, we may connect at that level first.

"**Live in harmony with one another**" (v. 16a). We need to do what we can "to keep the unity of the Spirit in the bond of peace" (Eph. 4:3b). "**Do not be proud, but be willing to associate with people of low position. Do not be conceited**" (v. 16b). Do not be 'stuck up.' Neither when we are young nor when we are old should we be proud and haughty. We are not celebrating the underdog; we are not celebrating the overdog. But we are to be willing—because our tendency is to go the other way—to associate with persons of low position. These are persons of low position as far as the eyes of men are concerned, not low in the eyes of God. Paul warns us against the temptation to be prideful and feel good about ourselves because of association with persons at a 'higher' level and finding our 'self-worth' and 'self-esteem' in that connection rather than finding our worth in Christ.

"**Do not repay anyone evil for evil**" (v. 17a); that is not the spirit of Christ. "**Be careful to do what is right in the eyes of everybody**" (v. 17b). We are to watch how we walk. Be circumspect, and do not say, 'My heart is pure, and I can do this sort of thing.' That is presumptuous—that attitude can cause a great deal of harm in the body of Christ. "**Be careful to do what is right in the eyes of everybody.**" We have to take into consideration how others will view our actions and not leave ourselves wide open for criticism. We have to be circumspect and watchful. We are not supposed to be 'bound up and uptight.' It is the principle of being wise as serpents and harmless as doves.[21]

"**If it is possible, as far as it depends on you, live at peace with everyone**" (v. 18). If it is possible, as far as it depends on you, live at peace with everyone—but it is not peace at any price. As far as we are concerned, as far as we can go, we should be at peace with all men. Do not have any cliques, grudges, or enemies. A Christian should not have any enemies except those who make a reproach about their walking with the Lord. "**Do not take revenge, my dear friends, but leave room for God's wrath**" (v. 19a). Understand that God is working; let God handle it. If we do not leave it to God, we are being presumptuous. "**For it is written: 'It is mine to avenge; I will repay,' says the Lord**"

---

21. *Matthew 10:16.*

(v. 19b). On the contrary, instead of avenging ourselves, since pride is involved in that, we are to think of God's providence. Paul says, **"On the contrary: 'If your enemy is hungry, feed him; if he is thirsty, give him something to drink. In doing this, you will heap burning coals on his head'"** (v. 20). The overall teaching here comes back to verse 9: **"Hate what is evil; cling to what is good."** Here, it says, **"Do not be overcome by evil, but overcome evil with good"** (v. 21). Anywhere we encounter evil, in ourselves and in others, in the church and in the world, we should overcome evil with good. We should discern God's purpose and have faith in Him as we overcome evil.

This is the way in which love will operate, and this is the way in which Christ's kingdom will be advanced. This is the way that we can give ourselves wholly to the Lord.

16

SACRIFICE

The Way to Life

2003

Romans 12:1–8

¹Therefore, I urge you, brothers, in view of God's mercy, to offer your bodies as living sacrifices, holy and pleasing to God—this is your spiritual act of worship. ²Do not conform any longer to the pattern of this world, but be transformed by the renewing of your mind. Then you will be able to test and approve what God's will is—his good, pleasing and perfect will.

³For by the grace given me I say to every one of you: Do not think of yourself more highly than you ought, but rather think of yourself with sober judgment, in accordance with the measure of faith God has given you. ⁴Just as each of us has one body with many members, and these members do not all have the same function, ⁵so in Christ we who are many form one body, and each member belongs to all the others. ⁶We have different gifts, according to the grace given us. If a man's gift is prophesying, let him use it in proportion to his faith. ⁷If it is serving, let him serve; if it is teaching, let him teach; ⁸if it is encouraging, let him encourage; if it is contributing to the needs of others, let him give generously; if it is leadership, let him govern diligently; if it is showing mercy, let him do it cheerfully.

REVIEW AND INTRODUCTION

"PRESENT YOUR BODIES A LIVING SACRIFICE" (v. 1b KJV). Sacrifice is the way to life. We want to think about sacrifice as the way to life, and see how it applies to us. Paul, in the letter to the Romans, lays out the gospel for us—the gospel of the grace of God to us in Jesus Christ our Lord. This is the way we are brought out of sin and death, and we are told what sin is. God has made a clear revelation of Himself: "For since the creation of the world God's invisible qualities—his eternal power and divine nature—have been clearly seen, being understood from what has been made" (Rom. 1:20a). In the creation, there is a clear general revelation of the existence and nature of God, and the law of God written in our hearts.[1] And yet, we have not sought Him diligently or understood Him because we lack faith/understanding. We have turned to the creation for satisfaction, and finding none, we have gone to excess in every kind of unrighteousness. "Therefore God gave them over in the sinful desires of their hearts" (Rom. 1:24a), to a darkened mind, to corrupt desires—spiraling downward into the pit. All nations throughout history, all persons throughout history, have been in the state of sin and death, and all stand in need of the gospel.

Those who have heard the Word of God spoken through the prophets, through covenant promise, and those who have not—Jews and Gentiles alike—are all under sin.[2] And God, through Christ our Lord, has provided the way by which we may come to Him. A righteousness that comes from God through Jesus Christ is presented to us in the gospel. "This righteousness from God comes through faith in Jesus Christ to all who believe" (Rom. 3:22a). And this is a righteousness received by faith, not by our own works, so that from beginning to end, it may be the mercy of God. Abraham was saved through faith,[3] and this is how it was from the beginning, in Adam. "Sin entered the world through one man, and death through sin" (Rom. 5:12); righteousness comes through one, even Christ.

Salvation through vicarious atonement goes all the way back to Adam being covered by the coats of skin.[4] This has always been the way of salvation. There is one and only one way—through Jesus Christ, our Lord, who became a sin offering for us.[5] "The Lamb of God, who takes

---

1. *Romans 2:14–15.*

2. *Romans 3:9.*

3. *Romans 4:3.*

4. *Genesis 3:21*; Gangadean, *The Biblical Worldview,* 295–309; Gangadean, *The Westminster Confession,* 149–156; Gangadean, *The Westminster Catechisms,* 193–198.

5. *2 Corinthians 5:21.*

away the sin of the world!" (Jn. 1:29b). He was a propitiation for our sin. He satisfied the justice of God by His sacrifice of Himself, once and for all, on the cross. And God has applied that to our hearts. He has brought us into a new relationship with Him through Christ. We are not under the law; we are under grace.[6] Though we struggle with sin remaining in us, it is through Jesus Christ, our Lord, and the Spirit given by Christ, that we have deliverance from the sin that remains in us.[7] And we have every blessing that there is in Christ, so that we can say, nothing "will be able to separate us from the love of God" (Rom. 8:39b), and that "all things work together for good" (Rom. 8:28a NKJV).

This gospel includes the covenant people, Israel. All who are chosen of God, as has always been true, are saved. The nation of Israel itself will be saved in God's due time. Just as the Gentiles have received mercy through Israel, now Israel will receive the mercy of God through the Gentiles, that God may be praised in everything. There is no searching out of His wisdom.[8] He owes a debt to no one. In all of His dealings, His grace and mercy to us through Jesus Christ our Lord is displayed.

THE BURNT OFFERING:
Living Sacrifices as Our Reasonable Act of Worship

On the basis of this gospel, Paul says, "**I beseech you therefore**" (v. 1a KJV). That "**therefore**" has reference to what is laid out before—the mercy of God. "**I urge you, brothers, in view of God's mercy,**" as we have briefly summarized it, "**to offer your bodies as living sacrifices, holy and pleasing to God—this is your spiritual act of worship**" (v. 1). The word *spiritual* comes from the root term *logos—logikos*—meaning a *reasonable* or *logical* act of worship. It is interesting to note how *logic* and *spiritual* are connected—almost interchangeable. In the King James Version, it is rendered as "**your reasonable service.**" This is what is reasonable.

"For we are God's workmanship, created in Christ Jesus to do good works, which God prepared in advance for us to do" (Eph. 2:10). Scripture is given to prepare us for this, and pastors are given to teach

---

6. *Romans 6:14.*

7. *Romans 7.*

8. *Romans 11:30–33.*

us the Scriptures in order to equip us for works of service.[9] From the beginning, we were to engage in works of service. We are called to work six days to glorify God, to uncover His glory in all creation, and to rest in anticipation that this work will be completed. We were to give ourselves wholly to the work of God, because God is the God of all of life—one God over all. He is to be loved with the whole heart. We were always to serve God with our whole heart. And we sin, yet we are restored to God through Jesus Christ all the more. "You are not your own; you were bought at a price" (1 Cor. 6:19b–20a).

We are to serve God with our whole heart. And to serve God with our whole heart, we are given, in Scripture, the figure of a burnt offering.[10] This is what Paul is alluding to here. It was always the case that we were to love God with our whole heart—"with all your heart and with all your soul and with all your strength" (Deut. 6:5b). With our whole being, utterly and fully, we are to love God and serve Him. That state of being is to be as a burnt offering. Our lives are to be consumed in service to God. The burnt offering has two aspects: for sin and for righteousness. Christ died for sin. "God made him who had no sin to be sin for us" (2 Cor. 5:21a). He was wholly consumed by our sin on the cross. And because we are forgiven in Christ, we are called, a second time, to serve God wholly as a burnt offering. Christ's sacrifice on the cross and our sacrifice are interconnected. They assume one another. Because we did not serve God with our whole heart, Christ served God and died as a sacrifice, and we are now called back to serve God with our whole heart. **"As living sacrifices."** This is not a sacrifice that is killed, burned, and then done away with; it is a **"living sacrifice."** The whole burnt offering is a picture, signifying that our whole being—presently and through time—is to be offered up as a *living* sacrifice to God. **"Holy and pleasing to God—this is your spiritual act of worship"** (v. 1b). This is our reasonable, spiritual act of worship.

So our sacrifice now, in view of the mercy of God, is based on the one sacrifice of Jesus Christ—once and for all. When we think of living a life of sacrifice, we are to think of it on the basis of the life of Jesus Christ, with Him as our example. There is a uniqueness in Christ's death. He, and He alone, bore the wrath of God for us—no one else. "He treads

---

9. *2 Timothy 3:16–17; Ephesians 4:11–12.*

10. *Leviticus 1, 6:8–13.*

the winepress of the fury of the wrath of God Almighty" (Rev. 19:15b). No one else could do that for us. But He was also obedient, even unto death.[11] He is our example. So, in a twofold way—on the basis of His sacrifice once and for all, and His entire life being one of sacrifice and obedience to God—we are to be a living sacrifice. Jesus Christ, our Lord, is our example in obedience to God. It is not something we are called to do in some abstract way, apart from Him. This is the *reasonable* act of worship of our Lord Jesus Christ. So we are not asking too much, we are asking what is reasonable—what is only logical. In this sacrifice, we are called not to "**conform any longer to the pattern of this world**" (v. 2a). As Paul speaks about sacrifice in all of this letter to the Romans, we will see that what follows can be understood in terms of what it means to live a sacrificial life—a living sacrifice—how sin is to be put away, and how self-life and self-indulgence are to be put away. All of this must be read with this one idea in mind: to put away self-indulgence and to live for God.

RENEWING OF THE MIND:
Sanctification by Knowing the Truth

Living a sacrificial life for God is manifest in not being conformed any longer to the pattern of this world: "**Do not conform any longer to the pattern of this world**" (v. 2a). The word *conform* comes from the root word *schema*—a form, a fashion. It means to be pressed and squeezed into a mold. But Paul says, in contrast to that, we are to be transformed: "**But be transformed by the renewing of your mind**" (v. 2). The word *transform* comes from the Greek word *morpho*—from which we get *metamorphosis*—to undergo a change in form. Not conformed to this world, but transformed. The world embodies everything that the self-life is, and we have lived in that way. We have desired that way, and there are things in us that still find it enticing. It is subtle, crafty, and deceiving. It surrounds us and we are continually being drawn in. And it speaks—it resonates with things within us. It does not come out boldly and say, 'This is the world, follow me.' It is seductive: 'This is the *real* source of pleasure and enjoyment in life. Go this way.' The way of the world is antithetical to sacrifice.

---

11. *Philippians 2:8.*

Living Sacrifice Versus Conformity to the Patterns of This World

The way we would think about making a sacrifice is to say, 'I am giving up ways that are comfortable and comforting and pleasurable.' And a sacrifice requires us to give that up. We are to give up the ways in which we have been conformed to the world. 'Everyone else is doing it this way. This is normal. This is natural. This is the standard. This is what we are accustomed to.' We must stop thinking in terms of what we are accustomed to or expect. We are not to be conformed to that way by the massive pressure that there is in the world around us. The world is pressuring us in this way, in every way, including all the music that we have listened to and enjoyed. Even the world has its own way of speaking about ideals and sacrifices—up to a point.

The world has its religiousness. The world has its spirituality. The world has its set of values that can imitate and try to say, 'This is the way to do it.' Do not be conformed to the world. Do not be squeezed into that mold. Watch. Be careful. **"Do not conform any longer to the pattern of this world, but be transformed by the renewing of your mind"** (v. 2a). We have to start to think differently and start to recognize that this is our ordinary expectation. This is the thing that keeps us from the sacrifice that we should make—the living sacrifice. Certainly, no one would say that this world is living out that living sacrifice in light of God's mercy. There are persons who, by the common grace of God, may do notable works. Albert Schweitzer did.[12] But in his quest for the historical Jesus,[13] he undermined the teaching of Jesus Christ.[14] His conclusions centered upon man's glory, man's righteousness, which is contrary to what Paul spoke of earlier in Romans 1 and 8.

---

12. Albert Schweitzer was granted the Nobel Peace Prize in 1952 for his humanitarian work, including providing medical care in West Africa. He became a symbol of selfless service and was a strong advocate for peace during the rise of the nuclear age.

13. Albert Schweitzer, *The Quest of the Historical Jesus*, trans. John Bowden (Minneapolis: Fortress Press, 2001).

14. Albert Schweitzer stripped Christ of His divinity, portraying Him as a human being influenced by Jewish eschatological expectations regarding the imminence of the kingdom. According to Schweitzer, Christ underwent crucifixion believing that His death would trigger God's establishment of the kingdom. Ultimately, Schweitzer concluded that Christ remains a historical figure inaccessible to us due to our biases and uncritically held assumptions. What remains for believers, in his view, is to imitate Christ's ethical goal of instilling reverence for life by pursuing a life of service, compassion, and the alleviation of suffering. However, this ethical approach detaches our work in the kingdom from the glory of God.

Albert Schweitzer's view of the gospel is not the righteousness of God spoken of by Paul.

Many have claimed their own righteousness. Many have their own martyrdom. Many are willing to be martyrs for their causes, and they can outdo us in many ways. But it is not according to the righteousness that is in God. So watch out. Do not think the world does not have its own language and its own ways of speaking about sacrifice. It can be very enticing—so enticing that the whole world has gone that way—outside of Christ. Paul says, **"Be transformed by the renewing of your mind"**—by the Word of God. We are to be transformed by the fundamental truths of God. They are to be meditated upon and applied. We are to be taught and instructed in them by the work of the pastor-teachers summed up in the Historic Christian Faith[15]—which is the work of the Holy Spirit through the pastor-teachers. Just as they did in Acts 15, concerning the question whether one must be circumcised to be saved, we are to come to the truth.

The Lord has brought challenges to the Church throughout history. And He has enabled the pastor-teachers by the work of the Holy Spirit—in and through all the multitudes of mixed motives and outward disparate circumstances—to make progress in understanding His truth. And we will yet make progress. The Holy Spirit will lead us into all truth.[16] We are to have that truth. We are to know the truth well. We are to know the reasons for the truth. We are to know how falsehood has been reasoned against. And you know what? It takes a certain amount of sacrifice to give ourselves to this—to take time and energy and to focus our minds so that we might be renewed and transformed by the renewing of our minds. The slothfulness of our minds is contrary to that spirit of sacrifice, diligence, and discipleship. We need to take time and make the effort to understand the Word so that we might be renewed. We are to speak often with one another about these things—about the basic things and about the less basic things in light of the more basic things—and not let our talk be flitted away. "Let your conversation be always full of grace, seasoned with salt" (Col. 4:6a) because "the days are evil" (Eph. 5:16b). We must make the most of the time that we

---

15. Gangadean, *The Westminster Confession,* xix–xxix, 349–351; Gangadean, "Paper No. 16: The Historic Christian Faith," in *The Logos Papers,* 103–114.

16. *John 16:13.*

have. "Do not conform any longer to the pattern of this world, but be transformed by the renewing of your mind" (v. 2a). There are many instances in Scripture where we are instructed about this.

THE LANGUAGE OF SACRIFICE:
Diligently Seeking the Lord and His Kingdom

The Hidden Treasure and the Pearl of Great Price

In Matthew 13:44–46, we have the teaching about the hidden treasure and the pearl of great price.[17] Let me quickly bring these parables to your attention. "The kingdom of heaven is like treasure hidden in a field. When a man found it, he hid it again, and then in his joy went and sold all he had and bought that field" (Matt. 13:44). The sacrifice is for something of great value—a treasure so great that you would sell everything you have for it. That is the language of sacrifice. You are giving your all for this kingdom. The kingdom and its glories are such a treasure. As our minds are renewed and we see what this kingdom is—in contrast to the kingdoms of this world—we will not just settle down and think, 'Well, we are here for a while, we die, and then we go on.' When we see how this kingdom is to be realized, when we have been renewed in our minds and understand the kingdom, we will treasure it in such a way that we *will* make sacrifices for it. We will go and sell everything we have, that we might possess it. "Again, the kingdom of heaven is like a merchant looking for fine pearls. When he found one of great value, he went away and sold everything he had and bought it" (Matt. 13:45–46). These are parallel parables. Just as the parables of the mustard seed and the leaven teach that the kingdom will grow to its fullness, so these parables teach of the sacrifice that must be made to possess the kingdom.

Jesus said, "And from the days of John the Baptist until now the kingdom of heaven suffers violence, and the violent take it by force" (Matt. 11:12). There is something violent about a sacrifice. There is something violent about what happened to Christ on the cross. There is something violent in taking up your cross daily and following Him. There is a violence against the self-life. One must use force to possess it.

---

17. Gangadean, *The Gospel of Matthew,* 179–198.

You must sell all you have to possess it. This is what Scripture teaches us: "He is a rewarder of them that diligently seek him" (Heb. 11:6b). Our seeking must be diligent. It cannot be casual. It cannot be every now and then. It must be diligent.

Examples in Scripture: Athlete, Soldier, and Farmer

There are examples in Scripture of this diligence and sacrifice.[18] There is the athlete, running in a race—running to win. There is a pressing forward. Paul speaks of that race: "I press on to take hold of that for which Christ Jesus took hold of me. . . . Forgetting what is behind and straining toward what is ahead, I press on toward the goal to win the prize for which God has called me heavenward in Christ Jesus" (Phil. 3:12b, 13b–14). There is also the soldier, who endures hardship for Christ. The life of a soldier is not the easy, ordinary circumstances of life. It is not about relaxing in front of the TV, watching the game with beer and nuts, and saying, 'Hey, this is a good life. This is what it is all about. Praise Jesus.' This is a soldier. There is also the farmer, who is working in his field. All these are figures of speech that tell us how we are to be striving in this sacrifice. "He is a rewarder of them that diligently seek him." (Heb. 11:6b KJV).

Diligently Seeking Versus Double-Mindedness

The Scripture instructs us against being double-minded:

> If any of you lacks wisdom, he should ask God, who gives generously to all without finding fault, and it will be given to him. But when he asks, he must believe and not doubt, because he who doubts is like a wave of the sea, blown and tossed by the wind. That man should not think he will receive anything from the Lord; he is a double-minded man, unstable in all he does (Jas. 1:5–8).

We want to have it both ways. 'Yes, if it does not cost me too much.' That is not the language of sacrifice. 'If it does not cost me too much, I will buy this pearl of great price.' Your mind has not been renewed. You are not in your right mind. The world would say to us that we are not in

---

18. *2 Timothy 2:3–6.*

our right mind, as Festus said to Paul. "At this point Festus interrupted Paul's defense. 'You are out of your mind, Paul!' he shouted. 'Your great learning is driving you insane.' 'I am not insane, most excellent Festus,' Paul replied. 'What I am saying is true and reasonable'" (Acts 26:24–25). He was speaking of the truth of Scripture—believing in the resurrection. The world says, 'Much learning has made you mad. Your mind has been so renewed, you are mad.' No—you have to be not in your right mind to pass up the pearl of great price. You have to be not in your right mind to pass up the invitation of the King to come into the kingdom. You have to be not in your right mind to fail to watch daily and to let things take you by surprise—not having a clue as to what is going on and living as if this world and its fashion will not pass away, because you have been fashioned by it, and you think it is going to last. So, who is in their right mind?

The brothers of Jesus thought He was not in His right mind. "When his family heard about this, they went to take charge of him, for they said, 'He is out of his mind'" (Mk. 3:21). They wanted to take Him and restrain Him. They came in, calling for Him. So, who is in their right mind? We must ask ourselves the question: 'You got your mind right?' Sometimes, we have to dig hard and suffer until we get our mind focused. Some of you know what I am talking about—Paul Newman's story in *Cool Hand Luke*.[19] We can be double-minded. We cannot say, 'Yes, that is great—but only if it does not cost me.' We are to be a living sacrifice. It is going to cost all we have. And if we are double-minded, we will not possess it. We will be infants—immature. We will miss the chance to possess the pearl of great price.

---

19. In reference to the following dialogue in *Cool Hand Luke*, dir. Stuart Rosenberg (1967; Burbank, CA: Warner Home Video, 2010), DVD. Captain: "You run one time, you got yourself a set of chains. You run twice, you got yourself two sets. You ain't gonna need no third set, 'cause you gonna get your mind right.'" Guard (after forcing Luke to dig and re-fill the hole repeatedly): "You got your mind right Luke?" Luke (eventually, exhausted and broken): "I got my mind right, boss."

DISCIPLINE FOR GODLINESS IN ALL AREAS OF LIFE

In Food, Exercise, and Money

Jesus said that we are to take up our cross daily and follow Him.[20] Just think of the life of discipline. Think of what it is to be disciplined in the area of diet. Or do you say that is a lost cause? 'Forget it. It is over. It's not going to happen.' Or think about exercise. There is a certain perseverance you have to have to stay with it, do you not? But there comes a time when you have stayed with it for a while, and you get over certain humps. You reach a certain level. And if you keep going steadily, you find yourself bumping up into another level after a while. And there is an ease that comes as you persevere through the initial difficulty—and then it goes on. And there are benefits. "For physical training is of some value, but godliness has value for all things, holding promise for both the present life and the life to come" (1 Tim. 4:8). So let us pursue godliness and not neglect bodily exercise. Or think about savings. And we might throw up our hands and laugh and say, 'What are you talking about, savings? I do not even have enough money to pay for groceries. What am I going to save?' A nickel, a dime—that is what you can save. It is an attitude. It begins with baby steps. And then eventually you can save a dollar a week. And then five dollars a week. It does not have to be all or nothing. It is the attitude—the mentality of saving. Rather than spending our money on things, indulging ourselves, and using up all that we have, we exercise discipline. These are easy areas to relate to: food, exercise, and money.

In Disciplined Study and Interpersonal Relationships

But discipline also applies to reading Scripture and to studying diligently. Setting aside time requires discipline and sacrifice. You have to give up one thing to gain another. Discipline involves the way in which we think about others—forbearing and forgiving—not judging, not gossiping, and restraining ourselves and exercising self-control. There is discipline in not indulging ourselves to say whatever first comes to our mind. There is discipline in not speaking whatever we feel. A life without discipline is a life of self-indulgence. It is not the thoughtful

---

20. *Luke 9:23.*

life, not the life that renews our minds for the sake of the kingdom. We are not to think more highly of ourselves than we ought. We are to appreciate the gifts given to others, to encourage them in their development, and to value them according to the glory that God has given, so that we might care for one another. Paul says, **"For by the grace given me I say to every one of you: Do not think of yourself more highly than you ought, but rather think of yourself with sober judgment, in accordance with the measure of faith God has given you"** (v. 3). He says many other things here about interpersonal relationships in the church, all in the context and the spirit of the sacrificial life.

In our self-life, we make judgments without knowledge because it comes easily, it is pleasing to us, and it satisfies our ego. We cannot make judgments without knowledge. That is self-indulgence; it is not the life of the cross. We have to discipline ourselves not to say what is evil or wrong to a third party, but to take it to the person to whom we should speak. We should not seek to get a certain comfort and ease in sharing with a third party. 'Do you know what is happening?' We let it out. It requires a certain amount of discipline to hold it in, deal with it properly, and pray for the person before we speak. There is the life of self-indulgence, which is the way of the world, or there is the life in Christ—a living sacrifice.

In Worry and Complaining

How about worrying? How about complaining? These are forms of the self-life. It reveals where our hearts are when we give ourselves to worrying and complaining. It is not the fruit of the Spirit. It is not God-centered. It is not godly. It is not God-focused. "If anyone would come after me, he must deny himself and take up his cross daily and follow me" (Lk. 9:23b). Worrying and complaining are part of the self-life.

In Prayer

How about prayer? "And pray in the Spirit on all occasions with all kinds of prayers and requests. With this in mind, be alert and always keep on praying for all the saints" (Eph. 6:18). If we prayed to God as much as we talked to men, or about men, we would be so much more pleasing to Him. And if we prayed to God *before* we talked about men, we would be so much more pleasing to Him. We should put that as a limiting factor on ourselves: 'Until I pray to God about this, I will not talk to others about this matter.' 'Before complaining about it, I will pray about it.' A certain amount of self-control and discipline is needed in this.

In Tithing

How about our money, our tithing? We are to be faithful in our tithing. This is a regular matter. These are ordinary matters. These are daily matters. Just be faithful in these. The money does not belong to you. It is God's. "Will a man rob God? Yet you rob me. But you ask, 'How do we rob you?' In tithes and offerings" (Mal. 3:8). God calls it stealing when we do not render to Him the tithe. And it is an expression of the self-life to hold on to the tithe that belongs to the Lord. And the Lord knows this. He takes note of this. And there is no way we can justify it. It is a simple, straightforward act of obedience and worship. Let us not indulge our self-life by holding on to the money God has entrusted to us.

In Witnessing

How about our witness? We are to prepare ourselves, make the most of every opportunity, and learn how to witness. We might say, 'When I open my mouth, the words do not come out right.' We need to come back and talk with others who have witnessed and who have shown some ability in witnessing. We can ask them, 'I said this, but what do you think I could have said?' We need to make the time and effort to learn—to invest time and effort, as opposed to using that time and effort for other things we want to do. All of this is part of the life of discipline.

THE LIFE OF SERVICE:
Fellowship, Work Habits, and Quality of Work

How about our work, our work habits, and the quality of our work? We need to see whether we make excuses easily about the work that we do. We need to see whether we learn to work hard and get it done right. We should keep quality control in our work rather than needing to have someone standing over us and watching us. Do it right; do it well. This is pleasing to the Lord. Do not cut corners. This is how Paul speaks of work in Romans 16. He speaks often about his fellow workers. That is the context in which fellowship occurs: two fellows in one ship, rowing in the same direction—*fellowship*. It is not one rowing while the other is being carried. Fellowship is not just good times together. It is not *gemütlichkeit*.[21] It is not merely having a shared meal and enjoying each others' company. That is not the essence of fellowship. That is a celebration of fellowship. But fellowship is where you are a fellow worker in the kingdom of God. You are a worker. Listen to how Paul speaks about his fellow workers: "Greet Priscilla and Aquila, my fellow workers in Christ Jesus" (Rom. 16:3). "I commend to you our sister Phoebe, a servant of the church in Cenchrea . . . she has been a great help to many people, including me" (Rom. 16:1–2b). These are the people who are to be commended—those who work hard in the kingdom of God. Those who desire to see the kingdom advance. Those who are investing their lives in the work of the kingdom. Priscilla and Aquila went to the point of risking their lives for Paul.[22] "Greet Mary, who worked very hard for you" (Rom. 16:6). It seems that special notice is given to the women in this passage. "Greet Urbanus, our fellow worker in Christ, and my dear friend Stachys" (Rom. 16:9). "Greet Apelles, tested and approved in Christ" (Rom. 16:10a). He was approved by the way in which he conducted himself.

Do people see your life and say, 'Now there is someone who works hard, in the Lord, for the kingdom'? We are not to simply work hard in our own way. That is the way of the world. Anyone will do that. So, let us not say we are living up to worldly standards when we work hard. We work hard *in* the kingdom, not merely for our own affairs. "Greet Tryphena and Tryphosa, those women who work hard in the Lord. Greet my dear friend Persis, another woman who has worked very hard in the Lord" (Rom. 16:12). Are you known as a hard worker in the Lord? Or are you only a hard worker in your own affairs? When we ask, 'How are you doing in your work in the Novitiate?'[23]—what are we really asking? 'If someone were to grade your work on a particular job,

---

21. *Gemütlichkeit* describes a feeling of comfort, relaxation, and well-being, often in a social setting. The term goes beyond just physical comfort—it's about creating a welcoming, pleasant atmosphere where people feel at ease and content.

22. *Romans 16:4.*

23. Gangadean, *The Westminster Confession,* 389–390.

would it be an A, B, C, D, or F? Or F minus?' Some students manage to get an F triple minus. Thirty out of 50 is an F. But some get ten out of 50. What is that? Lord, have mercy. Sometimes, while grading college students, I have to say, 'Well, I will give you an F at 30 rather than an F at 10. But I cannot be more merciful than that.' What is the quality of our work? 'We did well here, but we did not do too well there, and it all evens out, so we get a C minus.' That is not how it goes. We are to do well across the board. We are to work consistently, work hard, and work thoughtfully. We should work with insight and thoughtfulness. That is the other part of work. When the ax is dull, you have to use twice as much strength. But if the ax is sharp, if you can think clearly about it, you can get it done with less effort. That is all part of being a hard worker, a diligent worker, a wise worker.

We are to take up our cross and live the life of sacrifice in all aspects of our life. There is pride to be dealt with, there is lust to be dealt with, there is envy, and, of course, there is sloth. Paul says, "Never be lacking in zeal, but keep your spiritual fervor, serving the Lord" (Rom. 12:11). Keep the fire burning. We are to be burning in zeal and not slack. In this context, where he speaks about never lacking in zeal and never being slothful, the slothful person is one who is hesitant about getting involved. *Opnios* is the Greek term. He is hesitant; he is slow; he is loath to act; he delays. He is tardy, indolent, and finds work irksome; in so doing, he is irksome to others. He is grievous and slothful. Sloth is against working hard. Even if we are slaves, we are to work hard because we are doing it as unto the Lord. It may be unfortunate that we have to do it as a slave rather than in some other way, but there is work to be done—someone has to shovel the manure. Whether you do it as a slave or as a free man, it is to be done as unto the Lord. We should work hard. The world says, 'Indulge, take it easy; the best thing that you can have is money so that you do not have to work.' No, you may not have to work at some things, but there are other things you would work at even more. You should *always* be working hard, with all your might, as unto the Lord. We have to reckon with our work ethic and our work standards. We must be transformed by the renewing of our minds. We must recognize that we excuse ourselves from this. We work hard in our own way rather than for the kingdom. We are to live a life of service; we are members of the body of Christ. We are to work in hope and not give up.

Some of us have fallback positions. Here are three fallback positions: First, we might say, 'The gospel will not go out in America and in the West, but it will go out in Africa and Asia.' You wish. What reason do you have for thinking that? Have you allowed yourself to indulge that thought and not work hard here for change? Second, some of us have the fallback position of guns: 'If things get really bad, we have guns, and we will take ourselves to the hills and defend ourselves.' When this is a fallback position, we are not working hard. Third, here is my fallback position: We are a small band of survivors going across the desert. It is the *Lawrence of Arabia* fallback position. Even if no one else goes, and there is only a small band going, we are going to go, and we are going to make it, even if we die trying. It would be nice to have a great number go with you. But one way or another, you give yourself to that work.

SACRIFICIAL SERVICE

Husbands Love Your Wives: Sacrifice for Them

Here is another area of work: "Husbands, love your wives, just as Christ loved the church and gave himself up for her" (Eph. 5:25)—sacrifice. I hear men commending their wives week after week for all the hard work they are doing. Sometimes, I think, 'Okay, guys, are you leading as an example in hard work? What is the deal here?' You can be thankful for your wife's work—and indeed, you should be—but if need be, you should be praying, 'Lord, help me to be working hard, setting the pace, and setting the example.' Now everyone is going to say, 'Oh boy, I better not say that anymore because what else is he going to be thinking?' But guys, be men.

If you are going to take the lead and have that position of covenant head in your home, you have to live a sacrificial life for your wife—bringing the Word to her, taking the initiative, and taking the leadership. "As Christ loved the church and gave himself up for her to make her holy, cleansing her by the washing with water through the word, and to present her to himself as a radiant church, without stain or wrinkle or any other blemish, but holy and blameless" (Eph. 5:25b–27). You continue to bring the Word of God to your wife. She is beautiful outwardly, but she needs to be beautiful inwardly—with the Word. And do not be so taken by the beauty of your wives that you fail to see or cultivate that inner beauty, which is to come through loving and serving Christ and being conformed to Him. But you will not be able to live the sacrificial life for your wife, in the least, until you are able to submit your life to God.

This is an area of sacrificial service—very close to all of us. We are not to give ourselves over to self-indulgence in our marriages. Even in the intimate relationship of marriage, we can be selfish and self-indulgent—pleasing self rather than pleasing the other for their good. We may please the other so that we may, in turn, be pleased. But we should expect that we should live this life of sacrifice as a constant. And when we live this life of sacrifice as a constant, we can then be in a position to understand what sacrifice is above the constant, above the regular, in the special circumstances.

Individual and Group Projects: Over and Above the Regular

God willing, we will soon be engaged in building a church building. That is something you do not do every day—maybe once in the lifetime of a congregation. That is going to require special effort. That is going to require sacrifice in giving as we are able to give. For some, it will be more time and energy in the actual building. For others, it will be money. But we will be calling upon you to see what you are prepared to give and what you can commit to give. And on the basis of what you are committing to do, we will determine what we can do with the church building. Because as we go to get loans from the bank, pledges are seen by the loan officers, and that is taken into account as to whether they will support us or not. And the size of the building and the size of the rooms will depend on the giving we can do. We will build as small as we can afford. But if people pledge themselves to this—in time, energy, and money—we will be able to do more. We should not expect that we will be able to sacrifice on the special occasions if we have not been sacrificing on the regular occasions of daily life. God calls us to a life of sacrifice.

INVESTING OUR LIVES IN THE KINGDOM

Last of all, we are to invest our whole lives—not just our money. We are to invest our lives in the kingdom of God. We are to invest strategically—that is, wisely, considering the larger picture. Some of you want to change your occupation and go into teaching. Some of you want to undertake degrees. That is a significant step. Think about how you are doing it, why you are doing it, and how it can best serve in the kingdom of God. What are the needs? Do not just think, 'What are my gifts? What do I like?' I recently spoke to someone considering a PhD. They were asking, 'What would be a fun thing to do?' I was on another wavelength: 'What would be the useful thing to do? How would this best equip you to serve in the kingdom of God?'

This is investing your life. This is not just investing in stocks. This is investing your life in the work of the kingdom of God. And it should be done wisely, thoughtfully, and prayerfully, with urgency, fervency, and a willingness to sacrifice. And we will not make those sacrifices if we do not already live as a living sacrifice. We must sacrifice daily in every aspect of our lives. **"I urge you, brothers, in view of God's mercy, to offer your bodies as living sacrifices, holy and pleasing to God—this is your spiritual act of worship"** (v. 1).

May God grant us the grace to do so.

17

ALL AUTHORITY IS FROM GOD

Submission in Love—Overcoming Evil with Good

1994

Romans 13

¹Everyone must submit himself to the governing authorities, for there is no authority except that which God has established. The authorities that exist have been established by God. ²Consequently, he who rebels against the authority is rebelling against what God has instituted, and those who do so will bring judgment on themselves. ³For rulers hold no terror for those who do right, but for those who do wrong. Do you want to be free from fear of the one in authority? Then do what is right and he will commend you. ⁴For he is God's servant to do you good. But if you do wrong, be afraid, for he does not bear the sword for nothing. He is God's servant, an agent of wrath to bring punishment on the wrongdoer. ⁵Therefore, it is necessary to submit to the authorities, not only because of possible punishment but also because of conscience.

⁶This is also why you pay taxes, for the authorities are God's servants, who give their full time to governing. ⁷Give everyone what you owe him: If you owe taxes, pay taxes; if revenue, then revenue; if respect, then respect; if honor, then honor.

⁸Let no debt remain outstanding, except the continuing debt to love one another, for he who loves his fellowman has fulfilled the law. ⁹The commandments, "Do not commit adultery," "Do not murder," "Do not steal," "Do not covet," and whatever other commandment there may be,

are summed up in this one rule: "Love your neighbor as yourself." ¹⁰Love does no harm to its neighbor. Therefore love is the fulfillment of the law.

¹¹And do this, understanding the present time. The hour has come for you to wake up from your slumber, because our salvation is nearer now than when we first believed. ¹²The night is nearly over; the day is almost here. So let us put aside the deeds of darkness and put on the armor of light. ¹³Let us behave decently, as in the daytime, not in orgies and drunkenness, not in sexual immorality and debauchery, not in dissension and jealousy. ¹⁴Rather, clothe yourselves with the Lord Jesus Christ, and do not think about how to gratify the desires of the sinful nature.

INTRODUCTION:
Our Reasonable Service—Applied to Authority

IN ROMANS 12, PAUL SAYS THAT WHEN WE UNDERSTAND God's mercy to us, the only reasonable thing to do is to present our bodies as a living sacrifice and give ourselves wholly to God, which is our reasonable service. Paul spells out what it is to give oneself wholly to God; it involves a specific way for each one of us in the general context of the law. That is, Paul speaks about the gifts and diversities that exist in the body, and how each one of us has a particular place in the body. He says that we are to overcome evil in the world by doing good. In the last remark in Romans 12:21, he writes, "Do not be overcome by evil, but overcome evil with good." Paul speaks in the context of love. In verse 9, he says, "Love must be sincere. Hate what is evil; cling to what is good"—in pursuit of the good. That is always the general context in which we must understand: in pursuit of the good, we love and overcome evil with good. And now, we apply this still further to those who are in authority.

ALL AUTHORITY IS FROM GOD:
How Should We Respond?

The Law Applied: Honor to Whom Honor Is Due

In Romans 13, we have an application of the fifth commandment to honor your father and mother.[1] We are to give honor to whom honor

---

1. *Exodus 20:12.*

is due.[2] Paul explicitly says, **"If respect, then respect; if honor, then honor"** (v. 7b). Still more specifically, he makes the application of honoring the political authorities. Paul speaks about the ones who **"bear a sword,"** but it is not restricted to those; we are to submit to all authority, whether within the Family, Church, State, or work. Paul begins, **"Everyone must submit himself to the governing authorities, for there is no authority except that which God has established"** (v. 1a). Authority is not something that has been or can be established by human beings. God established authority by virtue of creation; no human being has that power, and no human being has the power to merely put themselves in a position of authority. We will see that not only the structure of authority, but a specific person put in a specific position of authority has to do with God's providence. Paul says, **"There is no authority except that which God has established,"** whether in the home between husband and wife, parents and children, at work between employer and employee, within the State, or in the Church. I will give some examples to help focus our thinking.

Nero, who was a political authority, persecuted the Church. How should the Church respond? The Jews in the time of Jesus, in response to Rome, sought to be released from that authority. Hitler carried out the genocide of the Jews. Stalin established the Gulag to persecute dissenters. Nebuchadnezzar wiped out the city of Jerusalem and took the people captive. These are errant ministers who, in their lives, came short in moral conduct. This is just to name some of the political applications. How should we respond to authority, particularly political authority? We will see that it is not limited to political authority only; the principles carry over to other areas of authority.

Rebellion Brings Judgment

The Scripture says, **"There is no authority except that which God has established;"** and more specifically, **"The authorities that exist have been established by God"** (v. 1b). Not only have the offices been established by God, but the persons in the offices have been established by God. Paul draws several conclusions from this, one being that we are not to rebel against authority. In light of the fact that all authority

---

2. Gangadean, *The Westminster Catechisms*, 247–254; Gangadean, *Philosophical Foundation*, 221–229.

is from God, what should our response be? Here, Paul says not to rebel: **"Consequently, he who rebels against the authority is rebelling against what God has instituted"** (v. 2a). The emphasis seems to be on the structure of authority. Paul continues, **"And those who do so will bring judgment on themselves"** (v. 2b). Because it is instituted by God, rebellion against authority is a sin against God. When Paul says that those who rebel against authority **"will bring judgment on themselves,"** that has to do with the judgment that God will bring. God may bring judgment *through* political authority, but it may also come apart from political authority.

The Need for Discernment

There are a lot of problems immediately felt about this. Every one of us has been in a place where we are under some authority, and we think the authority is unjust, improper, inadequate, wrong, evil, and harmful. We want to discern what this passage is saying. Is Paul saying that we should simply, without qualification, submit and not rebel? That is what we have to work through, and that is one of the reasons why we should have some discussion afterward. Think about all the examples and counterexamples you want to raise; this would be a very good time and occasion to do so.[3]

A Vital Question: The Historical Context Under Roman Authority

Paul had a special reason for emphasizing submission to authority in this letter. The Jews had often made insurrections against Roman authority, and they carried it to such a point that they were expelled from Rome in Paul's day. Think about the response of the Christians, who were also under Roman authority, and were persecuted. Let us get some clear examples fixed in mind. In A.D. 70, the Jews rebelled against Roman authority, and the Roman General, Titus, came in, destroyed the city, and dispersed the people. That dispersion continued for about 1,900 years. The Jews had a special concern about this because the Romans were Gentiles, they were nonbelievers who were ruling over them, and the law said, "Be sure to appoint over you a king the Lord your God

---

3. Gangadean, *Philosophical Foundation*, 221–229.

chooses. He must be from among your own brothers. Do not place a foreigner over you, one who is not an Israelite" (Deut. 17:15). How can the Jews square this Word with the reality that the Gentile rulers were over them? Remember, this was the point of contention for which they sought to trap Jesus: for teaching allegiance to God rather than to Caesar. They used that against Jesus, though they themselves objected to being under Roman rule. They asked the question, "Is it right to pay taxes to Caesar or not?" (Matt. 22:17b), and Jesus said, "Whose portrait is this? And whose inscription?" (Matt. 22:20b).[4] It was a very lively question and a question that had very dreadful consequences in that day. If we keep that in mind, we can see the vitality of what Paul is saying. Not only did the Romans rule over the Jews, but Christians were also subject to various forms of persecution—and increasingly so—not only in Paul's day, but much more broadly just before the destruction of Jerusalem, and especially after the destruction of Jerusalem, when it became apparent that Christians were not merely another sect within Judaism. They had their own independent systems. Then the full force of Rome came down on the Church, first in Rome under Nero, and then empire-wide under other emperors. How should we respond?

THEREFORE, SUBMIT—DO NOT REBEL:
Having a Heart of Submission

Remember, there was a time when the prophets were telling the Israelites to submit to Nebuchadnezzar, and they did not submit; they rebelled and were carried away.[5] Then we have the example of Daniel and how he conducted himself in the kingdom of Babylon. I do not think we can say, in any sense, that Daniel rebelled against the authority of Babylon. We have to keep these examples in mind when we try to make further applications. With regard to the authority of the Pharisees, Jesus said, "The teachers of the law and the Pharisees sit in Moses' seat. So you must be careful to do everything they tell you. But do not do what they do, for they do not practice what they preach" (Matt. 23:2–3). So there is a qualification to submitting to the teachers of the law and the Pharisees: "Do not do what they do."

---

4. Gangadean, *The Gospel of Matthew,* 349–367.

5. *Jeremiah 27:6–8, 29:4–7; Ezekiel 17:11–21.*

A Universal Context: Carnal Freedom to Indulge the Old Nature

There is a universal concern about submission to authority. This concern comes out toward the end of Romans 13 when Paul says, **"Rather, clothe yourselves with the Lord Jesus Christ, and do not think about how to gratify the desires of the sinful nature"** (v. 14). That is, in the name of 'Christian liberty,' which is really carnal freedom to indulge the old nature, we want freedom from authority. Whether it is within the Family, at work, the State, or elsewhere, we often resist, rebel, and put aside authority, because there is something in us that we want to indulge—our old nature. We want the authorities themselves to serve our desires, and this is the kind of king that was being sought in Jesus' day. A Messiah, who would deliver them from the oppression of Rome, one who would heal their diseases, one who would feed them with bread, one who would even raise them from the dead, deliver them from toil, strife, and death—*carnal* freedom, not freedom from moral evil/sin. If you want freedom from sin, be willing to accept natural evil, in God's providence, as a call to repentance in our lives.[6] There is something within us, as believers with sin remaining in us—the old nature—that resists and does not like anyone telling us what to do, because we do not want to do God's will, we want to do our own will. There is very good historical reason, and not only historical, but permanent reason, for us to take heed to this injunction—that the authorities that exist are established by God.

God's Order Before and After the Fall: Natural, Civic, and Redemptive Orders

We should note that there was an original authority within the Family before the Fall—structured into the very nature of things. There is an order within each person in terms of what function of human personality rules over the other aspects. The *thinking* over the *desires* and the *will* is a natural order that God has established. That function—thinking and having insight—is why those who possess insight in a particular area are naturally in positions of leadership within that area. The original arrangement of ordering was altered by the Fall. After the Fall occurred, in due time, God established new orders for dealing with evil. He

---

6. Gangadean, *The Biblical Worldview*, 311–328.

established the State to deal with evil externally, and He established the Church to deal with evil internally. The State bears the sword to externally eliminate evil when it gets to the outward manifestation and affects others.[7] The Church deals not with the physical sword, but with the sword of the Spirit, the Word of God—preaching, teaching, exhorting, encouraging, and applying that Word, to bring deliverance from evil inwardly.[8] These are the two institutions that God established after the Fall because of the existence of evil. We always have to keep in mind the reality of evil when we speak about the State. As I understand the idea of the State, it is the one that bears the sword, as it is referred to in this passage. I would say that the *essence* of the State is not to rule in a general way, in leading and guiding, but to bear the sword. The parental authority is not one that bears the sword; the master is not one who bears the sword; the church leadership is not one that bears the sword—but they govern and rule. So, we can make a distinction between *governance*, which is broader, and the State, which is a specific form of rule. Paul's application seems to concentrate on the State because he speaks about paying taxes, although he does speak of rendering respect and honor to all.[9]

Alternatives to Rebellion: Non-Violent Means

There are reasons for Paul to exhort the believers in a godly response to authority by establishing, first of all, that all authority is from God, and therefore, we are not to rebel against it. There are many other responses, short of rebellion. You can find all kinds of responses, such as resisting (which may not be the same as rebellion), disobeying, non-cooperation, and seeking to change. We will see how to deal with all of those; there are different degrees of obedience. It is one thing to pay taxes, it is another thing to render respect and honor to a person by following their example. The latter is a much stronger sense of submission to authority. In rendering honor by following one's example, we recognize the insight that person may have. We begin to see that when Paul says *rebel*, he means something fairly explicit—seeking to

---

7. Gangadean, *The Westminster Confession*, 253–262.

8. Gangadean, *The Westminster Confession*, 275–283.

9. *Romans 13:7*.

overthrow by the use of force. Paul says that we are not called to use force, but there may be many other things which we may have the freedom to do and should try to do.

Reasons for Submission to Authority: Learn to Live by the Word of God

Paul warns us, then, that rebelling against the authority is rebelling against what God has instituted—it is to rebel against God, God's governance, and God's leading. God gave to the people Saul as king, after they were crying out for a king, and then they did not want to have the king. That was not appropriate. It was part of God's rule in their lives, because of where they were spiritually, what they had attained to, and what they were seeking. God was dealing with them, ruling over them in such a way as to humble their hearts, so that they might learn to obey Him. We will see there are times when we are born under authority, as in the case of our parents, or the case of the State, and there are other times when we put ourselves under authority, where we call out for a certain kind of king, or a certain employer, or in marriage. We have to discern those distinctions in thinking about how we are to respond, keeping in mind that we want to learn to live by the Word of God. We want to crucify the flesh with its passions and desires.[10] We want to grow in the knowledge of God. If we insist on our *rights*, apart from the concern to know God, then everything is going to get twisted in our minds, and we will find ourselves straining under authority.

Fear of Authority and A Matter of Conscience

Paul gives two basic reasons for submission to authority, possibly three. One is the fear of punishment, and the other is conscience. The third may be consequences in terms of positive good. He says in verse 3, **"For rulers hold no terror for those who do right, but for those who do wrong. Do you want to be free from fear of the one in authority? Then do what is right, and he will commend you. For he is God's servant to do you good"** (vv. 3–4a). Rulers are God's servants. Just as persons who preach the gospel are God's servants, so rulers are God's servants. The purpose is not to do their own thing, but to be servants

---

10. *Galatians 5:24.*

of the people, and they are to do good for the people. That is one of the reasons they should be paid if they give themselves to full-time rule. Because rulers are under God, they are obligated to live and work by the law of God. The question comes up, 'What if they are not, in various ways, obeying God's law?' How are we to respond? We will have to think through and wrestle through that area.

Paul says that the one in authority is **"an agent of wrath to bring punishment on the wrongdoer"** (v. 4b). That is the purpose of the authorities that are instituted, and in that sense, it seems that he is speaking primarily about the State. Therefore, we have no need to be afraid of them, but we should submit to them. This is another reason for us to submit. Now, we might start exploring examples afterward, other forms of authority, and current examples of our own political situation and how we might operate. Seeing that discussion will be coming up, I will not pursue that in greater detail now.[11] Paul says, **"But if you do wrong, be afraid, for he does not bear the sword for nothing. He is God's servant, an agent of wrath to bring punishment on the wrongdoer"** (v. 4b). He concludes from this, that since God institutes authority, and it is for our good, and for conscience' sake, therefore, we should submit. If we do not, we will bring God's judgment on ourselves, and this judgment may come through those who exercise the sword, and therefore, there is fear of punishment.

Submission as a Religious Duty: Obedience from the Heart

There are two motivations: a positive motivation for obeying and submitting, and a negative motivation for obeying, or not disobeying. Either way, Paul says we are to submit ourselves to the governing authority. **"Therefore, it is necessary to submit to the authorities, not only because of possible punishment but also as a matter of conscience"** (v. 5). Submission to authority is not just a matter of "civil duty," but it is a matter of *religious* duty. It is not a matter only of outward obedience, as Paul wrote to the Ephesians: "Obey them not only to win their favor when their eye is on you, but like slaves of Christ, doing the will of God from your heart" (Eph. 6:6). We are to be careful that we do

---

11. For a fuller exposition on the nature of authority, see: Gangadean, *Philosophical Foundation*, 221–229, and the forthcoming series on *The Natural Moral Law: The Foundation for Lasting Culture, Volumes 1–6*.

not twist this passage and say, 'Well, I'm going to grin and groan and just minimally obey.' We have to reckon with both sides of obedience: outward obedience and obedience from the heart. In our fallen state, it is understandable that the negative motivation for obedience might also figure in. We might say that if we do not obey God's will, death will come upon us, spiritual death, and we will go deeper into death. If we disobey God and get into trouble, we should repent and turn back and start obeying now; if we do not and try to escape our difficulty, we will go deeper into it. So, there is a negative motivation, not just from the State, but from the way in which God orders and rules the world. But this is a positive motivation; God's dealing with us, our loving Heavenly Father, for our good. Therefore, for conscience' sake, we should obey.

Following Christ's Example

Sometimes, therefore, we have to watch how we speak about those who are in authority, and Paul comes to that point. Regarding the authorities, he says, "**This is also why you pay taxes.**" Now, again, he is speaking about political authority here. You do not pay taxes to your parents. (Or do you?) You do not pay taxes to your boss. You pay tithes in the church, but it is not quite the same as paying taxes where someone might come after you with a sword if you do not. Paul says, "**This is also why you pay taxes, for the authorities are God's servants, who give their full time to governing**" (v. 6). The authorities need to be paid, "for the laborer is worthy of his hire" (Lk. 10:7 NKJV). So we should pay taxes. Now the question will be raised, 'What about taxes that go beyond what is required?' The human heart is *extremely* skillful in arguing for its own interests, not wanting to give an *inch* above what is required. We have to look at our heart condition. Yes, we should pay taxes. Remember that Jesus, in part of His humbling and submitting Himself, paid the temple tax—God provided. Jesus said to Peter, "But so that we may not offend them, go to the lake and throw out your line. Take the first fish you catch; open its mouth and you will find a four–drachma coin. Take it and give it to them for my tax and yours" (Matt. 17:27). Jesus was asking, 'Should the Son of God be taxed?' He had asked Peter, "From whom do the kings of the earth collect duty and taxes—from their own sons or from others?" (Matt. 17:25b). The

Son of God was here, God was His Father—should the Son be taxed? No! But He said, nevertheless, so that we do not cause offense to men, we do so. He was the Son of God in human form, and He submitted to the ordinances. This is the example of our Lord Jesus. So, we should take His example into account when we begin to ask, 'How far should we go in submitting to authority?'

LIMITS OF AUTHORITY

Sphere Sovereignty: A Natural Limitation

We should ask ourselves the question: What are the limits of authority? First of all, we should understand that there is a built-in limit, in that there are multiple authorities. Therefore, one authority does not step into the realm of another. Masters are obeyed at work as masters, but not as governors. Parents are obeyed as parents, but not as rulers. Rulers are obeyed as rulers, but not as parents. There is a natural limitation of authority due to the fact that God has established multiple authorities. We can call this *sphere sovereignty*.[12] Each authority is sovereign in its sphere, and one is not to step over and beyond into another sphere; there is a limitation in that sense. That is why the Lord could say, "Render therefore to Caesar the things that are Caesar's, and to God the things that are God's" (Matt. 22:21b KJV). So, while we affirm the reality of authority, we do not overextend the authority and then create additional difficulties for ourselves. Each authority is naturally limited by the existence of others.

The Intended End of a Sphere of Authority

A second limitation is the *intended end* of the authority; the intended end is to do good. When those in authority begin to subvert the very purpose for which that authority is ordained, then there comes a serious question of whether that is the authority before God. There is a serious question when the authority begins to *violate* the very end for which it is ordained. Marriage is ordained to a particular end. When one party

---

12. Abraham Kuyper, *Lectures on Calvinism* (Grand Rapids: Eerdmans, 1931), 79–80. Kuyper teaches that God has ordained distinct spheres of life (such as the church, family, state, and education), each with its own authority directly under God, not subordinate to others.

in the marriage violates the end for which marriage is ordained, they are no longer properly in that position. There are reasons for parents being in a position of authority. When parents *violate* the very reason they are given a position of authority, for instance, in the abuse of children—instead of nurturing the children as authority understood properly—the State steps in and makes a judgment.

In the American Revolution, it was said, "Governments are instituted among Men, deriving their just powers from the consent of the governed, that whenever any Form of Government becomes destructive of these ends, it is the Right of the People to alter or to abolish it, and to institute new Government."[13] So we see the reasoning going on there. The limitation of authority is in terms of the ends. The claim was made in the Declaration of Independence that the people of the United States suffered a long series of abuses, and they listed, in the document, many of the abuses that they had suffered. They said that there comes a time when, before men and God, we must declare our cause.[14] We have to go back and ask, was the American Revolution justified? The Founding Fathers were using the violation of the purpose of Britain's authority as the reason to declare independence, and whether it was a *proper* use of that reason or not, we will have to see. The point is that violating the intended ends is another way in which we understand the limit of authority. **"For he is God's servant to do you good"** (v. 4).

Requiring Us to Do Evil: God's Law as a Limit

Another limit on authority is that no authority can require you to do what is against God's will—summed up in the Commandments. Authority is given within the context of the law; all authorities are ordained of God and, therefore, cannot violate the law of God. The law of God is another major protection. We might say that one authority cannot *require* us to do evil. The authority may do evil, in which case we have to go back to the question: Is the authority violating the purpose for

---

13. Thomas Jefferson, *The Declaration of Independence* (July 4, 1776).

14. "When in the Course of human events, it becomes necessary for one people to dissolve the political bands which have connected them with another, and to assume among the powers of the earth, the separate and equal station to which the Laws of Nature and of Nature's God entitle them, a decent respect to the opinions of mankind requires that they should declare the causes which impel them to the separation." Thomas Jefferson, *The Declaration of Independence* (July 4, 1776).

which it was ordained? For example, one purpose of the State is the protection of human life.[15] Then, we must go through argumentation to see if there is a long train of abuses that have led to injustice. And we have to look at other authorities, under which we are living, and see whether there is an opportunity to appeal and seek change.

Authority Is Limited by Insight

Authority is based on insight, especially authority in the fullest sense, where you follow the *example* of another. Everything is not spelled out in detail, but because someone has insight, their very lives become an example, and that carries authority. That is more than just doing what an authority tells you to do. The Lord made that distinction with the Pharisees: "You must obey them and do everything they tell you. But do not do what they do" (Matt. 23:3a). The full sense of authority is where we *emulate*, we follow the example of the person. But for those in authority who lack insight, we should not be honoring them by following their example. So, that is a limit of authority.

DISCERNING GODLY RESPONSES TO AUTHORITY

There is the question of submission to authority and its qualifications. There is a possibility of seeking change from *within* an institution as opportunity allows. We are not asked *not* to seek change. Where we do have the freedom, we can use it. However, it is wise to use it in a godly way. And even then, we must be careful and respectful. We may seek change of an illegitimate authority by leaving, where we have the freedom to do so. We can leave one country for another. In some cases, we cannot just pick up and go; the relationship is more binding, lifelong, and "until death do us part," as in the case of marriage, unless something is occurring in the marriage that violates the central purpose of it.[16] So, there is a way that is not the same as rebelling against the authority; one may leave.

It is always to be kept in mind that if we, the people of God, would obey His law, far from being submitted to others in authority, in

---

15. Gangadean, "Paper No. 27: The Limits of the State," in *The Logos Papers,* 165–169.

16. Gangadean, *The Westminster Confession,* 263–273.

God's providence, *believers* would be ruling and reigning with Christ, and would be in the position of authority. A lot of this discussion is happening in the context where there may be others in authority who are not believers. But what we should expect, and what should motivate a lot of our thinking about this, is that if we, the people of God, *individually*—as in the case of Joseph in Egypt and in the case of Daniel in Babylon—or *corporately*—the people together—were obedient, we would be in a position of leadership and would not be the tail of the culture. That has to be part of our understanding in thinking about the question of how we respond to authority.

GIVE EVERYONE WHAT YOU OWE HIM:
Especially the Continuing Debt to Love

Paul sums this up by saying, "**Give everyone what you owe him: If you owe taxes, pay taxes; if revenue, then revenue; if respect, then respect; if honor, then honor**" (v. 7). There is a whole range of things that may be due. It may be regarded as minimal to maximal, or it may be regarded as various. There are different things due to different people. We could give honor to the one in authority, and if that person is a wise, just, and benevolent ruler, we may want to honor them in terms of *emulating* them and not just giving taxes, which are the minimal sense of what is due.

In verse 7, Paul says, "**Give everyone what you owe him,**" and in verse 8, he says, "**Let no debt remain outstanding, except the continuing debt to love one another**" (v. 8a). He broadens this whole area of our duty of obedience to God and our service to others by saying that there is a debt that is permanent, and it is to all human beings, not just to some; and that is the debt of *love*. In that debt of love, we seek the welfare and the good of others. Just as government is to seek our good, and we have an obligation and a duty to be submitted to them as part of seeking the common good, so also, we are to think about applying the law of God in our relationships with our fellow man. "**Let no debt remain outstanding.**" Pay what you owe, but there is one debt owed to all, that will always continue, in every circumstance: "**the continuing debt to love one another, for whoever loves others has fulfilled the law**" (v. 8b). You see, Paul is still speaking in the context of the law—submission to authority is the fifth commandment—but the other Commandments still hold. He is giving an explication and an application, in detail, pressing that the law is God's way for us to come into the fullness of blessing that He has. Not by way of *earning* it, because we are justified freely through Christ, and on the basis of His righteousness, we are blessed and we learn to obey. We should keep that in mind.

Love Is a Summary of the Law

Some persons have attempted to set aside the law of God as permanently binding. Some have tried to make distinctions between the love of God and the law. They want to say, 'Love is binding, but the law is not binding.' This passage gives a categorical 'no' to that distinction. Paul says, **"The commandments, 'Do not commit adultery,' 'Do not murder,' 'Do not steal,' 'Do not covet,' and whatever other commandment there may be, are summed up in this one rule: 'Love your neighbor as yourself'"** (v. 9). **"Whatever other commandment"** includes do not lie, honor your father and mother, remember the Sabbath Day, to keep it holy. Notice that love is a *summary* of the law of God. I will say it once again: Love is a summary. Notice the term used here: *summed up*. The relation between love and the law is that love is essentially a *summary* of the law. The Commandments themselves are a summary of all that God requires of us. We are never, in our thinking, to separate love from the law. Many want to use the word *love* and reduce it to a feeling only. It certainly involves a feeling; it involves our thinking, our feeling, and our doing—it involves our whole being. That is why Jesus says, "Love the Lord your God with all your heart and with all your soul and with all your mind and with all your strength" (Mk. 12:30). To reduce it to one part of our being, and separate it from the others, is an unbiblical view of love. It is a form of self-deception if we separate it that way, and perhaps with that, self-justification.

Paul establishes the permanent binding nature of the law, as summed up in love, and that there is not a distinction between the two. The law opens up more fully what is contained in love. Love is not merely a *motivation*, as if the law does not involve motivation, as if the law were just an outward act and not an inward thought. The law *always* involves the whole of our being. We are not to say merely, 'Love is the motivation that leads you to keep the law.' The law is summed up in love, and this is the one debt binding on us all *continually*.

"Love does no harm to its neighbor" (v. 10a). But it is not just in the negative: "does no harm." The commandments are stated in the negative form: "You shall not kill," but they are always to be understood as having a positive side: Do good to your neighbor. "Love does no harm." Love does what is good, and we are to overcome evil by doing good and obeying the law.

The first part of Romans 13 is a continuation from Romans 12 regarding our service to God, and now it is applied to authority. We should keep in mind that after the fourth commandment—concerning work and rest—the first item on the agenda for our work is the fifth commandment—seeing that authority is properly structured. If we do not have the right persons in authority, there will be no end of trouble. That is why I think it is very appropriate to put the fifth commandment after the fourth. The fourth commandment says that the goal will be accomplished, the work will be completed, the Sabbath will be realized, and the work of dominion and filling the earth with the knowledge of God will be accomplished. The way to fulfill the fourth commandment is by proper authority, and Paul is warning us to be submitted to authority.

SUBMIT, UNDERSTANDING THE PRESENT TIME:
This Is the Time of Salvation

Paul then gives another reason for obedience in verses 11–14. He says, "And do this, understanding the present time . . ." (v. 11a). It is an eschatological motivation—the motivation of what our goal is and what our hope is. He says, "The hour has come for you to wake up from your slumber, because our salvation is nearer now than when we first believed" (v. 11b). He uses the word *salvation* in the full sense of the term. It is not justification only, it is not personal sanctification only, but salvation in the sense of the whole kingdom of God coming in its fullness in all the earth. This is the time; they have waited for the promise almost 4,000 years, since the time of Adam. Now Christ has come, and the gospel is going to the ends of the earth, and the gates of hell cannot withstand the onslaught of the Word of God, preached fully, preached clearly—"our salvation is nearer now than when we first believed." We are to understand that the day is at hand, the night is passing, and we are to give ourselves more fully to obedience. We are not to be discouraged and say, 'Oh, the Lord is waiting long.' No—*this* is the day of salvation, *this* is the time, and we are called to seek first the kingdom of God and His righteousness and give ourselves more and more fully; obedience should be increasing more and more. We should be speaking more often with one another, as Scripture says: "Not forsaking the assembling of ourselves together, as is the manner of some, but exhorting one another, and so much the more as you see the Day approaching" (Heb. 10:25 NKJV). That is how the day approaches: as we encourage one another daily in the way of God, in the Word of God, as we are increased with zeal and give ourselves more fully, as Paul says, "Let us throw off everything that hinders and the sin that so easily entangles, and let us run with perseverance the race marked out for us" (Heb. 12:1b). We are to "press on to take hold of that for which Christ Jesus took hold of me" (Phil. 3:12b). Paul is using this to urge our obedience and love, the hope of the blessing of salvation, the promise made to Abraham: "In you all the families of the earth shall be blessed" (Gen. 12:3b NKJV).

Paul calls upon us to understand the present time: **"Our salvation is nearer now than when we first believed. The night is nearly over"** (vv. 11b–12a). It is not just an individual night, it is a night where darkness covered the earth; there was a spot of light in Israel, but darkness was over the rest of the earth. Night was there, but now, **"the night is nearly over; the day is almost here"** (v. 12a). Dawn is coming—beautiful dawn—and bringing light where there was no light before and life where there was no life before.

Engaging in the Spiritual War: Put Off the Deeds of Darkness and Put On the Armor of Light

Paul urges this general understanding to come to a particular application. He says, **"So let us put aside the deeds of darkness"** (v. 12). Let us put aside the way we used to live, our old pattern of life, all those things that we were engaged in and that still cling to us. **"Let us put aside the deeds of darkness and put on the armor of light"** (v. 12b). Let us put on the armor for engaging in spiritual warfare, to take every thought captive. That involves being prepared through the teaching of the Word by the pastor-teachers, and being prepared for works of service. It involves not living as the Gentiles do, in terms of the way they handle education, or the way they handle family. Family is given in the context of dominion, and dominion is for the knowledge of the glory of God; we are to give ourselves to that work. We are to put aside the old way of life, the way of darkness, and put on the armor of light.

"**Let us behave decently, as in the daytime**" (v. 13a), in contrast to a life of self-indulgence, sexually and otherwise, and not in pride and envy. Paul says, "**Not in orgies and drunkenness, not in sexual immorality and debauchery, not in dissension and jealousy**" (v. 13b). We are to put on the Lord Jesus Christ. "**Rather, clothe yourselves with the Lord Jesus Christ, and do not think about how to gratify the desires of the sinful nature**" (v. 14). All of this we see perfectly embodied in Jesus Christ in the way He lived.[17] We are to look closely at the way Jesus lived. We are to see Jesus taking every thought captive and ruling at the right hand of God, ruling through His Holy Spirit to advance the kingdom in all the earth. We often restrict the work of Christ, not noticing Jesus taking thoughts captive and ruling and advancing the kingdom. We cannot afford to live in a narrow, confined view of the work of Christ, but we are to seek the kingdom of God in all the earth.

Fantasizing About God's Ideal

In Romans 12:1, Paul says, "Therefore, I urge you, brothers, in view of God's mercy, to offer your bodies as living sacrifices, holy and pleasing to God—this is your spiritual act of worship." He urges us to understand our particular calling in God and give ourselves to that calling. Paul urges us to overcome evil by doing good in particular responses to the government, and broadly speaking, in the whole obedience to the law of God. We are to understand that *this* is the time of salvation; *this* is when the gospel goes into all the earth. We should be thinking of ways in which we can carry the Word of God into *every* dimension of life as fully as we possibly can. This is what we should be fantasizing about. We should not keep our old fantasies as some way of escaping natural evil, either with some*one* or some*thing* or some*place*. Hawaii does not cut it; it is not paradise. Romantic love with another person is not going

---

17. *The Gospel of Matthew,* Surrendra Gangadean.

to satisfy. Hiking out in the mountains is not going to cut it. There is no perfect 'job' or circumstance out there that is going to cut it for us.

Fantasizing is idealizing, and it crosses the line very quickly into idolizing. John says, "Dear children, keep yourselves from idols" (1 Jn. 5:21). Let us watch our fantasy life. We are made to fantasize; we are made to fantasize about *God's ideal*. We have been expelled from the Garden; we have been driven out. Even after the conversion of Adam and Eve, they had to be driven out by God, and not only driven out, but blocked from coming back in. We cannot go back to the Garden. We have to go through labor and work to attain the end of the earth being filled with the knowledge of God. We should be fantasizing about how this can come about. We should be meditating on and delighting in the goal of the earth being filled with the knowledge of God. We should be finding ways to engage more and more in that work. "Therefore, I urge you, brothers, in view of God's mercy, to offer your bodies as living sacrifices, holy and pleasing to God—this is your spiritual act of worship" (Rom. 12:1).

—

18

LOVE AND LAW
Application to the Details of Life

1994

Romans 14

[1]Accept him whose faith is weak, without passing judgment on disputable matters. [2]One man's faith allows him to eat everything, but another man, whose faith is weak, eats only vegetables. [3]The man who eats everything must not look down on him who does not, and the man who does not eat everything must not condemn the man who does, for God has accepted him. [4]Who are you to judge someone else's servant? To his own master he stands or falls. And he will stand, for the Lord is able to make him stand.

[5]One man considers one day more sacred than another; another man considers every day alike. Each one should be fully convinced in his own mind. [6]He who regards one day as special, does so to the Lord. He who eats meat, eats to the Lord, for he gives thanks to God; and he who abstains, does so to the Lord and gives thanks to God. [7]For none of us lives to himself alone and none of us dies to himself alone. [8]If we live, we live to the Lord; and if we die, we die to the Lord. So, whether we live or die, we belong to the Lord. [9]For this very reason, Christ died and returned to life so that he might be the Lord of both the dead and the living.

[10]You, then, why do you judge your brother? Or why do you look down on your brother? For we will all stand before God's judgment seat. [11]It is written:

"'As surely as I live,' says the Lord,

'every knee will bow before me;

every tongue will confess to God.'"

[12]So then, each of us will give an account of himself to God.

[13]Therefore let us stop passing judgment on one another. Instead, make up your mind not to put any stumbling block or obstacle in your brother's way. [14]As one who is in the Lord Jesus, I am fully convinced that no food is unclean in itself. But if anyone regards something as unclean, then for him it is unclean. [15]If your brother is distressed because of what you eat, you are no longer acting in love. Do not by your eating destroy your brother for whom Christ died. [16]Do not allow what you consider good to be spoken of as evil. [17]For the kingdom of God is not a matter of eating and drinking, but of righteousness, peace and joy in the Holy Spirit, [18]because anyone who serves Christ in this way is pleasing to God and approved by men.

[19]Let us therefore make every effort to do what leads to peace and to mutual edification. [20]Do not destroy the work of God for the sake of food. All food is clean, but it is wrong for a man to eat anything that causes someone else to stumble. [21]It is better not to eat meat or drink wine or to do anything else that will cause your brother to fall.

[22]So whatever you believe about these things keep between yourself and God. Blessed is the man who does not condemn himself by what he approves. [23]But the man who has doubts is condemned if he eats, because his eating is not from faith; and everything that does not come from faith is sin.

ADIAPHORA IS NOT TO BE CONFUSED
WITH THE LAW OF GOD

IN ROMANS 14, PAUL CONTINUES THE CONCERN to know the good, perfect, and acceptable will of God; he continues the call to walk by the law of God and continues the call to walk in love. In the heart of this chapter, he says, **"If your brother is distressed because of what you eat, you are no longer acting in love"** (v. 15a). There is a continuation in Romans 14 of the application of the law of God into the most minute and delicate details of life. There is no sense of any abstraction in this chapter. A discussion is occurring about what is called the *adiaphora*, which is the Greek term for *non-righteous*. This is not the *unrighteous*, which is morally wrong, but the *non-righteous*—the things that are neither right nor wrong; things that are morally neutral.

The concern is that if we understand what love is, if we understand what the law of God is, we will understand what is the proper boundary of the law and not overextend the law into the area of the *adiaphora*—things that are neither right nor wrong. These are things like the food we eat, what we drink, and so on. But we will also not overextend the *adiaphora,* the neutral, into the law. This calls us, as we sang in Psalm 119F,[1] to dedicate ourselves to the law of God—"And in Thy statutes evermore I'll deeply meditate." We are called to think continually in light of the law of God and to learn how to apply it in the most delicate and intimate details of our consciousness and of our life.[2] That is what it is to walk in love. In the prior chapter, Romans 13, Paul says, "Let no debt remain outstanding, except the continuing debt to love one another" (Rom. 13:8a). Now we see this application going further. Remember: If we understand the will of God, the law of God, and the love of God, we will understand the application in terms of the boundary, and we will not overextend the law into the non-righteous, or over-expand the non-righteous in terms of indulging in the fleshly desires. Romans 13 ends with this: "Rather, clothe yourselves with the Lord Jesus Christ, and do not think about how to gratify the desires of the sinful nature" (Rom. 13:14). Sometimes, out of a desire to gratify the desires of the sinful nature, we *overextend* the boundaries of the *adiaphora.*

In Unbelief and Sin, We Overextend Both

In our unbelief and sin—actual unrighteousness and sinful behavior—we overextend in both directions. But we should know that these overextensions are not symmetrical. The way we deal with an overextension of the law into the area of the non-righteous is a matter of weakness of faith/conscience. The way we deal with the overextension of the *adiaphora*, the non-righteous, into the law, is a matter of sin, and requires it be dealt with as such.

I will give you a couple of real and lively examples to help us see. For decades, some segments of the Church have wrestled with the question of alcohol. Where does alcohol belong? Should ministers of the gospel take a vow to totally abstain? Almost every year for the past 40 to 50 years, discussion has taken place on this topic. It has been thought of in such a way that it has not been settled. That failure to settle the alcohol

---

1. *Psalm 119:48, 119F, The Book of Psalms for Singing.*

2. Gangadean, *The Gospel of Matthew,* 39–114.

question has meant that understanding the line between the law and the non-righteous is not clearly seen. That has encouraged, in turn, some to take the non-righteous and overextend it into the realm of the law and indulge their carnal desire. It goes both ways, and whole churches have been destroyed because of the antinomy between legalism and antinomianism. What Paul is speaking about here is a very pertinent, very live issue. We are not doing it with meat offered to idols,[3] but it is being done in other areas, because the carnal nature is still the same, unbelief is still the same, and Paul calls us to know the will of God and to walk in love by doing it.

Overextension of the Law in Legalism

Overextension is not a mere abstract issue that may be down the road one of these days. As we open this up, we will see that we use standards to judge and evaluate in terms of our thinking process. We use non-biblical standards and turn things that are neutral into wrong (legalism) and things that are wrong into neutral (antinomianism)—it goes on continually. The larger way in which this problem has been manifested is in the case of legalism: overextending the boundaries of the law to the neutral area—*adiaphora*. For example, some might say, 'You cannot go to watch a certain movie, you cannot wear certain clothes, the dress must come down a certain length' and so on—legalism. Legalism excuses us from true obedience to the law,[4] because we think that by detailing these elements, we are obeying the law, but we are really indulging the flesh.

---

3. *1 Corinthians 8.*

4. Christ, in the Sermon on the Mount, addressed this problem of legalism. The Pharisees and Teachers of the Law were too strict and too lax—too lax in understanding the principle of the law and too strict in emphasizing the particular application without upholding the principle. In legalism, the law is obeyed in a way that promotes the self-life.

Overextension of the *Adiaphora* in Antinomianism

Antinomianism[5] is the other side of this antinomy,[6] which says that the law does not apply to us now. For example, some say, 'Keeping the Sabbath day does not apply to us, only what is repeated in the New Testament is binding to us' and so on. Antinomianism opens up another area to indulge the carnal nature, the fleshly nature. So legalism and antinomianism are twins, sharing the same assumption. There is a failure to understand God's law; there is a failure to deeply meditate on the law and understand. In legalism, the Church has done terrible battery through overextension on things that are neutral. Because of the psychological harm caused by arbitrary legalistic applications, some have reacted by rejecting all limitations and restrictions. But antinomianism is not the alternative. That is what I mean by the *asymmetry*. The way we handle making something that is neutral into a matter of law (legalism) is different from the way we handle something that is a matter of law being made into neutral (antinomianism). Let us not confuse those two.

Paul's Focus on Legalism

In terms of the relation between legalism and antinomianism, in this passage, we are looking specifically at the overextension in one way only. Here, we are looking at legalism in the overextension of the law into the area of the neutral (*adiaphora*). In legalism, we make something that is neutral, like eating meat, into a matter of law by condemning it as wrong. Legalism was the specific concern that the Church was dealing with in Paul's time, along with the larger concern about the general boundaries of the law. These are connected with the larger concerns about doing the will of God, and the still larger concern about seeing the mercy of God—understanding sin and death. We are to understand

---

5. The error that, being set free from having to obey the law to be justified, God's law no longer binds and guides the conduct of believers. It is the rejection of God's law in favor of man's law (autonomy), whether private or by tradition, as the measure of holiness or piety. It denies the universal and perpetual nature of the law as the way of life.

6. Antinomies are contrary positions, both of which can be false at the same time because they share a common assumption. Examples include: capitalism and communism; this-worldly and other-worldly; all is eternal and none is eternal; skepticism and fideism; literalism and allegoricalism; virtue is the good and happiness is the good. Antinomies are a source of recurrent conflict within and between cultures.

what we have faced in the past, what we are facing now, and what we continue to face. We are to use biblical categories to think about our lives, and become more aware that obedience to the law is not only reading the Scripture and prayer, which are occasional, but meditating on the law day and night.

Using Biblical Categories to Understand

When we meditate, as we think about events and experiences, let us use biblical categories to think about them. This is how Paul begins Romans 12:

> Therefore, I urge you, brothers, in view of God's mercy, to offer your bodies as living sacrifices, holy and pleasing to God—this is your spiritual act of worship. Do not conform any longer to the pattern of this world, but be transformed by the renewing of your mind (Rom. 12:1–2a).

We are to learn to think in biblical categories, and we are to put away the old patterns and habits of thinking that we naturally fall into without even realizing. We are to learn to identify these old patterns and habits. We are to catch ourselves and see whether we are thinking on the surface of things or whether we are using biblical categories to understand what is really going on.

ADDRESSING LEGALISM:
How to Respond to Brothers of Weak Faith

Application: Eating Meat Offered to Idols

This application is not addressing whether we eat meat or only vegetables; this is not the general vegetarian question, though that is an example of overextension. This application has to do with meat offered to idols and the question of whether you are acknowledging and worshiping the idol by eating the meat. In that practice, the meat was offered in dedication to an idol; therefore, one might think that partaking in eating the meat would be almost like partaking in a pagan sacramental meal. It was pretty closely connected for recent converts. You can see how someone might have questions about this, especially someone coming out of and just barely escaping paganism, and all the practices that have gone on with paganism in connection with the practice of eating meat offered to idols. The festivities connected with this practice included sexual debaucheries and fertility celebrations. Celebrations of 'love' and 'receiving one another' is what they called it. One can always put a very nice face on human debauchery.

Response: Accept and Do Not Judge on Disputable Matters

The concern here, then, is about eating meat or not eating meat. Right at the beginning, to those who do eat meat, Paul says, **"Accept him whose faith is weak"** (v. 1a). He acknowledges two things. First, he acknowledges that their faith/understanding is weak, and they are overextending the law to what is neutral—legalism. It is a weakness of faith; it is a lack of understanding of the proper bounds of the law. Paul establishes this in the very first statement. Second, Paul establishes that they are to be accepted. We are dealing with a weakness of faith. We are not dealing with something that is morally wrong, where we overextend a neutral into the law. This is overextending the other way—it is not a symmetrical relationship.

Paul says the way to deal with this person, because they are not sinning, is that they are to be accepted. He says, **"Accept him whose faith is weak, without passing judgment on disputable matters"** (v. 1). What Paul means is that we do not try to, at this point, argue with the person. Do not pass judgment, and do not necessarily go around saying, 'Your faith is weak, and here is why your faith is weak,' giving out the arguments to prove them wrong. That is not the way in which the faith is built up. The building up of their understanding needs to be done, to be sure, but it is not on this matter, because this matter is disputable. When we begin with the foundation and build up from the foundation,[7] we will find that this matter will be taken care of—foundational matters are clearer.

Paul says, **"Accept him whose faith is weak, without passing judgment on disputable matters."** He continues, **"One man's faith allows him to eat everything, but another man, whose faith is weak, eats only vegetables"** (v. 2). Notice, **"whose faith is weak,"** Paul is clear in

---

7. Gangadean, *The Epistle to the Hebrews*, 83–98, 253–369.

identifying that this person's faith is weak. So, how should the one who is weak be viewed, and how should the one who is strong be viewed? Paul says, **"The man who eats everything must not look down on him who does not, and the man who does not eat everything must not condemn the man who does, for God has accepted him"** (v. 3). A lot of things concerning our personal relationships are *spoiled* by judgments regarding neutral matters.

God Has Accepted Them

It is also true that we do things that are morally wrong, and our brothers and sisters bring this to our attention, and that can spoil relations. But we are not to generalize this treatment about weakness of faith and not judging to say, 'There should be no judging whatsoever.' Antinomianism becomes another way to indulge the flesh. The pattern in judging is asymmetrical; it does not go both ways equally. Paul says the one must not look down on, and the other one must not condemn or judge—**"for God has accepted him."**

It is very rough on the person whose faith is weak to think that someone else is sinning. This person thinks that the other person is actually sinning. They may think, 'How can I possibly relate to this person who is sinning?' Paul goes on later in the text to show how that should be dealt with. Here, he says first that we must not judge others, God has accepted them. Later on, we will see that he is going to ask the person with stronger faith *not* to do those things that will cause his brother, who is weak in the faith, to stumble. That is how Paul deals with it here and gives many reasons. But initially, he says not to condemn the one who does eat, and the one who eats must not look down on his brother whose faith is weak. I know of issues like these that have come up in other churches, and they have caused great rifts and bad feelings between people. But *not all* bad feelings are caused by overextension. Sometimes people really do things that are wrong, and it is brought to their attention, and they have bad feelings, but that is not the same as dealing with disputable matters.

God Is Judge, Not Us

Another reason for not judging is that God is the judge—we are not the judge. God is abundantly able to bring His judgment to bear on that situation. Paul says, **"Who are you to judge someone else's servant? To his own master he stands or falls. And he will stand, for the Lord is able to make him stand"** (v. 4). Think of an earthly situation where that master is concerned. It could be someone at work who is picking on you and continues to pick on you, yet your supervisor is allowing it to continue. Why is he allowing it? Is he blind? Is he not noticing? He is the supervisor; he is supposed to know these things, yet your supervisor is not saying anything. **"To his own master he stands or falls."** Let the one who is in the position of authority make the judgment. Ultimately, God is in the position of authority, and it is impossible for Him to err in His judgment.

God Can Make Them Stand

Paul says, **"And he will stand, for the Lord is able to make him stand."** First, God has accepted us. Second, God is the judge. Lastly, God is the one who gives grace. We should consider these things when we approach this area of judging another. The Lord can and does strengthen the faith of the weak brother so as to enable them to overcome their lack of faith.

ANOTHER APPLICATION:
Sacred Days Versus Understanding the Commands of God

Sacred days are another application we have then and now: **"One man considers one day more sacred than another; another man considers every day alike"** (v. 5a). There used to be a lot of religious festivals and holy days, particularly within the Jewish calendar. So some would say, 'You *must* observe these holy days.' Others would say, 'No, those were shadows of what was to come; it has passed now that Christ has come.' Yet people still have these convictions from the past, and we must reckon with these convictions. Paul says, "Therefore do not let anyone judge you by what you eat or drink, or with regard to a religious festival, a New Moon celebration or a Sabbath day. These are a shadow of the things that were to come; the reality, however, is found in Christ" (Col. 2:16–17). In some cases, we see that it is from the Gnostic pagan eras that the impositions of holy days have come in. In any case, one way or another, the purity of the law of God that we speak of is found in Psalm 119: "In thy commandments which I love, I'll find the joy

I've claimed."[8] If we understand the commands of God—the proper boundaries and extensions—we will find joy in that command. The commands of God may be subjectively obscured for one reason or another, and we must come back and discern. The problem is at the level of understanding God's commands and their implications.

CHRISTIAN LIBERTY OF CONSCIENCE:
Living Our Convictions Before the Lord for We Are His

The rule set in this passage is this: **"Each one should be fully convinced in his own mind"** (v. 5b). Later on, we will see that we are not to violate our conscience, but at the same time, our conscience is not Lord, to be extended over all. We cannot make our conscience the rule for everyone. We are not to go against our conscience, but we cannot make our conscience the rule for everyone. Christians have the liberty of conscience, which consists in not being required to do anything which is against our conscience. It is more restrictive; it usually keeps us from doing certain things, or being required to do certain things, that we believe are against our conscience—it restricts us from positively doing anything wrong. Let us say I believe that everyone should wear a tie on the Lord's Day. I might come to church wearing a tie, but I cannot make my conscience the law for everyone else and have everyone else wear a tie. If our conscience is not properly informed of the law of God, it may bind us within certain limits that are applicable to ourselves but not to others. We have to watch that. The pattern seems to be this: we receive the teaching, and we hear it to a certain extent. Then we go along for a week, or two, or a month, and a circumstance comes up, and we begin to remember the Word that was taught, and then learn to apply it in that circumstance. **"Each of them should be fully convinced in their own mind"** (v. 5b). We are living before the Lord. Paul says,

> **He who eats meat, eats *to the Lord*, for he gives thanks *to God*; and he who abstains, does so *to the Lord* and gives thanks *to God*. For none of us lives to himself alone and none of us dies for himself**

---

8. *Psalm 119:47, 119F, The Book of Psalms for Singing.*

alone. If we live, we live *to the Lord*; and if we die, we die *to the Lord*. So, whether we live or die, we belong *to the Lord* (vv. 6b–8).[9]

We should be persuaded in our own minds before the Lord. We are not living out of someone else's convictions; we are living out of our own convictions, and our convictions should be before the Lord. When a person overextends the law to the neutral area in legalism, it is because they believe that this is what the Lord would have us do. But when a person overextends conscience into the area of law, and believes that because 'their conscience is pure' they can indulge the flesh, it is a violation of liberty of conscience. Someone could *try* to use that exact same argument, and someone *has* used that same argument, and has *destroyed* a church, which is one of the reasons we, as a church, are here today.[10] People have tried to use the argument under liberty of conscience, and we have to say, 'Let us look at the law of God to see if this is indeed within the law.' It is one thing to go one way (conscience as a negative guide); it is a different thing to go the other way (conscience is law and a positive guide). It is one thing to *restrict* your liberty because of conscience, but it is another thing to *expand* your liberties because of conscience. Let me repeat that again: it is one thing to restrict your liberties—that should be the case in the weakness of faith context. It is another thing to expand your liberties into the realm of the law. It is so very close; we might try to switch from one to the other. Paul is calling us to see that what we do should be done before the Lord.

Some people do things and do not even try to make an attempt to say, 'This is what I believe the Lord would have me to do.' We should say, 'I will be guided by what the Word says.' This is perhaps more what is being addressed here. We should say, 'This is what I believe the Lord would have me to do, and these are the reasons why I am convinced of it.' If we attempt to give reasons from the Scripture, in that respect, we are showing regard for the law and regard for the Lord who has given the law—that regard is understandable; that is the way it should be. We are living unto the Lord because He died for us. We can watch and see whether someone is claiming to act because the Lord wanted them to

---

9. Emphasis added.

10. This is referring to the break with the RPCNA in 1987. This incident will be documented in a forthcoming account of the history of Westminster Fellowship and the justification for starting a new work in the year 2000.

do it or whether they are merely indulging their sinful nature without regard for scriptural justification. Whatever we do, we should do out of conviction before the Lord, and not disregard His law.

CHRIST OUR LORD IS OUR JUDGE:
All Will Give an Account to God

Paul gives another reason why we should not judge and expands on the earlier reason that God is the judge. He says,

> **For this very reason, Christ died and returned to life so that he might be the Lord of both the dead and the living. You, then, why do you judge your brother? Or why do you look down on your brother? For we will all stand before God's judgment seat (vv. 9–10).**

Paul is speaking about judgment that does not always occur in this life. The fact that judgment does not always occur in this life—and *ultimately* does not occur in this life—does not mean it will not occur. Christ has died, He is raised from the dead, He is God, He is Lord both of the living and the dead. All will appear before Christ the Lord and must give an account of themselves to God.[11] That is a pretty awesome thing. Each person must come before the throne of God and give an account to God for what they have done. We should say it extends even to every idle word that we might speak. Jesus says, "For every idle word men may speak, they will give account of it in the day of judgment" (Matt. 12:36 NKJV). That should cause each one of us to fear the Lord for ourselves and, in doing so, to recognize, 'That person is going to have to stand before God and give an account for every detail of life.'

The believer's guilt is covered through the blood of Christ, but that does not mean the works and thoughts will not be judged. You will not be condemned; as Jesus said to the woman caught in adultery, "Neither do I condemn you; go and sin no more" (Jn. 8:11b NKJV). Our idle words will be judged as sin. You know how easy it is to speak idle words; it just flows out; it just naturally comes out; you don't have to do anything. So Paul gives this reason for why we should not judge: "**For we will all stand before God's judgment seat . . . each of us will**

---

11. Gangadean, *The Westminster Confession*, 337–342; Gangadean, *The Epistle to the Hebrews*, 355–369.

give an account of himself to God" (vv. 10b, 12). A father cannot give an account for his children, a husband cannot give an account for his wife, and a daughter cannot give an account for her mother. God judges each one of us individually for everything we have done. That includes this attitude of looking down on our brother. The secrets of our hearts will be revealed by Jesus Christ.

WALKING IN FAITH AND LOVE

Do Not Put a Stumbling Block in Your Brother's Way

Paul calls us to stop passing judgment on one another; he says, "**Therefore let us stop passing judgment on one another. Instead, make up your mind not to put any stumbling block or obstacle in your brother's way**" (v. 13). This whole pattern of living, particularly where we indulge our freedom in a way that causes hurt to others, is regarded as a "**stumbling block.**" Instead of making the way plain, we are putting a stumbling block in the way. It is like hiking on a trail, and you step on a stepping stone to help get you going, but it slips, and you stumble and fall; it becomes something slippery, something treacherous. Many of you have hiked, and you know what we are talking about. You stand on something, you think it is firm, and it slips out from under you, and you collapse and fall. Perhaps you hurt yourself very badly. We are not to put a stumbling block in our brother's or sister's way. Indulging in our freedom often involves putting a stumbling block in someone else's way.

Remember, the stumbling block is about indulging in *legitimate* freedom. Someone could use that exact same argument of Christian freedom *falsely* to indulge the flesh. The sense Paul is speaking of is when there is something that really is neutral, and you are free to do it, but you are not going to exercise it because of the well-being of your brother or sister. Someone may be *claiming* something is neutral, but it is, in reality, forbidden by the law. Question 99.6 of the *Larger Catechism* says that not only the sin itself is forbidden, but, "together with all the causes, means, occasions, and appearances thereof, and provocations thereunto." We are to be careful about these things, whether it applies to drinking, or smoking, or whatever else. We could make some medical arguments against some of these things, but the proper concern in

Paul's argument is the moral argument: if it is causing someone else to stumble, you are not walking in love. We might insist on our freedom in a way that harms another person. Paul is saying that this is not the way we should live. Do not **"put any stumbling block or obstacle in your brother's way."**

Paul reiterates, **"As one who is in the Lord Jesus, I am fully convinced that no food is unclean in itself"** (v. 14a). This brings up another element, not just meat offered to idols, but the question that the Jews wrestled with about clean and unclean animals—the distinction that the Lord did away with at the time of the expansion of the gospel. We can understand someone who is a pious Jew, brought up in this, seeing someone eat bacon, an unclean meat, and saying, 'That is not to be done!' Yet the Lord has declared all meats clean, and Paul says, **"As one who is in the Lord Jesus, I am fully convinced that no food is unclean in itself."** Let us say that God is gracious, opens the door, and brings in a lot of Jews who have been raised in pious households. We come to have lunch together and someone brings pork ribs, and the new convert is gasping on the floor. But we say, 'Paul says he is fully convinced that no food is unclean, come on, get with the program!' No, we are not to operate that way. Restrictions fall on you, as the stronger person, to bear with those who are weak.

"But if anyone regards something as unclean, then for him it is unclean. If your brother is distressed because of what you eat . . ." (vv. 14b–15a)—or what you drink, or what you smoke. Here, we are called to live in righteousness; if one person is doing something, it may cause the other person to be distressed. It is *insensitive* not to be aware of the distress that is being caused. Paul says, **"You are no longer acting in love"** (v. 15)—period. The loving thing to do is to recognize that distress. Paul gives arguments for this: **"Do not by your eating destroy your brother for whom Christ died"** (v. 15b). Christ died for this one, and you are going to insist that you cannot give up participating in this for your brother? Look at the love of Christ, and look at your love. Remember, you are not to refrain because it is morally wrong; you are not binding your conscience. You cannot be asked to bind your conscience in that way, but your conduct, which is distressing, can be addressed. **"Do not by your eating destroy your brother."** Notice that strong word: *destroy*. Your actions may break the fellowship, and cause the person to withdraw. It may cause the person to say, 'We can't know anything about the law of God, what's the use?' So they get discouraged, fall out of fellowship, and are destroyed. See how the law gets into the very delicate parts of our lives—the line between *adiaphora* and righteousness; non-righteousness and righteousness. **"Do not by your eating destroy your brother for whom Christ died."**

"Do not allow what you consider good to be spoken of as evil" (v. 16). That does not mean stand up and defend it. 'I'm not going to let eating ribs ('my good') be taken from me! Man, I've worked hard to win this freedom to eat ribs. My wife knows how to make the best ribs in town, and I'm not about to let that go!' It does not mean that we should not let evil be spoken of by defending it. What it means is that we do not overextend to neutral areas that which would cause offense. Paul says, **"For the kingdom of God is not a matter of eating and drinking . . ."** (v. 17a). You are not *required* to eat the ribs, you are not *required* to smoke that cigar, you are not *required* to drink that wine. But you are required to pursue **"righteousness, peace and joy in the Holy Spirit"** (v. 17b)—that is required. To restrict yourself from what is not required is different from failing to do what *is* required. So Paul is saying, 'Righteousness, peace, and joy is what is required. The other things you are free to do are not required.' Our concern is to pursue the kingdom of God. Build up the kingdom and be at peace with your brother. Do not cause distress and anguish. You are not binding your conscience, I remind you, but you are recognizing the weakness of another. What you are to do is not argue about specific disputable matters, but build one another up on the foundational level, and keep building there, which is certain, until the person matures enough to properly understand the law.

"Because anyone who serves Christ in this way is pleasing to God and approved by men" (v. 18). The Lord wants us—certainly, always, and under all circumstances—to be pleasing to God. There is no question about that. When our ways please the Lord, He makes even our enemies be at peace with us. We will be approved by men—believer and nonbeliever. We will certainly be approved by other believers, but sometimes by nonbelievers also, when they see us walking in this way and not indulging our desires of the sinful nature spoken of at the end of Romans 13.

Seek What Leads to Peace and Mutual Edification

"Let us therefore make every effort to do what leads to peace and to mutual edification" (v. 19). Certainly, we must do what is required by righteousness, but when we have peace and fellowship with others, there will be joy there, too. "Do what leads to peace and to mutual edification." Do what leads to building each other up. Often, we do not recognize our own sinful desires and we indulge in them, instead of doing what leads to mutual edification. There are times when we define ourselves in secondary, tertiary ways. We take that which is perhaps a fourth or fifth-level aspect of our being, such as gender or ethnicity, and we make it a first level aspect of our being. We reverse that order, we set standards on that basis, out of order, and we lose the difference between *adiaphora* and righteousness. Then we set up new systems of laws because we did not accept God's law about the nature of persons.

Sometimes, we define persons in terms of feelings. We become violently defensive when we feel someone's feelings are not being regarded, because it feels like a disregard of a *person*. We come flaming out of our caves to their defense, like Don Quixote tilting at windmills.[12] And boy, do we feel righteous about that. But that is not the righteousness of God. "Let us therefore make every effort to do what leads to peace and to mutual edification." We may think we are building someone up, but we have not given ourselves to think deeply about the law of God, and we are not really building them up. We may even kill someone in the name of God; Jesus was killed because we had zeal without knowledge. So, let us do "what leads to peace and to mutual edification." We are to meditate deeply on the law of God, think through it, work through it, and discuss it. It is the standard of our peace, righteousness, and joy in the Holy Ghost.

Again, Paul says, "Do not destroy the work of God for the sake of food" (v. 20a). We are to build up the work of God, the kingdom of God; we are to "seek first his kingdom and his righteousness" (Matt. 6:33). Do not destroy the work of the kingdom because of food. "All food is clean" (v. 20). The concern is the area of the neutral, and those who are weak overextending the law into the area of the neutral for whatever variety of reasons. Paul makes this clear: "All food is clean,

---

12. Miguel de Cervantes, *Don Quixote*, trans. Edith Grossman (New York: HarperCollins, 2003).

but it is wrong for a man to eat anything that causes someone else to stumble" (v. 20b). Here, Paul is saying that it is *wrong*. It is wrong to eat meat or eat anything that causes someone else to stumble. He says, "It is better not to eat meat or drink wine or to do anything else that will cause your brother to fall" (v. 21). Paul says in 1 Corinthians 8:13, "Therefore, if what I eat causes my brother to fall into sin, I will never eat meat again, so that I will not cause him to fall."

"So whatever you believe about these things keep between yourself and God" (v. 22a). That is, do not pass judgment on disputable matters; keep it between yourself and God. Do not make a remark that humiliates the other person. "Blessed is the man who does not condemn himself by what he approves" (v. 22b). There is a blessing for those who are strong in faith. "But the man who has doubts is condemned if he eats" (v. 23a). If he doubts that this is the will of God, if he thinks that it should not be done, and then still eats, he condemns himself, because he is not doing it out of respect for God. He is saying, 'Well, I believe this is wrong, but I'm going to do it, because I want to be accepted by others. I love the praise of men. I want to be admired.' Of course, we do not come out and say those words. "But the man who has doubts is condemned if he eats, because his eating is not from faith; and everything that does not come from faith is sin." (v. 23). Everything that does not come out of an understanding of God's will and submission to His will is sin.

Sin includes what is contrary to the law of God *objectively*, and also what is contrary to the law of God *subjectively*. If I believe something is contrary to the law of God, and I do it, that is sin. Whatever is not of faith is sin. We see how that captures both the objective law of God and the subjective. If I believe something that is contrary to the law of God, then I am simply wrong, and I need to be called out on that and shown from Scripture that it is wrong. The Lord applies His Word in this area so that we might learn, in all dimensions of our relationships, to walk in love with one another.

19

UNITY FOR FULLNESS
Seeking the Good for and with Others

Romans 15

EDITOR'S NOTE

The sermon audio recording on Romans 15 is not currently in the possession of The Logos Archives. We have used the existing handwritten outline and the post-sermon discussion to provide an accurate portrayal of the main content of the sermon. Although it is unfortunate to be unable to use the sermon's transcription for this chapter, it renders a rare opportunity to convey an additional dimension of Pastor Gangadean's approach to imparting teaching.

Dialogue was his preferred method for addressing theological and existential issues. It allows for greater attention to each person's particularities and perspective, and it shows how the Word of God is sharper than any double-edged sword in taking thoughts captive in a live setting that is relevant and intelligible to all involved.

This dialogue exchange conveys his patient, careful, open, and presuppositional approach to dialogue. He proceeds step by step in the discussion to secure the most basic and central idea. The discussion follows a pace that is both fluid and focused. The interlocutors pursue the topic from their understanding, and Pastor Gangadean reframes the focus through questions so as to render the engagement edifying while taking their concerns and ideas into account. This process may take the majority of the time in many cases, but it ultimately shows how, by proceeding presuppositionally, we can make progress in securing foundational pieces that can later be used to make further progress in this and other contexts.

The understanding of the congregants present limits the extent and depth of the dialogue. Out of care to feed the flock, Pastor Gangadean did not press much further ahead from where the congregants were. The aim is to edify them where they are and gradually over time enable growth in keeping with their faith. This dialogue is not to be used to assess his understanding of Romans 15 per se, but to highlight his gifting as a teacher and care as a shepherd of the flock. Pastor Gangadean modeled what to 'please his neighbor for his good, to build him up' looks like from he who is more mature to those who are weak.[1]

May this brief dialogue serve the reader in understanding Rational Presuppositionalism in action and applying the elements present to find meaning in subsequent discussions and settle long-standing disputes.

OUTLINE

1. Weak and strong believers.

    i. Question: What is it to please his neighbor for his good? To build him up.

    ii. All work together for good (Rom. 8:28).

    iii. Cling to what is good (Rom. 12:9).

    iv. Christ's example.

    v. Endurance and encouragement of the Scriptures: have hope (For what? Unity in purpose).

2. Unity in purpose for the glory of God.

3. Accept one another (Rom. 14:1) for the gospel/kingdom's sake. Christ became a servant to confirm promises to the Patriarchs (all families of the earth will be blessed).

    i. Gentiles glorify God (praise, rejoice, hope) as it is written again and again and again. The Gentiles will hope in Him.

4. God of hope, joy, and peace (based on trust). Overflow with hope.

5. Competent to instruct one another. This letter is on some points part of proclaiming the gospel to the Gentiles (Rom. 1:1–6).

---

1. *Romans 15:1–2.*

6. The privilege, progress, and program of preaching the gospel (Rom. 15:17–22).

7. Plan to visit Rome on the way to Spain.

   i. Enjoy your company and assistance on the way.

   ii. Mentality in sharing blessings.

   iii. God's timing and blessing in his coming to Rome.

8. Call to join in the struggle through prayer.

POST-SERMON DISCUSSION:
The Meaning of Pleasing One's Neighbor for Their Good

Pastor Gangadean: "Each of us should please his neighbor for his good, to build him up" (v. 2). What is the meaning of this passage? How do you understand it?

Congregant 1: Affirming the good in another person is inherently pleasing to them. When you affirm their good, you uphold their dignity, which brings them satisfaction.

Pastor Gangadean: Do you think affirming their dignity is the good, or part of the good, and that affirming the dignity of another is satisfying? What would you understand affirming the dignity of the other to mean?

Congregant 2: Anything that provides them with the opportunity to grow spiritually rather than merely making them feel good on a psychological level.

Pastor Gangadean: There are two things in your answer: First, what is *the good*, as it says, "**Each of us should please his neighbor for his good, to build him up.**" Second, whether the good is pleasing. Maybe we could hold the second part until we establish the first. There is another verse in Romans—let's look back at that briefly: "And we know that in all things God works for the good of those who love him" (Rom. 8:28a). There is that idea again. In Romans 12:9, Paul says, "Love must be sincere. Hate what is evil; cling to what is good." Here, the term *good* is used three times in passages that are central. We need to understand that and see where difficulties may arise.

Congregant 1: When you encourage them for their good, you should encourage them to have their identity in Christ and not in another person, and to seek the approval of God rather than another. I see that often people try to please each other. We should look to pleasing God first. First, we must be responsible to God. If our identity is placed in Him, then our relationships with others will flow from there.

I am learning from my own experience that I sought my husband's approval before God's, and that was my sin. It brought nothing but destruction to my marriage. Many times, children seek the approval of their parents to such a degree that they do not have their identity in Christ. I think this also happens among peers—it carries into every relationship.

Congregant 3: It demands a lot of patience. If we keep our objective in mind—When I go out for coffee with my students, I sit and listen as they share about their lives. There are so many moments when I think, 'Oh, no, don't do that.' But, I have realized that they can only change their behavior once they change their knowledge. Until their understanding changes, their actions will not change.

It is a patient process of loving them and being emotionally sensitive to where they are coming from and the turmoil they are experiencing. I cannot discount or disapprove their experience; I have to be sensitive to them. They should know that I love them—I hope. If I do something that makes them doubt that I love them, then I am at fault; I am the problem in that case. Loving them is like walking a gentle line—you cannot give in or disregard what you ultimately know to be true.

By patiently suggesting these things, they may change their minds. Many students discussed the movie *Philadelphia*.[2] If you have not seen it, I cannot explain it without going into extensive details. For those who have, the film only left you with two choices: one was to disregard the person, hate them because of their actions and lifestyle, and dismiss them altogether. The other was to embrace the person with compassion and, therefore, to embrace the lifestyle. They only left you, from a worldly point of view, with two choices. Of course, there is another option for believers, and they never bring that one up. But I think that is part of showing dignity to the person as a creation of God, which is the idea that they have a mind, they can think, and I have to reason

---

2. *Philadelphia*, dir. Jonathan Demme (Los Angeles: TriStar Pictures, 1993).

with them. I have to spend time, be patient, and go through these things repeatedly, knowing the ultimate goal.

Congregant 2: The idea of self-sacrifice comes up here in connection with Christ and the first verse—not pleasing ourselves, just as Christ did not please Himself. We should not necessarily put ourselves out at the expense of another's well-being or spiritual growth. Also, we can know what is good for our neighbor, even if our neighbor does not know what is good. Their perception of what is good is not necessarily aligned with what is truly good for them.

Congregant 1: Maybe it is not so much that *we* know, but rather, that Christ knows. Instead of placing ourselves in what I would consider an arrogant position—that we know—we need to let God work through those circumstances.

Congregant 2: We should never deny that we can know human nature. We can know what is good for all human beings, at all times, and in all places. If we keep this first and foremost in our minds, and direct all our actions toward that, we will, in effect, be doing what is good for all.

Pastor Gangadean: Does this passage cause us to know what the good is? Does it expect us to know what the good is?

Congregant 4: That is first and foremost. Before you can take the speck out of someone else's eye, you need to remove the log that is blocking your own vision.

Pastor Gangadean: Does that mean we can know what the good is for all persons? I think that is the primary question. If we *cannot* know the good, but Christ can know it, and we claim to know the good, that would be arrogant. If we *can* know the good and *should* know it, then that would not be arrogant—it would be part of pleasing our neighbor "for his good" (v. 2). That is exactly where the struggle is.

The question of the mote and the beam in the eye is a secondary question. First, we must ask the question of knowing what the good is. Regarding thinking that we can know what the good is, maybe we could ask, does this passage expect that we can know the good? For example, when it says, "**I myself am convinced, my brothers, that you yourselves are full of goodness, complete in knowledge and competent to instruct one another**" (v. 14). This is where much of the conflict is right now. Firstly, it is not clear that we agree on whether we can know the good. Secondly, if we can know the good, it is not clear that we agree on what the good is. Unless those questions are settled first, we cannot settle these other questions, which deal only with the psychological results of an earlier dispute. Does this require us to know the good if we are to please our neighbor for their good?

Congregant 5: Yes.

Pastor Gangadean: We can know the good? Do you have any reservations or questions? Then, what is this good?

Congregant 4: The knowledge of God—that is the only good, the ultimate goal.

Pastor Gangadean: What do we understand by the knowledge of God?[3]

Congregant 1: It is a relational type of thing. It is difficult because sometimes you are talking to people who are in the same boat as you, yet you are talking about things in very different ways. I think that is where the greatest struggle comes.

Pastor Gangadean: Exactly, that is why I am trying to draw attention to this. How do we understand the knowledge of God? I think we probably find a lot of agreement that the good is the knowledge of God in certain circles, but could we also find disagreement on how we understand what that knowledge is?

Congregant 5: It is the goal for which we are to live, as opposed to being part of the process.

Pastor Gangadean: Explain, please.

Congregant 5: A typical view that we deal with all the time is that heaven is the goal, and the knowledge of God is merely the means to get there. We say the knowledge of God is not only the means but it is also the goal. "Heaven and earth will pass away, but my words will never pass away" (Matt. 24:35). To know Him is the only eternal, lasting thing for anyone, as opposed to some type of physical destination or vision of God, which is a temporal thing; it is distorted.

---

3. Gangadean, *The Biblical Worldview*, 109–124; Gangadean, *The Westminster Confession*, 353–357.

Pastor Gangadean: Do you think that is pretty heavy-duty stuff being imported into and imposed upon this passage?

Congregant 5: It is what I grew up with my entire life.

Pastor Gangadean: That was assumed.

Congregant 5: Assumed.

Pastor Gangadean: Taught, assumed, and brought into this passage. Will we please people differently if we have these different views of the goal?

Congregant 5: Absolutely. Yes, you are a little more direct and honest with them.

Pastor Gangadean: For example, what might be the difference in how we please another person and build them up if the goal or the good is seen differently?

Congregant 5: Discipleship.

Pastor Gangadean: Discipleship?

Congregant 1: Many people assume the attitude, 'If you love one another and God is love, then you are okay.' Loving means tolerance, and tolerance means accepting many things that are detrimental, not only to ourselves in this fleshly life, but also to our ultimate relationship with the God of all creation.

Pastor Gangadean: Yes. Acceptance of a certain sort is detrimental. Is that right?

Congregant 1: Acceptance of a type that eventually leads us to ignore Scripture altogether.

Pastor Gangadean: Worldly acceptance.

Congregant 1: Worldly acceptance. I think that is, unfortunately, a byline in many parts of the body of Christ. I will not deny that they are still the body of Christ because, in many ways, they still absolutely do pursue the Word. However, it is easy to look at some Scriptures systematically while ignoring others. A good example is predestination—some ignore certain passages, which then changes their view of how they came to know Christ and who God is.

Pastor Gangadean: In this passage, and in Romans 15 as a whole, is there anything that helps us understand the goal? When I spoke about 'importing into'—discussions about the goal being imported into the passage—we can say, 'Oh well, we believe this,' it becomes very easy for us to import it into the passage and impose it on the passage. Do we see things in the passage that cause us to reckon with the goal or the good?

Congregant 2: Three things seem to be connected: knowledge, instruction, and teaching.

Pastor Gangadean: Where do you get the knowledge referenced in this passage?

Congregant 2: In the passage you have read: "**I myself am convinced, my brothers, that you yourselves are full of goodness, *complete in knowledge and competent to instruct one another*"** (v. 14).[4]

Pastor Gangadean: Is that the goal?

Congregant 2: That is the foundation for everything that was written in the passage—written to teach us—and, in connection with that, the idea of endurance, perseverance, and hope. We have knowledge, teaching, and hope. It seems as if the context is something present, a current reality, rather than something otherworldly.

Pastor Gangadean: When you refer to "**complete in knowledge and competent to instruct one another,**" is that the good being spoken of there, or is that a means to the good? You mentioned endurance and so on—is that a means to the good—a virtue—or is that the good? Or is that distinction itself being imposed on the passage?

Congregant 2: It says, "**full of *good*ness, complete in knowledge.**"[5] I don't think that is being imposed.

Pastor Gangadean: I see.

Congregant 2: That is just the sense of the term.

Pastor Gangadean: That is, if we have that knowledge, we can share it with others and instruct them.

---

4. Emphasis added.

5. Emphasis added.

Congregant 2: That is what I think it should be.

Pastor Gangadean: I was thinking about verses 5–6: "**May the God who gives endurance and encouragement give you a spirit of unity among yourselves as you follow Christ Jesus, so that with one heart and mouth you may glorify the God and Father of our Lord Jesus Christ.**" Unity enables us to glorify God. Then in connection with that passage, we have Jesus' example: "who for the joy set before him he endured the cross" (Heb. 12:2). The joy set before him is in bringing the nations to Christ. So the motivation to deal with some of these differences in a godly way, work through them, and handle them properly, seems to be the promises made to the Patriarchs. What is that promise? How should we understand the promises made to the Patriarchs?

Congregant 3: The promise made to Abraham? All the nations will be blessed.

Pastor Gangadean: This passage seems to focus on that promise: "**Therefore I will praise you *among the Gentiles*; I will sing hymns to your name**" (v. 9b).[6] He says it again and again and again. The joy set before Him in bringing many sons to glory, bringing the nations to know, and bringing the earth to be filled with the knowledge of God. Now, that seems to be central in the passage, not imposed; it is a central motivation. And in connection with the promise to the Patriarchs being central, so is having hope that we will attain to that promise. "**May the God of hope fill you with all joy and peace as you trust in him, so that you may overflow with hope by the power of the Holy Spirit**" (v. 13). Filled with the hope that the promise will come about.

So we are motivated to *endure*, to work through the problem, and come to a resolution in connection with seeking to please the other: "**please his neighbor for his good**" (v. 2). Build them up in connection with this way of understanding the good. Now, is this a common understanding of the good? Is this our *actual* understanding of the good? I do not mean just verbal agreement. I think our group is inclined to agree verbally to this, but verbally agreeing is not the same as *actually* understanding and believing. Perhaps we can deal with it at two levels. First, in general, is this commonly understood?

---

6. Emphasis added.

Congregant 1: I have got a lot of things going on in my mind right now, but one of them was the glory of God. We talk about glorifying God, but it has to have content, and that content is seeing and affirming that which is already there. The problem is that we do not see it. The affirmation of seeing what is there and the meaning that God has revealed in His creation. I see the glory of God as being seen and affirmed. When you see and affirm that good, that glory of God, it is full of content. Many people can verbalize and say, 'Praise to God' or 'Glory to God,' but it lacks content. They are not seeing meaning, and they are not seeing the intricate relationship of all the different things in creation in the fullness therein.

Regarding pleasing the neighbor and building him up, our idea of love is faulty. I think pleasing your neighbor is speaking the truth in gentleness. That pleasing is not the pleasing that we tend to think in a more worldly sense. It is speaking the truth in love, and perseverance in speaking that truth. Gentleness is always there. It is not a condescending act, as it says, one who is strong ought **"to bear with the failings of the weak"** (v. 1a).

Pastor Gangadean: Could two persons believe they are loving each other, and seeking the good for each other, yet be causing a lot of pain to each other?

Congregant 5: Yes. It happens more often than not; it is called marriage, isn't it? [*laughter*]

Congregant 3: You don't even have to get that far. How about Barnabas and Paul?

Pastor Gangadean: Exactly. That is an excellent example. Because I think that is where the fault lines are. We can think about that example. They were companions together for so long, and yet they parted. They parted over what?

Congregant 1: Mark.

Pastor Gangadean: John Mark. Specifically what? Whether they should take John Mark on the next trip. What had happened before?

Congregant 1: He bailed out.

Pastor Gangadean: Yes, he bailed out earlier. Paul did not want to take John Mark because he thought it was unwise, but Barnabas wanted to take him. Do you see how this idea of **"please his neighbor for his good"** (v. 2) is working itself out here?

Congregant 1: Sure.

Pastor Gangadean: Now, I do not know if you want to even touch the question of whether you think one was right in that situation?

Congregant 1: Could it have been God's way of allowing them to go their separate ways for the purpose of speaking to different groups?

Pastor Gangadean: Suppose that were an effect of it, would that still leave the question unanswered whether it was right? Could they have gone separate ways without having a sharp dispute?

Congregant 5: Yes, exactly.

Pastor Gangadean: What was the dispute about? What do you think the dispute was about?

Congregant 5: Pride.

Pastor Gangadean: Pride, I think, is a psychological term that *may* be reflecting an earlier difference. That is what I was trying to get at, to get to that earlier difference. Let us analyze that a little bit.

Congregant 5: It is their view of the good, and when they pursue it to its fullest; there is a difference in beliefs, and pride gets in the way . . .

Pastor Gangadean: Okay. They have differences. Can you identify what the differences are to see how we may have different views of the good? Because that was one of the outstanding disputes in Scripture, the dispute between Barnabas and Paul.

Congregant 1: Did Paul feel that if John Mark had done it once, he would do it again? Did Paul actually feel like John Mark was not even a disciple in the truest sense?

Pastor Gangadean: That he was not a believer?

Congregant 1: That he was not a believer.

Pastor Gangadean: I do not get the impression from the passage that Mark's status as a believer was questioned, but Paul questioned John

Mark's preparation. Later on, Paul said, "Get Mark and bring him with you, because he is helpful to me in my ministry" (2 Tim. 4:11b). It is interesting to notice how Paul is thinking here. He is thinking about the ministry and what will further advance that ministry. Over and against thinking about the ministry, it is possible to think about the person. It seemed that what was going on was that Barnabas—the son of encouragement, the son of consolation—was wanting to affirm the person rather than the ministry.

Paul was looking at the goal of the ministry. Do you know what hung on that situation? Our sitting here today, I believe, hung on Paul's decision not to take John Mark. The gospel going to Europe hung on that decision. The way the gospel went to Europe is that Paul took Silas, and both of their backs were beaten open, and they were thrown into prison. Both of them were able to pray and sing praises to God in the prison. In that context, the prison was shaken, the gospel was preached to the Philippian jailer, and he came to the Lord.[7]

That was the beginning of the mission in Europe. Remember, Paul had tried to continue in Asia Minor, and the Holy Spirit was preventing him. Then he had that vision in the night, someone from Philippi saying, "Come over to Macedonia and help us" (Acts 16:9b). Now the question is, given John Mark's weakness in turning away under affliction, would he have been able to stand up as Silas did when his back was beaten open? I think the indication was that he would not have been able to. Later on, after he was encouraged and nurtured by Barnabas, Paul said, "Get Mark and bring him with you, because he is helpful to me in my ministry" (2 Tim. 4:11b).

Notice, he is not just profitable to Paul, as if that were the end. It is for the ministry and the goal, the purpose for which God had called him. Sometimes, that kind of difference is made without the goal and the means being kept in mind—the immediate means, in this case. I think certainly John Mark became part of those means: "he is profitable to me for the ministry."[8] But the immediate means of being able to endure hardship, given the mission, was not being kept in mind by Barnabas.

Barnabas was affirming personhood. Sometimes, the value of the person seems so great that it seems that Paul was denying it. I think

---

7. *Acts 16:16–40.*

8. *2 Timothy 4:11* KJV.

that was one of the reasons why the dispute was so sharp. That difference between, I believe, the prophetic and the priestly,[9] insofar as the priestly is not grounded in the foundation of the prophetic—that difference comes up again and again. It comes up in our understanding of the goal. It rips us apart. We need to back up and understand what the good is. That is why I speak about the foundation being laid, and building on that foundation.

Congregant 1: That is really key.

Pastor Gangadean: It is.

Congregant 1: Now that you say that, I am thinking about how many times I have heard churches dispute over whether to concentrate on people or programs.

Pastor Gangadean: Programs may or may not be defined in terms of the goal properly understood as the knowledge of God. The dispute between people and programs is because of an antinomy. Sometimes there are disputes among our triune personality: the prophetic, priestly, and kingly. If the prophetic is functioning properly, the goal will be set properly. But the prophet can be a false prophet, the priest can be an unholy priest, or the king can be an unrighteous king. Often, the conflict is due to the prophet not having done the work properly. Or even when it is done properly, the conflict may be between the priestly and the kingly—people and programs.

The same kind of dispute arises in education between techniques/skills and self-esteem. That is why I think this passage says, "**Each of us should please his neighbor for his good, to build him up**" (v. 2). It is important to understand this. And it seems that the passage is speaking about the Gentiles coming in connection with the earth being filled with the knowledge of God. That is an important part of it.

Congregant 2: The good is very often described as glorifying God as opposed to the knowledge of God.

Pastor Gangadean: Are you asking how glorifying God is connected to the knowledge of God?

---

9. Gangadean, *The Unity of the Church*, 72–73, 134–136, 247–248, 275, 287–289; Gangadean, *The Contradictoriness of Sin*, 37–52.

Congregant 2: Well, how do we establish a solid, undeniable, irrefutable connection there?

Pastor Gangadean: Who wants to take a shot at it?

Congregant 2: Often people speak of glorifying God as something that we do. We glorify God from our actions.

Pastor Gangadean: What does glorifying mean?

Congregant 2: Well, if it does not have that sense of giving something to God, what sense must it have?

Pastor Gangadean: Well, the Confession says that "God hath all life, glory, goodness, blessedness, in and of himself; and is alone in and unto himself all-sufficient, not standing in need of any creatures which he hath made, nor deriving any glory from them, but only manifesting his own glory in, by, unto, and upon them" (WCF. 2.2).

Congregant 2: It seems as if it is something that man is not giving but receiving in the form of a revelation in terms of an understanding.

Pastor Gangadean: Okay, well, here are a couple of passages: (1) "And they [the seraphim] were calling to one another: 'Holy, holy, holy is the LORD Almighty; the whole earth *is* full of His glory'" (Is. 6:3).[10] (2) Isaiah 11:9 says, "the earth will be full of the *knowledge* of the LORD as the waters cover the sea."[11] I would like to think that is a way of understanding it. To know the greatness of His wisdom, power, justice, and goodness and to make that known is to glorify God. I believe that is consistent with the Confession and the Catechisms.[12] Man's chief end is to glorify God.[13] The answer to the first petition of the Lord's Prayer is "that God would enable us, and others, to glorify him in all that whereby he maketh himself known" (SCQ. 101).[14]

Congregant 2: It is comprehending the revelation.

---

10. Emphasis added.

11. Emphasis added.

12. Gangadean, *The Westminster Confession,* xxix–xxxii, 347–348; Gangadean, "Paper No. 115: Doxological Christianity," 595–596; "Paper No. 118: Eschatology (Seven Points)," in *The Logos Papers,* 603–607.

13. SCQ. 1.

14. Gangadean, *The Westminster Catechisms,* 100.

Pastor Gangadean: Knowing the revelation of God ourselves, *and* making it known. The process of knowing it, and responding in praise to God.

Congregant 2: Making it known—now, that helps to connect with the idea of something we *do*—something we are doing on our part, or at least it is being done through us.

Pastor Gangadean: Yes.

Congregant 5: You cannot make it known, or as you say, give Him glory for who He is, unless you comprehend it for yourself.

Pastor Gangadean: Yes. These are basics, and we need to keep concentrating on the basics in all of these passages so we might become established. Okay, let us leave it here, and we will pray. [Congregant 2], would you please ask God's blessing in our time to come?

Congregant 2: Thank you, Lord, for bringing us together in this way. Thank you for Your Sabbath, for the understanding of the hope that the Sabbath brings. Help us, Lord, to know You and keep Your way so that we may glorify You. Help us, Lord, to keep to the basics, to understand Your foundational way, that we may build on that, to the illumining of our minds through the Holy Spirit. Lord, help us to grow in understanding of unity so that we, as the Church, may reach all nations. Amen.

20

TEAMWORK

The Theological Basis for Fellowship

1994

Romans 16

¹I commend to you our sister Phoebe, a servant of the church in Cenchrea. ²I ask you to receive her in the Lord in a way worthy of the saints and to give her any help she may need from you, for she has been a great help to many people, including me.

³Greet Priscilla and Aquila, my fellow workers in Christ Jesus. ⁴They risked their lives for me. Not only I but all the churches of the Gentiles are grateful to them.

⁵Greet also the church that meets at their house.

Greet my dear friend Epenetus, who was the first convert to Christ in the province of Asia.

⁶Greet Mary, who worked very hard for you.

⁷Greet Andronicus and Junia, my relatives who have been in prison with me. They are outstanding among the apostles, and they were in Christ before I was.

⁸Greet Ampliatus, whom I love in the Lord.

⁹Greet Urbanus, our fellow worker in Christ, and my dear friend Stachys.

¹⁰Greet Apelles, tested and approved in Christ.

Greet those who belong to the household of Aristobulus.

¹¹Greet Herodion, my relative.

Greet those in the household of Narcissus who are in the Lord.

¹²Greet Tryphena and Tryphosa, those women who work hard in the Lord.

Greet my dear friend Persis, another woman who has worked very hard in the Lord.

¹³Greet Rufus, chosen in the Lord, and his mother, who has been a mother to me, too.

¹⁴Greet Asyncritus, Phlegon, Hermes, Patrobas, Hermas and the other brothers with them.

¹⁵Greet Philologus, Julia, Nereus and his sister, and Olympas and all the saints with them.

¹⁶Greet one another with a holy kiss.

All the churches of Christ send greetings.

¹⁷I urge you, brothers, to watch out for those who cause divisions and put obstacles in your way that are contrary to the teaching you have learned. Keep away from them. ¹⁸For such people are not serving our Lord Christ, but their own appetites. By smooth talk and flattery they deceive the minds of naive people. ¹⁹Everyone has heard about your obedience, so I am full of joy over you; but I want you to be wise about what is good, and innocent about what is evil.

²⁰The God of peace will soon crush Satan under your feet.

The grace of our Lord Jesus be with you.

²¹Timothy, my fellow worker, sends his greetings to you, as do Lucius, Jason and Sosipater, my relatives.

²²I, Tertius, who wrote down this letter, greet you in the Lord.

²³Gaius, whose hospitality I and the whole church here enjoy, sends you his greetings.

Erastus, who is the city's director of public works, and our brother Quartus send you their greetings.

²⁵Now to him who is able to establish you by my gospel and the proclamation of Jesus Christ, according to the revelation of the mystery hidden for long ages past, ²⁶but now revealed and made known through the prophetic writings by the command of the eternal God, so that all nations might believe and obey him—²⁷to the only wise God be glory forever through Jesus Christ! Amen.

INTRODUCTION

WE COME TO THE END OF THIS EPISTLE, AND Paul gives com-
mendations and greetings to those who are in Rome. Paul has
laid out the gospel to the Romans quite fully, explicitly, extensively,
and in depth. It is said to be the most systematic portion of the Scripture in terms of laying out the doctrine. As we have gone over the
Epistle to the Romans for the past five months, we have seen that this
is a book that we can go over again in another couple of years with a
lot of profit. We saw how Paul applies the gospel's teaching in terms
of our committing ourselves to God to serve the Lord. We saw how
the doctrine translates into doing the will of God in various contexts,
such as serving one another, in political applications, and submission
to authority. We saw how Paul dealt with *adiaphora*—things that are
neither right nor wrong—and he applied the doctrine to all sorts of
relationship dimensions connected with the gospel. The *gospel* specifically
has this bearing on us: how we are to live in all the details of our lives.

GREETINGS:
The Doctrine of Fellowship Illustrated

Paul now comes to the very end of the epistle, where he sends his
greetings. Again, the theme of the gospel comes through in his message.

> I commend to you our sister Phoebe, a servant of the church in
> Cenchreae. I ask you to receive her in the Lord in a way worthy
> of the saints and to give her any help she may need from you, for
> she has been a great help to many people, including me (vv. 1–2).

In this section, verses 1–16, Paul is commending and greeting, and he
begins with the word *greet* or *salute*. Paul ends that section in verse 16
by saying, "Greet one another with a holy kiss. All the churches of
Christ send greetings." I think in this section we have the doctrine of
the fellowship of believers illustrated—not taught, but *illustrated*. We see
how this doctrine works itself out in our relationships with one another.

First, Paul speaks about their sister Phoebe, a servant; some suggest a
'deaconess,' who had special administration over the sick and the poor,
and he commended her to the believers in Rome. She was a servant of

the church in Cenchreae, on the Isthmus of Corinth. There are two towns, one facing toward Asia and one toward Europe; this is the one facing Asia. Corinth is that strip of land on the Greek Peninsula. Phoebe is a servant of that church, but she is coming to Rome. She is needing help, and he calls the believers there to receive her **"in a way worthy of the saints."** This is what is expected of saints: to help others and to forward them in their work in the Lord. **"I ask you to receive her in the Lord in a way worthy of the saints and to give her any help she may need from you, for she has been a great help to many people, including me."**

FELLOWSHIP ON THE BASIS OF TRUTH:
Sharing in the Work of the Lord

One of the things we will see in these 16 verses is the basis of fellowship and joy. It seems to be always connected with the work of the Lord. Fellowship is between believers who are united in their work in the Lord. So here, at the beginning of this greeting and commendation, we find Paul commending Phoebe for her work in the Lord—**"for she has been a great help to many people, including me."** Paul recognizes her work, commends her, and wants the others to support her in her service. This view will become more explicit as we go through the illustration. This is not the teaching of doctrine—elsewhere, this doctrine is taught—but this is the *illustration* of how fellowship is based on sharing together in the work of the Lord, and the blessing and joy that comes from sharing that work. I say that because some people think of fellowship as something other than sharing in the work of the Lord. Some think that fellowship is just having good times together, but fellowship in the Lord is not just this. The church has a 'fellowship dinner,' as if fellowship is not occurring at the times when you are working—that is not the biblical view of fellowship. In Paul's greetings, we will see that fellowship involves, or is shown in, working together for the common goal of advancing the kingdom of God. That fellowship, in turn, is based on truth.

In the second part of Romans 16, Paul says, **"Watch out for those who cause divisions and put obstacles in your way that are contrary to the teaching you have learned"** (v. 17). On the one hand, there are those who are working hard together and have joy and fellowship in this work, and then there are those who are causing division and presenting obstacles that are contrary to doctrine. Those are the two main points in Romans 16, and we will have to learn how to apply this to our lives.

Those Who Labor in the Lord

"Greet Priscilla and Aquila, my fellow workers in Christ Jesus. They risked their lives for me." (vv. 3–4a). This passage shows how far and extensive this work had gone—Priscilla and Aquila were ready to risk their lives for Paul. Some of us are not ready to risk a few bucks, or even some time, for others. These persons were ready to risk their very lives for Paul—not just Paul in any circumstance, but Paul in terms of his intense involvement with the work of the Lord. Priscilla and Aquila were Jewish believers who had lived in Rome. Because of uprisings in Palestine, an edict went out during the time of Claudius, ordering that the Jews were to be removed from Rome.[1] So Priscilla and Aquila had left Rome, and had further contact with Paul. They were tentmakers, like Paul, so Paul had spent some time working with them. We hear of Priscilla and Aquila also in the Book of Acts.[2] They had suffered for the gospel in a particular way by risking their lives for Paul. So we have Phoebe, who "has been a great help to many people." There is the fruit, the actual fruit, being manifested. And we have Priscilla and Aquila; this is the basis on which Paul commends and greets others.

Paul says, "Not only I but all the churches of the Gentiles are grateful to them" (v. 4b). When people serve the Lord in this common way, there is a lot of thankfulness that occurs from others who are serving in the same way. "Greet also the church that meets at their house" (v. 5a). The greeting to churches in the homes of particular individuals occurs three or four times in this chapter. There were not yet church buildings in those days; they met in homes. The church members did not number 1,000 or 10,000 as some churches do today. We are not elevating this circumstance to be permanent, but we are noticing that it occurred, it was appropriate then, and it could be appropriate at other times. When we see situations, such as we have, of people meeting together in a home, we can affirm that this was the case in the early

---

1. *Acts 18:2.*

2. *Acts 18:1–3, 18–19, 24–26.*

church without making it a norm for all time. What we are saying is that this is okay.[3]

"**Greet my dear friend Epenetus, who was the first convert to Christ in the province of Asia**" (v. 5b). Epenetus was a believer, and nothing is said of his work *per se*, but there is a greeting to him, and he was among the firstfruits of Paul's labor. Some have thought there is a contradiction in the Bible because of someone else who was said to be the first convert in Asia.[4] But Epenetus was among the first converts and may have been a member of that household that was the first. There is also a question of whether it was Asia or Achaia. So once in a while, people will point out apparent contradictions in the Bible, and this verse has been used to ask, 'Who is the first?' If we look at it closely, we will see that there is no contradiction here.

"**Greet Mary, who worked very hard for you**" (v. 6). I want you to notice that women are noted for their work. There is Phoebe, there is Mary, and it seems that the women are particularly noted for their *hard work*, and couples are noted, along with men. Paul says, "**Greet Mary, who worked very hard for you.**" There is fellowship among people involved in working hard in the Lord, and there is joy that comes with the salutation.

"**Greet Andronicus and Junia, my fellow relatives who have been in prison with me**" (v. 7a). Paul notices when suffering is shared. Priscilla and Aquila risked their lives for him, and here, Andronicus and Junia were fellow Jews, and they had been in prison with him. They went through part of that suffering with Paul for the sake of the gospel. For that sake, Paul was giving his life, so when they were involved with him in risking their lives, it was for the sake of the gospel. This kind of actual, demonstrated commitment should be present in the body of Christ. And when that commitment is present, then there is fellowship, and there is joy in that fellowship. "**They are outstanding among the apostles, and they were in Christ before I was**" (v. 7b). That does not mean that they were apostles, but they were noted among the apostles, and were in Christ before Paul was. There are certain things that Paul notes: "**they were in Christ before I was.**" Perhaps they had been there

---

3. Westminster Fellowship did not incorporate as a church until 2000. In 1994, Pastor Gangadean preached the sermon series on Romans at his home.

4. *1 Corinthians 16:15.*

and had been praying for Paul, and now he recognizes God's grace in their lives.

"**Greet Ampliatus, whom I love in the Lord. Greet Urbanus, our fellow worker in Christ, and my dear friend Stachys**" (vv. 8–9). The King James Version says, 'my beloved.' Perhaps that carries a connotation that is different from 'my dear friend,' but I think the idea is ultimately the friendship that Paul enjoys with these believers. Notice that even though he does not specify 'the work' in each case, the whole chapter is laced with this concern about those who are with him in the work.

"**Greet Apelles, tested and approved in Christ**" (v. 10a). Here is someone who has undergone the process of testing and has shown themselves to be a faithful person in the Lord, and Paul singles this person out and is thankful for him. "**Greet those who belong to the household of Aristobulus**" (v. 10b). Again, this is not necessarily a church, but Aristobulus and his household, and households could be fairly extensive in those days. "**Greet Herodion, my relative. Greet those in the household of Narcissus who are in the Lord**" (v. 11). These persons are showing they are in the Lord by their walk.

"**Greet Tryphena and Tryphosa, those women who work hard in the Lord**" (v. 12a). There again, women who work very hard. Then he says, "**Greet my dear friend Persis, another woman who has worked very hard in the Lord**" (v. 12b). Paul had friendship with women, and the friendship is connected with working together in the Lord. Fellowship—that is, friendship—is demonstrated in terms of working together in the Lord.

"**Greet Rufus, chosen in the Lord, and his mother, who has been a mother to me, too**" (v. 13). When Peter said to Jesus that they had left everything to follow Him—father and mother and others—Jesus replied that they would have all of these things multiplied—with persecution.[5] Somehow, the Christian life cannot escape persecution, one way or another. But here, Paul—having lost perhaps many of his immediate family—has found a mother to him, one who cared for him in this way. Again, notice the place of women and their work, their ministry, and their role in advancing the kingdom of God in this way.

"**Greet Asyncritus, Phlegon, Hermes, Patrobas, Hermas and the other brothers with them**" (v. 14) A whole bunch of guys put together

---

5. *Mark 10:28–30.*

are greeted. "**Greet Philologus, Julia, Nereus and his sister, and Olympas and all the saints with them**" (v. 15). This is perhaps another cluster of believers.

"**Greet one another with a holy kiss. All the churches of Christ send greetings**" (v. 16). There has been some misunderstanding about this 'holy kiss.' People have abused that teaching. Other places in Scripture speak about greeting one another with the holy kiss: 1 Corinthians 16:20, 1 Thessalonians 5:26, and 1 Peter 5:14. The idea of this greeting, in the Greek term, seems to mean *to embrace* or *to enfold* in the arms. In any case, the spirit of it is that we are to greet one another in the Lord. Now, sometimes, there are difficulties in fellowship between believers. In the Epistle to the Philippians, Paul beseeches two women to get along together in the Lord: "I plead with Euodia and I plead with Syntyche to agree with each other in the Lord" (Phil. 4:2). Sometimes, women who are working in the Lord can have strains with each other, and he beseeches them to get along in the Lord.

THE THEOLOGICAL BASIS FOR FELLOWSHIP:
Walking in the Light

Let us take a minute to look at the underlying doctrine, biblical principles, and teachings behind fellowship. Fellowship is on the basis of truth—period. And not just truth, but *walking* in the truth. 1 John 1 speaks about fellowship:

> That which was from the beginning, which we have heard, which we have seen with our eyes, which we have looked at and our hands have touched—this we proclaim concerning the Word of life. The life appeared; we have seen it and testify to it, and we proclaim to you the eternal life, which was with the Father and has appeared to us. We proclaim to you what we have seen and heard, *so that you also may have fellowship with us.* And our fellowship is with the Father and with his Son, Jesus Christ. We write this to make our joy complete (1 Jn. 1:1–4).[6]

---

6. Emphasis added.

The teaching is on the basis of the Word proclaimed. Our joy in the Lord is connected with fellowship, and fellowship is connected with the truth. Please notice how John speaks of fellowship: "Our fellowship is with the Father and with his Son, Jesus Christ." Fellowship with each other comes out of our fellowship with the Lord. Whenever you attempt to have fellowship with each other without each person being in fellowship with the Lord, it will be a *strain*. Try as hard as you can to get the fellowship with each other without having it first with the Lord; it will not happen! When there is a fellowship problem with each other, it is because there is first a fellowship problem with the Lord. We should, first and foremost, use that strain as the occasion to come back and ask what is going on with our fellowship with the Lord. We have to see whether the fellowship is on the basis of truth, not on the basis of *feeling*. I have to explicate that and perhaps in some discussion to follow we can look at that. We have to be very, very careful about this distinction. Paul warns us in Romans: **"Now I urge you, brethren, note those who cause divisions and offenses, contrary to the *doctrine* which you learned, and avoid them"** (Rom. 16:17 NKJV).[7]

John continues,

> This is the message we have heard from him and declare to you: God is light; in him there is no darkness at all. If we claim to have fellowship with him and yet walk in the darkness, we lie and do not live out the truth. But if we walk in the light, as he is in the light, we have fellowship with one another, and the blood of Jesus, his Son, purifies us from all sin (1 Jn. 1:5–7).

Notice, he never says that perfection is necessary for fellowship, but that we must be walking in the light. Part of walking in the light means we are willing to come into the light and have our lives examined, to see whether what we are doing is in accordance with the light. John 3:21 says, "But whoever lives by the truth comes into the light, so that it may be seen plainly that what he has done has been done through God." Those who resist coming into the light, and stop short of examining their lives in light of the written Word of God, have something else going on. That is where the fellowship begins to break down.

---

7. Emphasis added.

We all have sin. "If we claim to be without sin, we deceive ourselves and the truth is not in us" (1 Jn. 1:8). While we all have sin, we may not have the particular sin that someone else is saying that we have. Job had sin, but it was not the particular sin that others were saying that he had. In the end, Job had not seen his sin and had to acknowledge his sin. But Job was asked to pray for those who had accused him of other sin. We have to handle this doctrine carefully. All of us have sin, but it does not mean we have the particular sin that other people say we have. We must confess our sins, name them, and acknowledge them; we cannot excuse or minimize them. There is a strong tendency to *accuse* and to *excuse*. Those are antinomies, and we are instructed to do neither in the Lord's Prayer.[8] "If we confess our sins, he is faithful and just and will forgive us our sins and purify us from all unrighteousness" (1 Jn. 1:9). If we confess our sins, we will name the sin and not take it back and attempt to justify it later. Notice the pattern: God will forgive, and He will purify. In the Garden, He forgave the sin of Adam and Eve, and He will purify them. And He will not purify them of the fruit sin merely, but the root sin. He will purify us of the deep unbelief, failing to seek God, and failing to know what is clear about God. It takes all the suffering of natural evil to bring us out of our deep unbelief.[9] He will purify us from *every* sin. These things will not go away by themselves. God is the searcher of hearts. He is the purifier.[10]

We have to deal with things that happened 20 years ago, 30 years ago, even 40 years ago. The Patriarchs, who sold Joseph out of envy, had to deal with what they had done. God will "purify us from all unrighteousness." That is why natural evil continues with us until the day we die. That is one of the reasons we die; the curse is there to call us to think deeply about basic issues.[11] If we excuse our sin in self-deception and self-justification and blame others for it, we are just postponing the inevitable—we have to deal with our sin. God is holy; God's holiness does not go away. That is why sin, left to itself, will not go away—God will continue to deal with our sin. Our fellowship with

---

8. Gangadean, *The Westminster Catechisms,* 97–106.

9. Gangadean, *The Westminster Confession,* 161–166; Gangadean, *The Westminster Catechisms,* 45–49; Gangadean, *The Biblical Worldview,* 311–328.

10. Gangadean, *The Epistle to the Hebrews,* 203–234.

11. Gangadean, *The Biblical Worldview,* 283–294.

one another can become more and more joyful as we deal with our sin. Our fellowship is first with God, and this is a continuing fellowship.

Our fellowship with one another in the Lord is on the basis of a new family. Paul says, "my brothers," "my beloved," and "my mother in the Lord." In Matthew, Jesus speaks about family relationships.

> While Jesus was still talking to the crowd, his mother and brothers stood outside, wanting to speak to him. Someone told him, "Your mother and brothers are standing outside, wanting to speak to you." He replied to him, "Who is my mother, and who are my brothers?" Pointing to his disciples, he said, "Here are my mother and my brothers. For whoever does the will of my Father in heaven is my brother and sister and mother" (Matt. 12:46–50).

That is how fellowship occurs. Fellowship occurs on the basis of doing the will of God, on the basis of truth. We have to ask ourselves, 'Is what we are doing consistent with the will of God?' We have to search out whether our lives are consistent with the will of God—in *deed*, and in *spirit*, and, insofar as we can search motives, in our motives also. We may be very sincere in thinking about what we are doing but we have to ask: Is this according to the Word? Remember there can be sincerity, or zeal, without knowledge. Jesus gave this example, and the contrast is very stark. His disciples are present. His mother and brothers are present. And he points to his disciples and says, "Here are my mother and my brothers. For whoever does the will of my Father in heaven is my brother and sister and mother." This is a teaching of the Scripture concerning fellowship.

The Scripture says, "Do not merely listen to the word, and so deceive yourselves. Do what it says" (Jas. 1:22). It is possible to be in the church, to hear the Word year after year, and yet not understand it and not do it. Fellowship is on the basis of truth. Fellowship is with those who are in Christ and who are actually putting the Word into practice. Joy in fellowship is had by those who *labor* in the Lord. Fellowship is not had by those who, in a minimal sense, say, 'I'm still a Christian; I've not outright denied the faith.' The joy in fellowship comes, in the positive sense, to those who labor in the Lord. That is where the joy in fellowship comes. When you are with fellow believers who are working hard together in the Lord, it is like being on a team! You are working *together* with others and pulling in the same direction—there is real joy and pleasure connected with working together in that way.

Two persons may both say that they are working hard in the Lord, but they are going in separate directions, and we have to come back and see whether the standard being used is biblical. That is where we come full circle: "If we walk in the light, as he is in the light, we have fellowship with one another" (1 Jn. 1:7a). We have to see whether what we are doing is according to the Word of the Lord. We confess that we hold the Scripture to be the final authority. We must come back and search the Scriptures, and by good and necessary consequences, show the basis of our work and fellowship. It is not enough to say, 'I have this feeling about it.' You have to *show*, and the way it is shown is by *reasoning* from the Scriptures. Our fellowship is with the Lord, and then with each other, as we walk in the light.

PAUL BESEECHES US:
Negative Application of the Principle of Fellowship

Contrary to the Doctrine

In the second part of Romans 16, we have a *negative* application of this principle. **"I urge you, brothers, to watch out for those who cause divisions and put obstacles in your way that are contrary to the teaching you have learned"** (v. 17a). Watch out, mark them, and take note of them. Paul beseeches us; this is not optional; he is urging it upon us to notice this. **"Watch out for those who cause divisions and put obstacles in your way that are contrary to the teaching you have learned."** The King James Version says, **"contrary to the doctrine which ye have learned."** We speak about a certain doctrine here; we are not just starting from scratch with the Scriptures. We spoke about the Westminster Confession as a standard, and we profess belief in this.[12] If we profess the doctrine, but do not live according to it, it is very likely because we do not understand the doctrine. And when that occurs, divisions will occur, and obstacles will be put in the way. Those obstacles and divisions are **"contrary to the teaching you have learned."**

---

12. Gangadean, *The Westminster Confession,* xix–xxix, 349–351; Gangadean, "Paper No. 16: The Historic Christian Faith," in *The Logos Papers,* 103–114.

An Application of Church Discipline

Paul says, "**Keep away from them**" (v. 17b). In Titus, also, this element comes in. What we have here is an application of church discipline. In Titus 3:10–11, Paul says, "Warn a divisive person once, and then warn him a second time. After that, have nothing to do with him. You may be sure that such a man is warped and sinful; he is self-condemned." The Westminster Confession says,

> For the better attaining of these ends, the officers of the church are to proceed by admonition, suspension from the sacrament of the Lord's Supper for a season, and by excommunication from the church, according to the nature of the crime and demerit of the person (WCF. 30.4).

This is part of what the Confession teaches about church discipline. When someone continues with a principle that is thought to be godly but is actually not according to the Word of God, that has to be removed. The officers of the church are to first give a warning. If the person continues not to heed the warning, a censure is placed, which is more formal, and they may perhaps be barred from the Lord's Table, because the Table of the Lord speaks about our unity. The principle they are holding to is contrary to unity, and the censure is for their good, and for the honor of Christ, and for the reclaiming of the offending person, and for preventing the wrath of God on the church. If they continue to resist after the censure, it becomes excommunication. Paul says, "Have nothing to do with him" (Tit. 3:10b), and he says, "**Keep away from them**" (v. 17b). Otherwise, they will infect the whole lump.

Appetites of the Flesh

Paul puts this in this context: "**For such people are not serving our Lord Christ, but their own appetites**" (v. 18a). The King James Version says *belly*, but I think the idea of *appetites* is a little bit broader than *belly*; it has to do with the appetites of the flesh, the desires of the flesh. They are not serving according to the Spirit. We are all going to serve certain desires. We will either be slaves to righteousness or slaves to evil. We all have feelings, and we are all going to act on those feelings. The question is whether the feelings are godly or whether they are ungodly. They are godly or ungodly in terms of the goal to which they are directed. Such people serve "**their own appetites.**" There is a sense in which we have a natural appetite to be removed from natural evil. The people sought the Lord Jesus when they thought He would provide food, heal their bodies, and raise the dead. Great multitudes sought Him, but He said, "Do not work for food that spoils, but for food that endures to eternal life, which the Son of Man will give you" (Jn. 6:27a). The people welcomed Moses when he delivered them from the bondage of Egypt, but as they went through other stages, they did not welcome him anymore. It showed that they were serving their own appetites. Remember, this is within the community of those who profess belief and within those who would follow Christ. It is not just the out-and-out debauched levels to which some unbelief attains.

The Need to Think Critically

Paul continues, "**By smooth talk and flattery they deceive the minds of naive people**" (v. 18b). They use smooth talk, flattery, and enticing words, but it is not reality, because the life, as God calls us to live, is not there. Those who are uncritical and would love to hear smooth talk and flattery will fall for it. This is where the feelings are operating. They make you feel good and you live by those feelings. But the person is not being critical. Just because it makes you feel good does not mean it is right. There is a lot of smooth talk and flattery out there, and behind that smooth talk and flattery is none other than the devil himself. Paul comes to that next.

Deal with Divisions: Concern for Our Witness

One of the things Paul is warning them about is their witness. "**Everyone has heard about your obedience, so I am full of joy over you**" (v. 19a). The report of the obedience of the believers in Rome had spread. It was a witness—a matter of honor to the Lord—and Paul did not want the name of God dishonored. When a church goes sour, it brings dishonor to the name of the Lord. Paul was concerned that these divisive matters be dealt with, so that they would not corrupt the whole Church and spoil the witness. If, for example, people have heard of our obedience, and then sin among us is allowed to go on and spoil the work, it will bring dishonor to the Lord and dishonor to the doctrine. We need to deal with divisions in a godly way.

Be Wise Concerning the Good

"I want you to be wise about what is good, and innocent about what is evil" (v. 19b). There is a place for being *simple* in the sense of *harmless*. This is the same idea as "be wise as serpents and harmless as doves" (Matt. 10:16b NKJV). The Lord does not commend us for being simple. The only time He commends us for being simple is concerning evil, in the sense of being harmless. He wants us to be wise as serpents—all of us—and we cannot excuse ourselves from that in any way. "I want you to be wise about what is good"—specifically understanding the good and seeking the good—"and innocent about what is evil." As we live this way, "the God of peace will soon crush Satan under your feet" (v. 20a). God will bring peace to us—both among each other and with Him. Satan would love, through false teachings, through beguiling words, and through whatever source, to stir up divisions, stir up animosity, stir up difficulty between believers, and stir up strife. He is masterful at stirring up divisions. Those who are uncritical are like sitting ducks for this cunning and craftiness. But if we will be wise concerning what is good, and watch carefully, we will soon see God crush Satan under our feet.

SALUTATION OF OTHERS AND BENEDICTION

Now there are other greetings given: "The grace of our Lord Jesus be with you" (v. 20b). This is the grace that Paul has spoken about in the gospel. We hope in that grace of God, and in none other—not in ourselves, not in situations out there—but in the grace of God, trusting that He will be gracious to us and merciful to us for Jesus' sake. He died for us, to forgive us, and He will cleanse us. We wait on the Lord in that grace—and in His grace, we will overcome.

> Timothy, my fellow worker, sends his greetings to you, as do, Lucius, Jason and Sosipater, my relatives. I, Tertius, who wrote down this letter, greet you in the Lord. Gaius, whose hospitality I and the whole church here enjoy, sends you his greetings. Erastus,

who is the city's director of public works, and our brother Quartus send you their greetings (vv. 21–23).

Paul closes with a benediction. "**Now to him who is able to establish you by my gospel . . .**" (v. 25a). It is one thing to begin, it is another to be established, firm, rooted, not going to be blown over, not going to dry up and blow away. If we persevere by God's grace, in that Word of God, we will be established in the gospel, and the gospel is the whole teaching we have heard coming through Romans—the whole system of doctrine.

> **Now to him who is able to establish you by my gospel and the proclamation of Jesus Christ, according to the revelation of the mystery hidden for long ages past, but now revealed and made known through the prophetic writings by the command of the eternal God . . . (vv. 25–26a).**

The gospel is contained for us in the Scriptures and in the writings and teachings of the prophets and apostles. It is revealed "**so that all nations might believe and obey him**" (v. 26b). It is always the case, throughout the gospel, that this gospel is for all the nations: "Therefore go and make disciples of all nations" (Matt. 28:19a). We have to keep in view what it is going to take to make disciples of all nations. Many individuals back off from this view; it may be acknowledged theoretically, but they hold an amillennial view and another view of what the goal is—and it is not that the earth is to be filled with the knowledge of God. They let a lot of things slip. The intellectual life—which is necessary and fundamental in order to gain understanding of God's revelation—they let slip. They do not hold that the earth is to be filled with the knowledge of God.

All men are to know. What is it going to take to bring all men to know? Remember, it was at the time when the believers were ready to go in to take the Promised Land that they turned back in fear, and they said, 'We can't do it.' Their faith—their understanding of God's will, purpose, and revelation—was not such that they thought they could take the land, and so they turned back. That generation remained in the wilderness for 40 years, but the younger generation went into the Promised Land. God is able to establish us. This is the God who wants this gospel to go to all nations, so that all might believe and obey Him.

"To the only wise God be glory forever through Jesus Christ! Amen" (v. 27). The wisdom of God is revealed in His dealings, and the glory of His wisdom is to be seen and praised. This is most deeply, fully, highly, and completely revealed in the person and work of Christ—not only while He was on earth, but also as He sits at the right hand of God, reigning. This is the truth of God.

21

TEAMWORK

From Doctrinal to Practical to Personal

2013

Romans 16 KJV[1]

[1]I commend unto you Phebe our sister, which is a servant of the church which is at Cenchrea: [2]That ye receive her in the Lord, as becometh saints, and that ye assist her in whatsoever business she hath need of you: for she hath been a succourer of many, and of myself also.

[3]Greet Priscilla and Aquila my helpers in Christ Jesus:

[4]Who have for my life laid down their own necks: unto whom not only I give thanks, but also all the churches of the Gentiles.

[5]Likewise greet the church that is in their house. Salute my well-beloved Epaenetus, who is the firstfruits of Achaia unto Christ.

[6]Greet Mary, who bestowed much labour on us.

[7]Salute Andronicus and Junia, my kinsmen, and my fellow-prisoners, who are of note among the apostles, who also were in Christ before me.

[8]Greet Amplias my beloved in the Lord.

[9]Salute Urbane, our helper in Christ, and Stachys my beloved.

[10]Salute Apelles approved in Christ. Salute them which are of Aristobulus' household.

---

1. This sermon was originally preached from the King James Version, and to maintain its original flow of thought, we have retained that translation in the text.

[11]Salute Herodion my kinsman. Greet them that be of the household of Narcissus, which are in the Lord.

[12]Salute Tryphena and Tryphosa, who labour in the Lord. Salute the beloved Persis, which laboured much in the Lord.

[13]Salute Rufus chosen in the Lord, and his mother and mine.

[14]Salute Asyncritus, Phlegon, Hermas, Patrobas, Hermes, and the brethren which are with them.

[15]Salute Philologus, and Julia, Nereus, and his sister, and Olympas, and all the saints which are with them.

[16]Salute one another with an holy kiss. The churches of Christ salute you.

[17]Now I beseech you, brethren, mark them which cause divisions and offences contrary to the doctrine which ye have learned; and avoid them. [18]For they that are such serve not our Lord Jesus Christ, but their own belly; and by good words and fair speeches deceive the hearts of the simple. [19]For your obedience is come abroad unto all men. I am glad therefore on your behalf: but yet I would have you wise unto that which is good, and simple concerning evil.

[20]And the God of peace shall bruise Satan under your feet shortly. The grace of our Lord Jesus Christ be with you. Amen.

[21]Timotheus my workfellow, and Lucius, and Jason, and Sosipater, my kinsmen, salute you.

[22]I Tertius, who wrote this epistle, salute you in the Lord.

[23]Gaius mine host, and of the whole church, saluteth you. Erastus the chamberlain of the city saluteth you, and Quartus a brother.

[24]The grace of our Lord Jesus Christ be with you all. Amen.

[25]Now to him that is of power to stablish you according to my gospel, and the preaching of Jesus Christ, according to the revelation of the mystery, which was kept secret since the world began, [26]But now is made manifest, and by the scriptures of the prophets, according to the commandment of the everlasting God, made known to all nations for the obedience of faith: [27]To God only wise, be glory through Jesus Christ for ever. Amen.

OPENING REMARKS

WE COME NOW TO THE END OF ROMANS. It has been a wonderful journey. There have been many blessings of the preaching from so many others.[2] It is truly a blessing to hear the Word of God preached. I am often the one preaching, so I am especially blessed to hear the Word preached by others. For those who are being prepared by giving heed to God's Word over the months and years, it is a blessing to see how this truth comes out. We will be continuing next week in Luke. I will preach one week, and the other men will preach the following week. In Logos, we will have preparation for preaching.[3] I sent out an email to the Logos group. Please read and study Luke carefully and come prepared to discuss it in a way that can enrich the preaching. I need your help. We need one another's help in this, so please do. That is not to take away from the other reading and study that we are doing on world history in Logos.[4]

TEAM AND WORK:
Each Is to Do Their Work in Season

Our focus today is on teamwork. Teamwork consists of two parts—*team* and *work*. We will pay attention to each part, and we will see what it is to *not* be on the team and to work contrariwise. Hopefully we will all be instructed through this, that we might be more faithful in glorifying God and not self.

In Romans 16, Paul is getting personal. He is giving personal recognition to particular persons. Up to this point, he has been doctrinal, then practical, and now he is personal. But he is personal in a way that builds on the doctrinal and the practical. We see a theme here, as we find in other places in Scripture, that each person is given a measure of faith,[5] and that we are to think soberly and thoughtfully, and that we are not to compare ourselves with one another.[6] We are not to think, 'If I am not the eye, I am not part of the body,' but we are to do the work God has given to us. We should not try to run ahead beyond our measure

---

2. As part of the *Practicum* in preparing others to lead in the work of the ministry, Pastor Gangadean only preached on four chapters in Romans in 2013. The rest was done by several men undergoing preparation.

3. Logos Theological Seminary.

4. The content of the courses taught in Logos Theological Seminary will be undergoing publication in the upcoming years.

5. Gangadean, *The Epistle to the Hebrews*, 321–337.

6. *Romans 12:3.*

of faith, nor lag behind. Each part is to do its work in season, that is, at the appropriate time. We are not to lag behind so that "though by this time you ought to be teachers, you need someone to teach you" (Heb. 5:12a).[7] We are not to run ahead and think of ourselves as having more faith and understanding than we, in fact, do.

PERSONAL RECOGNITION:
Honoring Unique Contributions in the Body of Christ

Paul has spoken of visiting Rome. What is remarkable about this passage is that he has not met a number of the people there. Certainly, some of these persons have traveled, and he has met them elsewhere—as will become clear—but he is writing to the church in Rome, and many he has not met. And yet, Paul knows them by name and speaks of each one in particular ways, recognizing their unique place, their contribution, and what they have done in the body of Christ.

We are going to go through the names of the people and what they did. We will see that he speaks about their work, or the providence of God in their lives, or their relation to either Paul himself, to the church, or to God. All of these things are finely mentioned and carefully distinguished in each case. We see the work and the fruit being acknowledged, and that honor is to be given to those who work faithfully. In 1 Corinthians 16, Paul speaks about honoring those who work, and in 1 Thessalonians 5:12–13, he says to especially note "those who work hard among you, who are over you in the Lord and who admonish you. Hold them in the highest regard in love because of their work."

The work may or may not be done by one who occupies an office. The important thing is that service is being done. The first mentioned is Phoebe: "**I commend unto you Phebe our sister, which is a servant of the church which is at Cenchrea**" (v. 1). Some have wondered and thought perhaps she was a "deaconess" in an office. It is not sufficiently clear from the Word to say that since she is a servant in the church, she is, therefore, in an office. The important thing is that she is serving, and we are able to serve even if we are not in an office, and that is the ordinary way in which one comes into an office. You concern yourself with serving, and when it is being done to a certain extent, degree, or

---

7. Gangadean, *The Epistle to the Hebrews*, 83–98.

recognition for time, then you may be asked to serve in that way. The important thing is to keep our eyes on the *service*. Jesus was among us as one who *served*.[8] Jesus washed His disciples' feet, and He was not recognized in terms of an office, though He did have the office of Messiah and the offices of prophet, priest, and king.[9] Phebe is a servant of the church in Cenchrea. Apparently, she is coming to Rome, and Paul knows her from elsewhere. I believe Cenchrea is in the southern part of Greece. Paul says, "**That ye receive her in the Lord, as becometh saints, and that ye assist her in whatsoever business she hath need of you**" (v. 2a). Here is where others are to serve her; Paul is asking for the church in Rome to help her do her service.

Notice there are many women named, and Paul begins with Phebe in speaking about being a servant in the church. There is ample room to serve; again, you do not have to be in an office to serve. The important thing is the service. Phebe is receiving commendation for her service, and she is to be received—she certainly is a saint. Paul says, "**assist her in whatsoever business she hath need of you**," then he goes on, "**for she hath been a succourer of many, and of myself also**" (v. 2b). Notice that she has been of help to others and to Paul. A "**succourer**" is one who is assisting, succoring, nurturing, and helping along. This service is needed; people need to be succored. Paul says, "**she hath been a succourer of many, and of myself also**." Sometimes the work is directed toward Paul, but often it is directed toward others in the church. Paul recognizes a whole range of services; it is not just limited to what a person has done for him personally. He notices the work that Phebe is doing by the grace of God, seeks to encourage her, and asks others to encourage her in concrete ways—including material support.

Then he says, "**Greet Priscilla and Aquila my helpers in Christ Jesus**" (v. 3). They appear in several places throughout the New Testament writings, and you get the sense that they are a really strong couple in the Lord—both of them. There may have been a particular relation between Priscilla and Aquila—Priscilla's name is mentioned first. It may be that she has a particular gift, and perhaps there is no contest between her and her husband. I thought of it this way: her husband is like the trunk of a tree, and she is like a vine that is wrapped around,

---

8. *Luke 22:27.*

9. Gangadean, *The Westminster Catechisms*, 163–168.

and can flourish because of his presence. It is a wonderful combination, and it comes out wherever they are mentioned. Paul speaks of them as **"my helpers in Christ Jesus."** They are helpers to Paul particularly, in a specific way, to a certain extent: **"Who have for my life laid down their own necks"** (v. 4a). Think of that—that is remarkable. That is outstanding. To go to such an extent: **"for my life laid down their own necks."** And the result of their service is recognition: **"unto whom not only I give thanks, but also all the churches of the Gentiles"** (v. 4b). Paul gets it precisely right; he gets right at the heart in recognizing the sacrificial work of others. He continues, **"Likewise greet the church that is in their house"** (v. 5a). Priscilla and Aquila served in this way; they opened their house to the church. Apparently, they moved around; they had been in Rome, they were expelled, they had been elsewhere, and perhaps now they are returning to Rome after the initial expulsion, and they are having a church meet at their house. They serve with what they have—with *all* they have—including, not just the house, but laying down their own necks. Try to imagine what that was like. We get the sense of a couple serving in the Lord. They are serving together, and it is beautiful, it is powerful, it is vital, and it is multifaceted.

One of the things that we need to recognize is that this is the first generation of Christians, and among the first generation of Christians, some are the first to be Christian in a certain place. Paul takes note of this and brings it to the attention of others. It is something special to him—first-generation Christians. Who were they? Here, they are being named, and we are to think about them. We are heirs of their service, as those who come after us are to be heirs of our service in the Lord. It is a rich tradition that we participate in and forward in the earth.

"Salute my well-beloved Epaenetus, who is the firstfruits of Achaia unto Christ" (v. 5b). That is, in the Corinthian Peninsula, the southern part of the Greek mainland. Epaenetus is said to be the firstfruits of Achaia. There were others who were first to come to Christ in other places, but here Paul notes Epaenetus. There was no one before Epaenetus in this place; he was a spiritual pioneer. He did not have the encouragement of a tradition behind him. He heard the truth, by the grace of God, and responded to it, and God led him. Epaenetus is called here **"my well-beloved."** Notice the word *my*—Paul uses various terms, sometimes *my beloved*, sometimes *the beloved*, or sometimes simply *beloved*. All of these nuances are interesting to notice. We might not be able to figure out all that is there, because there is so much history going on here. But certainly, those persons to whom Paul spoke heard these terms in a particular way—just as John referred to himself as the disciple whom Jesus loved, the disciple who *leaned* on Jesus at the table of the Lord's Supper, the one who got to the tomb first, before Peter. John was not rubbing it in with Peter. (Although I do wonder . . .) **"Salute my well-beloved Epaenetus, who is the firstfruits of Achaia unto Christ."** Epaenetus would have taken note and thanked the Lord for the grace in his life, and Paul's recognition probably warmed his heart.

"Greet Mary, who bestowed much labour on us" (v. 6). To others, Paul speaks about *labor*, but here he says *much labor*. Mary is singled out in a particular way. You should not think, 'Why did she get singled out? Why can't I get singled out?' That is not the spirit of it. One day, we will know what this *much labor* was, but all we need to know now is that she **"bestowed much labour on us."** She did not just labor in the church elsewhere, but he says, **"on us"**—Paul is included.

"Salute Andronicus and Junia, my kinsmen, and my fellow-prisoners, who are of note among the apostles, who also were in Christ before me" (v. 7). Paul says four things about them: they are his kinsmen, they were fellow prisoners (they suffered with him), they are of note among the apostles, and they were in Christ before him. Paul seems to take special note of the timing of when persons came to believe. We may wonder why. It was probably because he had persecuted the Church, and he had his regrets about that. Yet he did not dwell on the past; he would press forward. Paul said to the Corinthians, "But by the grace of God I am what I am" (1 Cor. 15:10a). And he said to the Galatians, "God, who set me apart from birth and called me by his grace, was pleased to reveal his Son in me so that I might preach him among the Gentiles" (Gal. 1:15–16a). How patient Christ was with Paul—of all people—who had led in the persecution of the church. Paul always turns the mirror back and reflects the glory of Christ. That is what it is all about.

"Greet Amplias my beloved in the Lord" (v. 8)—that is all Paul says. **"Salute Urbane, our helper in Christ, and Stachys my beloved"** (v. 9). Twice now he says, **"my beloved."** We get a sense of Paul's affection when he speaks about his yearning for the people. We see that same yearning in David when he was undergoing persecution. He could not join the people in going up to the house of the Lord to worship, although he wanted to.[10] There is a special blessing in being with the people of God. I remember once, after being away, hearing a whole congregation singing the Psalms. Later, I remembered being in that group, back East, singing the Psalms, and I remember longing to be there again and to join with them.[11] Paul speaks about yearning to be with the people of God, and that comes through in these words: "**Salute Apelles approved in Christ**" (v. 10a). He is a workman who need not be ashamed. He is one approved in Christ.

"**Salute them which are of Aristobulus' household**" (v. 10b). Paul embraces them as a group. "**Salute Herodion my kinsman. Greet them that be of the household of Narcissus, which are in the Lord**" (v. 11). There are households, groups, and churches that are meeting together. "**Salute Tryphena and Tryphosa, who labour in the Lord**" (v. 12a). Again, he notes their labor. Notice this theme being repeated directly or indirectly. "**Salute the beloved Persis, which laboured much in the Lord**" (v. 12b). She is not *my beloved* here, she is "**the beloved.**" She is loved. By whom? She is loved by the church, certainly—and she is loved by God. Persons are singled out in various ways. Again, about Persis, Paul says, "**which laboured much in the Lord.**" It is labor—much labor—it is hard work, and we will come back to the idea of *teamwork*.

"**Salute Rufus chosen in the Lord, and his mother and mine**" (v. 13). What a personal touch. Paul had suffered the loss of so much. Jesus said, "And everyone who has left houses or brothers or sisters or father or mother or children or fields for my sake will receive a hundred times as much and will inherit eternal life" (Matt. 19:29). This is an instance of these words spoken by Jesus. How do you think Rufus felt, and how do you think his mother felt, when they were greeted this way? "**Salute Rufus chosen in the Lord, and his mother and mine.**" Sometimes, people think that those who have "doctrine" are not personal and tender. It is just not true. Some people think that if you are "doctrinal," you are not practical. That is not true. Doctrine is the foundation. Some

---

10. "When I remember these things, I pour out my soul in me: for I had gone with the multitude, I went with them to the house of God, with the voice of joy and praise, with a multitude that kept holyday" (Ps. 42:4 KJV).

11. After leaving a Psalm-singing church in 1987, through no fault of his own, he was unable to worship in a church that held to exclusive psalmody, as there was no other such church in Phoenix until the founding of Westminster Fellowship. The Psalms were the delight of his soul. His love for the Psalms will be better appreciated when his commentary on the Psalms is published.

people say that Paul was "anti-woman." That is just not true. You do not get *any* sense of that here. This is the real Paul, taken all together.

"Salute Asyncritus, Phlegon, Hermas, Patrobas, Hermes, and the brethren which are with them" (v. 14). Paul knows of this group, and he knows them by name, yet he has not been to Rome. I do not think he had met all of them, but he had heard of them and knew them by name—that is so remarkable. Paul had been inquiring about each one; that is how he would know about them.

Perhaps Priscilla and Aquila had come from Rome, and when Paul inquired after them, they told him about these others. I often find myself asking about people *you* have met and to whom you are witnessing—asking you to tell me about them and what you know of them. I inquire closely, to know who your father, mother, and grandfather are. It is part of wanting to know and to see how the Lord is working in a person. Paul probably did something like that—to get to know these persons and to be able to greet them by name. He took an interest in them and longed to go to Rome to build them up in the faith.

"Salute Philologus, and Julia, Nereus, and his sister, and Olympas, and all the saints which are with them" (v. 15)—another group. He concludes this portion by saying, **"Salute one another with an holy kiss. The churches of Christ salute you"** (v. 16). Sometimes we may greet one another with an embrace or a handshake. Sometimes we may greet one another the way we see the French do it—they kiss on each side of the face or make a gesture toward that. In any case, it is a holy kiss—an expression of receiving another person, embracing another person with a kind of regard and affection. He calls it a **"holy kiss."** Now, this can always be distorted, and in the next verse, he will speak about those who distort things.

This is a team, and they are working together. The hard work being done by those who are noted reflects a *work ethic*. A work ethic comes from a life habit—from past practices—and it begins early in life and continues. It is first manifest in obeying your parents and doing what they ask of you. It is manifest in self-control over impulses—to do your own thing—and in curbing those impulses. It is being able to 'mind your parents.' We can see that it becomes pretty clear early on who is able to mind their parents and who throws a tantrum to get attention and to control their parents. We sometimes see that in public; we see it often enough in the grocery aisle. We see who is operating and ruling. So this self-control—not yielding to one's appetite by throwing a tantrum and manipulating to get what we want—is where it begins: self-control and doing what your parents expect you to do.

As you get older, it is manifest in doing chores—being asked to do chores and doing them *fully*, doing them *well*, not cutting corners, and not being sloppy about it. I have memories of doing chores. I have memories of raking up leaves that fell under the lignum vitae tree[12] in Jamaica, where I once lived. Those are some of my earliest memories. Then there are other memories—like cutting grass to feed the goats. I mean, I liked to play, and I did play. But I remember doing work; I remember doing work both at the house and at school. I remember playing like crazy as I got into early high school. In grade school, too, you are just totally absorbed in play. You give it everything you've got! You play with all your might—that's what it is. But, by the grace of God, somewhere along the way, you pause—and you do your schoolwork. To this day, I'm not quite sure how that happened, but I remember playing soccer with anything that would move: kicking around a tennis ball, or even a cricket ball. We would kick it and cut it out at halftime, go to a back room, and study. At school, we had ranking—a competition system with first, second, third, et cetera. It was hard work—both in play and in study. And you do it well and thoroughly—to the Lord.

I remember working early, and throughout the years. And there was another person who did not work—but they wanted honor. That attitude carried all the way through their life. I noticed it over the years, and it has been 20, 30, even 40 years. But the first memory I have of it is this—two persons were working, and one person was not. So this work ethic starts in early childhood, and you are supposed to do it well. You notice those parents and kids where that is going on—the kids mind their parents the first time, not the third or the fifth. They do it, and they do it all, and they are expected to do it. That is where this work ethic begins, and it continues throughout life. If you do not get this work ethic, it becomes manifest. If you do not work like that when you get older, you will try to get rich off the system—a "get-rich-quick scheme," where you take advantage of the system, which is really taking advantage of other men's labor. It is stealing—getting credit for work when you are not doing the work, whether that credit

---

12. Lignum vitae (*Guaiacum officinale*) is known as the "tree of life."

comes in the form of money or in the form of honor. And in that, the Lord is not being glorified.

MARK AND AVOID THOSE WHO CAUSE DIVISION:
Good Will Overcome Evil

This work ethic applies particularly to diligently seeking and understanding. It is not just outward physical chores, but a kind of intellectual work of diligently seeking and understanding. Lack of this intellectual work to seek diligently and understand becomes manifest when we ask the questions: Can we bear fruit? Are we able to hold others accountable? Are we able and willing to hold others accountable for basic truths? Or, do we hold back in order to get the praise of men? Or are we simply neither able nor willing?

Someone spoke to me about a situation where they encountered a person who had left Westminster Fellowship, and the person continued to make criticism. The question came up about what it is to hold that person accountable or to direct them where they can be held accountable. Recently, that has been happening, and if you are not able and/or willing to hold the person accountable because you are not prepared to, for one reason or another, maybe because of your season of life, or whatever it is, you should turn that situation over to someone who is prepared. This is what Paul says of that situation: **"Now I beseech you, brethren, mark them which cause divisions and offences contrary to the doctrine which ye have learned; and avoid them"** (v. 17). Mark and avoid those who cause **"divisions and offences contrary to the doctrine which ye have learned."** That doctrine includes all the teachings contained in Romans prior to this chapter, beginning with the proclamation of the gospel, clarity and inexcusability, the law of God written on the hearts of all men—it is clear.[13] It includes the understanding of sin: no one

---

13. Gangadean, "Paper No. 102: The Clarity of General Revelation," 527–529; "Paper No. 41: What Is Clear About God," 225–229; "Paper No. 112: Why General Revelation Is Basic in the Christian Worldview," in *The Logos Papers,* 583–585; Gangadean, *On Natural and Revealed Theology,* 213–222; Gangadean, *The Epistle to the Hebrews,* 255–271.

seeks, no one understands, no one does what is right.[14] It includes the doctrine of justification by faith alone, Christ alone, apart from works.[15] There is a need for sanctification, for ongoing cleansing.[16] All of these doctrines are beliefs that they have learned from Paul, and they are learning them in this epistle. Those that cause divisions contrary to this teaching are to be **"marked"** and they are to be **"avoided."**

The way this transfers, in our context, is that when persons are to be avoided, they respond by saying, 'Are you *shunning* us?' Those are the exact words that have been used. 'Are you shunning?' We can respond this way: You have left, and if you want to discuss, you need to come back to discuss with the elders the point at which you differed with the doctrine—clarity. You need to continue the discussion about whether anything is self-attesting, whether the Word of God is self-attesting, whether reason, as the light of the logos in all men, is the self-attesting Word of God.[17] Do not dance around it, blame others, hold up that you are being short-changed, and declare, 'It is I who am the sophisticated one, I know how to deal with these things.' There is pride and arrogance that goes with being unwilling to be held accountable according to the vows you took—vow number four.[18] **"Mark them which cause divisions and offences contrary to the doctrine which ye have learned."**

The teaching we have received is not only the doctrine from Paul in the Epistle to the Romans; we have received the doctrine of Historic

---

14. *Romans 3:10–11; Psalm 14:2–3, 53:1–3*; Gangadean, *The Biblical Worldview*, 177–195, 46–52; Gangadean, "Paper No. 103: The Noetic Effect of Sin," 531–538; "Paper No. 146: The Biblical Worldview (Part VI)," in *The Logos Papers*, 741–745; Gangadean, *The Westminster Confession*, 99–110.

15. *Romans 3:28;* Gangadean, *The Westminster Confession*, 143–206; Gangadean, *The Westminster Catechisms*, 191–207.

16. Gangadean, *The Westminster Confession*, 161–166; Gangadean, *The Westminster Catechisms*, 45–49; Gangadean, *The Biblical Worldview*, 311–328.

17. Gangadean, "Paper No. 23: A Response to Critics of Clarity (Part I)," in *The Logos Papers*, 69–73; Gangadean, *Philosophical Foundation*, 293–309.

18. "Do you promise to submit in the Lord to the teaching and government of this Church as being based upon the Scriptures and described in substance in the Bylaws of Westminster Fellowship? Do you recognize your responsibility to work with others in the Church and do you promise to support and encourage them in their service to the Lord? In case you should need correction in doctrine or life, do you promise to respect the authority and discipline of the Church?" Gangadean, *The Westminster Confession*, 287–288.

Christianity.[19] This person who is concerned about being 'shunned' is now saying he does not believe in Calvinism and does not believe in hell. **"Now I beseech you, brethren, *mark* them which cause divisions and offences contrary to the doctrine which ye have learned; and *avoid* them"** (v. 17).[20] So if the elders have taken the discussion further, down to more basic assumptions, the discussion needs to go back to that point. You are not to pick up the discussion on a less basic concern. In other cases, are you *able* and *willing* to hold others accountable? We have had a discussion recently about what the visible Church is. It is spelled out in the Westminster Confession in a number of places.[21] To what extent have we studied the Confession carefully and taken in all the Confession has to say about it? If a phrase was taken out of context, you can get the whole context by studying it carefully. That is hard work. "Study to shew thyself approved unto God, a workman that needeth not to be ashamed, rightly dividing the word of truth" (2 Tim. 2:15 KJV).

John Nelson Darby took that passage and ran with it and divided the Word of God improperly in developing dispensationalism. He did not build on the work of the pastor-teachers that have gone before;[22] he was not teachable. This is one of the ways you can quickly see if someone is seeking and if they are teachable—if one is getting back to what Paul says in Romans 1:19–20:

> Since what may be known about God is plain to them, because God has made it plain to them. For since the creation of the world God's invisible qualities—his eternal power and divine nature—have been clearly seen, being understood from what has been made, so that men are without excuse.

I recently sent out to a number of people a reminder of a document that was discussed in July 2010: *Three-Stage Preparation for Membership*.[23]

---

19. Gangadean, *The Westminster Confession*, xix–xxix, 349–351; Gangadean, "Paper No. 16: The Historic Christian Faith," in *The Logos Papers*, 103–114.

20. Emphasis added.

21. Gangadean, *The Westminster Confession*, 275–283.

22. Gangadean, *The Westminster Confession*, 111–120.

23. There are three stages of preparation for membership: *Inquirer* (before beginning attendance), *Adherent* (first three months of attendance), and *Membership Vow*.

Before a person even comes to church, there is an *inquiry stage*, and we include the question of clarity in that stage. We may need to make this known and remind you of how this works. We need to do the hard work. We need to recognize that we may not have had a strong work ethic from early on, or that our hard work was done for other reasons.

Of these persons whom we are to mark and avoid, Paul says, **"For they that are such serve not our Lord Jesus Christ, but their own belly"** (v. 18a). I do not know if it is literally just for food, it may be for an easy life, or their own glory. Some preach Christ out of contention.[24] Paul is saying that the self-life is so subtle and so wrapped in self-deception and self-justification that it is hard to discern. But "the word of God is living and powerful, and sharper than any two-edged sword, piercing even to the division of soul and spirit, and of joints and marrow, and is a discerner of the thoughts and intents of the heart" (Heb. 4:12 NKJV). It pierces to divide soul—what is of the self-life—from spirit—what is

---

An *Inquirer* may be a new believer or a believer for some time. They should know—be acquainted with and assent to—the following before coming to Westminster Fellowship (WF). From General Revelation (GR), they should understand the clarity of general revelation and the inexcusability of unbelief. From Special Revelation (SR), they should be familiar with Genesis 1–3 and the Creation–Fall–Redemption worldview (CFR), as well as the Gospel of John. From Historic Christianity (HC), they should read the Westminster Confession of Faith (WCF) as the fullest expression of Historic Christianity and know the doxological focus of the WCF. They should also be able to understand Scripture passages in context and apply them against contrary positions: *Romans 1:20–21; 2:14–15; 3:10–12; Hebrews 11:6; Romans 6:23; Ephesians 2:1; Ephesians 2:8–9; John 4:24; Luke 9:23–24; Isaiah 11:9.*

An *Adherent* should review and deepen knowledge gained in the inquiry stage. From GR, they should be able to show some proofs from general revelation. From SR, they should read more books of the Bible. From HC, they should come to understand Reformed theology, especially TULIP and the *ordo salutis*. In addition, they should understand and practice prayer according to the Lord's Prayer and be able to derive and apply the Moral Law.

A person preparing to take *Membership Vows* should understand the doctrine of the church—what it is and is not—and its discipline, as based on the membership vows. They should understand the distinctives of WF in contrast to contrary positions in the current context. They should have read approximately half or more of the Bible. They should also be able to give the dialectic for the basics of GR (epistemology), SR (including the CFR Worldview, eschatology, and hermeneutics), and HC, and give the reasons for each.

The above is a rough draft only and is to be developed and made clearer in the near future.

Since the Church is for worship, misconceptions of God in false doctrines (idolatry) are serious. Lack in understanding basic things must be corrected before going on and may require going back. Since the Church is for discipleship, lack in a credible commitment to discipline must be corrected before going on and may also require going back.

SG, July 6, 2010.

24. *Philippians 1:15–17.*

of the Spirit of God. You can see patterns in a person's life. Remember, God is holy; He calls us to be holy. And He will purify us "as silver tried in a furnace of earth, purified seven times" (Ps. 12:6b KJV). We have spoken in the past about that purification process.[25]

Not only are they serving their own appetite, but Paul says that they deceive others: "**by good words and fair speeches deceive the hearts of the simple**" (v. 18b). The young, the trusting, the one who is not adequately prepared to understand the deceptiveness of our hearts—these are being deceived. "**By good words and fair speeches deceive the hearts of the simple.**" One of the concerns the elders have is that when things about a person have already been discerned, that person may present themselves in a certain light to the simple and deceive them. Unless you are able and willing to engage—and it must be both able and willing—all the more, avoid it. Otherwise, you can be drawn in and taken in by smooth words, flattery, and unbelief. These persons are not on the team. They are in the church and appear to be on the team, but they really have a different center of operation. They have not done the hard work of seeking and being teachable.[26] If someone does not know what is clear, but they are seeking, they will acknowledge that they do not know and submit to learning. It is not the case that one must know what is clear, but whether or not they will acknowledge the principle and submit to learning. This is where you see whether there is teachability or not. So there are some who are not on the team, and it is the self-life that dominates. As Paul says, they serve "**their own appetites,**"[27] their own advantage. They are benefitting from the work of others without getting the work done, and they are using it for the self-life.

This is part of a long-standing conflict between belief and unbelief; a conflict between self-life and autonomy, and submission to God. Paul says, "**For your obedience is come abroad unto all men. I am glad therefore on your behalf: but yet I would have you wise unto that which is good, and simple concerning evil**" (v. 19). That is in connection with "**deceive the hearts of the simple**" (v. 18b). Paul does

---

25. Pastor Gangadean spoke extensively of the sanctification process. Forthcoming are five volumes compiling his sermons on sanctification.

26. Gangadean, *The Biblical Worldview*, 69–87; Gangadean, *The Epistle to the Hebrews*, 167–201.

27. NIV 1984.

not just want them to remain simple, but simple regarding evil, and wise regarding the good. Remember the tempter in the Garden used this idea and enticed Eve *not* to be simple in regard to evil: "You will be like God, knowing good and evil" (Gen. 3:5b).[28] People do not like to be thought of as simple. They want to be 'sophisticated,' as part of an appeal to the self—we want to think of ourselves as wise.

Paul then says, **"And the God of peace shall bruise Satan under your feet shortly"** (v. 20a). This reaches all the way back to the promise given in the Garden—the first mention of the gospel.[29] This is the Focus of the Week: "And I will put enmity between you and the woman, and between your offspring and hers; he will crush your head, and you will strike his heel" (Gen. 3:15). He, the seed of the woman, and those who belong to Him, will overcome Satan in crushing his head underfoot, by taking thoughts captive—the lies that are spoken. "We demolish arguments and every pretension that sets itself up against the knowledge of God, and we take captive every thought to make it obedient to Christ" (2 Cor. 10:5). How aptly, at the end of this magnificent work on the gospel, Paul brings it all the way back to the original expression of the gospel in the Garden of Eden. Good will overcome evil; God will **"crush Satan under your feet."**[30] Good will overcome evil.

BENEDICTION, SALUTATIONS, AND DOXOLOGY

Immediately after, Paul closes by saying, **"The grace of our Lord Jesus Christ be with you."** It is by grace, it is not by our works. It is the grace of the Lord Jesus Christ that makes us who we are: "by the grace of God I am what I am" (1 Cor. 15:10a). He prays this like a benediction: **"The grace of our Lord Jesus Christ be with you. Amen"** (v. 20b). That is his closing; that is where Paul pauses. Then, those who are with Paul are expressing their greetings to the church. It says, **"Timotheus my workfellow, and Lucius, and Jason, and Sosipater, my kinsmen, salute you"** (v. 21). He mentions kinsmen three times. Paul had kinsmen who were in the Lord; what a blessing that is. I have no kinsmen in

---

28. Gangadean, *The Biblical Worldview,* 159–176.

29. Gangadean, *The Biblical Worldview,* 62–68, 286–288; Gangadean, "Paper No. 56: The Gospel (Summary)," in *The Logos Papers,* 303–313.

30. NIV 1984.

the Lord. But God is gracious, and He absolutely knows what He is doing. We can rest in that grace.

"**I Tertius, who wrote this epistle, salute you in the Lord**" (v. 22). Paul had some trouble with his sight going back a long time, and he often had persons who wrote the letters for him. "**Gaius mine host, and of the whole church, saluteth you**" (v. 23a). Gaius is Paul's host and the host of the church. "**Erastus the chamberlain of the city saluteth you, and Quartus a brother**" (v. 23b). And then again, the same words: "**The grace of our Lord Jesus Christ be with you all. Amen**" (v. 24).

We have before us the doxology, which is a blessing of God who has blessed us. The gospel has been the focus throughout all of the Epistle to the Romans.

> Now to him that is of power to stablish you according to my gospel, and the preaching of Jesus Christ, according to the revelation of the mystery, which was kept secret since the world began, But now is made manifest, and by the scriptures of the prophets, according to the commandment of the everlasting God, made known to all nations for the obedience of faith . . . (vv. 25–26).

This is what Paul sees as the result of the preaching of the gospel: "**made known to all nations for the obedience of faith**" (v. 26b). Obedience comes from faith, which is understanding, and all nations are to come to faith and obedience. Jesus Himself said, "Therefore go and make disciples of all nations, baptizing them in the name of the Father and of the Son and of the Holy Spirit, and teaching them to obey everything I have commanded you" (Matt. 28:19–20a).

Here is a reference to the law of God that embodies the love of God and our love for God. The law is resting under His throne in the Most Holy Place, in the tabernacle, in the temple. The law is central; "**for the obedience of faith**" (v. 26b). Obedience comes from understanding in all of life. Through obedience, we will glorify God, we will achieve the good, which is to know God and to make Him known.[31] Paul ends the letter: "**To God only wise, be glory through Jesus Christ for ever. Amen**" (v. 27). The Word of the Lord.

---

31. Gangadean, *Philosophical Foundation*, 171–177, 208–211; Gangadean, *The Biblical Worldview*, 109–124; Gangadean, *The Westminster Catechisms*, 109–111, 321–325; Gangadean, *On Natural and Revealed Theology*, 33–39, 127–139.

—

APPENDICES

—

THE DOCTRINE OF CLARITY

Inexcusability, Maturity, and Lasting Fruit

2000

Romans 1:16–32

[16]I am not ashamed of the gospel, because it is the power of God for the salvation of everyone who believes: first for the Jew, then for the Gentile. [17]For in the gospel a righteousness from God is revealed, a righteousness that is by faith from first to last, just as it is written: "The righteous will live by faith."

[18]The wrath of God is being revealed from heaven against all the godlessness and wickedness of men who suppress the truth by their wickedness, [19]since what may be known about God is plain to them, because God has made it plain to them. [20]For since the creation of the world God's invisible qualities—his eternal power and divine nature—have been clearly seen, being understood from what has been made, so that men are without excuse.

[21]For although they knew God, they neither glorified him as God nor gave thanks to him, but their thinking became futile and their foolish hearts were darkened. [22]Although they claimed to be wise, they became fools [23]and exchanged the glory of the immortal God for images made to look like mortal man and birds and animals and reptiles.

[24]Therefore God gave them over in the sinful desires of their hearts to sexual impurity for the degrading of their bodies with one another. [25]They exchanged the truth of God for a lie, and worshiped and served created things rather than the Creator—who is forever praised. Amen. [26]Because of this, God gave them over to shameful lusts. Even their women exchanged natural relations for unnatural ones. [27]In the same way the men

also abandoned natural relations with women and were inflamed with lust for one another. Men committed indecent acts with other men, and received in themselves the due penalty for their perversion.

[28]Furthermore, since they did not think it worthwhile to retain the knowledge of God, he gave them over to a depraved mind, to do what ought not to be done. [29]They have become filled with every kind of wickedness, evil, greed and depravity. They are full of envy, murder, strife, deceit and malice. They are gossips, [30]slanderers, God-haters, insolent, arrogant and boastful; they invent ways of doing evil; they disobey their parents; [31]they are senseless, faithless, heartless, ruthless. [32]Although they know God's righteous decree that those who do such things deserve death, they not only continue to do these very things but also approve of those who practice them.

CLARITY IS A DISTINCTIVE OF THE WESTMINSTER CONFESSION AND WESTMINSTER FELLOWSHIP

CLARITY IS A DISTINCTIVE OF THIS CONGREGATION. It is not a distinctive absolutely; it is a distinctive in terms of the emphasis we place on it. The opening words of the Westminster Confession of Faith speak about the clarity of general revelation: "Although the light of nature, and the works of creation and providence do so far manifest the goodness, wisdom, and power of God, as to leave men inexcusable ..." (WCF. 1.1). God has made His existence and nature clear so that men are without excuse.[1] Clarity and inexcusability have been affirmed in other congregations historically. Calvin spoke about this clarity and inexcusability; he explained it in a certain way.[2] The Church has wrestled over the years, to some degree, to make its witness to the world based on that clarity. This congregation has, as one of its distinctives,[3] the clarity of general revelation. Another distinctive is the goal of the Christian life that the earth will be filled with the knowledge of God.[4] In addition, we continue the historic practice of exclusive psalmody:

---

1. *Romans 1:20.*

2. Gangadean, *History of Philosophy,* 127–130.

3. Gangadean, *The Westminster Confession,* 345–395.

4. *Isaiah 11:9.*

the use of the Psalms in the worship of God.[5] We hold to the regulative principle of worship in the context of the Westminster Confession of Faith, which is the high-water mark of the Historic Christian Faith. So here is where we stand. We have taken vows of membership recently, and we want to bring into focus what we are about as a congregation of God's people.

CLARITY IS NECESSARY FOR INEXCUSABILITY

Clarity is a distinctive of this congregation. Clarity is not merely something nice. The doctrine of clarity—that is, the clarity of general revelation—is necessary. It is necessary to understand inexcusability. Paul says, in Romans 1:20, "**For since the creation of the world God's invisible qualities—his eternal power and divine nature—have been clearly seen, being understood from what has been made, so that men are without excuse.**" The sin for which men are without excuse is the sin of failing to know and acknowledge what God has made clear by His creation. This sin is universal. If we are to understand the universality and the nature of sin, we must give heed to the doctrine of clarity. That is so very basic. Without the clarity of general revelation, we cannot speak in any way about inexcusability. Without inexcusability, we cannot speak about sin. And without sin, we cannot speak about the need for Christ.[6]

If there is no sin for which all men are inexcusable—and I say by definition sin is inexcusable—then Christ has died in vain, and our faith is in vain. We believe Christ's death is central to our faith; it is central because Christ died for sinners, and all of us have sinned.

---

5. Gangadean, *The Westminster Confession*, 233–244; Gangadean, "Paper No. 105: The Regulative Principle of Worship," 545–546; "Paper No. 134: Worship, the Sabbath, and the Church," 679–682; "Paper No. 135: On Worship," in *The Logos Papers*, 683–684.

6. Gangadean, "Paper No. 102: The Clarity of General Revelation," 527–529; "Paper No. 41: What Is Clear About God," 225–229; "Paper No. 112: Why General Revelation Is Basic in the Christian Worldview," in *The Logos Papers*, 583–585; Gangadean, *On Natural and Revealed Theology*, 213–222; Gangadean, *The Epistle to the Hebrews*, 255–271.

Clarity Is Necessary to Understand Sin and Death and the Curse and Promise

This doctrine of the clarity of general revelation is necessary in order to understand the nature of sin and the result of sin. The Scripture says, "The wages of sin is death" (Rom. 6:23a). Scripture says, from the very beginning, in the Garden of Eden, "in the day that you eat of it you will surely die" (Gen. 2:17 NKJV). Scripture says, "And you He made alive, who were dead in trespasses and sins" (Eph. 2:1 NKJV). So, in order to understand the wages of sin is spiritual death, we have to understand sin; and in order to understand sin, we must understand clarity.

The sin we are speaking of is the sin that all men are involved in, including the first man, Adam.[7] Adam had the specific command not to eat of the tree of the knowledge of good and evil.[8] But Adam was tested by the tempter: "You will be like God, knowing good and evil"(Gen. 3:5b). Adam was being tested to see whether he understood the difference between the Creator and the creature: that God is eternal, and he is temporal; that God is infinite, and he is finite. It is that line between Creator and creature that Adam blurred. And it is this line that Paul speaks of when he says that they **"exchanged the glory of the immortal God for images made to look like mortal man"** (v. 23a). To understand sin and death, we must understand clarity. And to understand the curse—the presence of natural evil, the existence of toil and strife, and old age, sickness, and death—we must understand sin and inexcusability. Along with the curse, the promise is given—the promise of redemption, what salvation consists of, and what eternal life consists of. Romans 3:23 says, "For all have sinned and fall short of the glory of God." And Romans 3:10–11 says, "There is no one righteous, not even one; there is no one who understands; no one who seeks God." Sin is universal. Later in this sermon, we will speak about a particular sin that is universal to all and has the greatest consequence that we can imagine, even when we do not pay attention to it or see it in ourselves.

---

7. *Romans 3:10–11*; *Psalm 14:2–3, 53:1–3*; Gangadean, *The Biblical Worldview,* 177–195, 46–52; Gangadean, "Paper No. 103: The Noetic Effect of Sin," 531–538; "Paper No. 146: The Biblical Worldview (Part VI)," in *The Logos Papers,* 741–745; Gangadean, *The Westminster Confession,* 99–110.

8. *Genesis 2:16–17.*

What Is Clear? The Content of General Revelation

Specifically, according to Paul, what is clear is the invisible qualities of God. Romans 1:20 says, **"For since the creation of the world God's invisible qualities—his eternal power and divine nature—have been clearly seen, being understood from what has been made."** So, it is the invisible qualities of God that are seen from the things created. So he says, **"being understood from what has been made."** And these are not only seen but **"clearly seen"**—and it is so clear that **"men are without excuse."** Now, specifically, when it says, **"his eternal power and divine nature,"** it is referring to *all* the attributes of God. And the particular attribute that is singled out is the eternality of God's power. In all the universe, there is nothing eternal besides God. The heavens, the sun and the stars, are not eternal. Paul is saying the creation is made in such a way that it is clear it is not eternal. So, the attribute that distinguishes God from everything else, that sets God apart, that speaks of the holiness of God, is, first and foremost, His eternal power.

"In the beginning God created the heavens and the earth" (Gen. 1:1)—these are the opening words of Scripture. It is saying that the heavens and the earth had a beginning. The heavens are vast—stupendously vast. And yet, all of that came into being by the power of God—the almighty power of God—a power that is not exhausted in creating the world. Scientists are pressing further and further back. Some are saying, 'We are getting close to the very beginning. We are one trillionth of one trillionth of one second away from the beginning.' And there is a gap in there they cannot seem to cross over.[9] When you get that close, you know you are at the beginning. They are getting to background radiation and seeing what it is. And there is something about the greatness of this power being stretched out and forming the heavens and the earth. Well, it is God's eternal power that brought the universe into being. And the Scripture teaches that "the heavens declare

---

9. Pastor Gangadean is referring to the concept of a "gap" in two distinct senses. (1) The logical gap refers to being coming into existence from non-being, which is a logical impossibility that theoretical physicists cannot get around. (2) Modern science is committed to metaphysical naturalism, the belief that matter is the only substance that exists. This is distinct from methodological naturalism, where only natural causes can be used to explain the material world. The former denies the existence of spirit as a substance. The latter, however, only restricts explanatory accounts to natural causes without making metaphysical claims regarding the existence of spirit or God.

the glory of God; the skies proclaim the work of his hands. Day after day they pour forth speech; night after night they display knowledge. There is no speech or language where their voice is not heard." (Ps. 19:1–3). Nothing is hidden from the heat of the sun.[10] Of all things we can see and know, we can know that the sun is not eternal. And the sun is declaring, 'I am made.'[11] Therefore, all those who worship the sun are raising an idol and will be ashamed. The sun is not the Creator. The sun is not what delivers. It is God's eternal power that has brought it into being.

It is not only God's power that is clear but also God's wisdom. As we penetrate into the molecular substructure of the genes and of the cell, we are seeing a design that could not possibly have come about by chance. Particularly at this level, the deeper we study, the clearer it becomes. We could have said, on the surface of it, that it is clear enough. But no one has ever come close to coming up with anything approaching that level of complexity, diversity, and design. So, we see the wisdom of God in the things that are made. But it is not in the creation only that we see the attributes of God—we see the justice of God and the goodness of God in the way the world operates. We see not only the natural attributes of God, but the moral attributes of God.[12] All of these are clear. And they are so clear that men are without excuse for failing to see.

To What Degree Is Clarity Clear: Maximal or Minimal?

To what degree is the existence and nature of God clear? Well, it is clear enough that there could be no possible excuse for failing to see. The term *without excuse* is of Greek origin: *anapologētos*. It means being without *logia*—without reason, without any explanation. You have absolutely no objection to be made. Clarity is something that cannot be objected to. We might say that it is as clear as it could possibly be; it could not be any clearer. It is not just sufficiently clear—although it is certainly sufficient—it is *maximally* clear. It could not be any clearer. And it is precisely because it is maximally clear that there is no excuse

---

10. *Psalm 19:6.*

11. Gangadean, *Philosophical Foundation*, 73–80.

12. Gangadean, *The Westminster Confession*, 47–52.

for failing to see and failing to understand the existence and nature of God. For example, we say that there are no square-circles. That is clear. I do not think we can get much clearer than that, can we? There is no being from non-being.[13] That is an example of clarity. God is not both eternal and not eternal in the same respect at the same time. It is also clear that you do not know everything. Of course, neither do I. But that is clear. And the fact that you do not know everything and I do not know everything is an indication that the soul is not eternal—although it is everlasting. That is the kind of clarity we are talking about. And you can go on and on and on.[14]

Human beings have used every objection against the existence of God. They say, 'Maybe God exists, but it is not clear,' or, 'Maybe there is a proof that some few people, after several years, can get into focus.' That is not the kind of clarity we are talking about. The clarity we are talking about is the clarity that leaves men inexcusable. **"So that men are without excuse"** (v. 20b). The opposite is not possible. For that reason, we say that it is clear to reason. It is by reason we know that there are no square-circles. God has endowed us with reason so that we can know this.

To Whom Is It Clear?

Paul says, "All have sinned and fall short of the glory of God" (Rom. 3:23). This *all* includes everyone. No one is exempt from having sinned and fallen short of the glory of God. That means, explicitly, neither the believer nor the nonbeliever, neither the learned nor the unlearned, neither the wise nor the simple is exempt. If all have sinned, they have sinned in this way, and not in some other way. They have all sinned in failing to see what is clear. For that failure, there is no excuse.

Some may be inclined to say that the unlearned do not have the ability, time, or circumstance to see and know what is clear. But we can see that is not true for this reason: the unlearned are not diligently seeking to know God. *No one* is seeking to know God. And the learned certainly have the time and, if you want to put it that way, the ability to see what is clear. Yet they are not seeking God. They are finding

---

13. Gangadean, *Philosophical Foundation*, 63–68, 294–306.

14. Surrendra Gangadean, *Introduction to Philosophy: The Basic Things Are Clear to Reason* (Phoenix: Public Philosophy Press, forthcoming).

ways to strain and get away from the clarity of God's revelation. It is not a matter of learned or unlearned, but a matter of *willingness* to seek—diligently seeking God.[15]

The next time you ask me, 'What about the simple?', I will reply in this way: Is this 'simple' person diligently seeking? And are they able to see that there are no square-circles? Or do they need special revelation to see that? So, we will try to undo this apology for the simple that would try to excuse them from responsibility for knowing. If "all have sinned," and certainly all have sinned, they have sinned in this way: failing to see what is clear.

How Do We Know That We Have Failed to See What Is Clear?

How do we know that all have sinned? If we understand that God created the world originally very good, and it was without physical death,[16] then we can know that death is something that was imposed upon man. All men, both the learned and the unlearned, have to go through the travails of old age, sickness, and death. And God is calling us back through the curse. Physical death is not punishment for sin. It is spiritual death that is punishment for sin. "The wages of sin is death" (Rom. 6:23a). Remember, all men will be raised from the dead—believer and unbeliever. Therefore, physical death is a call back, and it is placed on all men. We might say that God is an 'equal-opportunity God.' He is not a respecter of persons. He has made it equally clear to all. Because He has given reason to all, all can and should see what is clear. And physical death is upon all, calling all back.

The clarity of general revelation is clear to all who diligently seek—both the learned and the unlearned. How is it that we fail to see what is clear? In Romans 1:21, Paul says, **"For although they knew God, they neither glorified him as God nor gave thanks to him."** He is speaking of those who at one time *knew* God, in either a strong or weak sense of the term. We can consider the case of Adam, who knew God when there was no sin in his life. Or we can consider those who at one time were in the faith and professed belief, perhaps having genuine faith but

---

15. Gangadean, *The Biblical Worldview*, 69–87; Gangadean, *The Epistle to the Hebrews*, 167–201.

16. Gangadean, *The Westminster Confession*, 14–18; Gangadean, *On Natural and Revealed Theology*, 179–193.

possessing simple understanding. We can consider covenant children, who were raised in the faith, and perhaps were not converted but had the teaching. Or we can consider those to whom the clarity of general revelation comes, yet they do not know. In whatever sense you want to take the term *knew*—in the weakest or the strongest sense—this is the case: **"Although they knew God, they neither glorified him as God nor gave thanks to him."** That is how sin came into the world, by not glorifying God as we should. "Man's chief end is to glorify God, and to enjoy him forever" (SCQ. 1). The first commandment calls us to "know and acknowledge God to be the only true God, and our God; and to worship and glorify him accordingly" (SCQ. 46). To glorify God involves coming to see Him as He is—as Creator and as Ruler—that He is good, as Creator, and that every good thing we have is from God.[17] And even in the difficult things that may come up, the painful things, even there, we can and should see the justice and mercy of God. He is calling us back. If we go through life neglectfully, not noticing the good and glorious things in life, or if we do notice them but we do not recognize that these are from God, then we will not give the glory to God as we should. **"For although they knew God, they neither glorified him as God nor gave thanks to him."**

Another thing that will happen is that we will not be thankful to God as we should be. Paul says, **"They neither glorified him as God nor gave thanks to him."** What we will do instead is take these things for granted. We will take them as given—as if they do not belong to God, as if we had some right to them in and of ourselves, and as if they are not daily being given to us from God. But our very breath, every day, is from God, and He will take things from us from time to time. But these good things that are in creation, that are around us all the time—even in the midst of difficult things—good things persist. And even these difficult things are God's mercy, calling us back. We should see these things as such and thank God. It is entirely possible for us to be unthankful in the midst of trials. We are not seeing what God is doing. We are not seeing the goodness of God to us in many ways. But these trials are working for us. And so, we can let things slip. At that point, we are not holding to knowing God as our good, our blessing. But we have held up something else as the blessing. So, we turn away

---

17. *James 1:17.*

from God when we do not glorify God as God, nor give thanks to Him for every good we have.

What Is the Effect of Not Seeing What Is Clear?

Paul says, **"Their thinking became futile and their foolish hearts were darkened"** (v. 21b). Their thinking became futile—or they became vain in their imaginations. We imagined, thought, or reasoned, without thinking very clearly, about what else is good, and we began to pursue that in the place of God, even as Adam put something else (Eve) as the good in the place of knowing God. So, what happens is our thinking becomes vain. It is not productive. It is not fruitful. What happens as we try to learn and understand in a world without God is that it makes less and less sense to us, if we are honest. And in order not to be honest, we have to deceive ourselves in various ways. The result of not seeing what is clear about God is that our thinking becomes futile. Our foolish hearts are darkened.

"Although they claimed to be wise, they became fools and exchanged the glory of the immortal God for images made to look like mortal man and birds and animals and reptiles" (vv. 22–23). Notice the progression. We change the glory of the immortal God—the infinite, eternal, and unchangeable wisdom, power, justice, and goodness of God—for a finite justice, a finite wisdom, a finite goodness. We come up with doctrines of God's justice that are distortions of God's justice, such as the popular view of hell as something external and imposed. Rather than seeing that God's justice is spiritual death that is present and operating within us now and going on forever.[18] We fail to see the divine justice. We do not recognize physical death as God's call back. We do not make sense of it. And we have this puzzle that is going on: 'If God is all good and all powerful, why is there evil?' And we take this to be some great problem that we cannot figure out. We cannot fathom it because we are not seeing what is clear—because we shut our eyes to what is clear. How many people do you know who have struggled with the problem of evil? Many have struggled with the problem of evil objectively, in a general way, as well as subjectively, as it presents

---

18. Gangadean, *Philosophical Foundation*, 195–197; Gangadean, *The Epistle to the Hebrews*, 357–371.

itself within our lives. And we struggle in this way because we do not see what is clear and we do not give thanks where we should.

With this emptiness and futility in our thinking—which we refer to as meaninglessness, or increasing meaninglessness—comes a condition of boredom and dissatisfaction. In this condition, we turn away from God and try to find our satisfaction in someone else. Let us take the height of romantic love as an example. Let us take Romeo and Juliet—and visit them five weeks later. 'How are you doing, Romeo? Where is Juliet?' 'I don't know. How should I know? Am I my wife's keeper?' The height of romantic love begins to slide downward. Another person cannot fill the emptiness. And going on trips around the world—that does not fill it. Doing literary criticism by itself—that does not do it. Playing video games—that just doesn't do it. And having astute philosophical discussions at papers and conferences—that does not do it. Nothing can fill the emptiness. And so our desires become dissatisfied. We press, and we press further. We go to excess, we go beyond the boundaries, and we transgress. And the first place in which we transgress is in sexual matters. Adam put the voice of his wife before God. He put her—in a natural way—before his relationship with God. He put the natural relation before God. Imagine that. Is that a surprise? "To Adam he said, 'Because you listened to your wife and ate from the tree about which I commanded you . . .'" (Gen. 3:17a).

Human beings, next to God, are the most glorious beings we know. So we try to find some kind of satisfaction in a relationship with another human being. But in the end, it fails. And either we add other things to the relationship to kind of make it along, or we tend to go to excess one way or another. **"They exchanged the truth of God for a lie, and worshiped and served created things rather than the Creator—who is forever praised. Amen"** (v. 25). And we might go to such a point that our desires are so inflamed that they become unnatural. **"Because of this, God gave them over to shameful lusts. Even their women exchanged natural relations for unnatural ones"** (v. 26). What we see in our society—the rise of unnatural sexual relations—is a result of this emptiness in life and the attempt to fill it with what cannot fill. **"Although they claimed to be wise, they became fools"** (v. 22). And God gives us up further, and we plunge into hostile relations with others because of envy, strife, deceit, and malice. **"They have become filled with every kind of wickedness, evil, greed and depravity. They** are full of envy, murder, strife, deceit, and malice" (v. 29a). We keep going further and further down. And whenever we are exposed because of our sin, we can become quite defensive. We may try to say, 'It is not sin,' or, 'It is none of your business,' and so on, until the point where we may not even be ashamed. We may boldly proclaim it. **"Although they know God's righteous decree that those who do such things deserve death, they not only continue to do these very things but also approve of those who practice them"** (v. 32). It becomes acceptable to sin in outlandish ways. It is approved and accepted to transgress and to flaunt it.

When our lives are empty of meaning, we become bored, dissatisfied, and we go deeper and deeper into excess. Notice that not everyone makes an image of God to look like an animal or a reptile. But the beginning of the progression, seen in verse 23, is when we imagine God to be like man, instead of seeing man in the image of God. Not everyone goes into certain degrees of depravity, but if we continue on in this progression as a people, we end in a cesspool of sin. Why is that? Because we fail to see what is clear, we fail to engage our reason to see what is clear about God, and men are without excuse. And notice how this has happened. Meaninglessness—the vanity of our thinking—is inherent in our failure to see what is clear. **"Their thinking became futile and their foolish hearts were darkened"** (v. 21). We find philosophers trying to strain to make some explanation to get away from God. One of the things I hear them talk about is 'tenseless time,' where time is neither past nor present nor future, in order to get around the idea of time being finite and having a beginning. It is what the Lord calls 'straining at gnats and swallowing camels.'[19] Their thinking becomes futile, impossible, and pretty soon, it will be swept away.

And of all persons, why are philosophers straining at gnats? Philosophers should be the ones who see what is clear at the basic level, and yet we find them straining at these things.[20] **"Although they claimed to be wise, they became fools"** (v. 22a). 'Tenseless time' is evidence of futility. And we find scientists, too, going to such lengths in order to preserve dogmatic naturalist theories—in biology, in the form of

---

19. *Matthew 23:24.*

20. Gangadean, "Paper No. 20: Christianity, Philosophy, and Public Education," in *The Logos Papers*, 127–133.

Orthodox Darwinism, and in theoretical physics, in the Oscillating Big Bang Theory: 'We are going to find the missing link, and we are going to find that missing mass if it kills us.' You know why? Because the mass has to be there in order for everything to come back together. 'We haven't found it yet, but we're going to go on—to neutrinos and other ghostly particles, and to rogue planets at the edge of the universe—to get this. But we *know* it is there. It has got to be there.' And you might crack your teeth in the cold of the Antarctic trying to find some creature that would be a missing link. People have gone to such lengths.[21]

Our thinking becomes futile, and our lives become empty, and we plunge, as individual persons and as a people, into greater depravity. "For the wages of sin is death" (Rom. 6:23a). And it starts with failing to see what is clear. There is fruit sin that is the result of root sin. And yet Jesus said that we do not have to live like this. And Paul said, "This righteousness from God comes through faith in Jesus Christ to all who believe" (Rom. 3:22a). We do not have any righteousness of our own to stand before God. But Christ, as the Lamb of God, has died in our place. And His perfect obedience, His perfect understanding, His perfect faith, are credited to our account. And we can come before God in Christ and be fully accepted.[22] We can find the life that we are longing for in Christ—and only in Christ.

Jesus said to the woman at the well, "Everyone who drinks this water will be thirsty again, but whoever drinks the water I give him will never thirst. Indeed, the water I give him will become in him a spring of water welling up to eternal life" (Jn. 4:13–14). Everyone who drinks of this water—all the emptiness of life, the boredom, the various things we use to fill the emptiness, and the many ways we try to cover it over—will thirst again. These things cannot satisfy us. But the Lord, who is the Creator of heaven and earth, the Word of God by whom all things were made, the Logos who is in the world—He will make the Father known. He will bring us back, He will restore us, and He

---

21. In 1911, Apsley Cherry-Garrard, part of the British Terra Nova Expedition to Antarctica, set out on a mission to collect emperor penguin eggs to study embryonic development, hoping to find a link between birds and reptiles. The temperatures were so frigid that Cherry-Garrard's teeth shattered from the chill. He later recounted the ordeal in his memoir, *The Worst Journey in the World*, highlighting the extreme hardships faced—including his teeth cracking due to the severe cold.

22. *Romans 8:1.*

will bring us to know God. And the life that we have in knowing God will never be dissatisfied; we will never thirst again. Indeed, He said that the water He gives will become in us "a spring of water welling up to eternal life" (Jn. 4:14b). In this, Jesus is saying that the water He gives is not just an initial drinking in of God. It will be a well of water springing up from within us—because the Holy Spirit is in us. And the Holy Spirit will enable us to understand His Word more and more, and to see the glory of God that fills the earth: "The whole earth is full of his glory" (Is. 6:3b). In that way, there will be a well—a spring of water—welling up to eternal life. Jesus said on the last and greatest day of the Feast, "If anyone is thirsty, let him come to me and drink. Whoever believes in me, as the Scripture has said, streams of living water will flow from within him" (Jn. 7:37b–38). This invitation is to all who are thirsty, who cannot be satisfied by anything in this world. Christ, the Word of God, has come to make God known. Christ came to die on the cross in our place, that our sins might be forgiven, and to send the Spirit into our lives—to bring us to life, to illumine our minds, and to give us understanding more and more, that we might see the glory of God that fills the whole earth and rejoice before Him forever. So, Christ will bring us to see what is clear. True repentance begins with acknowledging the emptiness of our lives because we have not sought the Lord—and seeing that we need to seek Him. Clarity is necessary for inexcusability.

CLARITY IS NECESSARY FOR MATURITY

Ephesians 4:13 says that the people of God are to be taught the Word of God "until we all reach unity in the faith and in the knowledge of the Son of God and become mature, attaining to the whole measure of the fullness of Christ." Imagine that—all the Church fully agreed. The Word of God is to be taught until that happens. And it will come to pass, because Jesus said it will. Jesus prayed perfectly. And Jesus said, "If you ask anything in My name, I will do it" (Jn. 14:14, NKJV). So we should understand that Jesus' prayer for the unity of the Church will be answered by the Father. It looks bad now, but we know that God has permitted evil and allows it to work itself out in history in order to deepen the revelation. So we are not to be taken aback. We continue to believe and press on, trusting that the Church will come to the unity of the faith. And in order to come to that unity of the faith, the Church must see what is clear, acknowledge its failure to see what is clear, and repent of that sin. In doing so, the process of understanding by which we see what is clear will be the same process by which we come to understand the divisions within the Church—and deal with them. By this process, we will "all reach unity in the faith and in the knowledge of the Son of God and become mature, attaining to the whole measure of the fullness of Christ" (Eph. 4:13).

Christ, who created the universe, is to fill the whole universe: "Him who fills everything in every way" (Eph. 1:23b). And He is going to fill everything in every way through His people who believe in Him—it will come about. Clarity is necessary for maturity to deal with the divisions in the Church and come to the unity of the faith and the full measure of the Son of God. In Hebrews 6:1–3, we see again how we need to come into maturity:

> Therefore let us leave the elementary teachings about Christ and go on to maturity, not laying again the foundation of repentance from acts that lead to death, and of faith in God, instruction about baptisms, the laying on of hands, the resurrection of the dead, and eternal judgment. And God permitting, we will do so.

Hebrews 5:12 says, "In fact, though by this time you ought to be teachers, you need someone to teach you the elementary truths of God's word all over again. You need milk, not solid food!"

You know that song that says, "You must have been a beautiful baby, 'cause baby, look at you now."[23] There is a greater beauty in maturity. What is happening? Why have you not grown up to maturity? Why are you still caught in this Peter Pan Syndrome? Why do you resist growing up and understanding? There is a beauty to childhood, but there is a greater beauty to adulthood. Otherwise, the Lord would not have us leave childhood. "When I was a child, I talked like a child, I thought like a child, I reasoned like a child. When I became a man, I put childish ways behind me" (1 Cor. 13:11). There are beauties and depths to be understood as a mature person that call us onward continually.

---

23. Bing Crosby, *You Must Have Been a Beautiful Baby,* recorded September 2, 1938, Decca Records.

Spiritual Maturity Is Not Common Grace Maturity

The spiritual maturity we are called to is not the maturity of common grace. Many people come to an ordinary maturity by common grace. Sometimes, compared to the immaturity we may see, we praise the maturity of common grace. But that is not the maturity God has for us. God has for us the maturity of being a teacher in the Church. "In fact, though by this time you ought to be teachers, you need someone to teach you the elementary truths of God's word all over again. You need milk, not solid food!" (Heb. 5:12). It is the maturity of coming into the full measure of the stature of Christ.[24] It is the maturity of grown-up sons who can take their inheritance in God. You do not get your inheritance when you are a child. It is reserved for you. You are under a trustee until you grow up, and then, when you can handle it, you receive it. Then you can do all sorts of creative things with what has been given. So that is the kind of maturity we are called to. The Church was called to wait in Jerusalem until they were endued with power from on high,[25] and then they were able to make disciples to the ends of the earth. That is part of the maturity of the Church as a whole through the ages. God calls us to maturity, and seeing what is clear is necessary for maturity.

Characteristics of the Lack of Spiritual Maturity

We should not still be going through life crises. We should not be tossed around in times of uncertainty. If we are, the basics are not yet in place. We have got to get back and see what is clear. You have to understand what faith is—how faith is a conviction based on evidence, not on sight. "Now faith is the substance of things hoped for, the evidence of things not seen" (Heb. 11:1 KJV).[26] Faith is the conviction based on the evidence of reason, by which we see what is not visible. We should not be tossed to and fro by every wind of doctrine. "Then we will no longer be infants, tossed back and forth by the waves, and blown here and there by every wind of teaching" (Eph. 4:14a). Some

---

24. *Ephesians 4:13* NKJV.

25. *Luke 24:49; Acts 1:8.*

26. Gangadean, *The Biblical Worldview,* 3–20; Gangadean, *The Epistle to the Hebrews,* 167–201, 271–286.

of these things should be settled. We should not be wondering, 'What is the outcome of the Church? Is Christ going to come and rapture us out of this? Or is Christ working through us to subdue all things to Himself in history?' Why should we be tossed back and forth with that question? That should be settled, and in a mature person, it would be.

Characteristics of Spiritual Maturity

A mature person is one who understands the commandments of God and has been taught to observe all that He has commanded.[27] A mature person is one who has been prepared through schooling, through discipline, through discipleship, to make disciples of others. "And the things you have heard me say in the presence of many witnesses entrust to reliable men who will also be qualified to teach others" (2 Tim. 2:2). A mature person is one who is steadfast—unmovable. You can come back after twenty years, and that person will continue to be there in Christ. And not only there in Christ, but flourishing—and that person will have fruit. A mature person is like "a tree planted by streams of water, which yields its fruit in season and whose leaf does not wither. Whatever he does prospers" (Ps. 1:3).

CLARITY IS NECESSARY FOR LASTING FRUIT

Clarity and Fruitfulness

Clarity is necessary not only for maturity but also for lasting fruit. In Matthew 13:23, Jesus said, "He produces a crop, yielding a hundred, sixty or thirty times what was sown." And in John 15:8, Jesus said, "This is to my Father's glory, that you bear much fruit." He also said in John 15:16, "I chose you and appointed you to go and bear fruit—fruit that will last." This fruit would be to His Father's glory. This is how we glorify God—as we know God and make God known. Perhaps in maturity, we speak about our own knowing of God, but that is inseparable from making God known and bearing fruit.

---

27. *Matthew 28:20.*

Clarity and Taking Thoughts Captive

In 2 Corinthians 10:5, Paul says that we are to "demolish arguments and every pretension that sets itself up against the knowledge of God, and we take captive every thought to make it obedient to Christ." That is part of maturity. That is part of bearing fruit.

Clarity and the Word of God

The Word of God is life unto life to those who believe, and death unto death to those who do not believe. The Word of God spoken—what is truly the Word of God, not something truncated, garbled, and unclear—will *always* have its effect. Isaiah 55:11 says, "So is my word that goes out from my mouth: It will not return to me empty, but will accomplish what I desire and achieve the purpose for which I sent it." That purpose can be unto life, or it can be unto death for those who casually hear and let it pass.

In order to bear fruit, we must answer the questions that people put to us—thoughts that are raised up against the knowledge of God. One of these is the problem of evil. We should give an answer for why there is evil in a way that is clear and satisfying.[28] Clarity is opposed to naturalistic science that dominates the academic world today, whether in anthropology, biology, physics, sociology, or history. Clarity is opposed to the various religions of the world that do not acknowledge God the Creator, whether it is Hinduism, which teaches that all is one and does not recognize the distinction between the Creator and the creature, or Buddhism, which teaches that all is *dukkha* (impermanent) and fails to see that God is eternal and that God imposed the curse—old age, sickness, and death. Buddhists fail to see that God created the world good—without natural or moral evil.

Other worldviews must be answered—whether it is shamanistic religions,[29] Native American religions, Islam,[30] or post-biblical Juda-

---

28. Gangadean, *Philosophical Foundation*, 145–161; Gangadean, *On Natural and Revealed Theology*, 141–147; Gangadean, *The Biblical Worldview*, 219–239; Gangadean, "Paper No. 7: The Problem of Evil," in *The Logos Papers*, 33–39.

29. Gangadean, "Paper No. 125: Shamanism," in *The Logos Papers*, 659–660.

30. Gangadean, *Philosophical Foundation*, 191–192; Gangadean, *The Westminster Confession*, 21–27, 37–41, 67–69, 129–130, 236–238; Gangadean, "Paper No. 91: Christianity and Islam," in *The Logos Papers*, 479–484.

ism.[31] I am careful to put it that way to distinguish biblical Judaism from post-biblical Judaism. The latter developed other views after the destruction of the temple—these views must be answered. Islam has existed for centuries. We must take the thought captive concerning the necessity for atonement, which Islam denies, in both Judaism and Christianity.

Clarity is also opposed to all the divisions in the Church. It is opposed to those who try to argue for the truth of God solely from special revelation, those who try to argue from the Resurrection to the truth of God—this is a failure to see that inexcusability is based on general revelation. Clarity is opposed to fideism; those who fail to see that faith involves evidence. Clarity is against those who would say, 'It is very probably true that God exists,' rather than saying it is clear that God exists so that men are without excuse. If we are to bear fruit, we must take these thoughts captive.

CONCLUSION

The doctrine of the clarity of general revelation is basic. It is necessary for understanding inexcusability, it is necessary for our maturity, and it is necessary for bearing fruit. This is one of the doctrines that we want to build on. And by God's grace, we will do so.

---

31. Gangadean, *Philosophical Foundation*, 193–194.

Appendix B

CONTRA VOLUNTARISM
On Knowing and Not Doing[1]

1995

Romans 1:18–25, 3:10–12

[1:18]The wrath of God is being revealed from heaven against all the godless-ness and wickedness of men who suppress the truth by their wickedness, [19]since what may be known about God is plain to them, because God has made it plain to them. [20]For since the creation of the world God's invisible qualities—his eternal power and divine nature—have been clearly seen, being understood from what has been made, so that men are without excuse.

---

1. This chapter is a lecture, not a sermon. Its intent is to provide the basic elements needed to address the voluntarist interpretation of human anthropology—the belief that individuals knowingly do evil and that the will overrides the intellect. This belief is widespread in the history of philosophy and the Church. It hinders the establishment of the inexcusability of unbelief and the necessity for Christ. As such, it needs to be addressed.

Although Pastor Gangadean did not write a single comprehensive response against vol-untarism, he was mindful of the dispute and addressed it throughout his sermons, teach-ings, and philosophical writings. The four steps outlined in the conclusion of this lecture are consistently applied in his biblical exposition, constituting a comprehensive response against voluntarism.

Upon completing the publication of all DRSS works, The Logos Foundation Editorial Board plans to synthesize that knowledge and formulate a single comprehensive response against voluntarism. In doing so, we hope this will be a significant step toward settling this issue, to secure greater agreement in the Church, and to move closer to attaining the unity of the faith (Eph. 4:13). For an initial attempt at addressing voluntarism, see: Gangadean, "Paper No. 120: Contra Voluntarism," in *The Logos Papers*, 611–647.

21For although they knew God, they neither glorified him as God nor gave thanks to him, but their thinking became futile and their foolish hearts were darkened. 22Although they claimed to be wise, they became fools 23and exchanged the glory of the immortal God for images made to look like mortal man and birds and animals and reptiles.

24Therefore God gave them over in the sinful desires of their hearts to sexual impurity for the degrading of their bodies with one another. 25They exchanged the truth of God for a lie, and worshiped and served created things rather than the Creator—who is forever praised. Amen.

3:10As it is written:

"There is no one righteous, not even one;

11there is no one who understands,

   no one who seeks God.

12All have turned away,

   they have together become worthless;

there is no one who does good,
   not even one."

INTRODUCTION:
Knowledge, Not Doing, and Its Implications

IN THE SERMON ON THE THIRD COMMANDMENT regarding integrity, we spoke about the concern of *saying and not doing*. In this sermon, we want to examine the concern of *knowing and not doing*. This is not exactly connected with the third commandment, but it has been an issue that has been around for a long time and the discussion has been heating up. Concerning *knowing and not doing*, the claim is made: 'We know what the will of God is, and we fail to do it.'

The Need for Proof by the World and the Church's Response

The *knowing and not doing* claim falls under the general area of faith and reason, which falls under the general discipline of epistemology, which deals with the questions: 'Is knowledge possible?' and 'How do I know?' The topic of faith and reason has been discussed in the Church for a long time. Nonbelievers—from outside—have pressed the Church by asking the question: 'Do you have knowledge of what you profess?' They have required proof from the Church, and the Church has not been forthcoming with a sufficient response.[2] On the other hand, a significant number within the Church—the voluntarists—respond, and say, 'We do know, but we do not do.' So the nonbelievers say, 'Show us how you know; give us the proof.' The Church has not been forthcoming with a response, and yet the voluntarists within the Church say, 'We do know and yet we do not do' while not being able to show/prove what they claim to know.

Important Implications at Stake

The question of *knowing and not doing* is not just a theoretical question. It has important doctrinal and existential implications. First, it has to do with our understanding of sin.[3] Sin is the failure to know what is clear, and if we do not understand what it is to know, then we have sin at a very basic level, and we are not dealing with sin at that level. Second, it has to do with apologetics; our witness to the nonbeliever. God calls us to give a reason for the hope that is in us.[4] He calls all of us to give a reason, yet the Church has been stumbling in this area for a long time. Third, it has to do with our own sanctification, because the Lord says that we are sanctified by knowing the truth: "Sanctify them by the truth; your word is truth" (Jn. 17:17). Fourth, it has to do with our understanding of the Word of God, reason, and authority. And lastly, it has to do with an attitude in the Church, an attitude best characterized as *anti-intellectual*, which ranges from a disregard for the life of the intellect, to a resistance of it, to a hatred and a despising of it. This, in turn, has to do with our very goal of the Christian life.[5] If the goal is the knowledge of God, and this knowledge involves the mind being used fully, then we can see how the questions of *knowing and not doing* and *what is knowledge* are intimately connected with very basic things.

---

2. Gangadean, "Paper No. 3: The Principle of Clarity," in *The Logos Papers*, 15–20.

3. *Romans 3:10–11*; *Psalm 14:2–3, 53:1–3*; Gangadean, *The Biblical Worldview*, 177–195, 46–52; Gangadean, "Paper No. 103: The Noetic Effect of Sin," 531–538 in *The Logos Papers*, 741–745; Gangadean, *The Westminster Confession*, 99–110.

4. *1 Peter 3:15*.

5. Gangadean, *Philosophical Foundation*, 171–177, 208–211; Gangadean, *The Biblical Worldview*, 109–124; Gangadean, *The Westminster Catechisms*, 109–111, 321–325; Gangadean, *On Natural and Revealed Theology*, 33–39, 127–139.

So, the question of *knowing and not doing* has implications regarding sin, apologetic witness, sanctification, our understanding of the Word of God and authority, and our attitude and our vision of the goal of the earth being filled with the knowledge of God. In making progress to settle this dispute, we will have to look at two things: the definition of knowing (the biblical view of knowledge), and the relation between knowing and doing.

The Doctrine of Clarity Applied to Long-Standing Controversies and Their Controversion

What is knowing? Often, there are difficulties in understanding what knowing is and the relation between knowing and doing. The prior question is *what is knowing?* Behind the epistemological question of knowing, and the question of *knowing and not doing*, is the question of self-understanding, or biblical anthropology.[6] Theology has to do with the doctrine of God, and biblical anthropology has to do with the doctrine of man. Biblical anthropology, or biblical psychology, asks what we are like as human beings. It addresses the inner-workings of our minds. This is the general area that we are concerned about when addressing the question of *knowing and not doing*.

The conflict concerning *knowing and not doing* can be compared to other doctrinal conflicts we have had in the history of the Church. For example, there has been the doctrine of the five points of Calvinism.[7] These points have been debated for a long time and are still debated in some places, and even disregarded in many others. In the doctrine of the five points, each point has been controverted—and some of you have done studies on this. I say this to help us realize that just because something has been controverted, and controverted for a long time, does not mean it is not clear or that we cannot know it. For example, the very existence of God has been controverted—and it still is—but that does not mean that it is not clear.[8] We have the Word of Scripture to tell

---

6. Gangadean, *The Unity of the Church*, 72–73, 134–136, 247–248, 275, 287–289; Gangadean, *The Contradictoriness of Sin*, 37–52.

7. Gangadean, "Paper No. 18: Salvation by Grace," in *The Logos Papers*, 119–122.

8. Gangadean, *Philosophical Foundation*, 71–161; Gangadean, *History of Philosophy*, 47–58; Gangadean, *The Westminster Confession*, 1–13; Gangadean, "Paper No. 3: The Principle of Clarity," 15–20; "Paper No. 39: Clarity," in *The Logos Papers*, 217–220

us that it is clear,[9] and we understand from general revelation that if it were not clear, there would be no sin, because we would be excusable.[10]

We should not allow controversy on a subject to dissuade us from engaging in knowing. Although doctrines are clear, they have been controverted; this has certainly been true about the five points of Calvinism. It has also been true about the doctrine of the Trinity, which is a very vital doctrine. There has been conflict about the hypostatic union—Christ as being fully God and fully man. There has been conflict about the charismatic doctrine of the Spirit:[11] what it means to be led by the Spirit, and whether one can know immediately, apart from the intellect. The doctrine of baptism[12] has also been controverted, as we saw this past week in the debate that we attended at the Church of the Redeemer.[13]

The issue of *knowing and not doing* has been heating up for quite some time, and is now becoming quite a hot issue. Many in the Reformed faith take the position that we *knowingly do evil*—that we know, and while knowing, we do not do. This position is known as voluntarism.[14] I would like to focus our attention on that question today, so that we are not caught between two opinions, but rather we can consider the Scripture carefully to come to a clearer understanding and resolution.

Affirming Clarity in Seeking Resolution

In the history of the world, there have been many views about the doctrine of man and what it is to be human. Sigmund Freud gave a view in which he spoke about the id, the ego, and the superego—and he made

---

9. *Romans 1:18–20; Psalm 19.*

10. Gangadean, *The Epistle to the Hebrews,* 255–269.

11. Gangadean, "Paper No. 122: Contra Charismatic Distinctive," in *The Logos Papers,* 651–653; Gangadean, *On Natural and Revealed Theology,* 227–228.

12. Gangadean, *The Westminster Confession,* 299–305; Gangadean, *The Epistle to the Hebrews,* 287–319.

13. As part of Pastor Gangadean's attempt to be connected with the larger Christian community, he often attended debates and speaking engagements in other Reformed churches, hoping to find common ground on clarity and the foundation. Although these engagements did not result in securing common ground with others, they served as an opportunity for growth and reflection on the necessity to take thoughts captive in instruction at Logos Theological Seminary and preaching.

14. Gangadean, "Paper No. 120: Contra Voluntarism," in *The Logos Papers,* 611–647.

the id, the element of desire, most prominent. Plato had a view set in a dualistic framework, in which he spoke about intellect, will, and the appetites. Aristotle had another view, in which he distinguished moral virtues from intellectual virtues. Abraham Maslow, the psychologist, had another view, speaking about the hierarchy of needs. Thomas Hobbes had a view that made man a pleasure-seeking ethical egoist. Buddhism has a view which says there is no self (*anatman*) and attempts to explain the nature of consciousness and how it arises. Hinduism has a view, Daoism has a view, and there are many other traditions. Even within Confucianism, we have the realist and the idealist schools.

What should we do? This controversy is not just in the world; it is in the Church. Should we avoid it? Should we say, 'There are giants in the land, we cannot take the land,' and let it go?[15] We should say, rather, that there is sin in us, and because of that sin in us,[16] we are not able to see as clearly as we ought. In other words, because we do not seek, we do not understand. We need to deal with the root sin and wrestle mightily against it. We need to overcome, as the Book of Revelation says: "To him who overcomes I will give the right to eat from the tree of life" (Rev. 2:7b)—or from the various forms in which life is represented.[17] I think God calls us to overcome through struggling with sin as unbelief and taking thoughts captive;[18] we are to come to know God.[19] Wrestling with this issue is meant to bring us to know God. One of the reasons we have to wrestle with it is because we are so very slow in seeking God.

---

15. *Numbers 13:31–33.*

16. *Romans 3:10–11; Psalm 14:2–3, 53:1–3*; Gangadean, *The Biblical Worldview,* 177–195, 46–52; Gangadean, "Paper No. 103: The Noetic Effect of Sin," 531–538; "Paper No. 146: The Biblical Worldview (Part VI)," in *The Logos Papers,* 741–745; Gangadean, *The Westminster Confession,* 99–110.

17. *Revelation 2:7, 11, 17, 26, 3:5, 12, 21.*

18. *2 Corinthians 10:4–5.*

19. Gangadean, *The Biblical Worldview,* 69–87; Gangadean, *The Epistle to the Hebrews,* 167–201.

POSITIVE STEPS IN SETTLING THE DISPUTE

Defining the Two Positions: Willful Rebellion Against What Is Known Versus a Lack of Knowledge

These are some prominent theologians within the Reformed faith who take a position on *knowing and not doing*: R. C. Sproul, John Gerstner, Greg Bahnsen, John Frame, Herman Dooyeweerd, Alvin Plantinga, Ronald Nash, and R. J. Rushdoony. These men all have positions on this question—not quite the same position, but they do have one.

Here are the two sides of the conflict. The first view, voluntarism, claims that we know God but fail to act—we know and do not do. Sin is rebellion of the will against what we know, and there is no lack of knowledge. The issue is not to be addressed primarily in the realm of knowledge. We may 'remind' a person of their knowledge, but essentially, the knowledge is there. That is also true for sanctification: it is not a lack of knowledge; what needs to be known is already known.

The second view is the position that the apparent issue between *knowing and not doing* is due to a lack of knowledge. The lack of knowledge can be accounted for in many ways, as will be explored in the next section. This position does not mean that some things are not known (denying clarity), or that the person is not culpable (denying inexcusability), but it means that more things—or certain other things—*need* to be known, and when those other things are known, then the person is set free to do what is right. "Then you will know the truth, and the truth will set you free" (Jn. 8:32). In this view, truth is both necessary and sufficient to do what is right.

Identifying Biblical Passages for Both Positions

What I would like to do is give the passages both for and against the view that we *know and do not do*. That is how the discussion has occurred with the five points of Calvinism: passages are lined up on one side and passages on the other, and we say, 'Well, where do we go from there?' Then we see how people try to make adjustments and work through their understanding of the passages, because they recognize that the Bible cannot be contradictory. Then we see whether the particular way they try to work through it is satisfactory or not. Finally, after addressing the apparent contradiction in the interpretation of the passages, we will provide several additional approaches to settle this dispute.

Passages for Knowingly Doing Evil: Voluntarism

One passage that is used to support voluntarism is Romans 1:21: **"For although they knew God, they neither glorified him as God nor gave thanks to him, but their thinking became futile and their foolish hearts were darkened."** Although they *knew* God, they did not glorify Him as God. So the interpretation of the voluntarist is that they *knew* and they failed to *do*.

Another passage is in the Book of Numbers regarding intentional sins.[20] There are sins of ignorance, and there are sins that are intentional, and the intentional sin is taken to mean that persons knowingly do evil. I think one of the interesting points about knowingly doing evil is not just that you knew it in the past, but that, while continuing to know and maintain the understanding, you are acting contrary to it. So, the problem is not in the knowing, but in the doing. In this view, there is a split between the intellect and the will. I will argue that there *is* a split in man, but it is *not* between the intellect and the will. The split is within the intellect itself—within the understanding. This is where biblical anthropology and psychology must come into the picture.

Another passage that is used is this passage about demons: "You believe that there is one God. Good! Even the demons believe that— and shudder" (Jas. 2:19). The demons declared about Jesus Christ, "I know who you are—the Holy One of God!" (Lk. 4:34b), and they were rebuked by the Lord.[21] This is interpreted as a case where rational beings—capable of rationality—have knowledge and do not do.

I recently heard another passage from Jonah being referred to. Jonah was told, "Go to the great city of Nineveh and preach against it" (Jon. 1:2a), and he rebelled and took off in the other direction. It is said, 'Clearly, this is an example of knowing and not doing; it is obvious.' These kinds of remarks and words are used as if the passage were so very obvious. Did Jonah know? Was there a lack of knowledge on his part? The response is, 'No, God told him what to do, and he just did not do it. He knew, and he rebelled against God.'

---

20. *Numbers 15:22–31.*

21. *Luke 4:35.*

Then there is James 4:17: "Therefore, to him who knows to do good and does not do it, to him it is sin."[22] Those are some of the passages *for* the voluntarist position. I would like you to consider whether there are other passages that you might add to these.

Passages Against Knowingly Doing Evil

One of the passages against voluntarism, at least on the face of it, is Romans 3:10–12, which says, **"There is no one righteous, not even one; there is no one who understands, no one who seeks God. All have turned away, they have together become worthless; there is no one who does good, not even one."** This is what I read this morning in Psalm 14:1–3. It is also repeated almost verbatim in Psalm 53:1–3. It is unique that this one thing is repeated twice in the Scripture. **"There is no one righteous, not even one; there is no one who understands, no one who seeks God."** This passage, on the face of it, would seem to indicate that there is a lack of knowledge.

In Luke 23:34, Jesus prays, "Father, forgive them; for they know not what they do."[23] We will see how voluntarists try to approach these passages to explain them in light of Romans 1:21. Then, the words of Jesus to His disciples after His resurrection on the road to Emmaus:

He said to them, "How foolish you are, and how slow of heart to believe all that the prophets have spoken! Did not the Christ have to suffer these things and then enter his glory?" And beginning with Moses and all the Prophets, he explained to them what was said in all the Scriptures concerning himself (Lk. 24:25–27).

In 1 Timothy 1:13, Paul says he persecuted the Church "in ignorance and unbelief." In 1 Corinthians 2:6–8, he said,

We do, however, speak a message of wisdom among the mature, but not the wisdom of this age or of the rulers of this age, who are coming to nothing. No, we speak of God's secret wisdom, a wisdom that has been hidden and that God destined for our glory before

---

22. NKJV.

23. KJV.

time began. *None of the rulers of this age understood it, for if they had, they would not have crucified the Lord of glory.*[24]

John 16:2 says, "A time is coming when anyone who kills you will think he is offering a service to God." They think they are doing God's service. They really do not know God, but they think they know God. Then John 17:17: "Sanctify them by the truth; your word is truth." We are made holy and devoted to God through knowing the truth. Jesus said to His disciples who believed in Him, "If you hold to my teaching, you are really my disciples. Then you will know the truth, and the truth will set you free" (Jn. 8:31b–32).

Explaining Passages for Knowing and Not Doing by Showing a Lack of Knowledge

We can see that there are passages that favor *knowing and not doing*, and there are passages that favor *not knowing and not doing*. We do not want to say that there is a contradiction in the Bible. One side has to explain their passages, maintain that the contrary sense is not viable, and also explain the contrary passages in a sense that fits with the rest of Scripture. I will try to show that the passages that speak about *knowing and not doing* can be explained ultimately in terms of *a lack of knowledge*.

The solution to this conflict is generally of two kinds: First, we can raise a question of the *content* of the knowledge, and second, we can raise a question of the *definition* of knowledge. The first approach is to raise a question about the content of the knowledge. It is said that they know, but what is it that they know? We can speak about them knowing general revelation but not special revelation. Or we can speak about the 'amount' that they know. Still, it ultimately has to do with the content of knowledge.

The second approach is to make a change to the classical definition of knowledge, and instead, advocate one of the other six definitions. The advocates of voluntarism have adopted differing understandings of what it means to know. No consensus has been attained.[25] In analyzing

---

24. Emphasis added.

25. These are some of the thinkers advocating variations of voluntarism: Aristotle, Peter Abelard, Duns Scotus, William of Ockham, R. C. Sproul, John Gerstner, Greg Bahnsen, John Frame, Herman Dooyeweerd, Alvin Plantinga, Ronald Nash, and R. J. Rushdoony.

each of the definitions, their insufficiency to comply with knowledge as proof for inexcusability will be shown. I will try to argue for the first definition as the only viable explanation that is actually operating in the allegedly voluntarist passages.[26]

(1) Strong Justification: Justified True Belief

The classical definition of knowledge is also known as strong justification. Knowledge requires justified true belief: we believe it, it is objectively true, and we have rational justification—or proof—for it. We can speak about weak and strong justification, but when we speak about the clarity of general revelation, clarity *requires* strong justification. It is clear if, and only if, the opposite is not possible. That means we should be able to show that *all* the opposing views are not possible. Otherwise, we have not achieved clarity. We might have achieved something true, but not clarity. The particular thing that makes us inexcusable is objective clarity.[27] Because this is the beginning of all knowledge for which we are accountable, and it is said to be clear,[28] I will argue that knowledge is justified true belief. We must be able to give justification.

One of the things we can do is to ask anyone who claims that it is clear to show it. If the existence and nature of God is clear, they would certainly know it—and as a believer, it cannot be said that they are 'suppressing' it—so they should be able to show it, to give proof. In doing so, we will see just what they mean by 'clear.' I think that is the most straightforward, upfront, first-step process for those who claim it is clear. We will find that they claim it is clear, and they can perhaps show one step in the proof. Maybe they can show that materialism is not true, but they have not shown that deism is false. They have not

---

26. (1) Strong justification—justified true belief. (2) Weak justification: immediate, intuitive, pretheoretical. (3) Salvitic-relational knowledge: belief without understanding or justification. (4) Seed of religion: bare knowledge of the attributes of God. (5) Knowledge of special revelation: all held responsible whether they paid attention to it or not. (6) Knowing without believing: knowing about a proposition without assenting to its truth. (7) Mystical knowledge: non-cognitive.

27. Gangadean, "Paper No. 102: The Clarity of General Revelation," 527–529; "Paper No. 41: What Is Clear About God," 225–229; "Paper No. 112: Why General Revelation Is Basic in the Christian Worldview," in *The Logos Papers,* 583–585; Gangadean, *On Natural and Revealed Theology,* 213–222; Gangadean, *The Epistle to the Hebrews,* 255–271.

28. *Romans 1:18–20.*

shown that dualism is false. Dualism was present in Plato and has influenced the Church.[29]

Even those who claim it is clear have not been able to *show* clarity. At crucial points, they appeal to Scripture to make their case. When we speak about clear general revelation, we cannot appeal to Scripture to make our case—it must be clear *objectively* from the creation. The two approaches that have been taken are: (1) Some affirm clear general revelation but then go to Scripture and effectively deny general revelation.[30] (2) Some say it is clear and do not go to Scripture, but they do not quite show the clarity of general revelation. They show the probability or possibility of clarity, but not the actuality.[31]

When we say one of our distinctives is the clarity of general revelation,[32] we are referring to both the Principle of Clarity[33] and general revelation.

(2) Weak Justification: Immediate, Intuitive, Pre-Theoretical Knowledge

Some, instead of providing strong justification by reason and argument, have pursued another conception of knowledge. They appeal to an intuitive sense—that by looking at the heavens, we can say, 'Of course God exists.' But others have objected and provided an alternative naturalistic interpretation in terms of the Big Bang. How do we respond to that? Of course, we look at the world, and the world *appears* ordered and created—but how do we disprove the opposing evolutionary view?

---

29. Gangadean, *On Natural and Revealed Theology,* 9–39; Gangadean, "Paper No. 106: The Good and Heaven," 547–556; "Paper No. 116: The Knowledge of God vs. The Hope of Heaven," in *The Logos Papers,* 597–598; Gangadean, *Philosophical Foundation,* 40–41.

30. A prominent example is fideist presuppositionalists, who use the transcendental argument for the existence of God to assert that all knowledge depends on the Triune God of the Bible and Scripture.

31. This is referring to classical apologetics. In classical apologetics the classical arguments for the existence of God are used while not overcoming the Enlightenment challenges of Hume and Kant against them. Classical apologetics does not use the classical arguments cumulatively in a logical sequence.

32. Gangadean, *The Westminster Confession,* 345–395.

33. Gangadean, *Philosophical Foundation,* 3–5, 287–292; Gangadean, *The Westminster Confession,* 1–13; Gangadean, "Paper No. 53: Common Ground (Part IV)," in *The Logos Papers,* 283–286.

How do we respond to Plato's divine maker, the *demiurge*, which forms but does not create?

Those who use immediate/intuitive/pre-theoretical justification as an example of 'knowledge' have a very weak sense of the term *know*, which does not qualify for the strong sense required by clarity. Bahnsen would say, 'Men know that the wrath of God is on them.' It is said that the common grace of God in the rain falling on the just and the unjust[34] is not just revelation, but it is knowledge. 'Men know it from within and they know it from outside.'

In this intuitive sense of knowledge, it is thought that we do not have to use any reasoning, because it is already known. In this view, the knowledge of God is not *mediated* knowledge; it is *immediate* knowledge. It is almost like perception. We see already that those who claim that it is clear have varying views of how we know. And already, that begins to clue us in that there is a problem here. For example, some would say that Sproul's proof of the existence of God is inadequate. Why is Sproul not producing sound proof if it is clear and he already knows? Is Sproul suppressing the truth of God, though he is a believer and trying his very best to give that proof? That does not add up.

(3) Salvific-Relational Knowledge: Belief Without Understanding or Justification

Some have interpreted the term *know* in Romans 1:21—"**although they knew God**"—to mean salvific-relational knowledge. We want to ask: since the same term is used in John 17:3, does that mean these people had salvific-relational knowledge? How do we know? Is the meaning of the term so clear—so obviously—on the face of it? "**For although they knew God, they neither glorified him as God**"? The word know is ambiguous—as we are showing by providing seven definitions of what knowledge means. We cannot settle the meaning of the term *know* by mere exegesis. Prior work in establishing what knowledge is must be required. Nonetheless, some would claim that exegesis settles the question and are ready to fold up and leave the discussion if anyone raises a question.

---

34. *Matthew 5:45* NKJV.

(4) Seed of Religion: Bare Knowledge of the Attributes of God

The fourth view is that this knowledge is *bare* knowledge of the existence and divine attributes of God rather than the *full* knowledge that all of creation declares the glory of God and the earth is full of His glory.[35] Some refer to this knowledge as bare minimum—the *semen religionis*. Calvin appeals to this[36] by saying that the seed of religion is hardly developed in anyone. When we say we know God, just what is it that we know? What is meant by *know* has not yet been resolved.[37] I will be reading to you a passage from John Frame later on which makes the point about how this conflict is not yet worked out. Can it be said that we have no misunderstanding mixed in with our knowledge?

We are going to look at several biblical examples and point out how there is all kinds of misunderstanding mixed in with understanding. Is the failure to *do* a result of the misunderstanding that is mixed in with our knowledge? Knowledge requires understanding; understanding can be in varying degrees—that is often forgotten. It can be minimal, it can be much greater, and also, with understanding, there can be misunderstanding mixed in. When it is said that 'they *know*, and the failure is due to not *doing*,' I'm going to respond and say, 'Is there misunderstanding, and is the disobedience the result of the misunderstanding?' I am going to raise that question about the knowledge of the demons and point out examples from Scripture that would lead us to believe that there is a lot of unbelief in the demons.

Another question should be raised regarding the claim that the knowledge of God 'gets through' and that it is actually believed. An alternative interpretation can be given to knowledge: while objectively true, it is not subjectively believed or understood. Alternative accounts of 'get through' can be conceived. You may speak about it being blocked before it gets through. You could say, yes, men suppress the truth, but not that it gets through; or it gets through and it is expelled; or it gets through and it stays in. The voluntarist claim is that 'it gets through and

---

35. *Psalm 19; Isaiah 6:3.*

36. "That there exists in the human mind, and indeed by natural instinct, some sense of Deity, we hold to be beyond dispute, since God himself, to prevent any man from pretending ignorance, has endued all men with some idea of his Godhead." John Calvin, *Institutes of the Christian Religion*, trans. Henry Beveridge (Grand Rapids, MI: Christian Classics Ethereal Library, n.d.), 43, https://www.ccel.org/ccel/calvin/institutes/cache/institutes.pdf.

37. Gangadean, *History of Philosophy,* 127–130.

stays in.' So, while believing—with nothing wrong with their understanding and intellect—people are acting contrary to their knowledge.

(5) Knowledge of Special Revelation: All Held Responsible Whether They Paid Attention to It or Not

Charles Hodge, in his *Commentary on the Epistle to the Romans*, says
that unbelievers know by the fact that they have an objective revelation
in the creation just as believers are said to know the will of God by
having the Scriptures.

> This revelation was indeed generally so neglected, that men knew
> not what it taught. Still they had the knowledge, in the same sense
> that those who have the Bible are said to have the knowledge of
> the will of God, however much they may neglect and disregard it.
> In both cases there is knowledge presented, and a revelation made,
> and in both ignorance is without excuse.[38]

This is one sense of the term *know*; having access to the truth makes us
partakers of that knowledge whether we make use of it or not.

(6) Knowing Without Believing: Knowing Without Assenting to Its Truth

There is yet another sense of knowing where one can understand a
view or belief system without assenting to its truth. This is commonly
practiced in teaching, where 'I know Hinduism, but I do not believe it.'

(7) Mystical Knowledge: Non-Cognitive

The seventh view refers to a non-conceptual, non-verbal, non-cognitive, mystical kind of knowing. The Buddhists speak about this kind of
knowing that goes beyond words and concepts.[39] This is enlightenment
that comes through a mystical experience.

---

38. Charles Hodge, *Commentary on The Epistle to the Romans* (Grand Rapids, MI: Wm. B. Eerdmans Publishing, 1993), 36.

39. Gangadean, *History of Philosophy,* 107–110.

Strong Justification: The Relevant Sense of *Know*

The word *know* has been used in several different senses. We have to remain alert to these definitions. The relevant sense—the most critical sense—is in terms of having a clear general revelation and knowing by reason and argument. I would argue that the relevant sense of knowing is that you must have *justified true belief*. Certainly, we must have it in terms of Psalm 19:1: "The heavens declare the glory of God; the skies proclaim the work of his hands." We need to show how the heavens declare the glory of God. Romans 1:20 says that what may be known of God is **"understood from what has been made."** The understanding involves an *inferential process*, not a direct perception, as in 'I perceive the wall.' Justification is therefore relevant.

BIBLICAL EXAMPLES SHOWING LACK OF KNOWLEDGE

We have examples to consider in Adam, Job, David, Peter, and Paul. We have examples of Pharaoh, Korah, the demons, Agrippa, Israel, Kadesh, the golden calf, and Nicodemus. We can see that the list of examples is quite long. We would say regarding Adam—and certainly in the case of Eve—that she believed what was false, and then she ate.[40] She believed what was false in two ways: "You will not surely die," and "You will be like God."[41] In that sense, there was unbelief in the understanding *before* the action of eating came about.

Adam and Eve: Determined Good and Evil for Themselves

We would say that both Adam and Eve had turned aside from pursuing the knowledge of God. We will see that this turning aside is more basic than their actions. Failure to seek and understand is the root from which the fruit sin arises. *None seek God.* When we fail to continue seeking God, we can lose the understanding that we do have. In the case of Adam and Eve, they had knowledge without any problem—there was no admixture of sin, and yet that very knowledge was not held on to. They believed what was false because they had not continued seeking.

---

40. Gangadean, *The Biblical Worldview*, 159–176.

41. *Genesis 3:4–5.*

At every moment of our lives, we are faced with two ways and only two ways. We will go one way or the other. At any moment, we are either seeking the Lord, walking in the Spirit, and focusing on God's purpose, or we are walking in the flesh, doing our own will, concerned primarily about our own happiness, and judging all things in terms of how they make us feel. There is no in-between place. We are either seeking to grow in the knowledge of God, or we are turning aside, walking in the flesh, determining good and evil.

Left to themselves, Adam and Eve did not continue to seek God. But as rational beings, they had to be seeking something, and so they turned aside to seek something else. They did not retain the most basic things about God that they should have retained, namely, that God is infinite and man is finite. God determines good and evil as Creator of the nature of things; man cannot be creator. They could and should have known—it is very clear that they are not infinite. They cannot be creators. There must be something infinite and eternal. They did not continue to hold on to that most basic knowledge. I would say, in the case of Adam and Eve, it was not that they were knowing and not doing; they lost their knowledge and turned aside to unbelief.[42]

Job: Failed to Know What He Should Have Known

In Job's case, he had gone very far in living a blameless and upright life. When God spoke to him about the creation,[43] Job came to repentance. He said, "My ears had heard of you, but now my eyes have seen you. Therefore I despise myself and repent in dust and ashes" (Job 42:5–6). The understanding there is that Job had gone further than anyone else, but he failed to continue to go as far as he should have, and there was a lack of knowledge on Job's part. He was blameless but not faultless. Of Job, it is said that he was blameless but not sinless, and his sin was revealed. There was a culpable lack of knowledge in Job. It is not that he knew these things and was arguing with God, but he failed to know things that he should have known. The problem is a lack of knowledge, a *culpable* lack of knowledge. In both Adam and Eve, there was a failure to seek, and in Job, there was a failure to seek.

---

42. Gangadean, *The Biblical Worldview*, 159–195.

43. *Job 38–41.*

David: Pursued Something Else in Place of Advancing God's Kingdom

In the case of David, he committed adultery. He knew adultery was wrong—yes, he covered it up, but the story begins, "In the spring, at the time when kings go off to war . . . David remained at Jerusalem" (2 Sam. 11:1). This shows that he had turned aside from pursuing what was good and that there was something else in his mind that he pursued as the good. In that context, whether he could resist the temptation is another matter. When David repented, he said, "Behold, You desire truth in the inward parts" (Ps. 51:6a NKJV), and "Then I will teach transgressors your ways" (Ps. 51:13a). We would say that in David, too, there was a lack of knowledge.

Notice we are not saying that he did not know, in some sense, that adultery was wrong and that he should have, even on that basis, not committed adultery. What we are saying is that his failure to withstand the temptation was due to a lack of knowledge of God and a lack of the pursuit of the goal. Again, David was not seeking the knowledge of God. That is why I read Romans 3:10–12: "**There is none who seeks after God.**"[44] This is a universal statement about *all* men, not in respect to special revelation, but in respect to general revelation. God is not going to say, "**There is no one who understands**" of all men, when only few have special revelation. Paul is speaking about *general revelation*. Some have tried to blunt this passage by saying, 'None understand special revelation.' The context of Romans 3 is general revelation. The context of Psalm 14 and Psalm 53 is general revelation.

Peter: Misunderstood the Work of the Messiah

Peter received the revelation from God: "You are the Christ, the Son of the living God" (Matt. 16:16b). Jesus pronounced a blessing on him, "Blessed are you, Simon son of Jonah, for this was not revealed to you by man, but by my Father in heaven" (Matt. 16:17b). Notice what happens. Jesus tells Peter that He will go up to Jerusalem to die, and Peter takes Jesus aside and rebukes Him, "Far be it from You, Lord; this shall not happen to You!" (Matt. 16:22b NKJV). Then Jesus rebuked Peter openly. He said, "Get behind me, Satan! You are a stumbling block to

---

44. *Romans 3:11* NKJV.

me; you do not have in mind the things of God, but the things of men." (Matt. 16:23b). What was going on there? There was a lack in Peter's understanding—he did not understand that the Messiah must die. It is possible to believe that someone is the Messiah but misunderstand what the work of the Messiah is. So one can get the understanding that Jesus is the Christ, not by one's cogitations, but by God's very revelation, and while having that revelation, one can misunderstand it. In the case of Peter, there was a lack of understanding. That is why Jesus said, "How foolish you are, and how slow of heart to believe all that the prophets have spoken! Did not the Christ have to suffer these things and then enter his glory?" (Lk. 24:25b–26). Jesus did not say, 'You believe, and you are in rebellion, resisting.' He said, "How foolish you are, and how slow of heart to believe all that the prophets have spoken!" It was a lack of knowledge.

We should do what Jesus did. That is, we should explain, with a lot of perseverance, and open the understanding of the people. That is what He did on the road to Emmaus. "Then he opened their minds so they could understand the Scriptures" (Lk. 24:45 NKJV). In response to those who say, 'They knew and rejected it,' we see that even the disciples, who were with Him three years, when He told them a number of times, point blank, that He is going to go up to Jerusalem and die, could not process it. The lack was not in the will following the intellect, the lack was in the intellect itself.

Paul: Acted in Ignorance and Unbelief

In Paul's case, he said, "Even though I was once a blasphemer and a persecutor and a violent man, I was shown mercy because I acted *in ignorance and unbelief*" (1 Tim. 1:13).[45] We have the words of Paul himself. He persecuted the Church. Some have said, 'Well, Paul knew general revelation; he just didn't know special revelation.' That is relevant in that what he was doing was due to a lack of knowledge, in this case, of special revelation. I would also argue that there was a misconception in Paul's mind, from general revelation, about the infinite justice of God, when he was trying to establish his own righteousness. Even as

---

45. Emphasis added.

he spoke about Jews, that they had a zeal without knowledge.[46] Not knowing the righteousness of God, but having righteousness by the works of the law. "Once I was alive apart from the law; but when the commandment came, sin sprang to life and I died" (Rom. 7:9). The law awakened that knowledge, that true understanding, of what God's requirements are.

We see Paul's example; he could be used for all the others who had persecuted the Church in the early days. "I acted in ignorance and unbelief." The ignorance was not excusable. It was *culpable*. It was blameworthy. He ought to have known. When Stephen preached, and they could not resist the wisdom by which he preached, they stoned him.[47] That is still described in terms of doing evil ignorantly in unbelief.

Pharaoh: In Unbelief Resisted and Denied God's Increasing Revelation

Pharaoh hardened his heart. God's increasing revelation came to Pharaoh, and he had to increasingly harden his heart in response. The hardening has to do with resisting and stopping the revelation from coming in. Pharaoh is emblematic of the human heart in its fallen condition, showing the depth of unbelief to which one may go—to neglect, avoid, resist, and deny the knowledge of God. This is especially shown in his rejection of God's mercy revealed in the curse—the death of the firstborn and drowning in the sea. God appointed Pharaoh for the very purpose of making His glory known, while Pharaoh remained in the darkness of unbelief. He did not know and acknowledge God as he should.

Korah: Unbelief Regarding God's Appointed Ruler

The rebellion of Korah was presumptuous, high-handed, and warned against explicitly, yet he still rebelled. Did Korah believe that Moses was the only one chosen by God? He did not. There was an element of unbelief. That is precisely what he did *not* believe. That is what was settled—or more settled—when they took Aaron's rod, along with the other rods, and put them before the tabernacle, and Aaron's rod "bud-

---

46. *Romans 10:1–3.*

47. *Acts 7.*

ded, blossomed and produced almonds."[48] This was his unbelief: "You have gone too far! The whole community is holy, every one of them, and the LORD is with them. Why then do you set yourselves above the LORD's assembly?" (Num. 16:3b). Korah's rebellion was due to unbelief.

Satan: Believes God's Existence but Misunderstands God's Nature

In the case of the demons, we will see that they profess certain things. In the Garden of Eden, Satan did not deny the existence of God, *per se*, but what Satan did deny was the nature of God. He said, "You will be like God, knowing good and evil" (Gen. 3:5b). Does he remember and realize that there is a radical distinction between the infinite and the finite? When Satan challenged God in relation to Job, did he believe in the perseverance of the saints?[49] When Satan worked to bring about the destruction of Christ, did he know and understand the Scripture? Did he know that the destruction of Christ would be the fulfillment of the prophecy? When we look at what the demons know when they say, "You are the Son of God!"[50] we have to ask ourselves about the meaning of what they understand. No doubt they believe that there is a being who exists and who is powerful, but whether they believe that being is so powerful as to be omnipotent, and that they are finite creatures—that question, I think, remains to be examined.[51]

Agrippa: Knew of the Prophets, but Did Not Understand Their Message

Agrippa did not believe what Paul was saying about the Messiah. Paul said, "King Agrippa, do you believe the prophets? I know you do" (Acts 26:27). We have to ask, in what sense does Agrippa believe? Does he really know and believe with understanding, so that the inference that follows is that he should believe what Paul said? Paul may have said this in a context of courtesy, as he did when speaking to the Athenians— quoting some of their own poets—appealing to what you might call

---

48. *Numbers 17:8.*

49. Gangadean, *The Westminster Confession,* 189–195.

50. *Luke 4:41.*

51. *The Contradictoriness of Sin,* Surrendra Gangadean.

their 'better knowledge' regarding what they *should* know, or what they profess to know, or what they claim to know. In any case, Agrippa did *not* believe what Paul was saying. He said, "Do you think that in such a short time you can persuade me to be a Christian?" (Acts 26:28b). He was not persuaded. It is not that he *knew* and did not believe.

Kadesh Barnea: Unbelief Regarding the Power of God

Was the case of the Israelites at Kadesh Barnea a case of knowing and not doing? The spies brought a false report and caused fear to come upon the people. This was a case of culpable ignorance. They should have seen that, even in light of the report, the Lord would deliver them, because He delivered them out of the power of Egypt. God provided. But there was the factor of a false report: "There we saw the giants . . . and we were like grasshoppers in our own sight, and so we were in their sight" (Num. 13:33, NKJV). In the context of slowness to understand the acts of God—for quite some time before this—you can understand their slowness to understand and trust in God. They saw the acts of God but did not see and know the nature of God. Psalm 78:22 says of the Israelites, "for they did not believe in God or trust in his deliverance."

Nicodemus: Failed to Understand the Need for Regeneration

Jesus said to Nicodemus, "Are you the teacher of Israel, and do not know these things?" (Jn. 3:10b NKJV). It is not that Nicodemus knew and was suppressing the truth. Nicodemus had known some of the basics, but he had taken the sign for the reality, the way many have, in the case of circumcision. Circumcision spoke about regeneration, of being born again. When Nicodemus had been called to practice circumcision, he had not heard or understood Moses and the prophets: circumcise your heart and not your flesh.[52] He did not understand that circumcision is a sign of regeneration and being born again. Nicodemus should have known this, and he overlooked it. Here are cases where we can say that it is not that they know and do not do, but there is a failure to know.

---

52. *Deuteronomy 30:6; Jeremiah 4:4.*

ALTERNATIVE EXPLANATIONS FOR
UNDERSTANDING 'KNOWING AND NOT DOING'

There are many ways in which we can claim to know and not do. (1) We could, as in the case of Peter, *have unbelief and not do*. Peter rebuked Jesus, saying, "Never, Lord! . . . This shall never happen to you!" (Matt. 16:22b NKJV). Peter did not confess Christ but denied Him three times. (2) Or we can *say and not do*, as in the case of the Pharisees: "Do not do what they do, for they do not practice what they preach" (Matt. 23:3b). (3) Or we can *hear and not do*, as in the case of believers, often hearing and not doing. James says, "Be doers of the word, and not hearers only" (Jas. 1:22a NKJV). (4) Or we can *want to do and not do*. Paul says, "For what I do is not the good I want to do; no, the evil I do not want to do—this I keep on doing" (Rom. 7:19). (5) Or unbelievers can *oppose and not do*. (6) Or we can *think we are doing and not do*: "a time is coming when anyone who kills you will think he is offering a service to God"(Jn. 16:2b). (7) Or we can *have trials of faith and not do*, when the unbelief that is in us comes to the surface and takes over: "In the spring, at the time when kings go off to war . . . David remained at Jerusalem" (2 Sam. 11:1). (8) Or we can *not do because of negligence*: "The worries of this life, the deceitfulness of wealth and the desires for other things come in and choke the word" (Mk. 4:19). (9) Or we can *not do because of ignorance*: "Who is this that darkens my counsel with words without knowledge?" (Job 38:2). There are many explanations for 'not doing.' To just say that they *know and not do* is problematic.

SUPPRESSION AND BELIEF:
Do Believers Suppress the Truth?

I want to ask other questions about this. Is it just nonbelievers who suppress the truth? Are there believers who suppress the truth? Is it only the nonbeliever suppressing the truth, or is the believer also suppressing the truth? When we were at the debate on baptism, I believe the truth was spoken by the Pedobaptists. Were the Anabaptists suppressing the truth? Would the Anabaptists say that the Pedobaptists were suppressing the truth? Are the Arminians suppressing the truth? Do they 'know deep down' that it is false, yet they say no to the truth? If you think that way, you will not engage more carefully with the arguments and objections raised by those with whom we disagree.[53]

ADMIXTURE OF BELIEF AND UNBELIEF IN THE BELIEVER

John Frame says, "The believer knows and does not know at the same time."[54] Frame's position is different from those who claim that the unbeliever knows and does not do. Frame is saying that the unbeliever knows and does not know. I want to read just a brief passage by Frame from *The Doctrine of the Knowledge of God*:

> The last paragraph represents the most adequate view of the matter that I know of. Yet the question remains a very mysterious one. Scripture says that the unbeliever knows and that he does not know. Scripture does not give us an epistemological elucidation in as many terms; that elucidation must be drawn carefully out of what Scripture says about other matters. And much more work remains to be done before we will have a formulation that is credible to the church (even the Reformed churches) generally. Van Til is at his best in his *Introduction to Systematic Theology* (24–27) where he admits the difficulty of the questions (something he does not often do) and rests content with a description of the natural man as "a mixture of truth with error" (27). I will continue to assume the truth of the analysis under j above, but I would not advise anyone to be dogmatic about the details. Certainly they should not be used as tests of orthodoxy.

In another passage he says, "The believer and the unbeliever differ epistemologically in that for the believer the truth is dominant over the lie, and for the unbeliever vice versa." Some of you remember when I drew the double circles in class.[55] Both belief and unbelief are present in each person—no one is fully conscious and consistent—but one is

---

53. The audio recording cuts off for a few minutes on this portion of the lecture, but we have the remainder of this chapter.

54. John M. Frame, *The Doctrine of the Knowledge of God, A Theology of Lordship* (Phillipsburg, NJ: P&R Publishing, 1987).

55. This is a reference to an illustration where, at the core of each person, there is either unbelief or belief operating. Outside of the core, there is belief in the unbeliever and unbelief

always more basic than the other. I think Frame comes the closest in this point to affirming the admixture in each person without articulating it specifically. We can, from understanding the old and the new nature, draw that inference.

HOW TO RESOLVE THE DISPUTE

(1) If You Know It, You Can Show It

I would suggest that the way to resolve this dispute is to ask those who claim that they do have knowledge, and it is clear, to show that clarity.

(2) Show the Relevant Lack of Knowledge

In any examples given to show knowing and not doing, we need to show the relevant lack of knowledge—whether it is the demons, or the case of James 4:13–17, or Jonah. Jonah says, "That is why I was so quick to flee to Tarshish. I knew that you are a gracious and compassionate God, slow to anger and abounding in love, a God who relents from sending calamity" (Jon. 4:2b). Jonah did not want the Lord to have mercy on the Ninevites, because Jonah knew that, at some point, the Ninevites were going to come in and destroy Israel. He wanted them to be destroyed before they destroyed Israel. Jonah had a lack of understanding when he was mourning over the plant that came up overnight and perished, but he was not willing to mourn over the Ninevites, on whom God had bestowed so much labor. We can identify the thinking that is going on in Jonah, and the Lord spoke to Jonah:

> You have been concerned about this vine, though you did not tend it or make it grow. It sprang up overnight and died overnight. But Nineveh has more than a hundred and twenty thousand people who cannot tell their right hand from their left, and many cattle as well. Should I not be concerned about that great city? (Jon. 4:10–11).

James says, "Therefore, to him who knows to do good and does not do it, to him it is sin" (Jas. 4:17, NKJV). This is said in the context of a person boasting: "Now listen, you who say, 'Today or tomorrow we

---

in the believer. The core belief displaces the other over time. This is part of our finitude, our temporality, and our changeability—the formal/larger aspect of our shared humanity.

will go to this or that city, spend a year there, carry on business and make money.' Why, you do not even know what will happen tomorrow. What is your life? You are a mist that appears for a little while and then vanishes" (Jas. 4:13–14). It is not the case that this person knows, and while knowing his life is a mist, he continues to say, 'Today or tomorrow we will go to this or that city, spend a year there, carry on business and make money.' He forgets; he is a forgetful hearer—there is such a category. It is not that they know, have that knowledge in their minds, and are continuing, or somehow they are actively suppressing the truth; we let a lot of things slip because we are not actively seeking the Lord.

These passages can be looked at and dealt with by showing the relevant lack of knowledge and pointing out that we do not seek, and we turn aside. This is true for all the examples listed above—whether Adam, Job, David, Peter, or Paul (before he was converted)—because we all share in the same sin: we do not seek God as we should, and we lose sight of God as the rewarder of those who diligently seek Him.[56] At any moment, we can be either seeking the Lord or not seeking the Lord. There is no in-between point. We can go from belief to unbelief by not continuing to seek the Lord. We come short and fail to see what we should do until the Lord tests us.

(3) The Split Is Within the Understanding, Between the Old and the New Nature

We need to explain that the split is within the understanding—between the old nature and the new nature—and that the failure to do is due to a lack of understanding and misunderstanding at the time of acting in unbelief. That is what we need to address when we affirm what Christ says regarding sanctification: "Sanctify them by the truth; your word is truth" (Jn. 17:17).

(4) Objective Clarity Is Sufficient for Responsibility

Knowledge does not have to actually 'get through.' We would not say that with Peter, the knowledge actually got through that Christ should suffer and then be raised, because Jesus told him point blank that Christ must suffer and Peter responded by correcting the Lord. Is it that he

---

56. *Hebrews 11:6.*

knew that Christ was going to suffer and then proceeded to say, "Far be it from you Lord"?[57] No, there was a misunderstanding in Peter, but he was responsible, and the Lord rebuked him.

Even for those who persecuted the Lord, He says, "Father, forgive them; for they know not what they do" (Lk. 23:34a KJV). It is culpable ignorance, and it is not just those who are crucifying the Lord, those driving nails in His hand. It is all of those who are participating in the process. Otherwise, Jesus would be praying only for those who are driving the nails in His hands. His prayer is relevant for those who persecute Him, in the spirit of the Beatitudes: "Blessed are you when people insult you, persecute you and falsely say all kinds of evil against you because of me" (Matt. 5:11).

Objective clarity is sufficient for responsibility, and we distinguish that from subjective clarity—whether it 'gets through.' The suppression can be the root-unbelief pushing against the remaining belief that is in us. There is going to be a suppression, just as belief suppresses unbelief in the believer, so unbelief suppresses the remaining belief in the unbeliever. There is a psychological state, but we need to recognize more clearly how to explain it. Just as people explain faith as something originated from us: 'We are choosing God.' I think they misunderstand the experience by not recognizing that God chooses us. God works in our hearts through regeneration;[58] God quickens us; God brings us to understanding and conviction, and then we have faith.[59] We do not understand our own experience; we think we know our hearts but do not know our own hearts.

CONCLUSION

We can overcome a good part of this conflict by (1) showing the relevant lack of knowledge. (2) Show that misunderstanding is a result of not seeking. (3) Show the split within the understanding itself. (4) Lastly, establish objective clarity and responsibility versus subjective

---

57. *Matthew 16:22* NKJV.

58. Gangadean, *The Westminster Confession,* 143–148; Gangadean, *The Westminster Catechisms,* 191–192; Gangadean, *The Epistle to the Hebrews,* 306–309.

59. Gangadean, *The Westminster Confession,* 143–206; Gangadean, *The Westminster Catechisms,* 191–207.

clarity. Our example should be that of the Lord. The Lord acted in such a way as to shut the mouths of those who opposed Him, so that "no one dared to ask him any more questions" (Lk. 20:40). It does not mean that they believed, but their mouths were shut. He pronounced judgment on those who had revelation, whether it got into them or not. "Woe to you, Korazin! Woe to you, Bethsaida!" (Matt. 11:21a). "Woe to you, teachers of the law and Pharisees, you hypocrites!" (Matt. 23:13a). The Lord explained to His disciples from the Scriptures on the way to Emmaus, He did not say that they knew, but that they should have known. "How foolish you are, and how slow of heart to believe all that the prophets have spoken!" (Lk. 24:25).

Keep in mind always that the goal is to make God known and to see the earth filled with the knowledge of God. The life of the intellect is very important, and it is out of this life of the intellect that holiness comes: "Sanctify them by the truth; your word is truth" (Jn. 17:17). Out of knowledge and holiness comes righteousness by which we obey. In so doing, I believe we will imitate the Lord and honor His Word.

Appendix C

ON THE NECESSITY FOR NATURAL THEOLOGY

With a Program to Engage Internal and External Objections to Christian Theism

2004

ABSTRACT

NATURAL THEOLOGY ATTEMPTS TO SHOW what can be known of God and man, and good and evil from general revelation. Skepticism maintains that this knowledge is not possible, and fideism maintains that proof is not necessary. The failure of skepticism and fideism to preserve meaning makes natural theology necessary. In addition, historic Christian belief in creation–fall–redemption requires natural theology in order to be meaningfully believed. To show what is clear (about God) from general revelation requires a clearer understanding of reason and presuppositional thinking. A program of natural theology to engage internal and external objections to Christian theism is offered.

INTRODUCTION

Natural theology attempts to show what can be known of God and man, and good and evil from general revelation. Skepticism, in general, maintains that knowledge is not possible; hence, natural theology is not possible. Fideism, in general, maintains that proof for one's first principles is not necessary; hence, natural theology is not necessary. Before engaging in its program, natural theology must show why proof is necessary and how knowledge is possible. The possibility, necessity, and extent of the knowledge of God become more evident in historic

Christian theism, which is based on the overarching and undergirding themes of creation–fall–redemption.[1]

THE NECESSITY FOR PROOF AND THE POSSIBILITY OF KNOWLEDGE

Skepticism: Knowledge Is Not Possible

In the history of skepticism, from ancient to contemporary, the basis of skepticism has shifted. At times, it is grounded metaphysically in various formulations of the problem of the one and the many. At other times, it is grounded epistemologically in variations of empiricism and rationalism. Most recently, it has been grounded in hermeneutics, in issues related to interpreting experience and constructing worldviews. From time to time, it has been grounded in the nature of knowledge itself, whether knowledge is discursive, cognitive, and propositional, or whether it is relational, mystical, and a matter of encounter.

Metaphysical Skepticism: No Object of Knowledge

Metaphysical skepticism denies that there is an object of knowledge. In the ancient world, this was done in two ways: either all is flux (becoming without being—Heraclitus, or all is *dukkha*, dependently co-arising—Buddhism), or all is permanent (being without becoming—Parmenides, or all is one, beyond all dualities—Shankara's *Advaita*). Where all is permanent, change is an illusion (*maya*). Where all is change, permanence is an illusion (no object, no self). Since knowledge of the world involves permanence and change (some change in permanence and some permanence in change), on the assumption that all is one (either change or permanence), knowledge is not possible. The dualism of Plato and Aristotle attempted to address the problem of permanence and change but left significant problems unresolved.[2]

---

1. *The Biblical Worldview*, Surrendra Gangadean.

2. Gangadean, *History of Philosophy*, 87–105.

Epistemological Skepticism: The Limits of Experience and Reason

Epistemological skepticism reckons with the limits of experience and reason as they have been used in the modern period (Enlightenment). Experience may come through ordinary sense experience (common sense), sense experience systematically pursued (science), or inner experience (intuition). Ordinary experience gives appearance, not reality (Is the ocean blue? Does the sun rise?). Furthermore, through sense experience, we cannot know that there is an external world or material substance (Berkeley), nor causality or a self as perceiver (Hume). Science does not attempt to show that the external world exists, that all is matter, or that matter is eternal. Naturalism is the methodological assumption of science and empiricism, held on pragmatic grounds, with a tentativeness that disinvites philosophical criticism. Intuition admits of no corrective process, but neither are the deliverances of intuition self-certifying. Truth (or goodness) is not always connected with beauty, and what is called enlightenment experience (nirvana, *samadhi*) becomes inescapably connected with interpretations that are irreconcilable.

Methodological doubt of ordinary (or extraordinary) experience led Descartes to what he took to be the first and indubitable truth of reason ("I think, therefore I am"), upon which he attempted to erect a superstructure of knowledge (foundationalism). But the *cogito* became doubted in light of monism (absolute idealism) along with the mind/body and subject/object distinctions.[3] The existence of the self is no more self-evident than the existence of God ("We hold these truths to be self-evident, that all men are created equal"[4]). Furthermore, the traditional proofs for the existence of God (ontological, cosmological, and teleological), taken separately, were found problematic at least, over a period of time.[5] And reason seemed to present us with equally coherent and incommensurable worlds (Leibniz and Spinoza).[6] Kant's synthesis of sense experience and reason left the world beyond appearance (the noumenal world), devoid of cognizable content, and open to the

---

3. Gangadean, *History of Philosophy,* 131–133.

4. Declaration of Independence, 1776.

5. Gangadean, "Paper No. 3: The Principle of Clarity," in *The Logos Papers,* 15–20.

6. Gangadean, *History of Philosophy,* 133–137.

speculation that followed.[7] Reason, with its tendency to universalize, was seen as incapable of grasping the particulars of the real world (Nietzsche) or the concrete situation in which all exists (Kierkegaard).

Hermeneutical Skepticism: Situatedness, Alterity, and Incommensurability

Far from reason being a transcendent standard that gives knowledge of an objective world in which we exist, hermeneutical skepticism holds that reason (as well as science) is itself subject to the situation in which we find ourselves. We are always historically situated and cannot transcend our history. The world we live in is constructed on the basis of our identities and language, grounded in our social context. There is no objective world in itself (anti-realism). The canons of rationality differ from one worldview to another. All is interpretation (Nietzsche). We are bound in a hermeneutical circle. Claims to objectivity are attempts to privilege one's own position for advantage over others. This is inevitably repressive of the other in the name of a common standard defined by one's own meta-narrative. Since all things are understood within the confines of one's meta-narrative, one must recognize incommensurability between worldviews, the reality of alterity, and the ultimacy of difference. This recognition is said to be the virtue of tolerance. Hermeneutical skepticism says our beliefs are inescapably without proof and should be recognized as such. Fideism acquiesces to this.

Fideism: Belief Without Proof of First Principles

Fideism applies to all interpretive belief systems that make no attempt to prove their first principles, especially in light of existing challenges to them. It applies to theism as well as to anti-theism, to science as well as to philosophy, to realism as well as to anti-realism, and to foundationalism as well as to anti-foundationalism. It occurs whenever the reasons given are not sufficient to rationally exclude competing views. While fideism applies to a wide range of views, most discussions have focused on theistic fideism, particularly on Christian fideism. Christians have attempted to give reasons for their beliefs, but in light of the challenges of skepticism, Christian fideism has responded by maintaining that

---

7. Gangadean, *History of Philosophy,* 151–158.

either reason (proof) is not necessary for belief, is not sufficient for belief, or is not called for by Scripture.

Reason (Proof) Is Not Necessary for Faith

That reason (proof) is not necessary for belief in God seems obvious since many believe without proof. Many maintain that faith, by definition, is not sight (proof), and many have no idea of the proofs as they have been given historically. Some have argued that reason is not necessary since belief in God is properly basic, like belief in the external world, for which proof seems irrelevant. Properly basic beliefs occur naturally under certain conditions if one's cognitive faculties are properly functioning. Natural belief in God is warranted without proof, although warrant may be weakened in the presence of objections if they are unanswered (Plantinga).[8] Again, reason is said to be unnecessary for faith since faith is said to precede understanding and that we must believe in order that we might understand. Having first believed, faith then seeks to understand (Augustine).[9] And again, reason is said to be unnecessary, since faith is by grace and not a work of human reason (Barth).

Reason Is Insufficient for Faith

Furthermore, reason is said to be insufficient for faith. The proofs do not seem to persuade most people to believe, nor does knowing move someone to act. People are said to know, deep down, the truth of God's existence and yet suppress this truth, and to know what is right yet still do what is wrong.[10] Reason is said to be finite and incapable of discovering or apprehending the mysteries of the faith, which remain paradoxes to the intellect even after they are made known by revelation. If some are able to come to the truth of first things through dialectic, this is not available to most (Plato's *Allegory of the Cave*) and is accessible only to a few minds that have been trained in metaphysics (Aquinas).[11] Faith is said to be inaccessible to reason. The individual before God, in his

---

8. Gangadean, *History of Philosophy*, 175–177.

9. Gangadean, *History of Philosophy*, 111–114.

10. See: "Prolegomena to Paul's Gospel: The Biblical Doctrine of Clarity and Inexcusability" and "Appendix B: Contra Voluntarism: On Knowing and Not Doing," in this book; Gangadean, "Paper No. 120: Contra Voluntarism," in *The Logos Papers*, 611–647.

11. Gangadean, *History of Philosophy*, 121–126.

unique particularity (Abraham called to sacrifice Isaac), has no guidance possible from reason, which deals in universals. Faith is a leap beyond reason (Kierkegaard).[12] Reason is said to be fallen and fallible, and its use, apart from revelation, leads man away from God. Reason is said to be conditioned by pre-theoretical commitments so that all proofs are, in the end, circular, reflecting one's presupposition. Lastly, reason itself is said to be insufficient for justification but is thought to itself require justification, which can be found only in God—specifically, in the Triune God of the Bible (Van Til/Bahnsen).

Reason Is Not Called for and Is Opposed by Scripture

There are reasons offered for fideism based on an appeal to Scripture. There are no proofs given in Scripture for the existence of God, so it is thought that no proof is necessary. This view assumes that everything needed by the believer is expressly given in Scripture and in a form that does not require good and necessary consequences. This view affirms the sole authority of Scripture (*Sola Scriptura*) over and against all other authorities, including reason and general revelation, not merely over all other appeals to special revelation and to persons as authorities. It is pointed out that there are warnings raised in Scripture against the wisdom of this world and against vain philosophy (*simpliciter*). Scripture is said to exalt the proclamation of things foolish in the eyes of the world, and this is understood in a way that excludes reasoning and persuasion. Furthermore, the fullness of blessing is said to be reserved for those faithful in this life who will, in life after death, see God face to face (beatific vision). The highest good, therefore, does not require and is not accessible to the life of reason.

THE NECESSITY FOR NATURAL THEOLOGY

The Inadequacy of Non-Cognitivism: No Experience Is Meaningful Without Interpretation

One response to the pressing weight of skepticism and fideism is to argue that the knowledge of God (and of the world) is not discursive,

---

12. Gangadean, "Paper No. 128: Abraham's Faith," 665–666; "Paper No. 129: Faith and Reason in the Life of Abraham" in *The Logos Papers*, 667–669.

to be attained by reason and inference. It is more akin to knowledge by experience, through acquaintance or encounter. It cannot be expressed in words or communicated to another through words; one must have the experience. This knowledge is non-cognitive (not a matter of true or false) and non-propositional (not to be argued for or against). It is immediate, direct, personal, relational, and mystical—like an embrace. While it is true enough that thinking is not the same as, nor a substitute for, experience, it is equally the case that experience is not the same as, nor a substitute for, thinking. They are two distinct but inseparable aspects of human knowledge. We do not simply experience, but we 'experience as.' An embrace has significance in light of assumptions about the other in the embrace—assumptions not derived from the experience itself, assumptions of which we may become more conscious and critical and perhaps change so that the significance of the embrace may change or deepen over time in one and the same person. No experience is meaningful without interpretation. Any appeal to experience stripped of interpretation becomes meaningless. The shift to non-cognitivism in order to possess knowledge, without engaging with the objections of skepticism and fideism and without engaging in natural theology, is in vain, since experience devoid of meaning is empty. A different strategy is required, one that can show the inadequacy of both skepticism and fideism, even as non-cognitivism is inadequate.

The Negative Value of Skepticism

Skepticism has value.[13] Its value is negative. Its lasting value is that it will not let fideism pass without identifying itself as such. Skepticism is aware of the arbitrariness of fideism when it claims to be objective and exclusive and finds that arbitrariness self-destructive. However, skepticism reaches an overextended conclusion (that no knowledge is possible) by assuming it has considered all relevant assumptions. There are assumptions that skepticism has not considered.

Skepticism Arises from Uncritically Held Assumptions

There are alternatives to the assumption of monism (either nothing is eternal or all is eternal). There are alternatives to ontological dualism

---

13. Gangadean, *History of Philosophy,* xxi–xxvii, 9–12.

(both matter and spirit are eternal). Theism, the view that only some (God the Creator) is eternal, is an alternative to both monism and dualism. There are alternatives to rationalism, to empiricism, and to the synthesis of the two, which recognize what is uncritically assumed in both. There are alternatives to science (pure facts without interpretation) and deconstruction (pure interpretation without facts). One can identify and distinguish pure experience or fact (for example, the embrace) from its significance, which is given by interpretation. If there were no alternatives to the assumptions it has considered, then skepticism would be granted. However, if it were granted and carried out consistently, skepticism would lead to nihilism, the destruction of all meaning by the destruction of all distinctions. Qualified skepticism ("this view is incoherent") is possible; total skepticism ("all views are incoherent") becomes self-referentially absurd.

The Positive Value of Fideism

Fideism, too, has value, and its value is positive. It recognizes the impossibility of nihilism to which skepticism leads and the inadequacy of pragmatism to overcome self-conscious nihilism. Positions of fideism purport to offer their adherents a meaningful vision of the world. A more self-conscious fideism maintains its right to exist by an exclusivist claim to truth and meaning. However, fideism wishes to make some distinction between faith and understanding. In the motto "faith seeking understanding," it is assumed that one can believe more than one understands. If it were possible to believe more than one understands, then one could believe what one did not understand. To open a gap between believing p to be true and understanding p is to affirm p while emptying p of meaning. In contrast, "I believe in so far as I understand" preserves meaning by noting the inherent connection between belief and understanding and faith and reason: I believe p as far as I understand p. There is more to understand of p, and I seek to understand more of p, but I do not, and cannot, believe more than I understand. If "faith seeking understanding" means "understanding seeking more understanding," there is nothing controversial here. By faith, I believe p to be true; by reason, I understand the meaning of p. As truth is inseparable from meaning, so faith is inseparable from reason. It is not the case that faith is static while understanding grows in "faith seeking understanding." Faith grows as understanding grows; faith is tested as understanding is tested.

Biblical Faith Is Inseparable from Reason, Understanding, Certainty, and Proof

Faith, in the theistic sense, is directed to what is invisible.[14] Faith is contrasted with sight, which is directed to the visible, but it is not contrasted with understanding, which is directed to what is invisible. Faith in Christian theism is the substance of things hoped for, the evidence of things not seen.[15] Since faith is inseparable from understanding, the certainty of faith is the certainty of understanding. The certainty of understanding in faith is not different from the certainty of understanding a proof for what is unseen. Fideism, therefore, insofar as it separates faith and understanding, empties faith of meaning and nullifies its purpose, which is to offer its adherents a meaningful vision of the world. However, insofar as it does not separate faith and understanding, it has the certainty of proof in its understanding. True faith, contrary to fideism, is inseparable from reason, understanding, certainty, and proof. Faith without reason and proof—that is, fideism—is empty of meaning. Fideism fails in the same way that skepticism fails. Both fail to preserve meaning. Both failures make natural theology necessary.

Historic Christianity Is Structured on the Biblical Worldview

There is a third set of reasons why natural theology is necessary. Historic Christianity is structured on the theme of creation–fall–redemption. The implications of each of these, when understood, require natural theology.

Historic Christianity Assumes the Reality of Sin

Since sin is a reality in Christianity, Christianity must give some account of sin. Unbelief is regarded as root sin. Unbelief is inexcusable because there is a clear general revelation of the existence and nature of God in creation. Since the creation of the world God's invisible qualities—his eternal power and divine nature—have been clearly seen, being un-

---

14. Gangadean, *The Biblical Worldview*, 3–20; Gangadean, *The Epistle to the Hebrews*, 167–201, 271–286.

15. *Hebrews 11:1* KJV.

derstood from what is made, so that men are without excuse.[16] Men are without excuse for unbelief of what is clear. If there is no clarity of general revelation for which one is held accountable, there can be no sin. But if there is clarity of general revelation, then presumably, one should be able to see what is clear. And since it is clear, one should be able to show what is clear, especially over and against objections that deny clarity. To see what is clear is to see why the denial of clarity fails. Christian theists, believing in the reality of sin, should be able to show what is clear. To do so would be to do natural theology.

Historic Christianity Affirms Divine Judgment on Sin

Historic Christianity not only affirms the reality of sin but also affirms divine judgment on sin. The wages of sin is death.[17] This death is present in unbelief in this life and in the life to come. This death is spiritual and inherent in unbelief. It is the meaninglessness that is inherent in the failure to see what is clear at the most basic level of all one's understanding. This death is also said to be everlasting. Everlasting death is a maximal consequence. Maximal consequence requires maximal inexcusability, which in turn requires maximal clarity. The contradiction of what is maximally clear is not logically possible. Maximal clarity can be avoided only by ceasing to think—that is, by giving up or denying reason itself. Natural theology in Christian theism must show maximal clarity.

Historic Christianity Affirms Redemption

Christ is the Lamb of God who takes away the sin of the world.[18] If sense is to be made of the death of Christ, by which sin and death are removed, then clarity and inexcusability must be shown by natural theology.

Historic Christianity Holds to Salvation by Christ Alone

Historic Christianity has been exclusivist, believing that redemption is through Christ alone. It also holds that Christ's redemption is for all peoples. If people are called away from competing worldviews to the

---

16. *Romans 1:20.*

17. *Romans 6:23.*

18. *John 1:29.*

Christian worldview, reasons for the truth of its exclusive claims that do not beg the question must be given. This requires natural theology.

Historic Christianity Holds to the Good as the Knowledge of God

Historic Christianity holds up the highest good and the goal of life as the knowledge of God. Creation and history reveal God. Through an age-long and agonizing spiritual war, good will overcome evil. The earth shall be full of the knowledge of God as the waters cover the sea.[19] If God's justice and mercy are to be understood, the inexcusability of unbelief must be understood. If we do not understand clarity, then we cannot understand inexcusability. But if we understand clarity, then we can show clarity. This is the work of natural theology.

WHAT IS REASON?

Some clarification in the understanding of reason is necessary to show more specifically how knowledge is possible. There are different senses of reason that must be kept clearly in mind whenever the term *reason* and its derivatives are used. First, there is reason in itself, which is to be distinguished from reason in its use and reason in us. There are different uses of reason and different aspects of reason in us.

Reason in Itself

Reason in itself is *the laws of thought*. These laws are, most basically, the law of identity (*a* is *a*), the law of non-contradiction (not both *a* and *non-a*, at the same time and in the same respect), and the law of excluded middle (either *a* or *non-a*). These have been commonly accepted, at a minimum, in the history of philosophy as the laws of reason and the laws of thought. The terms *finite* and *fallen* may apply to human users of these laws but not to the laws themselves. These terms may describe a failure to use reason critically rather than a failure of reason itself. When any of these laws are broken, reason is not being used, and thinking ceases.

---

19. *Isaiah 11:9.*

Reason in Its Use

Reason is used *to form* concepts, judgments, and arguments, which are the forms of all thought. Reason is used *critically* as a test for meaning. Meaning is more basic than truth; we must know what a statement means before we can know if it is true. When a law of thought is violated, there is no meaning. Reason is used *to interpret* experience in light of one's basic beliefs. Reason is also used *constructively* to build a coherent world-and-life view. The constructive use of reason is not the same as the critical use. Reason should be used critically first, to test one's basic beliefs for meaning, before constructing a worldview upon them. Likewise, the interpretive use must be distinguished from the critical use. Much confusion in hermeneutical skepticism can be avoided by observing these distinctions.

Reason in Us

Reason in us is *natural*, not conventional. It is universal—the same in all persons. It is a common ground between all worldviews. It is the source of coherence in constructing a worldview and in testing the meaning of its basic beliefs. It is the Common Ground by which thoughts (concepts, judgments, and arguments) are formed and the means by which experience is interpreted in light of basic beliefs. Reason in us, as Common Ground, is not historically situated; it is universal. This prevents incommensurability between worldviews, even when the basic beliefs of different worldviews are contradictory.

 Reason is *ontological*. It applies to being as well as to thought. There are no square-circles, no uncaused events, and no being from non-being. God is not both eternal and not eternal, at the same time and in the same respect. If reason did not apply to being, then statements could be true and not true, at the same time and in the same respect. If *a* could be *non-a*, then being could not be distinguished from non-being. All distinctions would lose meaning, and all meaning would be lost.

 Reason is *transcendental*. It is authoritative. It is self-attesting—the highest authority. It cannot be questioned because it makes questioning possible. A statement that violates a law of reason is not meaningful and cannot be true, regardless of its source.

 Reason is also *fundamental*. It is fundamental to other aspects of human personality. Thought supplies the belief concerning the good as the object of desire, and thought and desire move a person to act. It is knowing the truth that sets a person free.

Rational Presuppositionalism: Reason Testing Basic Beliefs for Meaning

Thinking is presuppositional. This follows from the nature of reason in itself, reason in its use, and reason in us. We think of what is less basic in light of what is more basic. We think of truth in light of meaning; we think of experience in light of basic belief; we think of conclusion in light of premises; we think of the temporal in light of the eternal, and the finite in light of the infinite. We must know what a statement means before we can know if it is true. If it violates a law of reason, it is not meaningful because reason, as the laws of thought, is transcendental—it is the test for meaning and, thus, of what can and cannot be true. If a statement is meaningless, it cannot be true because reason is ontological. If there is agreement on what is more basic (that reason is the laws of thought, universal, ontological, and transcendental), there can be agreement on what is less basic. However, if there is doubt that reason is ontological, disagreement is not even possible because skepticism here lapses into nihilism and the loss of meaning.

Since thinking is presuppositional, and reason, as the test for meaning, is most basic, this position can be described as Rational Presuppositionalism.[20] It is a position distinct from empiricism, rationalism, and fideistic presuppositionalism.

THE FIRST APPLICATION OF RATIONAL PRESUPPOSITIONALISM:
Show There Must Be Something Eternal

The first act of reason is forming concepts, and the most basic concept is about existence. Since existence is either temporal (with a beginning) or eternal (without a beginning), and since the eternal is more basic than the temporal, our most basic concept is about eternal existence. The possible judgments concerning what is eternal are four: all is eter-

---

20. Gangadean, *History of Philosophy*, 19–23; Gangadean, "Paper No. 101: Rational Presuppositionalism," 521–526; "Paper No. 52: Common Ground (Part III)," in *The Logos Papers*, 281–282; Gangadean, *On Natural and Revealed Theology*, 59–66.

nal, none is eternal, some is eternal, and some is not eternal. Can we know if there is something eternal? The following is offered as proof that something must be eternal.

1. Contradictory statements cannot both be true and cannot both be false (at the same time and in the same respect).

2. The contradiction of "some is eternal" is "none is eternal."

3. If nothing is eternal, then:

   All is temporal.

   All had a beginning.

   All came into being.

4. If all came into being, then being came into existence from non-being.

5. Being from non-being is not possible.

6. Therefore, the original "none is eternal" is not possible.

7. Therefore, its contradiction "some is eternal" must be true.[21]

Being comes from being alone. Non-being is the absence of being and of the power of being to cause to be. If being could come from non-being, then there would be no distinction between being and non-being (*a* could be *non-a*). Skepticism and nihilism are the result.

It is clear through reason, therefore, that something must be eternal. To doubt this, one must give up reason. To give up reason is to give up meaning. "There must be something eternal" is *maximally* clear. The opposite is not possible. To doubt what is maximally clear, one must give up reason. To give up reason is to deny one's nature as a rational being and, in doing so, to bring upon oneself spiritual death, which is meaninglessness.

---

21. Gangadean, *Philosophical Foundation*, 61–65; Gangadean, *History of Philosophy*, 40–44; Gangadean, "Paper No. 3: The Principle of Clarity," in *The Logos Papers*, 15–20.

THE PROGRAM OF NATURAL THEOLOGY

The Goal of Natural Theology

The goal of natural theology is to show what is clear about God and man, and good and evil from general revelation. It is to respond to all objections raised against the knowledge of God, proceeding from what is most basic in general revelation to what is equally basic in special revelation. It must show all that is clear from general revelation, which is necessary for inexcusability, as well as respond to philosophical objections to the doctrines of special revelation. What follows is an outline of the objectives by which this goal is to be achieved. The objectives state what must be done and indicate, only in the most general way, how this may be done.

Outline of Objectives

Objective 1: Show That There Must Be Something Eternal[22]

Since eternal is our most basic concept and since God is eternal, it must be shown that there must be something eternal. This first step is necessary but not sufficient to prove the existence of God. This proof is a modification of the ontological argument: what cannot be logically conceived cannot exist.

Objective 2: Show That Only Some Is Eternal[23]

Since God is Creator of all things, only some (God) is eternal. All else is temporal. This step uses the cosmological argument in a variety of ways.

 i. *The material world is not eternal* (vs. material monism). It is not self-maintaining in general (entropy), in its parts (sun and stars), and as a whole (the Big Bang oscillating universe or the inflationary universe).

---

22. Gangadean, *Philosophical Foundation*, 61–65; Gangadean, *History of Philosophy*, 40–44; Gangadean, "Paper No. 3: The Principle of Clarity," in *The Logos Papers*, 15–20.

23. Gangadean, *Philosophical Foundation*, 71–161; Gangadean, *History of Philosophy*, 47–58; Gangadean, *The Westminster Confession*, 1–13; Gangadean, "Paper No. 3: The Principle of Clarity," 15–20; "Paper No. 39: Clarity," in *The Logos Papers*, 217–220.

ii. *The material world exists* (vs. ordinary idealism—Berkeley). The cause of what I see is not my mind or another mind but outside all minds.

iii. *The soul exists*—the mind is not the brain (vs. material monism). A neural impulse is not a mental image, nor does the mental image perceive itself.

iv. *The soul is not eternal* (vs. ordinary dualism—Plato, and qualified non-dualism—Ramanuja). The soul goes through unique events in time (growth in knowledge, enlightenment, etc.).

v. *The soul exists* (vs. absolute idealism, *Advaita*—Shankara). The soul is neither unreal, that is, an illusion/*maya*, nor real/eternal.

Objective 3: Respond to the Problem of Evil[24]

If God is all good and all powerful, why is there evil? The teleological argument is used to respond to the problem of natural evil and moral evil.

i. Natural evil (toil and strife, and old age, sickness, and death) is not necessary. Original creation was very good, without natural evil (vs. origin by evolution, natural or theistic).[25]

ii. Natural evil is due to moral evil. It is imposed not as punishment but as a call back from moral evil. Suffering is a call to stop and think.

iii. Moral evil is permitted for a purpose; it is made to serve the good through deepening of the divine revelation.

iv. There is an ironic solution to the problem of evil, requiring understanding the nature of evil in light of the clarity of general revelation.

---

24. Gangadean, *Philosophical Foundation*, 145–161; Gangadean, *On Natural and Revealed Theology*, 141–147; Gangadean, *The Biblical Worldview*, 219–239; Gangadean, "Paper No. 7: The Problem of Evil," in *The Logos Papers*, 33–39.

25. Gangadean, *The Westminster Confession*, 14–18; Gangadean, *On Natural and Revealed Theology*, 179–193.

Objective 4: Show the Moral Law from General Revelation[26]

If there is no moral law that is clear from general revelation, then human responsibility and moral evil are not possible. This moral law must be *clear*, *comprehensive*, and *critical*.

    i. *The moral law is clear* because it is grounded in the fundamental features of human nature. It is grounded in the reality of choice, in the nature of thinking, in the natural unity of our being, in the work required to bring into being and sustain being, in being born ignorant, in being born human, in being born of a sexual union, in valuing and producing what is of value, in being born equal, and in being born changeable.

    ii. *The moral law is comprehensive* in that it applies to all choices and all aspects of human nature that come to expression in choice.

    iii. *The moral law is critical.* The consequence of observing the moral law is life, which means obtaining the good; the consequence of not observing the law is spiritual death, both individual and corporate.

Objective 5: From Deism to Theism[27]

Deism maintains that God creates but does not act in history. Theism—Judaism, Christianity, and Islam—maintains that God creates and acts providentially in history, including, specifically, in giving scriptures.

    i. God acts in history by imposing natural evil. Natural evil is not part of the original creation and is not inherent in moral evil.

    ii. Natural evil, as a call back from moral evil, requires redemptive revelation to show how God can be both just and merciful.

    iii. Special revelation must be consistent with general revelation and must show how God is both just and merciful.

---

26. Gangadean, *Philosophical Foundation*, 171–284; Gangadean, *History of Philosophy*, 61–69; Gangadean, *The Westminster Catechisms*, 215–267; Gangadean, *The Westminster Confession*, 207–221; Gangadean, *On Natural and Revealed Theology*, 127–139, 166–178.

27. Gangadean, *The Westminster Confession*, 14–18; Gangadean, *The Biblical Worldview*, xvii–xix.

    iv. Biblical revelation alone is consistent with general revelation and shows how God is both just and merciful.

Objective 6: Respond to the Root of Conflict Among Theists

Judaism, Christianity, and Islam profess to hold some basic scriptures in common. Since scripture is redemptive revelation, the conflict between them is rooted in their understanding of the divine nature—specifically, how God is both just and merciful in redemption.

    i. Judaism and Christianity affirm that God is both just and merciful by nature, and that mercy must satisfy divine justice by atonement. Islam affirms that God has no nature by which He is bound; mercy can set aside divine justice—there is no need for atonement.

    ii. Biblical Judaism affirms the justice and mercy of God in vicarious atonement through the death of another, as seen in the temple sacrifice on the Day of Atonement. Post-biblical Judaism affirms that atonement is achieved in and by oneself.

    iii. Christianity affirms the justice and mercy of God in vicarious atonement through human representation—Christ in the place of Adam. The lamb symbolically represented Christ, in whose death the reality of atonement is accomplished.

Objective 7: Respond to Rational Challenges to Doctrines of Christianity

Non-theists and non-Christian theists have objected to ecumenical doctrines in Christianity. If Scripture is divine revelation, it must be shown that these doctrines, while not originating from human reasoning, are in accordance with reason and consistent with all that can be expected from both general and special revelation.

    i. *The doctrine of the Trinity*[28] requires an understanding of what is meant in saying that "God is one."

---

28. Gangadean, *The Westminster Confession*, 47–60; Gangadean, *The Westminster Catechisms*, 119–127.

ii. *The doctrine of the Incarnation*[29] requires an understanding of the unity and diversity of natures in one person.

iii. *The doctrine of the Fall*[30] requires an understanding of the nature of moral evil (sin) and of representation.

Objective 8: Respond to Philosophical Questions in the Continuing Divisions Within Christianity

Redemptive revelation in Scripture assumes the reality of sin in the failure to understand clear general revelation. Understanding Scripture assumes an understanding of general revelation. Continuing divisions within Christianity reveal a lack of understanding of what is clear in general revelation. The perspicuity of Scripture rests on the clarity of general revelation.

i. There is continuing division concerning the sufficiency of vicarious atonement—grace versus works.

ii. There is continuing division concerning divine sovereignty in predestination and human freedom and responsibility.

iii. There is continuing division concerning hermeneutics: what is literal interpretation, and what is contextual interpretation.

iv. There is continuing division concerning the good: is the knowledge of God gained through a direct vision of God in heaven, or is it the knowledge of God gained through the work of dominion on earth throughout history?[31]

CONCLUSION

Natural theology, I believe, is not only possible—it is *necessary*. The external and internal challenges to Christian theism have accumulated through the Enlightenment period, although their roots go back to an-

---

29. Gangadean, *The Gospel of Matthew,* xv–xxxiv.

30. Gangadean, *The Biblical Worldview,* 159–239; Gangadean, *The Westminster Confession,* 99–110; Gangadean, *The Westminster Catechisms,* 141–152; Gangadean, "Paper No. 145–147: The Biblical Worldview," in *The Logos Papers,* 733–757.

31. Gangadean, *The Biblical Worldview,* 109–124; Gangadean, *The Westminster Confession,* 353–357.

cient history. The need for natural theology today is more urgent, if not acute, as ancient worldviews come face to face. All human beings need meaning, and neither skepticism nor fideism can provide that meaning for human beings as they become more epistemologically self-conscious and consistent. A deeper understanding of reason, leading to a deeper, clearer, and more consistent understanding of good and evil, can lead us out of our present impasse and toward a unity and fullness we had not thought possible.[32]

---

32. *The Unity of the Church*, Surrendra Gangadean.

Appendix D

_____

THE TASK OF
CHRISTIAN PHILOSOPHY
Serving All Areas of Dominion
by Laying Foundation

2002

ABSTRACT

CHRISTIANITY PRESUPPOSES THE CLARITY OF general revelation. Clarity is the basis of inexcusability, and sin—as unbelief—is inexcusable. If there is no inexcusability, there is no sin and no need for Christianity as redemptive revelation. There are many challenges to theism in general and to Christian theism in particular. Responses to these have not been based on the assumption of clarity and inexcusability.[1] It is the task of Christian philosophy to respond to what challenges the clarity of general revelation. Knowing what is clear implies being able to show that unbelief in what is clear is contrary to reason. Christian philosophy must respond to skepticism and fideism, to various forms of non-theism (material monism, spiritual monism, and dualism), and to various forms of non-Christian theism (deism, Judaism, and Islam). Christian philosophy must also respond to ethical views that challenge the clarity of the moral law given in general revelation.

---

1. Gangadean, "Paper No. 102: The Clarity of General Revelation," 527–529; "Paper No. 41: What Is Clear About God," 225–229; "Paper No. 112: Why General Revelation Is Basic in the Christian Worldview," in *The Logos Papers,* 583–585; Gangadean, *On Natural and Revealed Theology,* 213–222; Gangadean, *The Epistle to the Hebrews,* 255–271.

WHAT CHRISTIAN PHILOSOPHY MUST DO

Christianity presupposes the clarity of general revelation regarding the existence and nature of God, and the moral law written in the heart of man.[2] Christian philosophy must respond to the internal and external challenges to what is presupposed in Christianity. Christian philosophy must show that some things about God and man, and good and evil, are clear to reason, in contrast to all forms of skepticism and fideism. It must show that only some (God, the Creator) is eternal, in contrast to all forms of non-theism—nothing is eternal, or all is eternal. It must show that there is a moral law, grounded in human nature as created by God, in contrast to all forms of human autonomy.[3] In addition, Christian philosophy must respond to the internal challenges of theism (deism, Judaism, and Islam) and to the divisions within Christianity that are grounded in uncritically held assumptions.

Christian philosophy must justify the Christian notion of sin, death, and redemption by showing how sin (moral evil) is possible. It must show the connection between the clarity of general revelation and the inexcusability of unbelief. To show clarity, it must respond to the challenge of skepticism. There have been many responses to skepticism—from Plato to Plantinga, by Augustine and Aquinas, by Descartes and Kant, by Nietzsche and Quine, and by Wittgenstein and Derrida. Justification and warranted belief have been addressed, but the inexcusability of unbelief has not received sufficient attention.

Proofs for God's existence (if they succeed), or warrant for Christian belief, do not show clarity and inexcusability. Appeal to suppression of an instinctual knowledge of God does not show the inexcusability of unbelief. It does not show how alternatives to theism or to Christian theism are inexcusable (*anapologētos*, without reason).

Christian philosophy must fully defeat skepticism. If some things are not clear, then general revelation is not clear, and unbelief is excusable. Skepticism rests on uncritically held assumptions. In attempts to achieve knowledge, rationalism and empiricism fail to recognize assumptions and are vulnerable to doubt. Descartes' *cogito* requires more work to

---

2. *Romans 1:20, 2:14–15; Deuteronomy 30:11–14.*

3. Gangadean, *Philosophical Foundation*, 171–284; Gangadean, *History of Philosophy*, 61–69; Gangadean, *The Westminster Catechisms*, 215–267; Gangadean, *The Westminster Confession*, 207–221; Gangadean, *On Natural and Revealed Theology*, 127–139, 166–178.

establish the real existence of the self over against Vedantic idealism. Reid's common-sense realism requires more work to establish the real existence of the world over against Berkeley's idealism.

To overcome skepticism requires getting to the most basic level of thought. Reason, in itself, is the laws of thought (identity, non-contradiction, excluded middle). The laws of thought make thought possible. They cannot be questioned but make questioning possible. Reason, in its critical use, is a test for meaning. The meaning of a statement must be known before judging its truth. If a law of thought is violated, there is no meaning, and there can be no truth. Hence, there are no square-circles, no uncaused events, and no being from non-being. If we cannot know these things, nothing can be known. To avoid knowing some things, one has to deny reason itself. One cannot deny reason and retain any thought. Since we cannot avoid thought, we cannot deny reason. The attempt to deny reason to avoid what is clear is inexcusable.

The attempt to deny reason is an act contrary to human nature and is an act of self-destruction. To neglect, avoid, resist, or deny reason empties life of meaning, which leads to boredom and guilt, the state of spiritual death.[4] A Christian can argue that reason is the life of the logos (the Word of God) in all men.[5] To deny reason is to deny the life of God in man. The wages of sin is death.[6]

Suppose we can know some very basic things by reason. Can reason show the existence and nature of God? Can Christian philosophy answer the internal and external challenges to Christian theism? In light of the history of philosophy, is this not too daunting a task, foolhardy, an invitation to disaster? In reply, it can only be said that there is no choice if inexcusability requires clarity. The survival of Christianity as a vital cultural force requires that thoughts raised up against the knowledge of God be taken captive.[7] We can say, 'There are giants in the land,' and wander in the wilderness until we die,[8] or we can understand that the divine grace, which began redemption, is able to complete it. Christ

---

4. Gangadean, *The Gospel of Matthew*, xv–xxxiv; Gangadean, *The Westminster Catechisms*, 113–114.

5. *John 1:4.*

6. *Romans 6:23; Ephesians 2:1.*

7. *2 Corinthians 10:4–5.*

8. *Numbers 13–14.*

is the Lamb of God who takes away the sin of the world.[9] He is the Word of God who makes God known.[10] The earth is to be filled with the knowledge of God.[11] It is not rash, therefore, to think that Christian philosophy must answer the challenges to Christian theism.

Christian philosophy must show that it is clear that God the Creator exists. It must show that only some (God) is eternal, that is, without beginning, and that all else is temporal, that is, created, with a beginning. Christian philosophy must show that there must be something eternal, that only God is eternal; that matter exists (versus idealism) and that matter is not eternal (versus material monism); that the soul (self, mind, spirit) exists and that the soul is not eternal. In doing so, Christian philosophy must use all three classical arguments for the existence of God, in logical combination, with some revision to each. The ontological argument shows that there must be something eternal (whatever that may be); the cosmological argument shows that only some is eternal; and the teleological argument shows that kinds are specially created, and that evil in the world is not an argument against the existence of an all good, all powerful God. Ironically, the reverse is true.[12]

SHOW THE CLARITY OF GENERAL REVELATION:
Reformulated Proofs of the Classical Arguments

I will outline below what I believe is necessary in order to show that it is clear that God the Creator exists. Showing the clarity of general revelation is necessary because clarity is presupposed in the Christian concept of sin. If believers claim that something is clear, they should be able and willing to show this clarity. The program for showing clarity proceeds in defined stages, from the logically more basic to the less basic. If we understand what is more basic, we can understand what is less basic. If we agree on what is more basic, we can agree on what is less basic. Care is required to observe this simple principle in order to

---

9. *John 1:29.*

10. Gangadean, *The Gospel of Matthew*, xv–xxxiv.

11. *Isaiah 11:9; Habakkuk 2:14.*

12. Gangadean, *Philosophical Foundation*, 145–161; Gangadean, *On Natural and Revealed Theology,* 141–147; Gangadean, *The Biblical Worldview,* 219–239; Gangadean, "Paper No. 7: The Problem of Evil," in *The Logos Papers,* 33–39.

avoid needless disputes. This epistemological method can be described as Rational Presuppositionalism.[13] It recognizes that our set of beliefs forms a system (a worldview) and that less basic beliefs presuppose, or are supported by, more basic beliefs. Rational Presuppositionalism is a form of foundationalism but goes deeper than its classical form. Rational Presuppositionalism differs from fideistic presuppositionalism in that it not only uses reason to construct a coherent worldview from basic beliefs (taken for granted as true) but also uses reason critically at the basic level as a test for meaning.

THE ONTOLOGICAL ARGUMENT:
There Must Be Something Eternal

Christian theism affirms God as Creator of all things. "In the beginning God created the heavens and the earth" (Gen. 1:1). God is eternal, and all else is temporal. God created all things *ex nihilo*. From this idea of creation *ex nihilo*, the infinite wisdom and power of God are derived. Plato's divine maker is neither the creator of matter nor of the soul. The Demiurge is not infinite. To show that it is clear that God exists, it must first be shown that there is an eternal being, and secondly, that all else is temporal. To show that there must be something eternal, it must be demonstrated that the contradiction, 'Nothing is eternal,' implies that being would have to come from non-being, which is impossible.[14]

This form of ontological argument, from the concept of an eternal being to the necessary existence of an eternal being or substance, does not prove the existence of God, as Anselm's argument purports to. It argues that, if anything exists, something exists eternally. It does not show that something exists necessarily. That something exists is assumed by all in any discussion.

The value of beginning with this argument is that it makes explicit a process of argument which, if not agreed upon, prevents further discussion that would be fruitless. If there is no agreement on what is more basic, there can be no agreement on what is less basic. It is a

---

13. Gangadean, *History of Philosophy*, 19–23; Gangadean, "Paper No. 101: Rational Presuppositionalism," 521–526; "Paper No. 52: Common Ground (Part III)," in *The Logos Papers*, 281–282; Gangadean, *On Natural and Revealed Theology*, 59–66.

14. See: "Appendix A: The Doctrine of Clarity: Inexcusability, Maturity, and Lasting Fruit," in this book.

paradigm of what is clear to reason. If it is clear and not agreed to, it shows how one must deny reason to avoid what is clear. It demonstrates inexcusability.

THE COSMOLOGICAL ARGUMENT:
Only Some Is Eternal

If something must be eternal, is it that all is eternal in some form or other, or is only some (God, the Creator) eternal? If all is eternal, is it matter only (material monism), spirit only (spiritual monism), or matter and spirit (dualism)? In the history of worldviews, as alternatives to theism, no other kind of being has been asserted to exist. If there are forms, numbers, or laws, they are neither material nor efficient causes needed to explain change in the world. Perhaps one could attempt to construct a logically possible world (assuming there is no appeal to an unknown at the basic level) in which there are other substances, dimensions, or time and space relations. However, such views have not yet been put forward in a way that merits serious attention. We can safely focus on actual worldviews, held historically, until other worldviews are presented. Since matter (extended and non-conscious) and spirit (conscious and non-extended) are mutually exclusive and exhaustive, by the law of excluded middle, there is no reason to expect other views to emerge.

Material Monism: Matter Exists and Matter Is Eternal

Traditionally, metaphysics has been concerned with just three alternatives to theism, and historically, only three views have been exemplified: material monism in Western science, spiritual monism in Eastern mysticism, and dualism in Greek philosophy. It is appropriate to begin with material monism, which has been the most prevalent form of anti-theism in the West recently. Material monism asserts that all is matter in some form or other. There is no non-physical reality, no God, and no soul. All processes can be explained in natural terms only, including the origin of the cosmos, the existence of thought and perception, and the origin of all life forms.

What Christian philosophy must show is that the material world is not eternal and that it is not the only kind of reality. It must demonstrate that the material world is not self-maintaining—whether in general, in its parts (sun, stars), or as a whole (the Big Bang oscillating universe or inflationary universes). It must also show that thought cannot be accounted for by the motion of atoms in the brain and that, in perception, a mental image is not identical with the neural impulse (*a* is not *non-a*). Mental state terms cannot be analyzed without remainder into statements containing only behavioral terms. The structure and process (change) in the cosmos cannot be accounted for by natural or physical processes alone—neither in the starry heavens above nor in human consciousness within. These are outlines of cosmological arguments against material monism.[15]

The Natural Teleological Argument: Order in the World Is by Special Creation, Not Evolution

There are teleological arguments, based on natural design, against the evolutionary implications of material monism. The long-standing dispute between science and religion is due to uncritically held assumptions on the part of both. There are three issues in this dispute: first, is the dispute a matter of science, religion, or philosophy? Second, which assumption (uniformity or non-uniformity) best explains the data? Third, is a compromise position, such as theistic evolution, possible? Science assumes methodological naturalism, operating on the assumption that only natural causes exist and that all knowledge comes from sense experience. Religion assumes the existence of God and the authority of scripture. Neither side argues for its assumption but instead interprets the data in light of their first principle. Because the dispute rests on first principles, it belongs in the realm of philosophy, which must critically examine basic beliefs for meaning.[16]

After this dispute is resolved, the question becomes which assumption—uniformity or its alternative, non-uniformity—best interprets the data in the fields of geology, biology, and astronomy. In geology, the data of fossil beds, coal beds, sedimentary strata, mountain ranges, volcanic plateaus, ocean depths, and meteorological changes can best be explained by non-uniformity.

---

15. Gangadean, *Philosophical Foundation*, 71–100.

16. Gangadean, *Philosophical Foundation*, 87–89.

In biology, there are several stages in macro-evolution (amoeba to man). Can randomness and natural law account for each stage? How reasonable are the probabilities that life arose from non-life by chance and not by design? Is there a purely natural explanation for the transition from life to more complex life? Are there transitional forms from more complex life to hominids, or must we resort to punctuated equilibrium? Can the path of ascent from hominid to human be agreed upon, given the methods of research and reconstruction, the relation of language and thought, and the distinction between mind and brain? There are problems of logical gaps in each stage, not merely an exploiting of empirical gaps in favor of non-naturalism.[17]

Is there a third alternative? Theistic evolution attempts to mediate the dispute between historic theism and scientific naturalism. Is this third position possible without compromising fundamental features of both alternatives? Theistic evolution requires, over against historic theism, a revision of the concept of the soul as something infused into an already living being. The concept of creation as continuing in theistic evolution implies no unity of human nature and reduces differences in kind to differences of degree. Theistic evolution also requires a revision of the concept of God to make natural evil compatible with the goodness of God in creation. Over against scientific naturalism, theistic evolution requires God to guide the mechanism of the process of evolution (random micro-mutations), which would involve an intolerable degree of interference by non-natural causes.[18]

In the dispute between naturalistic science and special creation, the claim of incompatibility between the age of the heavens and the age of the earth rests upon the assumption of the uniformity (versus relativity) of time. Given the current understanding of the relation between gravity and time and an expanding universe, this source of dispute must be re-evaluated.

The arguments against material monism, and reflections on the dispute between science and religion, show that it is by no means clear that naturalism overcomes theism. Rather, naturalism must show that it does not deny reason in the meaning of its assertions. The objections

---

17. Gangadean, *Philosophical Foundation*, 90–96.

18. Gangadean, *Philosophical Foundation*, 98–100.

to material monism are fundamentally logical—arising from the nature of things—and not merely empirical.

Spiritual Monism: Spirit Exists and Spirit Is Eternal

Spiritual monism is the second major alternative and objection to theism. It asserts, in contrast to material monism, that reality is fundamentally spiritual and explains the physical as a manifestation of the spiritual. Epistemologically, it is a more radical form of empiricism, appealing to an inner experience of enlightenment or awakening as a self-certifying source of truth. In various forms of Hindu (Vedantic) thought and Buddhism, it begins with reincarnation and seeks release from the cycle of rebirth through an immediate awareness of what is taken to be ultimate reality. From the point of view of enlightened consciousness, reincarnation itself is seen as illusory (*maya*), or all distinctions of intellect vanish, including the distinction between enlightened and unenlightened consciousness.

Reincarnation assumes the eternal pre-existence of the soul, in contrast to theism, in which the soul is created. It is argued for on the basis of certain experiences (déjà vu, recollections from past lives, and manifestations of special powers not acquired by experience in this life). However, other explanations besides pre-existence are available, in addition to contrary evidence. The philosophical reasons for reincarnation have defeaters. There are other, and perhaps better, alternatives to no afterlife besides reincarnation. The karma theory of explanation, by accounting for any and every possible event *ad hoc*, has no predictive power and, therefore, explains nothing. Suffering for one's own karma is said to be fair, but it does not explain how suffering through innumerable rebirths without clarity of general revelation can be fair. And if it is clear, why is there a need for many lives to achieve this knowledge? If we have not learned through innumerable past lives, is reincarnation truly hopeful? Furthermore, is it possible to be finally released from rebirth if there has already been an infinite time in which to find release?[19]

Recourse is made to the illusory nature of the world (*samsara*) and the need for enlightenment to realize this. However, appeal to experi-

---

19. Gangadean, *Philosophical Foundation*, 103–105.

ence, including the experience of awakening, must be interpreted to be meaningful, and it has been interpreted differently across various traditions. A valid interpretation must be internally consistent, yet the interpretations of *Advaita* (absolute non-dualism of Shankara) and *Dvaita* (qualified non-dualism of Ramanuja) are admittedly incoherent in many ways.[20]

For Shankara, it cannot be explained in whose mind the illusion resides, how illusion concerning self-consciousness is possible, how the world can be neither a thing nor a thought, or how the world can be neither real (eternal) nor non-existent. Instead of giving up the assumption that all is one in favor of belief in the temporal reality of the world as created, Shankara moves to give up reason. The giving up of reason to avoid what is clear about God is inexcusable and results in the spiritual death of meaninglessness.

The claim by Ramanuja that the many selves are part of the one God encounters equal difficulties. Is the infinitude of God the sum of finite parts? Can the soul be finite and eternal? If all the parts are infinite, then each is complete in itself and not a part of another. And if some parts are finite (and temporal) while other parts are infinite (and eternal), why is this not creation and theism rather than pantheism?

Dualism: Matter and Spirit Are Both Eternal

A third major alternative to theism has been dualism—matter and spirit are both eternal. Christian theism encountered the Greek dualism of Plato and Aristotle as its first major challenge outside of Judaism. The clarity of general revelation, in opposition to dualism, has not been pressed, and aspects of ontological and ethical dualism have lingered in the Christian worldview. Augustine allowed a degree of Platonic thought, and Aquinas did the same for Aristotle. Christian philosophy must show that matter is neither eternal and independent of spirit, as in Platonic dualism, nor eternal and dependent on spirit (Prime Mover/pure actuality) as pure potentiality. The dualistic explanation of evil as the opposition of the body to the soul must be shown to be incoherent in itself and inconsistent with the goodness of creation in theism.[21]

---

20. Gangadean, *Philosophical Foundation*, 110–115.

21. Gangadean, *Philosophical Foundation*, 129–131.

THEISM:
The Nature of God and Preliminary Problems

At this point, the incoherence of the three major forms of "all is eternal" has been brought to attention. However, theism itself has been challenged as being incoherent. These challenges must be met if the clarity of general revelation is to be upheld. The nature of God, knowable from general revelation, must first be clarified in contrast to sub-theistic views such as pantheism, dualism, polytheism, and panentheism. Additionally, some preliminary difficulties must be addressed: How is creation *ex nihilo* different from being from non-being? How is the creation of matter and spirit (other than God) possible? How is creation not a unique event in time? And why did God create, as opposed to not creating, or why did God create this world instead of some other world?[22]

The Moral Teleological Argument: Both Moral and Natural Evil Serve the Good

The major problem historically facing theism has been the problem of evil. If God is all good and all powerful, why is there evil? David Hume's *Dialogues Concerning Natural Religion* explores several solutions, all of which are unsatisfactory: that God's goodness is perfect but incomprehensible; that the answer will be known in the afterlife; that there is more good than evil; that God is finitely powerful; or that God is morally indifferent. In the end, we are left with Philo's argument that natural evil in many forms is not necessary.[23]

Theists have appealed to free will as a solution to the problem of evil. They have generally accepted that natural evil is not necessary. Natural evil is due to moral evil; moral evil is due to free will; and free will is necessary for human dignity. But there are objections. Free will makes moral evil possible, not actual. Even if it is actual, that does not show that evil is necessary. Free will does not have to make moral evil possible (God is free without the possibility of evil, and man, in his final blessedness, is free without the possibility of evil). Furthermore, one can pass from innocence to virtue without any moral evil.[24]

---

22. Gangadean, *Philosophical Foundation*, 139–144.

23. Gangadean, *Philosophical Foundation*, 145–154.

24. Gangadean, *Philosophical Foundation*, 155–156.

Theism has a serious problem, at least, with explaining the existence of evil. To maintain the clarity of general revelation more is needed than simply stating that the problem is not a contradiction or that there is a reason, known to God but not to man, why there is evil in the world. An alternative solution is needed—an ironic solution to an ironic problem. To outline an ironic solution employing Rational Presuppositionalism, Christian philosophy must clarify the meaning of basic terms in the argument. Good and evil must be defined in relation to human nature as rational and in light of the inexcusability of unbelief. In this solution, moral evil, understood as unbelief, is permitted for a purpose. Moral evil serves to obscure revelation to the person in unbelief while also deepening the revelation of the divine nature for all to see. If moral evil is removed abruptly, the revelation will not be deepened. And if unbelief is not removed, the revelation will not be seen. Moral evil (unbelief), in every form and degree of admixture with belief, is allowed to come to expression in world history. Through history, good (belief) gradually overcomes unbelief.

Natural evil was not original in creation but was imposed by God to restrain, recall from, and remove moral evil. In this way, evil is made to serve the good. The assumptions of this solution must be scrutinized. Is there a clear general revelation so as to make unbelief inexcusable? Is there any other way to deepen the revelation apart from actual evil? Does the good (the knowledge of God) justify the existence of evil without denying its nature as evil?

By understanding good and evil more consistently, and by applying it to oneself, the irony of the solution can be seen:

1. If God is all good and all powerful, why is there evil in the world?

2. Because of all the evil in the world, I cannot see how God is all good and all powerful.

3. Because of all the unbelief in the world, I cannot see how God is all good and all powerful.

4. Because of all the unbelief in me, I cannot see how God is all good and all powerful.

5. Because I have turned off my reason, I cannot see how God is all good and all powerful.

We can call this solution the Ironic Solution, consistent with the nature of evil as presupposed by Christian theism from the beginning.

There Is a Moral Law Which Is Clear, Comprehensive, and Critical

Christian philosophy must address two final steps in showing the clarity of general revelation. It must answer the question of ethics and show the transition from general to special revelation. Ethics is concerned with giving a rational justification for an answer to the question: What is the good? Both skepticism and non-theistic alternatives challenge clarity. Christian philosophy must show that there is a moral law that is clear (because it is grounded in human nature), comprehensive (applying to all choices and all aspects of human nature), and critical (its consequence being a matter of life or death).[25] Consistent with Rational Presuppositionalism, Christian philosophy must begin with what is most basic in ethics. The good (the end in itself, the highest value, the source of unity) is assumed in all choice. It is distinct from virtue (the means to the end in itself) and from happiness (the effect of possessing what one believes to be the good). The good is grounded in human nature, which is itself grounded in one's view of what is real. Since it is clear that only some (God, the Creator) is eternal, God, as the creator of human nature, is the determiner of good and evil for man. God as determiner is opposed to man, understanding himself apart from God, as the determiner of good and evil. This is sufficient to rule out ethical egoism, utilitarianism, deontology, existentialism, and other forms of human autonomy.[26]

The moral law must address divisions among theists concerning the nature of God based on the nature of thinking (the less basic in light of the more basic). It must also address divisions within a person (lack of integrity) based on the unity of our nature. Work, as necessary for the good, requires hope that the good will be achieved. We are born ignorant and must be taught the good and the means to the good. Those

---

25. Gangadean, *Philosophical Foundation*, 171–284; Gangadean, *History of Philosophy*, 61–69; Gangadean, *The Westminster Catechisms*, 215–267; Gangadean, *The Westminster Confession*, 207–221; Gangadean, *On Natural and Revealed Theology*, 127–139, 166–178.

26. Gangadean, *On Natural and Revealed Theology*, 9–39; Gangadean, *Philosophical Foundation*, 171–183.

in authority must have insight into the good. We are born human, possessing the capacity to understand, and must be treated as having both the capacity and the responsibility for understanding. We are born of a sexual union, which is a natural sign of love and the commitment required by love. We naturally value things and, by the possession of talent, are obligated to create what is of lasting value in service to others. We are born equal as persons and have a natural obligation to do justice (to treat equals equally). Therefore, we are to know and speak the truth in order to achieve justice. We are born changeable and can misconceive the good. We are not to turn from the good in discontent due to such misconception or because of natural evil, which is a call to stop and think.[27]

The moral law knowable from general revelation is the same in content as the moral law given in special revelation. It is universal, perpetual, and the means to the good. It is not the means to redemption but makes manifest the need for redemption. Through redemption, one is enabled to seek the good through the way of life given in the moral law.

General Revelation Is Necessary for and Requires Special Revelation

The need for redemption and for redemptive revelation can be understood by considering the existence and nature of natural evil. Deism denies the necessity of special revelation by failing to understand the origin of natural evil (physical death). Physical death is not original in creation. God, as all-powerful and all-good, could, would, must have, and therefore did, create mankind without physical death (not to mention other forms of natural evil). Physical death is not inherent in moral evil. The inherent consequence of moral evil is spiritual, not physical, death. Physical death, therefore, is imposed by God because of moral evil as a call back from moral evil. A call back, as mercy, requires redemptive revelation to show how God can be both just and merciful. Mercy does not set aside divine justice but satisfies it. What would count as redemptive revelation must be consistent with what is clear from general revelation and must show how God is both just and merciful to man in sin. Biblical revelation, with its teaching on

---

27. Gangadean, *Philosophical Foundation*, 185–198.

vicarious atonement and the Christian interpretation, which finds both justice and mercy in Christ's atonement, satisfies the requirement for special revelation. Other scriptures and other interpretations do not meet these requirements.

RESPOND TO PAST AND CONTINUING CHALLENGES

If Christian philosophy can get this far, many of the external challenges posed by non-theism would have been met. Yet challenges remain: to show Christian theism in contrast to non-Christian forms of theism (Judaism and Islam); to settle long-standing disputes within Christian theism (e.g., free will vs. predestination); to answer objections put forward by Kant, Nietzsche, Marx, and Freud against popular distortions of Christianity (pietism, fideism, and otherworldliness); and to avoid reconstructions of Christian theism put forward by Kant, Schleiermacher, Hegel, and Ritschl, which fail to reckon with the clarity of general revelation.

SERVE ALL AREAS OF DOMINION:
Laying Foundation for the Glory of God

Finally, Christian philosophy must serve the good, not only negatively but positively. If eternal life is knowing God, and if through dominion the earth shall be full of the knowledge of God, Christian philosophy must serve all areas of dominion by helping to establish the philosophical foundations of the various academic disciplines on which each discipline must build. Philosophy of Art (aesthetics), Philosophy of Literature (hermeneutics), Philosophy of Science (natural and social), Philosophy of Law, Philosophy of History, and other areas must be worked out. If Christian philosophy is to be relevant and regarded, it must enable others to interpret personal and communal experience in ways that further the knowledge of God. Christian philosophy, therefore, has a task that is as necessary and demanding as it is rewarding.

INDEX

About the Author

Dr. Surrendra Gangadean (1943–2022) was a Professor of Philosophy at Phoenix College and at Paradise Valley Community College for 45 years. Additionally, he taught from the pulpit at Westminster Fellowship for almost 30 years and taught courses at Logos Theological Seminary for over 25 years. Courses he taught include: Introduction to Philosophy, Logic, Ethics, Philosophy of Religion, Eastern Religions, World Religions, Introduction to Christianity, Introduction to Humanities, Philosophy of Art, The Great Books, Philosophical Theology, Biblical Worldview, Biblical History, Church History, Systematic Theology, Biblical Hermeneutics, and Existential Hermeneutics. He received an M.A. degree in Literature from the Arizona State University, an M.A. degree in Philosophy from the University of Arizona, and a Ph.D. in Natural Theology from Reformed International Theological Seminary. He presented academic papers and public lectures on Natural Theology and the Moral Law. Dr. Gangadean was the organizing Pastor of Westminster Fellowship Church, and President of The Logos Foundation, which serves academic education in Liberal Arts and Theology.

www.ingramcontent.com/pod-product-compliance
Lightning Source LLC
Chambersburg PA
CBHW021602120626
46545CB00001B/28